Managing IT Outsourcing Performance

Hans Solli-Sæther
Norwegian School of Management, Norway

Petter Gottschalk
Norwegian School of Management, Norway

BUSINESS SCIENCE Reference

BUSINESS SCIENCE REFERENCE

Hershey · New York

Director of Editorial Content: Kristin Klinger
Senior Managing Editor: Jamie Snavely
Assistant Managing Editor: Michael Brehm
Publishing Assistant: Sean Woznicki
Typesetter: Sean Woznicki
Cover Design: Lisa Tosheff
Printed at: Yurchak Printing Inc.

Published in the United States of America by
Business Science Reference (an imprint of IGI Global)
701 E. Chocolate Avenue
Hershey PA 17033
Tel: 717-533-8845
Fax: 717-533-8661
E-mail: cust@igi-global.com
Web site: http://www.igi-global.com/reference

Library of Congress Cataloging-in-Publication Data

Managing IT outsourcing performance / Hans Solli-Saether and Petter Gottschalk, editors.
p. cm.
Includes bibliographical references and index.
Summary: "This book provides a collection of methodologies and tools that can be used in managing relationships and performance of IT outsourcing"--Provided by publisher.

ISBN 978-1-60566-796-6 (hardcover) -- ISBN 978-1-60566-797-3 (ebook) 1. Information technology--Management. 2. Contracting out. 3. Electronic data processing departments--Contracting out. I. Solli-Saether, Hans. II. Gottschalk, Petter, 1950- III. Title.

HD30.2.M3642 2010
004.068'4--dc22

2009010756

British Cataloguing in Publication Data
A Cataloguing in Publication record for this book is available from the British Library.

Table of Contents

Selected Readings

Foreword

"*Welcome to the age of constant alarm bells where surprise is all and no one can predict what will happen tomorrow*"[1]. When Ridderstråle and Bordström wrote this back in 2002, little did they know that, less than a decade later, business managers would be wondering daily whether there would *be* a tomorrow, let alone how it would look. Nowadays, industry news bulletins sound like war dispatches. Many are scared to turn on the nightly news, just in case another company has hit the road. At times like this, businesses have to be prepared for anything that might happen. And, if you are dealing with Information Technology (IT) outsourcing, that is the best reason why you should read this book: *Measuring IT Outsourcing Performance* prepares you to proactively design and manage your IT outsourcing venture.

The book is packed with relevant notions, tips and knowledge which will increase your awareness of the typical risks and challenges and will enable you to avoid falling into the most dangerous pitfalls. Solli-Sæther and Gottschalk even devised a maturity model that, in itself, can be used instantaneously as a roadmap to success: a series of stages that you should follow to make your business evolve and grow hand-in-hand with your outsourcing partners.

I should probably say at this point that, in a true outsourcing spirit, at first I thought I should ask somebody else to write this foreword for me. Then I realised that was probably not what the authors had in mind when they invited me to do this! So, I sat down at the desk of my hotel room, turned on my computer, accessed my Software-As-A-Service provider's platform, opened Microsoft Word, created a new "Foreword.docx" file and saved it to my quota on our IT supplier's server situated in a remote office location somewhere in Scotland. And there I was, ready to go! How's that for IT outsourcing?

As Editor-in-Chief of *Strategic Outsourcing, An International Journal* (*SOIJ*), I have been fortunate to be at the heart of the outsourcing scientific community, working with some of the world's most esteemed outsourcing experts. Over the past few years, I have seen this topic rise to the top of both scientists' and executives' agendas. In its first year alone, *SOIJ* generated over 7400 article downloads worldwide, clear evidence of the interest in this area. One of Volume 1's closing articles[2] identified the top 10 most urgent outsourcing research questions. One was the need to better address the challenges inherent with managing outsourcing performance. And then Solli-Sæther and Gottschalk's book appeared. Timely, to say the least!

Working with executives from various sectors responsible for sourcing and outsourcing projects, I have seen firsthand the virtues and shortcomings of existing knowledge and theories, when applied in the real world. Traditional tools for performance measurement seem inadequate when applied to outsourcing projects and as a result, many scholar and practitioners question the real success rate of these initiatives. Today's global financial crisis, however, is increasingly holding executives accountable for every decision, more than ever before. Consequently, all projects are scrutinised through the lenses of return on investment, cost/benefits and efficiency measures. There is no other way to put it: measuring and managing outsourcing performance is something we will need to become much better at in the future!

Managing IT Outsourcing Performance offers the nuts and bolts of managing outsourcing relationships while providing critically relevant insight from industrial case studies which demonstrate that what appears simple in theory may become extremely complex in reality. Whether you work with IT outsourcing or simply want to be "educated" on the subject, the balanced approach of presenting scientific theories side by side with practical experience makes the value of this book stand out shouting.

Solli-Sæther and Gottschalk start from the basics, offering a detailed yet easy to follow run-through of the seminal theories often used to explain how to answer the crucial "make or buy" question. Then, they build their argument all the way up to the complex stuff, providing several useful clues about how to manage global outsourcing relationships under the pressure of ever more demanding stakeholders. Their book looks at outsourcing from the perspective of the client-supplier relationship, suggesting how to measure and manage its performance to create a win-win environment.

Building and managing business today feels at times like playing the Hasbro's Jenga game, the one where you play with a tower made up of layers of wooden bricks and you need to take as many bricks as possible apart and place them to the top of the tower trying to go as high as possible: your company will become stronger if you can recognise what processes you can let go; it will lose its equilibrium, falling into pieces at the slightest mistake or trembling, as you let these processes go; and it won't be the 'tallest tower' in the market unless you have an idea of how to design and manage the structure of your network.

If IT is your Jenga's Tower or simply one of its wooden bricks, and if you want to be Hasbro' tallest, Darwin's fittest or Ridderstråle's and Bordström's funkiest business in the industry, this book gives you the rules of the game.

Friedman once said: *"It's all about combining the best of what computers can do with the best of what humans can do, and the constantly reintegrating the new best practices the humans are innovating back into the system to make the whole – the machines and the people- that much more productive"*[3].

Read this book and be prepared!

ENDNOTES

1 Ridderstråle, J., Bordström, K., (2002). *Funky Business*. Upper Saddle River, NJ: FT Prentice Hall

2 Busi, M., McIvor, R. (2008). Setting the outsourcing research agenda: the top-10 most urgent outsourcing areas. *Strategic Outsourcing, an International Journal, 1*(3), 185-197.

3 Friedman, T. (2005). *The world is Flat*. New York: Penguin Books.

Dr. Marco Busi
Editor-in-Chief,
Strategic Outsourcing an International Journal
CEO and Director of Research,
Carisma RCT Ltd., www.carismarct.com

Preface

Information technology outsourcing – the practice of transferring IT assets, leases, staff, and management responsibility for delivery of services from internal IT functions to third party vendors – has become an undeniable trend. In recent years, private and public sector organizations worldwide have outsourced significant portions of their IT functions to service providers onshore and offshore (e.g., Lewin & Peeters, 2006; Solli-Sæther & Gottschalk, 2007). Examples can be found in major organizations such as Scandinavian Airlines Systems, ABB, and Rolls-Royce. In a business perspective, outsourcing is motivated by the promise of strategic, financial, and technological benefits. The success of outsourcing, then, should be assessed in terms of attainment of these benefits (Lee, Miranda, & Kim, 2004). In a user perspective, outsourcing success is the level of quality of offered services.

This book is about managing IT outsourcing performance, focusing on relationship management, value creation and measurements. In addition to organizational and management issues, a number of other important topics and areas are covered in this book to shed light and generate new insights into the way forward for IT outsourcing. For example, value configurations may differ between outsourcing parties, creating challenges in connecting primary and secondary activities of client and vendor organizations

This book offers a comprehensive literature review of IT outsourcing based research. It provides methods, tools, and metrics for relationship management and for value creation and performance measurement. In order to understand the inherent complexities and the underlying constructs of relationship and performance management, three internationally based outsourcing relationships are presented.

The mission of this book is to:

- Identify outsourcing opportunities and threats.
- Provide an overview of organizational and management theories and practices of IT outsourcing.
- Demonstrate that a holistic approach to IT outsourcing is needed that recognizes and emphasizes the combination of several critical success factors. The theory-based factors presented have both divergent and convergent implications for management.
- Define stages of growth model for IT outsourcing, which can be used by companies to learn the path to improved relationships. By identifying development stages, scholars and practitioners have a framework within which they can diagnose the current situation and plan for future improvements in their outsourcing relationship.
- Emphasize the important role of knowledge for inter-organizational learning and innovation. An outsourcing arrangement between vendor and client seems dependent of knowledge transfer. With the changing business environments, the locus of value creation is no longer within the boundaries of a single firm, but occurs instead at the nexus of relationships between the parties. Outsourcing can add to the enterprise using unique organizational resources of both tangible and intangible nature.

- Classify company activities into value configurations for outsourcing. As people in the strategy field already know, the contingent approach to strategy implies that value chains, value shops, and value networks have very different value creation logic.
- Provide a model for strategic planning for outsourcing initiatives. The Y-model describes the current situation and the desired situation, thereby evaluating a gap between current and desired that should be reduced and closed by means of a new strategy.
- Provide an understanding of how a client company can benefit from outsourcing by explaining vendor value proposition, and further, explain how to manage the vendor relationship with an advantageous benefit/cost ratio. This includes a method for development and examples of how to measure IT outsourcing performance.
- Identify frameworks for outsourcing governance to establish effective relationships. A number of important issues are presented in this book, enabling the reader to select an appropriate management control system for the outsourcing relationship. This is important as responsibilities of management change after an outsourcing decision.

The generalizability of the findings in this book to the entire IT outsourcing market might be found problematic by some readers. We as authors have mainly used case studies in the European area and surveys in the Norwegian area, and we have used those studies to generalize it to entire outsourcing market. Some readers may have a problem with that, primarily because outsourcing is a global business practice. As we are very well aware, companies and governments engage in global outsourcing relationships.

The target audience for this book includes (but is not limited to):

- Graduate students, MSc, early researcher, and first year PhD, in management information systems, who will need to get an overview of research conducted in this area.
- Undergraduate students in systems development, who should learn about the intricacies of not only technical aspects of IT outsourcing, but also organizational and managerial aspects as well.
- Information systems designers, developers and programmers in public and private software organizations, who want to think in the big picture of IT outsourcing as they might get affected by an outsourcing arrangement.
- Project managers in IT projects, who will typically get involved when companies are outsourcing information systems and technology.
- CIOs and IT managers, who are responsible for outsourcing project, and later, for the success of the outsourcing arrangement.

INTRODUCTION TO CHAPTERS

This book is concerned with opportunities and threats managing IT outsourcing performance. It shows how companies can handle the complex business process of outsourcing by addressing issues such as critical success factors, stages of growth in outsourcing maturity, knowledge transfer between client and vendor. This book shows that understanding of costs, benefits and risks, influence IT outsourcing performance. Further, this book suggests performance measurements and a model for outsourcing governance.

First, Chapter 1 starts out by defining and describing IT outsourcing. Based on a conceptual understanding of this important business process, we present a sourcing universe, and we discuss some key aspects of the important outsourcing decision.

Based on outsourcing definitions explored in the first chapter, Chapter 2 identifies eleven theoretical perspectives for IT outsourcing. The primary purpose is to guide readers in understanding outsourcing projects according to attributes like outsourcing focus, goals and objectives, unit of analysis, outsourcing philosophy, and critical success factors.

Chapter 3 builds on Chapter 2 by developing eleven critical success factors in IT outsourcing, one for each theory. The theory-based factors have both divergent and convergent implications for management of IT outsourcing relationship, which require a contingent approach to outsourcing decision-making.

Chapter 4 introduces the concept of value configurations. A value configuration is the way an organization creates value for its stakeholders and clients. Three alternative value configurations exist for organizations. First, the value chain is a value configuration for sequential operations producing goods and services. Next, the value shop is a problem solving entity working in a cyclical fashion. Finally, the value network is connecting parties that exchange with each other. A company's value configuration may serve as a determinant and predictor for the extent of outsourcing. IT is not just another resource that should be managed like any other resource. Managing successful IT outsourcing implies that managers understand the specifics of any IT outsourcing candidate. Management has to understand the variety of IT activities, predict future needs, and understand IT economics. Furthermore, management has to identify sourcing options and analyze opportunities and threats associated with each of them. Such analysis should take place within the framework of strategic IT planning.

Chapter 5 introduces the evolutionary perspective of stages of growth models for IT outsourcing relationships. Such models are helpful to determine where an organization is, where it came from, and in what direction it is moving in terms of outsourcing relationship maturity. Stages of growth imply that there is a cumulative improvement over time, where continuous struggle and successes are more important than paradigm shifts.

In managing IT outsourcing performance it is important to understand costs, benefits, and risks as presented in Chapter 6. We discuss production and transaction economics, hidden costs and contract termination costs, and we will also take a look at benefits and risk behavior.

Chapter 7 discusses the importance of knowledge transfer in IT outsourcing relationships, both from a client, vendor, and relationship perspective.

In Chapter 8, we discuss the important issue of measuring IT outsourcing performance. In this chapter the vendor's value proposition is presented because outsourcing outcomes are dependent on the vendor's ability to create value for both parties in the relationship. A method for developing quantitative performance measurements is presented, and there are examples of scales measuring service quality, satisfaction, and the overall success of the relationship.

Building a governance model for successful management of IT outsourcing relationship in Chapter 9, we synthesize several of the perspectives discussed in previous chapters.

Finally, Chapter 10 is presenting an internationally based IT outsourcing case study in order to understand the inherent complexities and the underlying constructs of managing IT outsourcing relationships and the performance of these relationships.

This book has three sections. The first section, Chapters 1 and 2, provides background material to understand and analyze the phenomenon of IT outsourcing. This section covers topics such as outsourcing definitions, sourcing universe, opportunities (Chapter 1), and IT outsourcing theories (Chapter 2). The second section presents key topics in relationship management, value creation and measurement, as illustrated by Chapter 3 – 8 in the Figure 1. Managing IT outsourcing performance starts with a decision to outsource. To succeed in a relationship companies have to understand the critical success factors (Chapter 3), the stages of growth of the relationship (chapter 5), and how to transfer knowledge between the parties involved (Chapter 7). Measuring IT outsourcing performance (Chapter 8) is based on a thor-

Figure 1. Key topics managing IT outsourcing performance

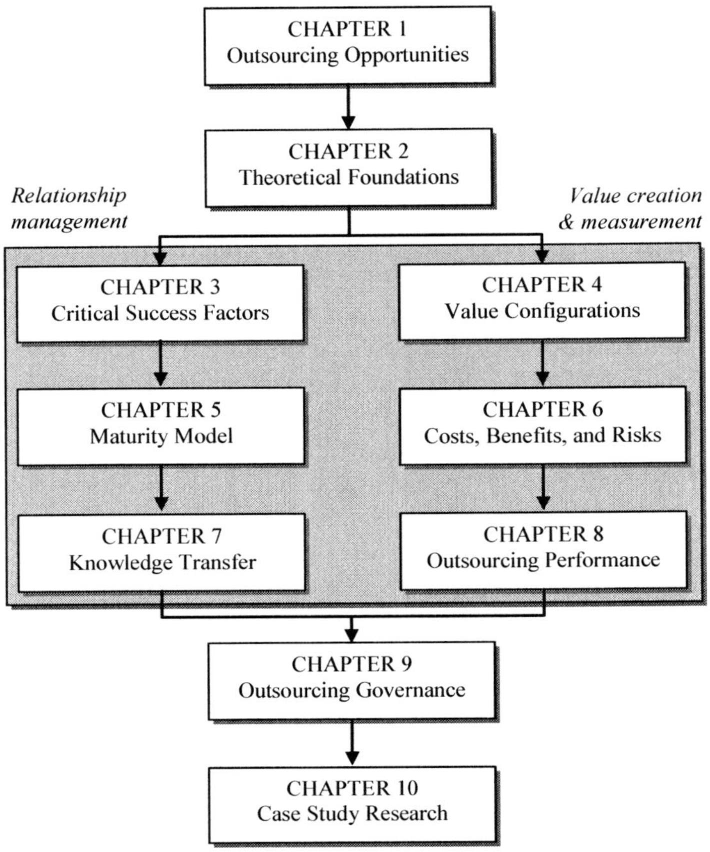

ough understanding of value creation (Chapter 4), and costs, benefits, and risks (Chapter 6). The second section of this book serves as foundation for the third section proposing an outsourcing governance model in Chapter 9, and finally for understanding of real world outsourcing cases in Chapter 10.

REFERENCES

Lee, J.-N., Miranda, S. M., & Kim, Y.-M. (2004). IT Outsourcing Strategies: Universalistic, Contingency, and Configurational Explanations of Success. *Information Systems Research, 15*(2), 110-131.

Lewin, A. Y., & Peeters, C. (2006). Offshoring Work: Business Hype or the Onset of Fundamental Transformation? *Long Range Planning, 39*(3), 221-239.

Solli-Sæther, H., & Gottschalk, P. (2007). *Rapport fra Outsourcingsundersøkelsen 2007* (National Survey). Oslo: Norwegian School of Management.

Chapter 1
Outsourcing Opportunities

In this chapter on outsourcing opportunities, a common conceptual understanding of important issues of the business practice of our interest is established. First, we take a look at how researchers have defined the term outsourcing. An updated outsourcing definition will serve as a common platform for understanding the sourcing universe presented in the following section. Next, we describe in more detail the building blocks of the sourcing universe – insourcing, information technology (IT) and information systems (IS) outsourcing, business process outsourcing, transformational outsourcing, and global outsourcing. At the end of the chapter, we discuss some key aspects of the important outsourcing decision.

OUTSOURCING DEFINITIONS

If a firm does not want to use its internal resources to build or operate information systems, it can hire an external organization that specializes in providing these services to do the work. The *process of turning over an organization's computer center operations, telecommunications networks, and/or applications development to external vendors is called outsourcing* (Laudon & Laudon, 2005).

DOI: 10.4018/978-1-60566-796-6.ch001

Loh and Venkatraman (1992a) define IT outsourcing as *the significant contribution by external vendors in the physical and/or human resources associated with the entire or specific components of the IT infrastructure in the user organization*. Vendors may contribute computer assets for the user from outside the organization. Alternatively, the ownership of certain computer assets of the user may be transferred to the vendor. Similarly, vendors may utilize their personnel to provide the required services, or the vendor may employ existing staff of the user. In their research, they attempted to explain the degree of IT outsourcing by using cost structures and economic performance. They found that the degree of IT outsourcing is positively related to both business and IT cost structures, and negatively related to IT performance. IT outsourcing was framed as a make-versus-buy decision, where contractual modes differ in the domain of influence within the corporation (Loh & Venkatraman, 1992a, 1992b).

Lacity, Willcocks, and Feeny (1996) define outsourcing *to dismantle internal IT departments by transferring IT employees, facilities, hardware leases, and software licenses to third-party vendors*. Hirschheim and Lacity (2000) define information technology outsourcing as the practice of *transferring IT assets, leases, staff, and management responsibility for delivery of services from internal IT function to third-party vendors*.

In research by Grover, Teng, and Cheon (1998), they define outsourcing of IS functions as *the organizational decision to turn over part or all of an organization's IS functions to external service provider(s) in order for an organization to be able to achieve its goals*. This decision-making approach is interesting because it focuses on an early stage of a long process. Resource-based theory and resource-dependence theory from the field of strategic management and transaction cost theory and agency theory from economics are used in order to describe its implications for outsourcing research and practice. The definition includes decisions about how to arrange external IT services. Using several theoretical perspectives of outsourcing, they presume that organizations attempt to make these decisions in their best interests. Similarly, Grover, Cheon, and Teng (1996) define outsourcing as involving *a significant use of resources – either technological and/or human resources – external to the organizational hierarchy in the management of information technology*.

Hu, Saunders, and Gebelt (1997) define information systems outsourcing as *a business practice in which a company contracts out all or part of its information systems operations to one or more outside suppliers*. Here we find that outsourcing is a practical issue that also has a significant impact on business organization. Even though outsourcing is a business practice, for IS executives acquiring outside services is an important strategic issue confronting their organizations. Thus, their theoretical perspective is strategic decision-making. In their research they have identified sources of influence in the adoption decision. One significant influence is the combined effects of external media, vendor pressure, and internal communications at the personal level among managers.

Outsourcing can be defined as *turning over all or part of an organizational activity to an outside vendor* (Barthélemy, 2003). Here outsourcing is the purchasing, from outside the organization, of IT services needed to perform business functions. According to Langfield-Smith and Smith (2003), outsourcing is *the contracting of any service or activity to a third party*. Both definitions are concerned with the inter-firm relationship, and the authors pay attention to how to deal with uncertainty and risk encompassed in outsourcing. Where Barthélemy is concerned with management expertise as a predictor of success or failure, Langfield-Smith and Smith are concerned with the design of management control systems.

Outsourcing is *a phenomenon in which a user organization (client) transfers property or decision rights over information technology infrastructure to an external (vendor) organization* (Levina & Ross, 2003). By using this definition, Levina and Ross direct their research at how vendors can deliver financial and managerial benefits to their clients that outweigh contracting costs and risks. But instead of using traditional economic theories, they apply the concept of complementarity in organizational design as well as the core competency argument in outsourcing and theories of client-vendor relationships. They explain variability in outsourcing outcomes by using relationship factors as predictors.

In this book we will use the definition proposed by Kern and Willcocks (2002), who define outsourcing as *a process whereby an organization decides to contract-out or sell the firm's IT assets, people and/ or activities to a third party supplier, who in exchange provides and manages these assets and services for an agreed fee over an agreed time period.* They focus on the key elements of the exchange and the relationship between different stakeholder groups. They recognize the influence of the environment and the atmosphere in which the interaction takes place. In their process-oriented approach, they are using Håkansson's (1982) interaction model to explain the client-vendor relationship of IT outsourcing.

Although Lacity and Willcocks (2000b) did not explicitly provide a definition of outsourcing, it seems that they are in line with this process-oriented approach. They introduced a relationship framework that focuses on relationship stakeholders, relationship types, and six phases (scooping, evaluation, negotiation, transition, middle, and mature phase) and activities related to these phases. In this perspective, IT outsourcing is viewed as a longitudinal process involving several stakeholder groups.

In Table 1, some of the definitions used in the research literature on IT outsourcing is listed. We find that many of the researchers did not define outsourcing. Among those who did, we have seen that definitions vary, both according to outsourcing perspective and according to theoretical perspective. In Chapter 2 will go further in the discussion of theoretical perspectives on IT outsourcing.

A SOURCING UNIVERSE

The suggested sourcing universe in Figure 1 recognizes that a range of assets can be outsourced in order to satisfy business objectives. Assets can refer to hardware, software, people, and processes, each of which can be separately examined. As the extent of assets outsourced increases, there will be an increasing need for cooperation between the outsourcing parties, because of increasing uncertainty. In the case of insourcing, the client company retains responsibility for the delivery of all IT service, bringing vendor resources in only to supplement internally managed teams. External delivery of services is relatively easy to manage and control, because the amount is not very high. In outsourcing, the responsibility for delivery of services, such as infrastructure operation and management, systems development and support, business process design and operation, and organizational change, is transferred to an external vendor. This external vendor can even be located overseas. As the complexity of these services increases, so does the uncertainty. And thus, the need for management control systems and trust in the outsourcing relationship increases. Characteristics of the transaction, environment and parties involved, can be used in the design of control systems (Langfield-Smith & Smith, 2003).

The term outsourcing can be studied further by using the opposite term of *insourcing*. Hirschheim and Lacity (2000), define insourcing as "the practice of evaluating the outsourcing option, but confirming the continued use of internal IT resources to achieve the same objectives of outsourcing." They studied six decision factors: decision scope, decision sponsor, evaluation process, year of decision, size of the organization, and decision outcome. Their research contributes to the IT sourcing research base by providing evidence that companies need not necessarily turn to outsourcing to improve IT performance. While outsourcing may be a preferred option for some organizations for various reasons, such as return-

Table 1. Examples of outsourcing definitions in the research literature

Literature reference	Outsourcing perspective	Theoretical perspective	Determinants of practice in IT outsourcing
Barthélemy (2003)	Turning over all or part of an organizational activity to an outside vendor	Management theory	Lacking management expertise underlies most failed outsourcing efforts
Grover, Teng and Cheon (1998)	Turning over IS functions to external service provider(s)	Strategic decision-making, economic theory	External services like applications development and maintenance, systems operations, networks and telecom management
Hirschheim and Lacity (2000)	Transferring IT assets, leases, staff and management responsibility to third-party vendors	Decision-making theory	Companies most likely outsource on a large scale when they are in poor financial conditions, have poor IT functions, or have IT functions with little status within the organization
Hu, Saunders Gebelt (1997)	Contract out all or part of its information systems operations	Decision-making theory	Combined effects of external media, vendor pressure, and internal communications at the personal level among managers
Kern and Willcocks (2002)	Contract out or sell to a third party supplier	Interaction theory	The elements of the interaction approach (services, information, financial, social), the parties involved, the environment, the atmosphere
Lacity and Willcocks (2000b)	Transfer to suppliers	Relational theory	Relationship stakeholders, relationship types, relationship phases and related activities
Lacity, Willcocks and Feeny (1996)	Dismantle internal IT departments by transferring to third-party vendors	Economic theory	Critical factors such as degree of technological maturity and degree of technology integration
Langfield-Smith and Smith (2003)	Contracting of any service or activity to a third party	Transaction cost theory, agency theory	Characteristics of the transaction, transaction environment and parties
Levina and Ross (2003)	Transfer property and decision rights to an external organization	Client-vendor relationship	Vendor efficiency is based on complementarities in organizational design, core competencies, and relationship management structures.
Loh and Venkatraman (1992a)	Contribution by external vendors	Neoclassical economics, procurement activities	Business and IT cost structures, IT performance

ing to core competencies or focusing IT staff on more business-oriented IT activities, Hirscheim and Lacity (2000) show that if cost reduction is the major objective, IT managers can oftentimes replicate a vendor's cost reduction tactics. Insourcing success, however, is predicated on a number of key issues, including aligning perceptions of and agendas for IT.

Lacity, Willcocks, and Feeny (1996) define total insourcing as the management and provision of at least 80 percent of the IT budget internally after evaluating the IT service market. The common element of the two definitions seems to be that customers evaluate the external IT services market before a sourcing decision takes place.

IT outsourcing has been defined as "a process whereby an organization decides to contract-out or sell the firm's IT assets, people and/or activities to a third party supplier, who in exchange provides and manages these assets and services for an agreed fee over an agreed time period" (Kern & Willcocks, 2002). If the costs represent more than 80% of the IT budget, this is called total outsourcing (Lacity et al., 1996). When the decision is to source selected IT functions from external provider(s), while still providing between 20% and 80% of the IT budget internally, this is called selective outsourcing. The vendor(s) becomes responsible for delivering the result of the selectively outsourced IT activities, while

Figure 1. A sourcing universe

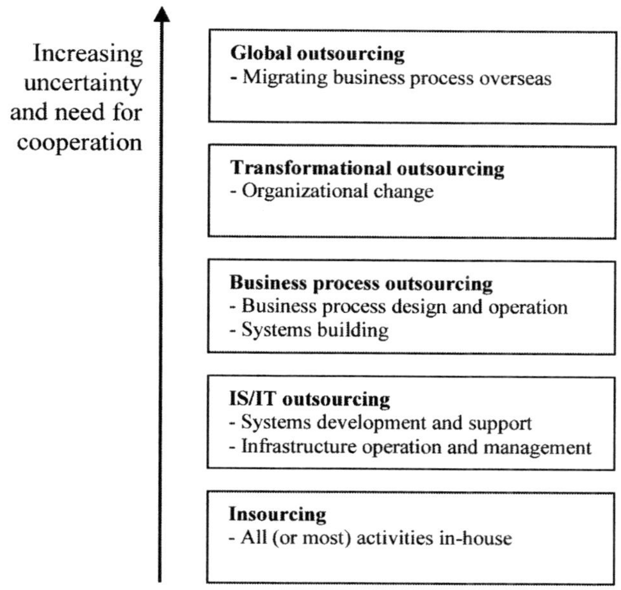

the customer remains responsible for delivering the result of the insourced activities. Traditional outsourcing is depicted by the customer having a one-to-one relationship with large IT service companies (e.g., IBM, EDS, CSC). This is the domain of very large companies due to the fact that both set-up and maintenance costs are expensive. Unlike traditional outsourcing, business application outsourcing offered by application service providers (ASPs) is targeted for the small and medium enterprises (SMEs). This is typically a one-to-many model, where an application will be offered to numerous customers across different sites. The emerging technologies coupled with economies of skills (rather than scale) make the ASP model a viable and affordable option for SMEs (Currie & Seltsikas, 2001).

BUSINESS APPLICATION OUTSOURCING

Dramatically reduced network cost due to the Internet and virtual private networks, the ever increasing supply of bandwidth, and advances in the security of Internet based transactions have led to the emergence of application service providers (ASPs), a new category of IT service firms. ASP can be defined as "an organization that manages and delivers application capabilities to multiple entities from a data center across a wide area network." User organizations can get access to software applications from one or more ASPs over the Internet for a subscription fee (Susarla, Barua, & Whinston, 2003).

In a typical business, we find several information systems applications. For example, Weill and Vitale (1999) identified an applications portfolio of 18 systems in a manufacturing business: budgeting, capital projects, customer complaints, debtors, general ledger, freight cost management, fixed assets, human resource management, inventory, market data, multi-plant accounting, office support, payroll management, pricing & sales, purchasing, sales forecasting, product safety system, and trading accounts management. These systems support tasks in peoples' jobs. For example, all systems help planning, investigating, coordinating, evaluating, supervising, staffing, negotiating, and representing to a varying extent.

User organizations can get access to software applications from one or more ASPs over the Internet for a subscription fee. A key selling point for ASP services involves a shorter time period required to implement new software applications. For businesses plagued by high turnover of information technology staff, inadequate organizational resources to maintain and upgrade existing IT applications, and large capital requirements for major IT implementation projects, the ASP business model could be an attractive alternative with its off-the-shelf IT applications subscription approach. Sophisticated ASPs have gone as far as offering enterprise resource planning, electronic commerce, and supply chain applications, which may involve integration with existing information systems in a user organization (Susarla et al., 2003).

While the ASP model has the potential to fundamentally change the manner in which IT services are provided to user firms, to date ASPs have had a limited success in signing up customers. Moreover, several customers of ASPs are unsatisfied with their service, which questions the viability of the ASP business model and selection of ASP as an enter strategy for IT outsourcing. Evidence points also to the fact that ASPs themselves have to rework their service strategies in response to market demand. It has been long recognized that market success depends on designing services to match customer needs and that customer satisfaction has a positive impact on market share and profitability. Satisfied customers are more likely to engage in positive word of mouth, thus lowering the cost of attracting new customers. Satisfaction based on successful exploration and exploitation of the vendor value proposition plays an important role in building other important assets for the firm. A focus on satisfaction is important for ASPs if they have to retain existing customers as well as attract new customers (Susarla et al., 2003).

This calls for an assessment of the determinants of client satisfaction with ASP and evaluation of the effectiveness of the ASP mode of service delivery over the Internet. Susarla et al. (2003) analyzed the determinants of satisfaction in ASP service provision. Their analyzes shows that the satisfaction with an ASP is negatively affected by the disconfirmation effect, but positively influenced by the perceived provider performance and prior systems integration, which is a measure of integration of organizational systems prior to using ASP services. Disconfirmation is the negative discrepancy between expectation and performance.

Further, perceived provider performance is positively influenced by the functional capability of the ASP and the quality assurance by the ASP, but negatively influenced by the prior systems integration. These findings suggest that, to be successful, ASPs must strive to reduce the disconfirmation effect faced by adopting organizations and to enhance the perceived quality of their solution, possibly through partnerships with leading IT vendors. Further, ASPs must improve the integration of their offerings with existing applications in user organizations, which may require alliances with IT firms that specialize in integration services. From a client perspective, an enter strategy of ASP selection may thus focus on integration with existing IT, performance delivery, and standards of software capability.

From a vendor perspective, the findings of Susarla et al (2003) indicate a need for ASPs to facilitate integration with existing IT in client organizations, ensure superior performance delivery, emphasize rigorous enforcement of service agreements, and ensure that their application meets standards of software capability. Their finding that ASPs are not evaluated on some of the prior experiences of the organizations is favorable to vendors, since it suggests that firms that are Internet savvy or that have a strong IT department are not going to have unreasonably high expectations from the ASPs.

A related area of exploration is an analysis of how organizational users form expectations about an ASP's services. The literature on outsourcing posits that the trade press, discussion with peers, consultants' forecasts, and the business strategy pursued by the company can contribute to the formation of expectations in the outsourcing context. As the IT outsourcing literature has documented, management defines the scope of the outsourcing and the sourcing criteria, while the IT department can provide insights on the technological reasons for outsourcing and judge the success of the outsourcing project in terms of performance outcomes that are met. Expectations that need to be realized in the outsourcing context may reflect the consensus among the different stakeholders in the organization (Susarla et al., 2003).

BUSINESS PROCESS OUTSOURCING

Business processing outsourcing is typically the outsourcing of a company's non-core or back-office business processes. Usually those processes are IT enabled (or should be IT enabled) and hence can be transformed by the use of a new or improved technology platform. The appeal of business process outsourcing is that it therefore attempts to involve a new support services model involving cost effective, scaleable, efficient services (Honess, 2003). The growth in demand for process outsourcing has also seen an expansion in the range of services being provided by suppliers. Processes typically outsourced include finance and accounting, procurement, human resources, contact centers, and other administrative functions. According to Feeny, Lacity, and Willcocks, (2005), successful outsourcing of back-office business functions requires the client to identify which competencies to assess, to undertake careful evaluation of supplier strengths, and to remain involved in the business processes.

Enterprise restructuring is expected to provide fertile ground for outsourcing in the business process outsourcing market segment. Some companies turn to outsourcing to foster change management during consolidation and integration. Consolidation, mergers and acquisitions result in integration needs for back-office processes, which are often met by outsourcing. Divested companies need to grow entire back-office functions from scratch and look to external services providers to provide this process-management capability. Business process outsourcing includes enterprise services (human resources, finance and accounting, payment services, and administration), supply management (buying processes, storing processes, and moving processes), demand management processes (customer selection, customer acquisition, customer retention, and customer extension), and operations. A typical business process outsourcing contract includes discrete project-based IT services, ongoing IT management services and general process management (Gartner, 2004).

Business process outsourcing often fills human resources (HR) practitioners with fear, but handled properly it can help the HR function become more efficient and strategic. Of all the business-related acronyms that are filtering through to the corporate consciousness, BPO – business process outsourcing – is certainly one that appears to be raising interest. Business process outsourcing, although often seen as the next evolutionary step in IT outsourcing, is also very different from it. BPO is about delegating the ownership, administration and operation of a process to a specialist third party in order to solve a business problem. And because BPO is about delivering outcomes – higher performing business processes – it aims to raise a client company's shareholder value (Strategic HR Review, 2004).

Business processes within a company can be broken down into three categories: core; business critical non-core; and finally non-core, non-critical. Core processes are seldom outsourced, because they are the very essence of the business and the area that requires the most investment. Critical and non-critical non-core processes may be suited for outsourcing to a third party supplier who will invest in them on the company's behalf. Process management has the highest expected growth rate in outsourcing. Business processing outsourcing is typically the outsourcing of a company's non-core or back-office business processes. Usually those processes are IT enabled (or should be IT enabled) and hence can be transformed by the use of a new or improved technology platform. The appeal of business process outsourcing is that it therefore attempts to involve a new support services model involving cost effective, scaleable, efficient services. The growth in demand for process outsourcing has also seen an expansion in the range of services being provided by suppliers. Processes typically outsourced include finance and accounting, procurement, human resources, and real estate (Honess, 2003).

TRANSFORMATIONAL OUTSOURCING

According to Linder (2004), the concept of transformational outsourcing is an emerging practice, where companies are looking outside for help for more fundamental reasons – to facilitate rapid organizational change, to launch new strategies and to reshape company boundaries. In doing so, they are engaging in transformational outsourcing: "partnering with another company to achieve a rapid, substantial and sustainable improvement in enterprise-level performance." Transformational outsourcing places the power to bring new capabilities to the organization squarely in the hands of executives who have and value those capabilities. In other words, the outsourcing partner provides a management team that is experienced in the capability that the organization seeking change needs. And those executives are empowered by the outsourcing process to implement the practices they bring with them.

Given the potential headaches of managing IT, it is tempting to hand the job over to someone else. Indeed, outsourcing once appeared to be a simple solution to management frustrations, and senior management teams at many companies negotiated contracts with large service providers to run their entire IT functions. At a minimum, these providers were often able to provide IT capabilities for a lower cost and with fewer hassles than the companies had been able to themselves. But many of these outsourcing arrangements resulted in dissatisfaction, particularly as a company's business needs changed. Service providers, with their standard offerings and detailed contracts, provided IT capabilities that were not flexible enough to meet changing requirements, and they often seemed slow to respond to problems. Furthermore, a relationship with a supplier often required substantial investments of money and time, which entrenched that supplier in the company's strategic planning and business processes. The company then became particularly vulnerable if the supplier failed to meet its contractual obligations (Ross & Weill, 2002).

Problems arose because senior managers, in choosing to outsource the IT function, were also outsourcing responsibility for one or more of the crucial decisions they should have been making themselves. Companies often hired outside providers because they were dissatisfied with the performance of their own IT departments – but that dissatisfaction was primarily the result of their own lack of involvement. In light of this track record, bigger companies, at least, are deciding to keep their main IT capabilities in-house. But many engage in selective outsourcing. Good candidates for this are commodity services – such as telecommunications, in which there are several competing suppliers and specifications are easy to set – and services involving technologies with which the company lacks expertise. Unlike decisions to outsource the entire IT function, selective outsourcing decisions are usually best left to the IT unit – assuming that senior management has taken responsibility for overall strategy.

Beaumont and Costa (2002) studied information technology outsourcing in Australia. They found that close to 40% of Australian organizations outsource one or more IT applications. Large organizations tended to outsource more than small ones. The three most important reasons for outsourcing were access to skills, improved quality and focus on core business. Four factors contributed to successful outsourcing: a tight contract, a partnership, a change process, and the IT manager's role changing from managing projects and operations to acquiring and managing the internal and external resources required to do the organization's IT work.

The traditional way of thinking in IT outsourcing is to move the current IT function out of the organization and let another organization handle it. There is no strategic thinking behind it, except the idea of solving a problem, saving some money or improving a function by means of some undefined solutions. The new way of thinking is to make IT outsourcing part of a strategic transformation of the IT function, where new tasks and roles are implemented to replace old tasks and roles. A classic example of this new way of thinking was the transformation of the IT function at British Petroleum (BP) in the 1990s. The IT function went through a fundamental transformation consisting of the following changes (Cross, Earl, & Sampler, 1997):

- *From systems provider to infrastructure planner.* The mission of the IT function shifted from developing systems to overseeing technical integrity and pursuing value creation and cost reduction opportunities through information sharing.
- *From monopoly supplier to mixed sourcing.* In 1991, outsourcing of operations, telecommunications, systems development, and IT maintenance began, as BP recognized that it was not essential that these were carried out in-house. Some local sites already had experience in facilities management, and, as contracts came up for renewal, lessons were recorded and a worldwide outsourcing program implemented.
- *From business standards to industry standards.* IT managers have long been concerned about coordinating various types of computing and communication equipment. However, throughout most of the research on IT infrastructure, the focus has been directed at creating and managing the internal infrastructure. Therefore, BP spearheaded a unique initiative to help create an external software market by being one of the early advocates and founding members of the Petrotechnical Open Software Corporation, which was joined by a number of oil companies such as Elf, Mobil, Statoil and Texaco.
- *From decentralized bias to centralized top sight.* The senior management team realized that the major benefit of centralized management of IT is not budget authority, but is in setting standards for infrastructure. While some IT resources still remain in the local businesses, it is the job of the top IT management team to provide the global perspective for infrastructure planning and cost control, which is here called top sight.
- *From systems analysts to business consultants.* A new skill set was defined for IT personnel. The new skill set has an equal balance between business, technical, and people skills. Such a radical change in the skill set of IT staff has been supported by a number of human resource initiatives such as skills testing, self-assessment, and personal development planning.
- *From craftsmen to project managers.* IT personnel no longer approach their job as craftsmen, viewing each job as a unique, customized process. Their task has switched to that of project managers, integrating and coordinating stakeholders involved in providing IT applications and operations.
- *From large function to lean teams.* Team orientation was stimulated in different ways. For example, staff was moved around the world to create global not local loyalties. A team building and

team-working program was introduced stressing the use of multifunctional teams and diluting the functional focus.

The IT budget was reduced from 360 million dollars in 1989 to 132 million in 1995 after this transformation. IT personnel were reduced from 1400 persons to 150 persons in these six years. Hence, a large portion of the reduced IT budget went to external outsourcing vendors. As this pioneering case of IT outsourcing illustrates, outsourcing can be more than a tool for cutting costs and improving organizational focus. Increasingly, it is a means of acquiring new capabilities and bringing about fundamental strategic and structural change.

According to Linder (2004), the concept of transformational outsourcing is an emerging practice, where companies are looking outside for help for more fundamental reasons – to facilitate rapid organizational change, to launch new strategies and to reshape company boundaries. In doing so, they are engaging in transformational outsourcing: partnering with another company to achieve a rapid, substantial and sustainable improvement in enterprise-level performance.

Transformational outsourcing places the power to bring new capabilities to the organization squarely in the hands of executives who have and value those capabilities. In other words, the outsourcing partner provides a management team that is experienced in the capability that the organization seeking change needs. And those executives are empowered by the outsourcing process to implement the practices they bring with them. Not all transformational outsourcing initiatives are alike. Linder (2004) identified four broad categories from her research on twenty companies that have attempted the practice. The four categories are:

- startups (outsource to rapidly scale up a new business)
- pathway to growth (outsource to fix a key process that stands in the way of growth)
- change catalyst (outsource to signal broad change and focus on adding value)
- radical renewal (outsource to improve core operating capabilities radically)

As executives get more experience with outsourcing, they are learning the tool's potential and beginning to wield it for more strategic purposes. Some will use it to shape and reshape their business models. Instead of massive, sweeping changes, many organizations will master the ability to use outsourcing to make continuous incremental improvements. But while the potential benefits are incontrovertible, the art of joining organizations with unique capabilities is extremely challenging and requires visionary leaders with strong hearts and a large capacity for hard work. By combining the tool's execution effectiveness with their own growing skills in partnering, leaders who display those characteristics will have a practical and realistic road map at their disposal for building strategic flexibility.

Transformational outsourcing is an emerging practice, but the track record of companies that have engaged in it is impressive. In Linder's study of 20 companies, 17 of them have been in place long enough to show results. Of that group, 13 have achieved dramatic, organization-level impact. To the extent that other companies can replicate such success, transformational outsourcing may become a more effective way of improving performance than major internal change initiatives, mergers and acquisitions, or joint ventures (Linder, 2004).

The key issue is new capabilities. In undertaking an internal initiative, a company has concluded that it lacks an important set of skills – otherwise it would not be seeking transformation. But it often proves too time-consuming to develop the skills internally. In a mergers-and-acquisition scenario, the company acquires the capabilities it lacks, but cultural clashes often interfere with its ability to use them effectively. An acquiring company seldom, for example, puts executives from the acquired company in charge of its own organization in order to learn from them. Similar cultural impediments make it unlikely that a company will transform itself with the expertise it gains in a joint venture. But transformational outsourcing places the power to bring new capabilities to the organization squarely in the hands of executives who have and value those capabilities. The outsourcing partner provides a management team that is experienced in the capability that the organization seeking change needs. And those executives are empowered by the outsourcing process to implement the practices they bring with them.

Transformational outsourcing is concerned with bringing new capabilities to the organization through important sets of skills. These skills can be found in knowledge work, and knowledge management emerges as an important discipline in transformational outsourcing. Executives have to lead a transformational outsourcing initiative much differently from the way they would manage conventional outsourcing.

GLOBAL OUTSOURCING

Since the mid-1990s global outsourcing – sometimes called offshoring – has been a fast growing aspect of the world economy. Venkatraman (2004) has defined the term offshoring as "the practice among U.S. and European companies to migrating business processes to India, the Philippines, Ireland, China and elsewhere to lower costs without significantly sacrificing quality." The strategic benefits for firms can be portrayed as a means to reduce costs, improve asset efficiency, and increase profits. Criticisms of outsourcing have often been in the areas of changing employment patterns, globalization of labor force, and its effects on individuals and organizations (Clott, 2004). For most companies, coordinating a far-flung network of business processes presents new challenges, e.g., security, culture and knowledge transfer. For global outsourcing the role of transaction costs is almost as significant as production costs (Qu & Brocklehurst, 2003).

The traditional outsourcing model implies a one-to-one relationship between client and supplier. Håkanson's (1982) Interaction Approach has been used as a basic framework describing the relationship between client and supplier. This model is previously used by outsourcing researchers (e.g., Lacity & Willcocks, 2000a; Kern & Willcocks, 2002) to described different aspects of the outsourcing relationship. As global outsourcing grows (Lewin & Peeters, 2006), several international service suppliers have established service centers or delivery centers overseas or in low cost countries. Today, we see a trend towards a global outsourcing model, as shown in Figure 2, where global vendor companies contract clients locally and produce services from their delivery centers in low cost countries. In this way suppliers get access to high qualified personnel at a low costs.

Based on experiences gathered from offshore projects at a global service supplier, we have identified some good practices and success factors using global outsourcing models with offshore delivery centers. The global service supplier has established large delivery centers in India and in Eastern Europe. Their motivation is to maintain margins in increasingly competitive markets and to get access to skilled resources. From the supplier's perspective, the key success factors of offshoring with global delivery centers can be summarized as follows:

- *Planning and project management are foundations to offshoring success.* When preparing offshoring, planning should be a priority. Typical problems are: no clear idea about distribution of

Figure 2. Client and vendor outsourcing model with delivery center

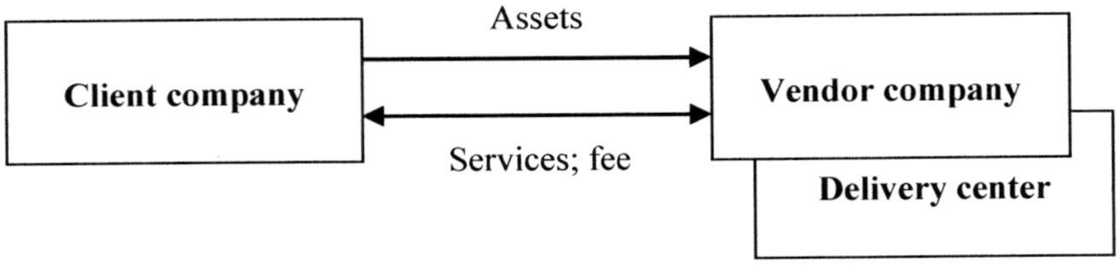

services, lack of expectation management towards client and team members, lack of communication plan or strategy, no plan for knowledge transfer. This may lead to dissatisfaction, misunderstandings, loss of important information, insufficient understanding of services and business. Planning should cover aspects such as: roles and responsibility onshore and offshore, team structure, the scope of work, key data and deliverables, what tools and language to use, infrastructure and resources needed, monitoring and control tools, issue management and project risk management, time and expense reporting, training needs, and schedules.

- *Use proven good practices and methods, and carefully select right leadership onshore and offshore.* Many projects have started offshoring without involving experienced resources, and they are spending time making templates and processes that already exists. Therefore, many projects have to learn by the same mistakes. It is important to utilize the knowledge and experience already in the organization. Initially, there is often a resistance towards offshoring among certain groups of stakeholders. The responsible for offshoring should be able to overcome this initial resistance by motivating clients and talk to them about opportunities.
- *Do not underestimate the importance of personal relationships.* The approach to creating personal relationships between onshore and offshore team may be challenge, e.g. in terms of culture, time, language, and geographical differences. The need for face-to-face meetings still exists and many people find it easier to talk and collaborate with someone over the phone if you have met.
- *Offshoring demands high focus on expectation management.* Expectation management towards the client, on all levels, is important to ensure adaptation to new processes and language requirements. Early offshoring projects developed a "cowboy style", but offshoring means introducing formal processes and communication. Even if formalities are accepted at higher management levels, the vendor may experience day-to-day problems adopting formalities to lower levels in the client organization.
- *Carefully plan knowledge transfer – especially on functional and business process knowledge.* There is great difference between projects who spent time in planning knowledge transfer, and those who did not. Planning of knowledge transfer leads to efficient mobilization of offshore team, and makes offshore team more independent and motivated. When no plan for knowledge transfer exists some of the aspects of the application are uncovered (especially functional understanding tends to be weak). As a result of this the offshore resources becomes dependent on support form onshore team.
- *Early offshore involvement increases responsibility and motivation.* Involving delivery center as early as possible promotes ownership and understanding. At the same time it gives delivery center time to gather resources and set up the infrastructure needed. This prevents time leg interpreting plans made onsite. Early involvement may also prevent loss of valuable information.

- *Offshoring increases the need for clear and specific communication.* Clear routines for communication should be established. Feedback improves collaboration and is important to obtain agreed upon deliveries. Communication is also about control over decisions being made. A communication plan must be stated in a formal document and must include: formal two-way feedback sessions, norms of how to control the flow of information between teams, meeting and reporting schedules, identification of team members on both sides, how to handle special risks or issues. Cultural differences make communication more challenging.

Outsourcing, whether it is with a local or a global partner, is a form of strategic alliance that has increased in popularity over the past decade. However, there is a level of risk associated with alliances, compared to in-house activities. Aspects that cause high risk include the difficulties inherent in gaining cooperation with partners who have different objectives, and the potential for opportunistic exploitation of the dependence relationship that exists between partners. Appropriate governance structures, including management control systems and the development of trust, may work to reduce risk and decrease failure (Langfield-Smith & Smith, 2003). In Table 2, we have examined the global outsourcing model using the framework developed by Langfield-Smith and Smith (2003). Designing governance structures in situations that span traditional organizational boundaries, including strategic alliances with suppliers, or outsourcing, one should consider characteristics of the transaction, the parties involved, and the environment. In addition, almost every control system involves some degree of trust that the individuals of concern will do what is best for the organization without any, or with only incomplete, monitoring of actions or results.

Client global outsourcing is demanding regarding specification of services and control of services delivered, and in terms of information, financial and social exchange. For long-term successful relationships knowledge transfer is an important issue. Client companies may have a challenge migrating business processes directly to a supplier overseas. An interesting global outsourcing model is coming up, contracting a global service supplier with delivery centers overseas. The global service supplier must handle the difficulties of changing environment and atmosphere of working together from different cultures, time, languages and geographical regions.

From a client perspective, one can go directly to a supplier in a low cost country meeting challenges such as contracting, specification and verification of services, and day-to-day communication. In building of trust, two key issues seems to be the transfer of knowledge about application and business processes, and the cultural, lingual, time, and geographical barriers when trying to build personal relationship with the offshore team. When contracting a local, but global service supplier with delivery centers abroad, some of these challenges of control and trust can be resolved more easily. The onshore team is responsible for handling most issues with offshore team. Although this, the importance of knowledge transfer still doesn't disappear. To successfully deliver services, both offshore and onshore team needs functional understanding of client business processes.

OUTSOURCING DECISION

How should firms organize their enterprise-wide activities related to the acquisition, deployment, and management of information technology? During the 1980s, IT professionals devoted considerable attention to this issue, primarily debating the virtues of centralized, decentralized, and federal modes of

Table 2. Control mechanisms and trust in global outsourcing relationships

Offshoring model	Transaction, actors, and environmental characteristics	Control mechanisms	Trust
Client – supplier in low cost country	• Resistance against offshoring can result in potential opportunities not taken • Starting offshoring without involving experienced resources • Time consuming planning process – gather resources and setting up infrastructure needed • Expectation management to ensure new processes and language requirements	• Contracting with offshore supplier needs special skills • Formal verification processes needed • Increases the need for clear and specific communication, meeting and reporting schedules	• Knowledge transfer enables trust in offshore supplier • Building personal relationship meets barriers such as culture, language, time, geographical locations differences
Client – global supplier with delivery center in low cost country	• Overcomes initial resistance because of local contract • Utilizing offshore experience and knowledge from other projects • Involve delivery center to reduce costs and get access to qualified personnel • Introducing formal processes and routines	• Supplier onshore team involved to improve collaboration and giving the best deliveries • Supplier onshore team is responsible for the result; and for knowledge transfer • Supplier onshore team ensures control, resource utilization, and ownership	• Trust is based on relationship with supplier onshore team • Communication between supplier onshore and offshore team necessary making the collaboration work

governance. Throughout the 1980s and 1990s, IT researchers anticipated and followed these debates, eventually reaching considerable consensus regarding the influence of different contingency factors on an enterprise's choice of a particular governance mode (Sambamurthy & Zmud, 2000).

Today, however, there are increasing signs that this accumulated wisdom might be inadequate in shaping appropriate insights for contemporary practice. The traditional governance logic has been turned upside down by utilizing other mechanisms, such as sourcing arrangements, strategic alliances, roles, teams, processes, and informal relationships, as the primary vehicles through which business executives orchestrate their IT organizational architectures.

Today's IT organization must grapple with the unrelenting challenges associated with: acquiring current technical knowledge; attracting, retaining, motivating, and leveraging an IT workforce; distilling the confusion amid a proliferation in IT products, services, and vendors; and, contracting and managing a variety of relationships involved with selective outsourcing. Increasingly, the providers of IT products and services are being viewed as both arms-length suppliers of cost-effective technology and as vibrant business partners with an unlimited potential to enhance a firm's IT and business capabilities. IT procurement has moved from being operational to tactical to strategic, amidst networks of alliances with IT vendors, consultants, and third party service providers being built and managed in order to leverage their associated assets, competencies, and knowledge.

The decision to outsource or insource enterprise-wide activities related to the acquisition, deployment, and management of IT represents one of the more complex choices facing a firm's managers. On the one hand, insourcing requires management to commit significant resources to a course of action, the effects of which may be costly to reverse, while forgoing numerous advantages associated with the marketplace. On the other hand, insourcing may be required for a firm to accumulate resources necessary to generate or maintain a competitive advantage.

The complexity of this decision is demonstrated in research conducted by Leiblein, Reuer, and

Dalsace (2002). They examined the relationship between governance choice and technological performance. In contrast to popular arguments suggesting that insourcing or outsourcing will lead to superior technological performance, they found that governance decisions per se do not significantly influence technological performance directly. Rather, observed differences in the performance of transactions governed by different organizational forms are driven by factors underlying governance choice. While the increasing rapidity of technological change and the increasing dispersion of knowledge suggest an increased role for outsourcing in the economy, the relationship between governance choice and performance is dependent on the distribution of relevant capabilities and the degree to which performance is driven by autonomous or systemic innovation.

Empirical evidence suggests that carefully crafted outsourcing strategies increase the overall performance of the firm. Outsourcing is generally considered as a very powerful tool to cut costs and improve performance. Through outsourcing, firms can take advantage of the best outside vendors and restructure entrenched departments that are reluctant to change. Outsourcing can also help focus on the core business. Since building core competencies and serving customer needs are critical to firm success, anything that detracts from this focus may be considered for outsourcing (Barthélemy, 2003).

CONCLUSION

In this chapter we have defined outsourcing as "a process whereby an organization decides to contract-out or sell the firm's IT assets, people and/or activities to a third party supplier, who in exchange provides and manages these assets and services for an agreed fee over an agreed time period" (Kern & Willcocks, 2002). An outsourcing relationship consists of a vendor (supplier) and a client (customer). The vendor is a firm that has the required technology in terms of hardware, software and services. This firm is sometimes called the source firm (Steensma & Corley, 2001) and sometimes called the outsourcer (Beamount & Costa, 2002). The client is a firm that desires the technology. This firm is sometimes called the sourcing firm or outsourcee.

The client company's decision to outsource technology, systems, and/or business processes to a vendor onshore or offshore is influenced by a number of factors. Later in this book we will discuss factors such as production economies, transaction economies, technological uncertainty, functional complexity, transaction specific investments, supplier presence, slack resources, and criticality of IT.

REFERENCES

Barthélemy, J. (2003). The Seven Deadly Sins of Outsourcing. *The Academy of Management Executive*, *17*(2), 87–100.

Beamount, N., & Costa, C. (2002). Information Technology Outsourcing in Australia. *Information Resources Management Journal*, *15*(3), 14–31.

Clott, C. B. (2004). Perspectives on Global Outsourcing and the Changing Nature of Work. *Business and Society Review*, *109*(2), 153–170. doi:10.1111/j.0045-3609.2004.00189.x

Cross, J., Earl, M. J., & Sampler, J. L. (1997). Transformation of the IT Function at British Petroleum. *MIS Quarterly*, *21*(4), 401–423. doi:10.2307/249721

Currie, W. L., & Seltsikas, P. (2001). Exploring the supply-side of IT-outsourcing: evaluating the emerging role of application service providers. *European Journal of Information Systems*, *10*(3), 123–134. doi:10.1057/palgrave.ejis.3000393

Feeny, D. F., Lacity, M. C., & Willcocks, L. P. (2005). Taking the Measure of Outsourcing Providers. *MIT Sloan Management Review*, *46*(3), 41–48.

Gartner. (2004). *Worldwide IT Services Market Definitions Guide*. Surrey, UK: Gartner Group.

Grover, V., Cheon, M. J., & Teng, J. T. C. (1996). The Effect of Service Quality and Partnership on the Outsourcing of Information Systems Functions. *Journal of Management Information Systems*, *12*(4), 89–116.

Grover, V., Teng, T. C., & Cheon, M. J. (1998). Towards a Theoretically-Based Contingency Model of Information Systems Outsourcing. In L. P. Willcocks & M. C. Lacity (Eds.), *Strategic Sourcing of Information Systems. Perspectives and Practices* (pp. 79-101). Chichester, UK: John Wiley & Sons.

Håkansson, H. (1982). *International Marketing and Purchasing of Industrial Goods: An Interaction Approach*. Chichester, UK: John Wiley & Sons.

Hirschheim, R., & Lacity, M. C. (2000). The Myths and Realities of Information Technology Insourcing. *Communications of the ACM*, *43*(2), 99–107. doi:10.1145/328236.328112

Honess, S (2003). Business process outsourcing. In J. Angel (Ed.), *Technology Outsourcing* (pp. 208-229). London: The Law Society.

Hu, Q., Saunders, C., & Gebelt, M. (1997). Research Report: Diffusion of Information Systems Outsourcing: A Reevaluation of Influence Sources. *Information Systems Research*, *8*(3), 288–301. doi:10.1287/isre.8.3.288

Kern, T., & Willcocks, L. P. (2002). Exploring relationship in information technology outsourcing: the interaction approach. *European Journal of Information Systems*, *11*(1), 3–19. doi:10.1057/palgrave/ejis/3000415

Lacity, M. C., & Willcocks, L. P. (2000a). Relationships in IT Outsourcing: A Stakeholder Perspective. In R. W. Zmud (Ed.), *Framing the Domains of IT Management: Projecting the Future Through the Past*. Cincinnati, OH: Pinnaflex Educational Resources.

Lacity, M. C., & Willcocks, L. P. (2000b). Survey of IT Outsourcing Experiences in US and UK Organizations. *Journal of Global Information Management*, *8*(2), 5–23.

Lacity, M. C., Willcocks, L. P., & Feeny, D. F. (1996). The Value of Selective IT Sourcing. *Sloan Management Review*, *37*(3), 13–25.

Langfield-Smith, K., & Smith, D. (2003). Management control systems and trust in outsourcing relationships. *Management Accounting Research*, *14*(3), 281–307. doi:10.1016/S1044-5005(03)00046-5

Laudon, K. C., & Laudon, J. P. (2005). *Essentials of management information systems - Managing the digital firm* (6th ed.). Upper Saddle River, NJ: Pearson Education.

Leiblein, M. J., Reuer, J. J., & Dalsace, F. (2002). Do make or buy decisions matter? The influence of organizational governance on technological performance. *Strategic Management Journal, 23*(9), 817–833. doi:10.1002/smj.259

Levina, N., & Ross, J. W. (2003). From the Vendor's Perspective: Exploring the Value Proposition in Information Technology Outsourcing. *MIS Quarterly, 27*(3), 331–364.

Lewin, A. Y., & Peeters, C. (2006). Offshoring Work: Business Hype or the Onset of Fundamental Transformation? *Long Range Planning, 39*(3), 221–239. doi:10.1016/j.lrp.2006.07.009

Linder, J. (2004). Transformational Outsourcing. *MIT Sloan Management Review, 45*(2), 52–58.

Loh, L., & Venkatraman, N. (1992a). Determinants of Information Technology Outsourcing: A Cross-Sectional Analysis. *Journal of Management Information Systems, 9*(1), 7–24.

Loh, L., & Venkatraman, N. (1992b). Diffusion of Information Technology Outsourcing: Influence Sources and the Kodak Effect. *Information Systems Research, 3*(4), 334–358. doi:10.1287/isre.3.4.334

Qu, Z., & Brocklehurst, M. (2003). What will it take china to become a competitive force in offshore outsourcing? An analysis of the role of transaction costs in supplier selection. *Journal of Information Technology, 18*(1), 53–67. doi:10.1080/0268396031000077459

Ross, J. W., & Weill, P. (2002). Six IT Decisions Your IT People Shouldn't Make. *Harvard Business Review*, (November): 84–91.

Sambamurthy, V., & Zmud, R. (2000). Research Commentary: The Organizing Logic for an Enterprise's IT Activities in the Digital Era - A Prognosis of Practice and a Call for Research. *Information Systems Research, 11*(2), 105–114. doi:10.1287/isre.11.2.105.11780

Steensma, H. K., & Corley, K. G. (2001). Organizational Context as Moderator of Theories on Firm Boundaries for Technology Sourcing. *Academy of Management Journal, 44*(2), 271–291. doi:10.2307/3069455

Strategic HR Review. (2004). Exercising due diligence in recruitment outsourcing. *Strategic HR Review, 3*(3), 10-11.

Susarla, A., Barua, A., & Whinston, A. B. (2003). Understanding the Service Component of Application Service Provision: An Empirical Analysis of Satisfaction with ASP Services. *MIS Quarterly, 27*(1), 91–123.

Venkatraman, N. V. (2004). Offshoring Without Guilt. *MIT Sloan Management Review, 45*(3), 14–16.

Weill, P., & Vitale, M. R. (1999). Assessing the Health of an Information Systems Application Portfolio: An Example From Process Manufacturing. *MIS Quarterly, 23*(4), 601–624. doi:10.2307/249491

Chapter 2
Theoretical Foundations

IT outsourcing as a theoretical as well as practical discipline is based on several other concepts and disciplines, as well as the relations between them – such as international business, marketing, psychology, technology management, strategic management, project management, knowledge management, finance, economy, organizations, traditional management, political science, and the behavioral sciences. Even though IT outsourcing is a practical issue in the end, organizational and management theories can be applied to enlighten the emerging business practices of outsourcing.

In this chapter, eleven organizational and management theories are presented according to attributes like outsourcing focus, aim, the unit of analysis, outsourcing philosophy, and critical success factors. A comparison of theories is presented in Table 1 and a comprehensive literature review of IT outsourcing based research is presented at the end of the chapter. The primary purpose of the chapter is to strengthen the theoretical understanding of IT outsourcing. This approach is adapted from Earl (2001). No claims are made that any one theory outperforms others. Each represents a particular theoretical orientation and a different form of organizational intervention of IT outsourcing. The theories are not mutually exclusive, and two or more of them can be applied to the same outsourcing arrangement. Application of different theories in a practical decision-making situation can lead to different outcomes.

DOI: 10.4018/978-1-60566-796-6.ch002

NEO-CLASSICAL ECONOMIC THEORY

Focus, Aim, Unit of Analysis

Neo-classical economic theory regards every business organization as a production function (Williamson, 1981), where their motivation is driven by profit maximization. This means that companies offer products and services to the market where they have a cost or production advantage. They rely on the marketplace where they have disadvantages. Neo-classical economic theory posits that firms outsource IT to attain cost advantages from assumed economies of scale and scope possessed by vendors (Ang & Straub, 1998).

In neo-classical economic theory, outsourcing may arise in two ways. First, outsourcing may arise through the substitution of external purchases for internal activities. In this way, it can be viewed as a discontinuation of internal production (whether it be production of goods or services) and an initiation of procurement from outside suppliers. To the extent this type of outsourcing reduces a firm's involvement in successive stages of production substitution-based outsourcing may be viewed as vertical disintegration. This seems to be the most commonly understood type of outsourcing. Outsourcing may also occur through abstention. Outsourcing need not be limited to those activities that are shifted to external suppliers. On the contrary, outsourcing may also arise when a firm purchases goods or services from outside organizations even when those goods or services have not been completed in-house in the past. In neo-classical economic terms, Gilley and Rasheed (2000) posed the question, "Making more by doing less?" Their study empirically examined the extent to which outsourcing of both peripheral and near-core tasks influenced the firm's financial and non-financial performance. In addition, the potential moderating effects of firm strategy and the environment on the outsourcing-performance relationship were examined. Results indicate that both firm strategy and environmental dynamism moderated the relationship between outsourcing and performance, whereas there was no significant direct effect of outsourcing on firm performance.

In neo-classical economic theory, both the distribution of income and the composition of output are endogenously and simultaneously determined by a general equilibrium of supply and demand. The underlying data on the supply side are parametrically given resource inputs and a given technology of production for transforming inputs into outputs; on the demand side, the data are specified in terms of a given distribution of ownership of inputs and a given pattern of preferences for final outputs (Gram, 2003).

Contribution to the Understanding of IT Outsourcing

Companies will justify their sourcing strategy based on evaluating possibilities for production cost savings. Thus, the question of whether or not to outsource, is a question whether the marketplace can produce products and services at a lower price than internal production. In the context of IT outsourcing, a company will keep its IT-function internally if this has production cost advantages, and it will outsource when the marketplace can offer production cost savings. However, defining outsourcing simply in terms of procurement activities does not capture the true strategic nature of the issues (Gilley & Rasheed, 2000). IT outsourcing is not only a purchasing decision – all firms purchase elements of their operations. This is done to achieve economic, technological, and strategic advantages. However, the economies of scale and scope argument would predict that outsourcing has little to offer to larger

Table 1. Comparison of theories

Theory / Attribute	Cost concerns					Resource concerns		Partnership concerns			
	Neo-classical economic theory	*Transaction cost theory*	*Contractual theory*	*Agency theory*	*Theory of firm boundaries*	*Theory of core competencies*	*Resource-based theory*	*Partnership and alliance theory*	*Relational exchange theory*	*Stakeholder theory*	*Social exchange theory*
Focus	Organization as a production function	Economic organization	Contract as a legally bound, institutional framework	Delegation of work	Determinants of firm boundaries	Firm-specific skills and know-how	Unique organizational resources of both tangible and intangible nature	Collaborative interfirm business relationships	Relational norms	Manage organizations more effectively	Social behavior
Aim	Profit maximization, obtained from economies of scale and scope	Governance structure; which transactions should be organized how	Facilitating exchange and preventing opportunism	Most efficient contract governing principal-agent relationship	Pursuing hierarchical control or market contracts	Organization of work and delivery of value	Leverage distinctive internal and external resources	Achievement of mutually compatible goals	Effective contract governance	Balancing interests of all stakeholders	Obtain positive economic and/or social outcomes
Unit	Company	Transaction	Contract	Contract	Company	Company	Company	Relationship	Relationship	Firm/ group/ individual	Individual/organizational
Outsourcing philosophy	Outsource when marketplace can offer production cost savings	Firms take sourcing decisions to minimize the sum of production and transaction costs	Contractual completeness reduces uncertainty and risk	Outcome based outsourcing contract reduces opportunism	Outsource if there are large markets for IT services available from vendors	Activities which are non-core should be outsourced to best-in-world suppliers	Outsourcing give client access to vendor resources	Pooling of resources to achieve mutually compatible goals	Collaborative actions can act to improve the client-vendor relationship	Upholding the principles of moral management will affect outsourcing success	Satisfaction is the overall approval of an outsourcing arrangement
Critical success factors	Integration and exploitation of IT services from vendor	Minimize settings in which opportunistic behavior is likely	Simultaneous use of contractual and cooperative mechanisms	Choosing a suitable agent, and monitoring the agent's work	Matching economic opportunities to individuals' efficiency	Define needs and manage services from vendor	Integrate and exploit strategic resources	Competence in finding, developing, and managing alliances	Develop and secure common norms	Efficient and effective communication with and between all stakeholders	Enable social and economic outcomes which outperform alternatives

firms, because they can generate economies of scale and scope internally by reproducing methods used by vendors. As documented by Levina and Ross (2003), there are other reasons for large firms to move into outsourcing, e.g. the vendor's efficiency is based on the economic benefits derived from the ability to develop a complementary set of core competencies.

TRANSACTION COST THEORY

Focus, Aim, Unit of Analysis

According to Henisz and Williamson (1999), transaction cost economics is a comparative contractual approach to economic organization in which the action resides in the details of transactions on the one hand and governance on the other. Given that all complex contracts are unavoidably incomplete (by reason of bounded rationality) and that contract as mere promise, unsupported by credible commitments, is not self-enforcing (by reason of opportunism), the question is which transactions should be organized how. Much of the predictive content of transaction cost economics works through the discriminating alignment hypothesis, according to which transactions, which differ in their attributes, are aligned with governance structures, which differ in their costs and competencies, so as to effect a (mainly) transaction cost economizing result. Implementing this requires that transactions, governance structures, and transaction cost economizing all be described.

Transaction cost economics concurs that the transaction is the basic unit of analysis and regards governance as the means by which order is accomplished in a relation in which potential conflict threatens to undo or upset opportunities to realize mutual gains (Henisz & Williamson, 1999). The problem of conflict on which transaction cost economics originally focused is that of bilateral dependency. The organization of transactions that are supported by generic investments is easy: classical market contracting works well because each party can go its own way with minimal cost to the other. Specific investments are where the problems arise.

Williamson (1979) identified three types of transactions according to specificity. Non-specific transactions have low asset specificity and are associated with the acquisition of commodities. Idiosyncratic transactions have high specificity. Mixed transactions have elements of both commodity and customization. Transaction specificity can be viewed alongside transaction frequency, a second major construct of transaction cost economics, which distinguishes occasional from recurrent transactions. Two frequency categories multiplied by three specificity types produces six discrete transaction types. It can be argued that the market is better for all but transactions, which are both recurrent and idiosyncratic. The third major determinant of transaction costs is uncertainty, compounded by the bounded rationality of humans and often associated with the complexity of the product to be acquired.

Uncertainty is recognized as a major determinant of transaction costs. It is compounded by the bounded rationality of humans and is often associated with the complexity of the product acquired. Given the cognitive limits of human actors, complex contracts, such as IT outsourcing contracts, are unavoidably incomplete. Contractual incompleteness poses problems when paired with the condition of opportunism – which manifests itself as adverse selection, moral hazard, shirking, sub-goal pursuit, and other forms of strategic behavior. Because human actors will not reliably disclose true conditions upon request or self-fulfill all promises, contract as mere promise, unsupported by credible commitments, will not be self-enforcing (Williamson, 2000).

Contribution to the Understanding of IT Outsourcing

In transaction cost economics, firms are hypothesized to take sourcing decisions to minimize the sum of production and transaction costs (Anderson, Glenn, & Sedatole, 2000). If transaction costs offset production cost advantages of the external supplier, the firm subsumes the activity – an outcome termed vertical integration or insourcing. Otherwise, it can be argued that the market is better for all transactions. The consistency of the empirical results seems startling in the light of two problems with this outsourcing philosophy. First, production and transaction costs are rarely neatly separable. Second, decision-makers are likely to be affected by wealth effects associated with sourcing, and thus unlikely to make decisions that strictly maximize firm profit (Anderson et al., 2000). Researchers have found that production cost differences seem more influential in sourcing decisions than transaction cost differences (e.g., Ang & Straub, 1998).

The transaction cost economics presumption is that economic actors attempt to forecast the potential for opportunism as a function of unfolding circumstances, and then take preventive actions in transactions where opportunism is likely to be high. Opportunism is an explanatory mechanism, not readily observable, and typically empirically untested. However, it is important because it has potential for enormous impact on economic performance (Jap, 2001). Opportunism is self-interest seeking with guile, and includes overt behavior such as lying, cheating and stealing, as well as subtle behavior such as dishonoring an implicit contract, shirking, failing to fulfill promises, and obligations. It is the equivalent of bad faith, the implication being that the party who is opportunistic is not trustworthy. In an outsourcing setting, opportunism may involve misrepresentations, unresponsiveness, unreasonable demands, and lying. The notion of opportunism is what differentiates transaction cost theory from alternative conceptualizations of the firm, such as agency theory, relational exchange theory, or resource-based view. Trying to minimize settings in which opportunistic behavior is likely becomes a critical success factor in IT outsourcing.

CONTRACTUAL THEORY

Focus, Aim, Unit of Analysis

An outsourcing contract provides a legally bound, institutional framework in which each party's rights, duties, and responsibilities are codified and the goals, policies, and strategies underlying the arrangement are specified. Every outsourcing contract has the purpose of facilitating exchange and preventing opportunism. Appropriate contractual arrangements can attenuate the leeway for opportunism, prohibit moral hazards in a cooperative relationship, and protect each party's proprietary knowledge. A complete contract reduces the uncertainty faced by organizational decision-makers and the risks stemming from opportunism on the part of one or more contracting parties. It provides a safeguard against ex post performance problems by restraining each party's ability to pursue private goals at the expense of common benefits. An incomplete contract may bring about ambiguity, which creates a breeding ground for shirking responsibility and shifting blame, raises the likelihood of conflict, and hinders the ability to coordinate activities, utilize resources, and implement strategies (Luo, 2002).

Outsourcing contracts are relational contracts characterized by long durations of interpartner dependency and enormous unanticipated contingencies in an uncertain environment. Outsourcing often involves highly idiosyncratic assets that give rise to high coordination costs and appropriation concerns.

The optimal contract completeness simultaneously requires opportunism mitigation and adaptation promotion. Transaction cost economics scholars commonly point to three categories of exchange hazards that necessitate contractual safeguards (or vertical integration): asset specificity, measurement difficulty, and uncertainty. Asset specificity emerges when sourcing relationships require significant relationship-specific investments in physical and/or human assets. The presence of these specific assets transform an exchange from a world of classical contracting into a world of neo-classical contracting in which the identity of parties is irrelevant into a world of neo-classical contracting in which the identity of exchange partners is of critical importance. For example, an information technology outsourcing provider may need to customize service offerings to the client's work setting. Similarly, the client may need to develop a unique understanding of the provider's procedures, approach, and language to effectively utilize their services. Difficulty in measuring the performance of exchange partners also generates market hazards. Markets succeed when they can effectively link rewards to productivity – that is, they can measure productivity and pay for it accordingly. Uncertainty, a third hazard, also challenges an exchange by requiring the parties to adapt to problems raised from unforeseeable changes. High levels of uncertainty in conjunction with measurement difficulty or asset specificity render contracting even more hazardous. This encourages more complex contracts (Poppo & Zenger, 2002).

However, a contract alone is insufficient to guide outsourcing arrangements. Cooperation is also needed. Cooperation is an improvement process through mutual forbearance in the allocation of resources, such that one party is made better off and no one is worse off than it would otherwise be. Cooperation is a necessary complement that overcomes long-term contracts' constraints in adaptation and execution and becomes an important vehicle that nourishes continuity and flexibility when change and conflict arise (Luo, 2002). Similar to Luo's argument that contract and cooperation are not substitutes but complements, Poppo and Zenger (2002) argue that contracts and relational governance are not substitutes but complements. They found that relational exchange arrangements supported by trust are commonly viewed as substitutes for complex contracts in interorganizational exchange, and that many argue that formal contracts actually undermine trust and thereby encourage the opportunistic behavior they are designed to discourage.

Contribution to the Understanding of IT Outsourcing

Kern and Willcocks (2000) have investigated contracts in IT outsourcing. The contract in outsourcing has been described as a mechanism that establishes the balance of power between the client and vendor. Contracts essentially have to be as airtight as possible, because research has shown that vendors tend to refer to it as their chief source of obligation. Vendors however would prefer to see the contract as a working document, giving them flexibility to suggest improvements and new services. This is the interest of most vendor companies, for their goal is one of profit margins. An IT outsourcing contract tends to be more complicated than other business contracts, resembling as it does a hybrid between an asset purchase and sale agreement, and a sale/leaseback agreement, in that there is a sale of assets or transfer of operations, transfer of employees, and a lease back to the customer of the information technology services that were divested. This legal complexity is evident in the detail and in the time typically invested in negotiating agreement. Third-party legal experts have for quite some time emphasized the need for a comprehensive contract, not only because it is their livelihood, but also because it basically becomes a reference point specifying how the client and vendor relate. Kern and Willcocks (2000) identified three common dimensions that can be a useful typology for analyzing control in IT: focus of control (directed at whom or what), measures of control (degree of control), and process of control (means of enforcing control). Using this typology as an underlying guide, Kern and Willcocks presented a post-contract management agenda as the focus of control. The greatest challenge that client companies face following the signing of the contract is the achievement and the enforcement of agreed terms. To accomplish the management agenda, an effective communication and operations structure has to be established in each organization and between both parties.

AGENCY THEORY

Focus, Aim, Unit of Analysis

Agency theory has broadened the risk-sharing literature to include the agency problem that occurs when cooperating parties have different goals and division of labor. The cooperating parties are engaged in an agency relationship defined as a contract under which one or more persons (the principal(s)) engage another person (agent) to perform some service on their behalf which involves delegating some decision making authority to the agent (Jensen & Meckling, 1976). Agency theory describes the relationship between the two parties using the metaphor of a contract. In an IT outsourcing relationship this is a client-vendor relationship and an outsourcing contract.

According to Eisenhardt (1985), agency theory is concerned with resolving two problems that can occur in agency relationships. The first is the agency problem that arises when the desires or goals of the principal and agent conflict and it is difficult or expensive for the principal to verify what the agent is actually doing. The second is the problem of risk sharing that arises when the principal and agent have different risk preferences. These problems are well known in IT outsourcing. An example might be that the client organization wants to reduce its IT costs, while the vendor organization wants to maximize profits. The agency problem arises when the two parties do not share productivity gains. The risk-sharing problem might be the result of different attitudes towards the use of new technologies. Because the unit of analysis is the contract governing the relationship between the two parties, the focus of the theory is on determining the most efficient contract governing the principal-agent relationship given assumptions about people (e.g., self-interest, bounded rationality, risk aversion), organizations (e.g., goal conflict of members), and information (e.g., information is a commodity which can be purchased). Thus the question becomes: Is a behavior-oriented contract more efficient than an outcome-oriented contract? Outsourcing contracts are to a great extent tied up to service level agreements, where the outcome of the service is the focal point.

The agency theory is applicable when describing client-vendor relationships in IT outsourcing arrangements. Typically, the client organization (principal) transfers property rights to the vendor organization (agent). In the context of IT, assets transferred might be infrastructure, systems and documentation, and employees. For a certain amount of money, the vendor organization provides services to the client organization. This implies a change in legal relationships, and IT services are carried out using a more formal transaction process. The status of personal relationships also changes, from that of a manager and a subordinate, to that of a client-manager and a vendor. According to agency theory, control mechanisms also change, from that of behavioral control, to that of outcome-based control. If both parties to the relationship are trying to maximize their utility, there is good reason to believe that the vendor organization will not always act in the best interests of the client. Monitoring and bonding activities in reducing agency costs include auditing, formal control systems, budget restrictions, and the establishment of incentive compensation systems which serve to more closely identify the manager's interests with those of the outside equity holder.

Contribution to the Understanding of IT Outsourcing

The original impetus for the development of agency theory was large corporations' separation of control from ownership. Thus, its focus was never on organizational boundaries, as with transaction cost theory. Agency theory's primary interest is not the decision to source via the hierarchy or via the market. Although all contractual arrangements contain important elements of agency, agency theory is essentially concerned with the delegation of work by the principal to the agent via a contract, whether or not they are both within the same organization. However, agency and transaction cost theories share several concepts, such as opportunism, uncertainty and bounded rationality, and there is a rough correspondence between transaction cost economics' hierarchies and markets and agency theory's behavior-based contracts and outcome-based contracts. The technological and business complexity of IT means that there may be a critical success factor for the principal in choosing a suitable agent and in monitoring the agent's work. Only the agent knows how hard he is working, and that can be especially important in multilateral contracting where one agent acts for several principals. This is often the case in IT outsourcing because of the market dominance of one (or a few) large firm(s). Given the difficulties of behavior-based contracts suggested by agency theory, it is reasonable to assume that the overwhelming majority of clients would insist on outcome-based contracts when acquiring IT products and services. Such a strategy can only succeed if the client can confidently specify current and future requirements. But accurate predictions by the client may not always be in the vendor's interests, since vendor account managers often are rewarded according to contract profitability, which is principally achieved through charging the client extra for anything that is not in the contract.

According to Hancox and Hackney (2000), the choice of contract type depends on the agency costs, which include the principal's effort in assessing the agent's performance and the agent's efforts in assuring the principal of his commitment. Agency theory holds that human beings act through self-interest and therefore, as contracting parties, they may have divergent goals. An important aspect of the theory is that both principal and agent wish to avoid risk when dealing with each other. The principal may prefer to place risk with the agent via an outcome-based contract, whereas the agent may prefer to avoid risk by having a behavior-based contract. Outcome-based contracts are claimed to reduce agent opportunism because the rewards of both agent and principal depend on the same actions. Behavior-based contracts need the principal to have sufficient information to identify two possible dangers: first, whether there is adverse selection (the agent does not possess the skills he claims); second, moral hazard – the agent is shirking. Sourcing via the hierarchy may reduce the overall risk, but agency costs also exist in hierarchies. Problems between agents and principals are greater in complex organizations with many managerial layers.

THEORY OF FIRM BOUNDARIES

Focus, Aim, Unit of Analysis

There has been renewed debate on the determinants of firm boundaries and their implications for performance. According to Schilling and Steensma (2002), the widely accepted framework of transaction cost economics has come under scrutiny as a comprehensive theory for firm scale and scope. At the heart of this debate is whether the underlying mechanism determining firm boundaries is a fear of opportunism (as posited by transaction cost economics), a quest for sustainable advantage (as posed by resource-based view theorists and others), a desire for risk-reducing flexibility (as has recently gained increased attention in work on options), or a combination of factors. Although perspectives on firm boundaries such as transaction costs or the resource-based view are based on fundamentally different motivations for pursuing hierarchical control over market contracts, they rely on common resource or context attributes as antecedents.

Contribution to the Understanding of IT Outsourcing

Schilling and Steensma (2002) explored how various attributes of technology to be sourced influence the governance mode chosen, and the intermediate mechanisms by which they do so. They found that uniqueness and difficulty of imitation are significantly related to the perceived potential for sustainable advantage. They also found that technological dynamism and difficulty of imitation are significantly related to the perceived threat of opportunism. In turn, consistent with a transaction cost perspective, the threat of opportunism increases the probability of outsourcing. Schilling and Steensma's findings suggest that the resource-based view, transaction cost economics, and an options perspective may play complementary roles in explaining firm technology-sourcing decisions. Firms may pursue resources that are unique or inimitable because of their potential to create a sustainable competitive advantage, but the uniqueness and inimitability may also create a potential for opportunism. The potential for opportunism and the degree of uncertainty associated with the technological resources then heavily influence the governance mode chosen. In sum, the results imply that the resource-based view explains why a firm pursues particular resources rather than others, but transaction costs and an options perspective better explain the governance mode undertaken for accessing the resources once they are chosen. Therefore, the theory of firm boundaries claims that resource-based view, transaction costs, and options perspectives each explain only a portion of managerial motivation for decisions on firm boundaries. The rationale supporting the choices firms make regarding technology sourcing is multidimensional; firms are not only seeking potential sources of competitive advantage, but are also seeking to avoid opportunism and to preserve or create flexibility (Schilling & Steensma, 2002).

According to Garicano and Hubbard (2003), some theorists have proposed that firms' boundaries reflect the division of labor across individuals. Whether a set of tasks is organized within one or multiple firms depends on the extent to which individuals specialize. While the particular trade-offs these theories emphasize differ from each other, together they represent a departure from the earlier literature: there is far less emphasis on specificity and far greater emphasis on issues related to the division of labor such as specialization and job design. This class of theories is important because it has the potential to explain firms' boundaries in a wide range of contexts where specificity is unlikely to have an important effect on individuals' incentives.

THEORY OF CORE COMPETENCIES

Focus, Aim, Unit of Analysis

According to Prahalad and Hamel (1990), core competencies are the collective learning in the organization, especially how to coordinate diverse production skills and integrate multiple streams of technologies. Since core competence is about harmonizing streams of technology, it is also about the organization of work and the delivery of value. The force of core competence is felt as decisively in services as in manufacturing. Core competence does not diminish with use. Unlike physical assets, which do deteriorate over time, competencies are enhanced as they are applied and shared. But competencies still need to be nurtured and protected; knowledge fades if it is not used. Competencies are the glue that binds existing businesses. They are also the engines for new business development. At least three tests can be applied to identify core competencies in a company. First, a core competence provides potential access to a wide variety of markets. Second, a core competence should make a significant contribution to the perceived customer benefits of the end product. Finally, a core competence should be difficult for competitors to imitate. The tangible link between identified core competencies and end products is what Prahalad and Hamel (1990) call core products – the embodiments of one or more core competencies. Core products are the components or subassemblies that actually contribute to the value of the end products. Core competencies are sometimes called firm-specific competence, resource deployments, invisible assets and distinctive competencies.

Quinn (1999) argues that core competencies are not products or "those things we do relatively well." They are those activities, usually intellectually based service activities or systems, that the company performs better than any other enterprise. They are the sets of skills and systems that a company does at best-in-the-world levels and through which a company creates uniquely high value for customers. Developing best-in-the-world capabilities is crucial in designing a core competency strategy. Unless the company is best-in-the-world at an activity it is someone else's core competency. The company gives up competitive edge by not buying that skill from a best-in-the-world source. Activities which are none-core should be outsourced to best-in-world suppliers.

Contribution to the Understanding of IT Outsourcing

Core competencies theory suggests activities should be performed either in-house or by suppliers. Activities, which are not core competencies, should be considered for outsourcing with best-in-world suppliers. Some non-core activities may have to be retained in house if they are part of a defensive posture to protect competitive advantage. Employees in non-core functions (even if not facing outsourcing) may feel excluded by the organization because they are a non-dominant discipline. An organization may view IT itself as a core competence. It seems that most successful companies have a good understanding of IT's potential. However, some organizations outsource IT even though they see IT as core and delivering competitive advantage. This may be because IT can be considered core at the corporate level, but some of its aspects, at lower levels, might be commodities. Thus the complexity of IT, and it's (at least in part) core nature, may make the contracting out of IT a particularly challenging exercise. The ability to define IT requirements and to monitor their delivery by third parties may be some of the core IT competencies that any organization must have if it is to outsource IT successfully. It can even be argued that the very acts of specifying and managing supply contracts can themselves give competitive advantage. It is critical that client organizations are able to define their needs and manage services from their vendors.

Since most supplier markets are imperfect, Quinn and Hilmer (1994) recommended that managers must answer three key questions about any activity considered for outsourcing. First, what is the potential for obtaining competitive advantage in this activity, taking account of transaction costs? Second, what is the potential vulnerability that could arise from market failure if the activity is outsourced? Third, what can we do to alleviate our vulnerability by structuring arrangements with suppliers to provide appropriate controls yet provide for necessary flexibilities in demand? When the potentials for both competitive edge and strategic vulnerability are high, the company needs a high degree of control, usually entailing the activity internally or through joint ownership arrangements or tight long-term contracts.

The belief that outsourcing of IT is only appropriate when IT is not considered a core function of the firm's industry was not held by executives interviewed by McLellan, Marcolin, and Beamish (1995). Core activities were defined by a firm's management as those that provided the competitive capabilities that lead to competitive advantage. This definition implies that a core activity is central to the competitive nature of the industry. The executives involved in outsourcing relationships clearly viewed the IT function as central to their competitiveness within the banking industry, yet the firms still choose to outsource much if not all of the IT activities.

Hancox and Hackney (2000) interviewed IT managers to find support for the core competencies theory in IT outsourcing. Contrary to vendors' marketing material and much of the literature on IT outsourcing, concentration on core competencies did not appear to be a strong motive for IT outsourcing among the sample organizations. No organization from either private or public sector had systematically examined its activities to identify core and non-core functions. Most organizations seemed to share the view of IT as a mix of core and non-core activities.

RESOURCE-BASED THEORY

Focus, Aim, Unit of Analysis

The central tenet in resource-based theory is that unique organizational resources of both tangible and intangible nature are the real source of competitive advantage. With resource-based theory, organizations are viewed as a collection of resources that are heterogeneously distributed within and across industries. Accordingly, what makes the performance of an organization distinctive is the unique blend of the resources it possesses. A firm's resources include not only its physical assets such as plant and location but also its competencies. The ability to leverage distinctive internal and external competencies relative to environmental situations ultimately affects the performance of the business. The resource-based theory is a useful perspective in strategic management. Research on the competitive implications of such firm resources as knowledge, learning, culture, teamwork, and human capital, was given a significant boost by resource-based theory – a theory that indicated it was these kinds of resources that were most likely to be sources of sustainable competitive advantage for firms (Barney, 2001).

The essence of the resource-based theory of the firm lies in its emphasis on the internal resources available to the firm, rather than on the external opportunities and threats dictated by industry conditions. Firms are considered to be highly heterogeneous, and the bundles of resources available to each firm are different. This is both because firms have different initial resource endowments and because managerial decisions affect resource accumulation and the direction of firm growth as well as resource utilization (Løwendahl, 2000).

Firms' resource endowments, particularly intangible resources, are difficult to change except over the long term. For example, although human resources may be mobile to some extent, capabilities may not be valuable for all firms or even for their competitors. Some capabilities are based on firm-specific knowledge, and others are valuable when integrated with additional individual capabilities and specific firm resources. Therefore, intangible resources are more likely than tangible resources to produce a competitive advantage. In particular, intangible firm-specific resources, such as knowledge, allow firms to add value to incoming factors of production (Hitt, Bierman, Shumizu, & Kochhar, 2001).

Transformational outsourcing, as indicated by Linder (2004), is an emerging practice to bring new capabilities to the organization. Resources are required to bring new capabilities, and resources bringing new capabilities can be found in an outsourcing vendor. In this context we apply the knowledge-based view of the firm that has established itself as an important perspective in strategic management. This perspective builds on the resource-based theory of the firm. According to the resource-based theory of the firm, performance differences across firms can be attributed to the variance in the firms' resources and capabilities. Resources that are valuable, unique, and difficult to imitate can provide the basis for firms' competitive advantages. In turn, these competitive advantages produce positive returns.

Contribution to the Understanding of IT Outsourcing

The value generation potential of an outsourcing relationship consists of three factors: client characteristics, the vendor-client relationship, and vendor characteristics. A key client characteristic is an understanding of how to manage resources that a firm does not own. A key in the vendor-client relationship is formal (contractual) aspect of the relationship. The third factor shaping the outsourcing value proposition is the vendor's own capabilities. From an outsourcing vendor's perspective, there are many potential opportunities and benefits for the client. These opportunities and benefits can be derived from the IT outsourcing vendor's value proposition. Important vendor characteristics include capabilities such as technical competence, understanding the customer's business, and relationship management. Levina and Ross (2003) stressed the importance of vendor characteristics in terms of the vendor value proposition. The concepts of complementarities and competencies explain that outsourcing vendors can increase productivity and reduce costs on client projects by applying a set of complementary application management competencies. They identified three complementary vendor competencies: IT personnel development, methodology development and dissemination, and customer relationship management.

Although it is generally accepted that IT is critical for information-intensive firms, not all members of top management teams attach the same degree of criticality to IT. Perceptions of the CIOs and CEOs of IT importance tend to be misaligned. While CIOs recognize IT as vital to an organization's strategy, CEOs with little background in IT tend to regard IS services as back-room operations, an expense to be controlled rather than a strategic investment to be capitalized. Generally, CEOs' perceptions of IT criticality are as important as, if not more important than, those of the CIOs' with respect to IS sourcing decisions because IS investments represent a significant financial outlay for corporations. Sometimes management policies and direction of IT use are dictated by the CEOs' psychological involvement and participation in IS. Thus, we would expect that the greater the perceived criticality of IT to the firm, the less likely the firm will outsource its IS services (Ang, 1993).

PARTNERSHIP AND ALLIANCE THEORY

Focus, Aim, Unit of Analysis

Alliances are broadly defined as collaborative efforts between two or more firms in which the firms pool their resources in an effort to achieve mutually compatible goals that they could not achieve easily alone (Heide & John, 1992; Lambe, Spekman, & Hunt, 2002). Resources here are defined as any tangible or intangible entity available for use by a firm to compete in its marketplace. When interfirm business relationships are collaborative, rather than adversarial in nature, a variety of types of these relationships may be classified as alliances, for example outsourcing.

According to Lambe, Spekman, and Hunt (2002), the popularity of alliances is growing. Alliances account for anywhere from 6 percent to 25 percent of the market value of the typical company. Yet, alliance success remains elusive. Studies find that as many as 70 percent of alliances are not successful. Thus, an important question for researchers and practicing managers is what makes alliances succeed? Lambe et al. (2002) argue that alliance competence contributes to alliance success, both directly and through acquisition and creation of resources. Using survey data gathered from 145 alliances, empirical tests provide support for the posited explanation of alliance success. They found alliance competence has three facets, labeled alliance experience, alliance manager development capability and partner identification propensity. Furthermore, consistent with competence-based theory and resource-advantage theory conceptualizations of a competence (a higher order resource that is a distinct combination of lower order resources), the researchers proposed that these three facets are the three lower order resources that collectively comprise the higher order resource of an alliance competence. That is, more of each of these three lower order resources will contribute to increasing a firm's competence in finding, developing, and managing alliances. Alliance experience is a resource that can be leveraged across an organization because it contributes to knowledge about how to manage and use alliances. Alliance manager development capability enables firms to plan and navigate the mechanisms of an alliance so that roles and responsibilities are clearly articulated and agreed upon. In addition, these managers have the ability to review continually the fit of the alliance to the changing environment to make modifications as necessary. Partner identification propensity enables firms to systematically and proactively scan for and identify partners that have the complementary resources that are needed to develop a relationship portfolio or mix that complements existing competencies and enables them to occupy positions of competitive advantage.

Furthermore, Lambe et al. (2002) posited that two specific types of resources affect alliance success: idiosyncratic and complementary resources. In terms of resource-advantage theory, complementary resources may be thought of as lower order resources that are brought to the alliance and idiosyncratic resources as the higher order resources that are developed by the alliance through the process of combining the complementary resources of the partner firms. Idiosyncratic resources are resources that are developed during the life of the alliance, are unique to the alliance, and facilitate the combining of the distinct lower order resources contributed by the partner firms. Idiosyncratic resources may be tangible, such as computers and cables, or intangible, such as developing a methodology or a process together. Similarly, some researchers refer to idiosyncratic investments or assets.

Das and Teng (2002b) studied how alliance conditions change over the different stages of alliance development to understand the development processes of strategic alliances such as an IT outsourcing relationship. They defined three stages in the alliance development process – formation, operation, and outcome stage. In the formation stage partner firms approach each other and negotiate the alliance. Partner firms then carry out the agreement and set up the alliance by committing various types of resources. The alliance is initiated and put into operation. Alliances will be formed only under certain conditions. These conditions include a relatively high level of collective strengths, a low level of interpartner conflicts, and a high level of interdependencies. Not only is the formation stage directly influenced by alliance conditions, the transition from the formation stage to the operation stage is also dictated by the same alliance conditions variables. During the operation stage, partner firms collaborate and implement all agreements of the alliance. The alliance will likely grow rapidly in size during this stage, somewhat akin to the growth stage of organizational life cycles. Other than the growth route, an alliance may also be reformed and/or terminated at this stage. During the outcome stage, alliance performance becomes tangible and can, thus, be evaluated with some certainty. There are four possible outcomes for an alliance at this stage – stabilization, reformation, decline, and termination. A combination of outcomes is also possible, such as a termination after reformation. Alliance reformation and alliance termination do not necessarily signal alliance failure. Reformation and termination may be the best option under certain circumstances, such as the achievement of pre-set alliance objectives. Alliance condition variables continue to play a decisive role in the outcome stage. The particular alliance outcome will depend on the condition of the alliance.

Das and Teng (2003) discussed partner analysis and alliance performance. An important stream of research in the alliance literature is about partner selection. It emphasizes the desirability of a match between the partners, mainly in terms of their resource profiles. The approach is consistent with the resource-based theory of the firm, which suggests that competitors are defined by their resources profiles. They found a lack of agreement concerning alliance performance. This lack of agreement reflects an underlying conceptual puzzle: what does effective alliance performance mean? There are two distinct loci of alliance performance in the literature: the alliance itself and the partners forming the alliance. On the one hand, when alliances are viewed as separate entities, alliance performance is the success of these separate entities – in terms of, say, profitability or growth rate. On the other hand, because partner firms use alliances to achieve certain strategic objectives, alliance performance ought to be measured in terms of the aggregated results for the partner firms.

Contribution to the Understanding of IT Outsourcing

Applying partnership and alliance theory client and vendor companies may pool their resources to achieve mutually compatible goals in an IT outsourcing relationship. Partnership has frequently been noted as a major feature of IT outsourcing. Partnership can reduce the risk of inadequate contractual provision, which may be comforting for clients about to outsource a complex and high-cost activity such as IT. However, in the relationship between vendor and client the latter may be over dependent on the former, and goals are not necessarily shared. A client may be more comfortable if it knows the vendor already. In partner selection, cultural compatibility is vital and shared values and objectives inform all stages of the partnership development process.

Hancox and Hackney (2000) interviewed IT managers to find support for the partnership theory in IT outsourcing. They found that few organizations claim to be in a strategic partnership with their IT suppliers. Partnership was more likely to be claimed in the area of systems development, where vendors needed to have a greater understanding of the organization, than in outsourcing of operations and IT infrastructure support.

RELATIONAL EXCHANGE THEORY

Focus, Aim, Unit of Analysis

Relational exchange can be defined as an interactive process where commitments are made, outcomes are observed, and further investments made, if outcomes meet or exceed expectations (Rokkan & Haugland, 2002). Based on previous interactions as well as expectations about the future, a mutual orientation develops resulting in a common language and mutual knowledge. The exchange is embedded in a normative structure that determines the functioning of the system. Patterns of behavior are taken for granted. The actors share common expectations about expected and accepted behavior, and collective interests are incorporated into the preferences and belief structures of the actors.

According to Lambe, Spekman and Hunt (2000), norms are important in relational exchange because they provide the governance rules of the game. These rules depend on the game, which from an exchange perspective has been described as either discrete or relational. Discrete exchange norms contain expectations about an individualistic or competitive interaction between exchange partners. The individual parties are expected to remain autonomous and pursue strategies aimed at the attainment of their individual goals. Pure discrete exchange is consistent with the underlying assumptions of neo-classical economic theory. In contrast, relational exchange norms are based on the expectation of mutuality of interest, essentially prescribing stewardship behavior, and are designed to enhance the well being of the relationship as a whole. In the evolutionary model of relational exchange, relational norm development takes place during an extended period of time through many interactions between the partners (Lambe et al., 2000). According to this theory, the key to determining how efficiently contract governance is carried out lies in the relational norms between the transacting parties.

Many classifications of norms have been proposed, but no one is regarded as dominant. Heide and John (1992) have proposed that relational norms are a higher order construct consisting of three dimensions: flexibility, information exchange, and solidarity. Flexibility, defines a bilateral expectation of the willingness to make adaptations as circumstances change. Information exchange defines a bilateral expectation that parties will proactively provide information useful to the partner. Solidarity defines a bilateral expectation that a high value is placed on the relationship. It prescribes behaviors directed specifically towards relationship maintenance.

Contribution to the Understanding of IT Outsourcing

Norms create expectations of behavior and imply a certain action and are shared by the actors. In long-term IT outsourcing relationships these norms might as well be formalized and included in contract between the parties. It is believed that society shares a number of common norms that make it necessary for contracts to contain certain features but not necessary to include statements about others. Yet norms vary a great deal between and within societies as is illustrated by international contracts where a foreigner's requirements as to what should go into a contract will often surprise us, but what we would not consider necessary to include may surprise them. Artz and Brush (2000) examined supplier relationships that were governed by relational contracts, and they found support for the relational exchange theory. By altering the behavioral orientation of the alliance, relational norms lowered exchange costs.

Kern and Blois (2002) considered the role of norms within networks by describing how BP Exploration outsourced its information technology function. This outsourcing venture led to the formation of a consortium of vendors, but the attempt was found to have failed. Kern and Blois suggested that central to the failure of the consortium was the issue of norms. In the case of BP Exploration, three problems arose. First, the consortium's members, though competitors, were expected to work closely with each other as the senior partner on some sites and as the junior partner on others. Yet neither BP Exploration nor any member of the consortium recognized in advance that the norms that they usually applied in their relationships with their clients would not be applicable to this situation. Consequently, their staff was working with norms that were at best not appropriate to the new situation and at worst made for difficulties. For example, a company's norms do not normally encourage the acceptance of flexibility, information exchange and solidarity in contacts with competitors, all of which are needed if sound relationships are to be developed between organizations. Second, BP Exploration's line managers conducted their relationships with the consortium members as if they were buying a commodity service. Yet a major reason for outsourcing was BP Exploration's desire to obtain a state of the art IT service. Its behavior towards the consortium was therefore based on norms that were inappropriate, relative to its stated objectives. The third problem was that one of the vendors was not familiar with European modes of operations and had a horrendous job trying to adapt to a non-US culture. Many factors led to BP Exploration being a less than successful experiment in outsourcing. However, a major contribution was a failure to recognize the need for establishing norms of behavior that were appropriate to the consortium form of organization (Kern & Blois, 2002).

SOCIAL EXCHANGE THEORY

Focus, Aim, Unit of Analysis

Social exchange theory was initially developed to examine interpersonal exchanges that are not purely economic. Several sociologists are responsible for the early development of this theory. These theorists view people's social behavior in terms of exchanges of resources. The need for social exchange is created by the scarcity of resources, prompting actors to engage one another to obtain valuable inputs. According to Das and Teng (2002a), social exchange can be defined as voluntary actions of individuals who are motivated by return they are expected to bring and typically, in fact, bring from others. Social exchange can be viewed as an ongoing reciprocal process in which actions are contingent on rewarding reactions from others. There are important differences between social exchanges and economic exchanges. Social exchanges may or may not involve extrinsic benefits with objective economic value. In contrast to economic exchanges, the benefits from social exchanges often are not contracted explicitly, and it is voluntary to provide benefits. As a result, exchange partners are uncertain as to whether they will receive benefits. Thus social exchange theory focuses on the social relations among the actors that shape the exchange of resources and benefits. While its origins are at the individual level, social exchange theory has been extended to organizational and interorganizational levels (Das & Teng, 2002a).

Social exchange theory postulates that exchange interactions involve economic and/or social outcomes. Over time, each party in the exchange relationship compares the social and economic outcomes from these interactions to those that are available from exchange alternatives, which determines their dependence on the exchange relationship. Positive economic and social outcomes over time increase the partners' trust of each other and commitment to maintaining the exchange relationship. Positive exchange interactions over time also produce relational exchange norms that govern the exchange partners' interactions. Implicit in these postulates, the four foundational premises of social exchange theory are: (1) exchange interactions result in economic and/or social outcomes, (2) these outcomes are compared over time to other exchange alternatives to determine dependence on the exchange relationship, (3) positive outcomes over time increase firms' trust of their trading partner(s) and their commitment to the exchange relationship, and (4) positive exchange interactions over time produce relational exchange norms that govern the exchange relationship (Lambe, Wittmann, & Spekman, 2001).

Contribution to the Understanding of IT Outsourcing

According to social exchange theory, satisfaction plays an integral role in relationships. Satisfaction in IT outsourcing relationships can be defined in terms of performance satisfaction, which is the level in which a transaction meets expectations of the partner's product and non-product attributes. Satisfaction can be the result from evaluating all aspects of a working relationship (not only the service level agreements). In such, satisfaction can be the overall approval of the success of the outsourcing relationship.

Firms who receive benefits that meet or exceed their expectations and are equal to or superior to outcomes available from alternatives, are likely to maintain and expand the relationship. Satisfaction serves as a measure of a firm's view of the outcomes of the relationship. While it may not capture a partner's estimation of available alternatives, it does provide insight into a relationship's overall performance (Lambe et al., 2001).

STAKEHOLDER THEORY

Focus, Aim, Unit of Analysis

The stakeholder approach to strategic management was introduced by Freeman (1984). According to Freeman a stakeholder is any group or individual who can affect, or is affected by, the achievement of a corporation's purpose. Stakeholders include employees, customers, suppliers, stockholders, banks, environmentalists, government and other groups who can help or hurt the corporation. For each category of stakeholder groups can be broken down into several useful smaller categories. Freeman's focus was to show how executives could use the stakeholder approach to manage their organization more effectively. In instrumental stakeholder theory, the role of management is seen as achieving a balance between the interests of all stakeholders. For each major strategic issue we must think through the effects on a number of stakeholders, and therefore, we need processes that take into account the concerns of many groups. It is argued that maintaining an appropriate balance between the interests of all stakeholder groups is the only way to ensure survival of the firm and the attainment of other performance goals. The normative condition is that managers must provide economic and other returns to stakeholders in order to continue engaging in wealth creating activities by virtue of the critical resources stakeholders provide to the firm.

Stakeholder theory is justified on the basis that firms have responsibilities to stakeholders for moral reasons, and that there is no priority of one set of interests over another. Upholding four principles: 1) honouring agreements, 2) avoiding lying, 3) respecting the autonomy of others, and 4) avoiding harm to others, are a necessary precondition for efficient working. And thus, stakeholder theories of the firm establish economic relationships within a general context of moral management.

According to Phillips, Freeman, and Wicks (2003), it is commonly asserted that the stakeholder theory implies that all stakeholders must be treated equally irrespective of the fact that some obviously contribute more than others to the organization. Prescriptions of equality have been inferred from discussions of balancing stakeholder interests and are in direct conflict with the advice of some experts on organizational design and reward systems. However, corporations should attempt to distribute the benefits of their activities as equally as possible among stakeholders in light of their respective contributions, costs, and risks. This interpretation of balance is called meritocracy, where benefits are distributed on the basis of relative contribution to the organization.

Stakeholder theory is a managerial conception of organizational strategy and ethics. The central idea is that an organization's success is dependent on how well it manages the relationships with key groups such as customers, employees, suppliers, communities, financiers, and others that can affect the realization of its purpose. The manager's job is to keep the support of all of these groups, balancing their interests, while making the organization a place where stakeholder interests can be maximized over time. The identification of stakeholder groups is currently among the central debates in the scholarly and popular press (Freeman & Phillips, 2002).

Contribution to the Understanding of IT Outsourcing

Contrary to the traditional understanding of the principal-agent relationship used in several IT outsourcing studies, a stakeholder orientation will include at least two new dimensions: 1) balancing interests of a number of stakeholders, and 2) the interpretation of the four moral principles that underlie stakeholder theory. Neglecting these dimensions, firms will have less satisfied stakeholders, and will show financial performance that is consistently below industry average (Shankman, 1999).

As indicated by some of the reviewed literature above, a stakeholder is defined and used differently in finance (issue of CEO responsibility to shareholders or stakeholders), law (requires ownership), and gaming (person who holds the bets). The term is also used and accepted by IT outsourcing practitioners and researchers, e.g. Lacity and Willcocks (2000a) who define a stakeholder as a group of people with aligned interests. According to Lacity and Willcocks, there are four distinct client IT stakeholder groups and three distinct vendor IT stakeholder groups. The groups identified are client senior business managers, client senior IT managers, client IT staff, client IT users, and vendor senior managers, vendor account managers, vendor IT staff. An additional group is the subcontractors. All stakeholder groups are presumed to have significant differences in expectations and goals regarding IT outsourcing. Thus, it is reasonable to propose that upholding the interest of these different stakeholder groups with the principles of moral management will affect the success of IT outsourcing.

REVIEW OF IT OUTSOURCING BASED RESEARCH

An extensive review of IT outsourcing based research has been conducted (see Table 2). Starting with major IS/IT journals, promising articles were followed back to their origin, whether based in articles, books, or dissertations. Previous research has investigated why companies outsource (e.g., Ang & Cummings, 1997; Lacity & Hirschheim, 1993), how companies manage outsourcing contracts (e.g., Elitzur & Wensley, 1998), and how to manage an IT outsourcing relationship (e.g., Kern & Willcocks, 2002; Kern, 1999). A few researchers have focused on individual level challenges in IT outsourcing (Ho, Ang,

Table 2. Review of IT Outsourcing based research

Title/ authors	Research method	Scope of the research	Key conclusions/ findings
"Determinants of information technology outsourcing: a cross-sectional analysis" (Loh & Venkatraman, 1992a)	Survey of 57 US firms	Degree of IT outsourcing explained by cost structures and economic performance	The degree of IT outsourcing is positively related to both business and IT cost structures, and negatively related to IT performance.
"Diffusion of information technology outsourcing: influence sources and the Kodak effect" (Loh & Venkatraman, 1992b)	Survey of 60 IT outsourcing contracts	Influence sources in the diffusion of IT outsourcing	Adoption of IT outsourcing is motivated more by internal influence than by external influence amongst the user organizations.
"The etiology of information systems outsourcing" (Ang, 1993)	Survey of 226 US banks	Development of a theoretical model of IS outsourcing synthesizing economic, managerial-behavioral, and institutional factors	The study found that external production cost advantages in the service provider markets motivates outsourcing of IS in both large and small banks). Large banks were affected by internal institutional influences of unbundling support services, while small banks were affected by the level of transaction cost present in outsourcing arrangements, as well as the external institutional influences.
"The information systems outsourcing bandwagon" (Lacity & Hirschheim, 1993)	Case studies of 14 companies that faced outsourcing decisions	Outcome and scope of outsourcing decisions	Practical advice for negotiating contracts and suggests that IT outsourcing does not always lead to cost reductions.
"Offshore systems development" (Ravichandran & Ahmed, 1993)	Conceptual	Examine offshore computing of complex system projects	A decision framework for offshore systems development addresses: a) the suitability of a project for offshore development, and b) the selection of the specific offshore site.
"Strategic outsourcing" (Quinn & Hilmer, 1994)	Conceptual, supported by several business examples	Ways to determine core competencies and which activities are better performed externally.	Companies can substantially leverage their resources by: 1) developing a few well-selected core competencies of significance to customers, 2) focusing investment and management attention on them, and 3) strategically outsource many other activities.
"How to manage an IT outsourcing alliance" (McFarlan & Nolan, 1995)	Case research	When to outsource and how to structure and manage the relationship	What determines success or failure is managing the relationship less as a contract and more as a strategic alliance.
"Financial and strategic motivations behind IS outsourcing" (McLellan et al., 1995)	Seven case studies in the banking industry	Why and how managers outsource IS functions considered 'core' to the success of the business	Firms were undertaking outsourcing to change organizational boundaries, to restructure, to mitigate technological risks and uncertainty, to access emerging technology, to manage IS department, and to business and IT strategy.
"Domestic and global outsourcing practices of America-s most effective IS users" (Sobol & Apte, 1995)	Conceptual	Offshore outsourcing of software development	Proposes a framework that links projects and sites, which also includes environmental agents whose actions affect resource availability at the sites. Agents identified are firms, governments, infrastructure providers, business environment, and international organizations.
"Decision to outsource information systems functions: testing a strategy-theoretic discrepancy model" (Teng, Cheon, & Grover, 1995)	Sample of 188 companies	Decision to outsource information systems	Decision to outsource is based on gap between actual and desired level of IS resource performance; manifested in the form of gaps in information quality and IS support quality.

continued on following page

Table 2. continued

Title/ authors	Research method	Scope of the research	Key conclusions/ findings
"IT outsourcing relationships: an exploratory study of inter-organizational control mechanisms" (Davis, 1996)	Exploratory case studies into two IT outsourcing relationships – Xerox/EDS, Kodak/IBM	Governance control mechanisms when firms were interested in developing a partnership model	Three governance control mechanisms – price, authority, and trust – appear when companies are forming partnership with their IT vendors.
"The risks of outsourcing IT" (Earl, 1996)	Unspecified methodology, based on discussions with senior executives and IT managers	Limits to IT outsourcing	Identifies 11 risks in outsourcing: weak management, inexperienced staff, business uncertainty, outdated technology skills, endemic uncertainty, hidden costs, lack of organizational learning, loss of innovation capacity, dangers of an eternal triangle, technological indivisibility, and fuzzy focus.
"The effect of service quality and partnership on the outsourcing of information systems functions" (Grover, Cheon, & Teng, 1996)	Survey of 188 IS executives	Relationship between IT outsourcing and its success.	Outsourcing success is found to be highly related to the degree of outsourcing of two IT functions, systems operations and telecommunications.
"The value of selective sourcing" (Lacity, Willcocks, & Feeny, 1996)	Conceptual	Sourcing scope, financial outcome	A framework to clarify sourcing options and aid managers in deciding which IT functions to contract out and which to retain in-house.
"Offshore outsourcing of software development and maintenance: A framework for issues" (Smith, Mitra, & Narasimhan, 1996)	Survey of 48 companies	Reasons for outsourcing, pros and cons of outsourcing, activities to outsource, comparison of domestic vs. global outsourcing	Empirical evidence on the extent to which outsourcing of various IS functions is being practiced, and the views of CIOs concerning the advantages, disadvantages and motives of IS outsourcing. Cost savings needed for global outsourcing is higher than saving needed for domestic. MIS executives play a very important role, and are involved in a large majority of IS outsourcing. Companies with relatively smaller MIS budgets are less likely to outsource than those with larger MIS budgets. Firms with centralized MIS functions are more likely to outsource globally.
"Strategic response to institutional influences on information systems outsourcing" (Ang & Cummings, 1997)	Survey of 226 US banks	Critical contingencies arising from competition that moderate institutional influences on information systems outsourcing	The propensity of banks to conform to or resist institutional pressures (on IS outsourcing) depends on the nature of institutional pressures, perceived gain in production economics, financial capacity to resist influences, and transaction cost considerations.
"Transformation of the IT function at British Petroleum" (Cross, Earl, & Sampler, 1997)	Longitudinal single case study, unspecified methodology	Transformation of the IT organization	A model of the transformed IT organization comprising seven components of transformation organized around purpose, process and people.
"Research report: diffusion of information systems outsourcing: a reevaluation of influence sources" (Hu, Saunders, & Gebelt, 1997)	Survey of 175 firms	Sources of influence in the adaptation of IS outsourcing	The combined effects of external media, vendor pressure, and internal communications at the personal level among managers, significantly influence the decision to adopt IS outsourcing.
"Achieving success in information systems outsourcing" (Saunders, Gebelt, & Hu, 1997)	Interviews of 34 managers who signed or administered their firms outsourcing contracts	Determinants of successful outsourcing	Primary reasons for outsourcing were technological considerations, cost savings, strategic considerations. Tight contracts were written for over three-fourth of companies reporting success.

continued on following page

Table 2. continued

Title/ authors	Research method	Scope of the research	Key conclusions/ findings
"Production and transaction economies and IS outsourcing: a study of the US banking industry" (Ang & Straub, 1998)	Survey of 243 US banks	Influence of production costs, transaction costs, and financial slack on outsourcing decisions	Banks were strongly influenced by production cost advantages in their decision to outsource. Transaction economies were much less of a determinant while financial slack was not significant explanatory.
"Game theory and IS outsourcing contracts" (Elitzur & Wensley, 1998)	Conceptual, using game theory	Identify critical issues negotiating outsourcing contracts	Six critical issues are identified as: transfer of assets, risk sharing, technology upgrade, duration of contract, relationship management, and calculation of fee.
"Towards a theoretically-based contingency model of information systems outsourcing" (Grover, Teng, & Cheon, 1998)	Conceptual	Using resource-based theory and resource-dependence theory from the field of strategic management, and transaction cost theory and agency theory from economics, they suggests implications for outsourcing research and practices	The phenomenon of IT outsourcing should be studied in an integrative manner.
"An empirical investigation of information technology sourcing practices: lessons from experience" (Lacity & Willcocks, 1998)	61 US & UK IT sourcing decisions	Management of computing and IS, measuring IS success, contract, strategic alliances, outsourcing of IS	First, selective outsourcing decisions had higher success rates than total outsourcing or total in-sourcing decisions. Second, senior executives and IT manager who made decisions together had higher success rates than either stakeholder group acting alone. Third, organizations that invited both internal and external bids had higher success rates than organizations that merely compared external bids with current IT costs. Forth, short-term contracts achieved higher success rates than long-term contracts. Fifth, detailed fee-for-service contracts had higher success rates than other types of fee-for-service contracts.
"Relationships in IT outsourcing: an exploratory research study of a conceptual framework" (Kern, 1999)	Survey of top 400 UK organizations, in-depth interviews in five case study organizations	Conceptual framework of IT outsourcing relationship	A multi-paradigmatic framework providing a comprehensive understanding of outsourcing relationships in terms of intent, contract, structure, interactions, behavior, and efficiency-outcome.
"Effect of partnership quality on is outsourcing success: conceptual framework and empirical validation" (Lee & Kim, 1999)	Survey of 74 outsourcing relationships	Investigating outsourcing partnership based on a social, rather than an economic, perspective.	Result indicates that partnership quality may serve as a key predictor of outsourcing success. Partnership quality was found to be positively influenced by factors such as participation, communication, information sharing, and top management support, and negatively affected by age of relationship and mutual dependency.
"Strategic outsourcing: leveraging knowledge capabilities" (Quinn, 1999)	Conceptual, using concept of core competencies and business examples	Designing core competence strategy	Outsourcing for short-term cost-cutting does not yield nearly as much as outsourcing for longer-term knowledge-based system or strategic benefits. Developing best-in-the-world capabilities is crucial in designing a core competency strategy. Unless the company is best-in-the-world at an activity, it is someone else's core competency.

continued on following page

Table 2. continued

Title/ authors	Research method	Scope of the research	Key conclusions/ findings
"IT outsourcing in insurance services: risk, creative contracting and business advantage" (Willcocks & Lacity, 1999)	Single case study	Risks in IT outsourcing	The case illustrates 10 major risk areas in IT outsourcing arrangements. Through awareness of risks and careful handling, the company studied was found to be achieving business advantage from a total outsourcing strategy.
"Modelling the price, performance, and contract characteristics of IT outsourcing" (Domberger, Fernandez, & Fiebig, 2000)	Analysis of 48 contracts for IT support and maintenance	Modeling the price, performance and contract characteristics that are relevant to IT outsourcing.	The study suggests that first-term contracts were more expensive than repeat contracts, possibly due to the higher risk and uncertainty often associated with newly awarded contracts.
"Making more by doing less: an analysis of outsourcing and its effects on firm performance" (Gilley & Rasheed, 2000)	Survey of 94 top executives in manufacturing firms	The study attempted to determine the performance implications of outsourcing strategies.	Although no direct effect of outsourcing on performance was detected, outsourcing interacted with firm strategy and environmental dynamism to predict performance.
"IT outsourcing: frameworks for conceptualizing practice and perception" (Hancox & Hackney, 2000)	Semi structured interviews with IT mangers from 13 public sector organizations and 7 local authorities in UK	Assess usefulness of four conceptual frameworks – core competencies, transaction cost economics, agency theory, and partnership – in an exploratory study of practice and perception of outsourcing	The study suggests that core competencies may not be a major issue in respect of ITO. Elements of TCE could be found. In terms of agency, the participants demonstrated some neutrality where they indicated that there was little perceived client conflict in contracting relations. Recognition of partnership was more usually found in public sector organizations, as local authorities had more additional constraints.
"The myths and realities of information technology insourcing" (Hirschheim & Lacity, 2000)	14 case studies	Generate insights into best sourcing practices by comparing successes and failures	Four archetypes of insourcing: 1) senior executives enable internal IT managers to cut costs, 2) IT managers terminate failing outsourcing contracts, 3) IT managers defend insourcing, and 4) senior executives confirm the value of IT.
"Contract, control and 'presentiation' in IT outsourcing: research in thirteen UK organizations" (Kern & Willcocks, 2000)	Findings from 13 UK-based organizations	The role of the outsourcing contract and its purpose for ensuring control over the client's outsourcing destiny	The contract has a legal function; the contract attempts to presentiate service levels; the contract assures client control over the outsourcing venture.
"Developing a framework for analyzing IS sourcing" (King & Malhotra, 2000)	Conceptual	Developing a framework for the consideration of internal markets as an alternative to IS outsourcing.	Identifies short term operational impacts (efficiencies, cost savings, service levels) mid term tactical impacts (performance, control, risk sharing), and long term strategic impacts (core competencies, learning competencies) that should be addressed both in research and practitioners' decision to outsource.
"Relationships in IT outsourcing: a stakeholder perspective" (Lacity & Willcocks, 2000a)	Conceptual	Customer-supplier relationships	An IT outsourcing relationship framework, that focuses on three key elements: 1) relationship stakeholders, 2) relationship types, and 3) six relationship phases and their related activities.
"Survey of IT outsourcing experience in US and UK organizations" (Lacity & Willcocks, 2000b)	Survey of 101 UK & US CIOs	Current market practices and experience	IT outsourcing continue to grow and evolve. Benefits of selective sourcing are: cost reduction, re-focus of in-house staff, improved IT flexibility, better quality services, access to scarce IT resources. Downside of selective sourcing includes: increased transaction costs, potential lack of integration, cooperation, and coordination among multiple sources.

continued on following page

Table 2. continued

Title/ authors	Research method	Scope of the research	Key conclusions/ findings
"Outsourcing innovation: the new engine of growth" (Quinn, 2000)	Conceptual, using concept of core competencies and business examples	How do you stay ahead, when everyone around is innovating?	Higher innovation return can accrue from outsourcing. Innovation calls for the complex knowledge that only a broad network of specialists can offer – resource limits, specialist talents, multiple risks, attracting talent, speed.
"Place, space and knowledge work: a study of outsourced computer system administrators" (Schultze & Boland, 2000)	Ethnographic fieldwork	Work practice of a group of outsourced computer systems administrators – the struggle to negotiate the place-space duality	The contractor's writing served to create an informational body that removed them from the confines of a particular place and technology. Allowing their "real" bodies to move on to newer technologies, responsibilities and organizations. The idealized place they yearned for was one that gave them security and safety through mobility and independence.
"On the performance of technology-sourcing partnership: the interaction between partner interdependence and technology attributes" (Steensma & Corley, 2000)	Survey of 95 sourcing arrangements	Technology attributes, organizational interdependence, sourcing performance	Using a knowledge-based perspective, a contingency model suggests that the imitability, uniqueness, and uncertainty with a technology interact with partner interdependence to influence sourcing outcomes (performance).
"Work outcomes and job design for contract versus permanent information systems professionals on software development teams" (Ang & Slaugther, 2001)	Empirical	Contract vs. permanent IS professionals	Work attitudes of contract professionals are more favorable than permanent professionals. Nonetheless, the contractors are perceived to exhibit lower in-role and extra-role behaviors and lower performance. In-depth interviews suggest that these results can be attributed to how organizations assign jobs to the two groups of professionals.
"Outsourcing information systems: drawing lessons from a banking case study" (Baldwin, Irani, & Love, 2001)	Single banking case study	Decision to insource or outsource IT/IS	Identifies motives for outsourcing decision to be strategic and organizational, political, technical, and economic.
"The hidden costs of IT outsourcing" (Barthélemy, 2001)	Survey of 50 companies	Identifying costs that managers can't pinpoint	Hidden costs are identified as: vendor search and contracting, transitioning to the vendor, managing the effort, transitioning after outsourcing (switching or reintegrating).
"Exploring the supply-side of IT outsourcing: evaluating the emerging role of application service providers" (Currie & Seltsikas, 2001)	Initial survey of 250 SMEs and case study among 28 ASPs	Exploring the supply-side of IT outsourcing; a comparison of traditional outsourcing and application outsourcing	ITO is moving into a industry centric wave. A shift from traditional one-to-one outsourcing relationship to a one-to-many relationship where an ASP provides an outsourcing solution to several clients remotely over the Internet or a VPN.
"The impact of the client-vendor relationship on information systems outsourcing success" (Goles, 2001)	Survey	Ascertain the components of an effective relationship, and explore the link between that relationship and outsourcing success or failure	A set of constructs that comprise a successful relationship was identified and tested. The study demonstrated that customers and vendors have different expectations for each party's responsibilities and behaviors. It also showed that each party measures success differently.
"Global information technology outsourcing" (Lacity & Willcocks, 2001)	Case studies	How to gain business advantage	Organizations must develop a comprehensive outsourcing strategy in order to achieve more than modest improvement of service and cost reduction. IT functions must develop a set of core capabilities that must be insourced.

continued on following page

Table 2. continued

Title/ authors	Research method	Scope of the research	Key conclusions/ findings
"The impact of knowledge sharing, organizational capability and partnership quality on IS outsourcing success" (Lee, 2001)	Survey of 223 IS managers in Korea	Relationship between knowledge sharing and outsourcing success	Knowledge sharing is one of the major predictors for outsourcing success. Organizational capacity to learn or acquire the needed knowledge from other organizations is a key source of successful knowledge sharing. Partnership quality is a significant intervening factor between knowledge sharing and outsourcing success.
"Culture, power and politics in ICT outsourcing in higher education institutions" (Allen, Kern, & Mattison, 2002)	Three British higher education institution (HEI) case studies	The impact of culture, organizational power and politics in outsourcing	Outsourcing represented a potential threat to academic culture. It was the outcome of intra-HEI power struggles, and it was also caused by departments increasing their fight to retain control over ICT. The ITO arrangements were highly politicised processes. Outsourcing service providers was used as change agents.
"Information technology outsourcing in Australia" (Beaumount & Costa, 2002)	Six exploratory interviews, survey of 277 informants	Identify reasons for outsourcing, and factors that contribute to success	Three most important factors for outsourcing were identified as: access to skills, improved service quality, and managers' ability to focus on core business activities. Factors most associated with success were cultural match and nature of contractual arrangement.
"Norm development in outsourcing relationship" (Kern & Blois, 2002)	Single case study, BP Exploration	The role of norms within networks	The need for establishing norms of behavior that was appropriate for the outsourcing consortium arrangement was not recognized by the parties involved. The failure of the consortium was the issue of "norms".
"Exploring relationships in information technology outsourcing: the interaction approach" (Kern & Willcocks, 2002)	Exploratory research into 12 organizations	Håkansson's (1982) interaction model applied on IT outsourcing relationships. Key elements are the interaction process, the parties involved, the environment, and the atmosphere.	The research identified certain factors in IT outsourcing relationships not captured satisfactory by the interaction approach, namely the centrality of the contract, the importance of formal processes, and the hidden cost of relationship management.
"The winners curse in IT outsourcing: strategies for avoiding relational trauma" (Kern, Willcocks, & van Heck, 2002)	Conceptual, re-analyzing longitudinal case research database of 85 IT outsourcing arrangements	Identifying the right supplier and contract bid	The Winners' Curse occurs when the winner of an auction or bidding event systematically bids above the actual value of the objects or service and thereby systematically losses. The experience places considerable pressure on an outsourcing venture and relationship to the point where re-negotiation or early termination becomes the only option.
"Do make or buy decisions matter? The influence of organizational governance on technological performance" (Leiblein, Reuer, & Dalsace, 2002)	Sample of 714 production decisions	Relationship between outsourcing decisions (governance choice) and technological performance	Neither outsourcing nor internalization per se results in superior performance. Rather, a firm's technological performance is contingent upon the alignment between firms' governance decisions and the degree of contractual hazards.
"Making the HR outsourcing decision" (Adler, 2003)	Extensive literature review and a single case study	What and when to outsource HR services	Six factors can help companies determine which HR process to outsource and which to retain: dependency risks, spillover risks, trust, relative proficiency, strategic capabilities, and commitment versus flexibility.

continued on following page

Table 2. continued

Title/ authors	Research method	Scope of the research	Key conclusions/ findings
"The information technology outsourcing risk: a transaction cost and agency theory-based perspective" (Bahli & Rivard, 2003)	Conceptual, using prior research as well as transaction cost and agency theory	Conceptualization of IT outsourcing risk	A framework for conceptualization and measurement of risk applied to IT outsourcing – scenarios, likelihood or risk factors occurring, risk mitigation mechanisms, and the consequences.
"The hard and soft sides of IT outsourcing management" (Barthélemy 2003a)	In-depth study of 50 IT outsourcing cases	The impact of hard (contract) and soft (trust) sides of IT outsourcing outcomes	Simple IT outsourcing may be managed with hard side only and complex IT outsourcing with soft side only. Simultaneously used, trust can take over from contract when the limits of the contract have been reached. IT outsourcing efforts managed through 'neither hard nor soft side' are doomed to fail.
"The seven deadly sins of outsourcing" (Barthélemy, 2003b)	Conceptual, based on in-depth analysis of 91 outsourcing efforts	Lessons learned from failed outsourcing	Reasons why outsourcing fail: 1) outsourcing activities that should not be outsourced, 2) selecting the wrong vendor, 3) writing a poor contract, 4) overlooking personnel issues, 5) losing control over the outsourced activity, 6) overlooking the hidden costs of outsourcing, 7) failing to plan an exit strategy.
"Portfolios of Control in Outsourced Software Development Projects" (Choudhury & Sabherwal, 2003)	Five case studies	Control in outsourced information system development projects	Portfolios of control are dominated by outcome controls, especially at the start of the project. Behavior controls are often added later in the project, as are controls aimed to encourage and enable vendor self control. Clan controls are used when the client and the vendor share goals.
"When subordinates become IT contractors: persistent managerial expectations in IT outsourcing" (Ho et al., 2003)	Mixed-method: 147 survivors of a single government IT organization	Persistence of managerial expectations in an IT outsourcing context where the traditional relationship between supervisor and subordinates changes to one of client-manager and contractor (client-vendor perspective)	Findings show that role overload, the presence of strong ties between manager and contractor, and the lack of prior outsourcing experience increased the persistence of managerial expectations. In turn persistence of expectations had a distinctive positive influence on managerial perceptions of contractor performance.
"Management control systems and trust in outsourcing relationships" (Langfield-Smith & Smith, 2003)	Single case study	Examine how control mechanisms and trust are used to achieve control of outsourced IT operations	Characteristics of the transaction, environment and parties, can be used in the design of control systems and trust in outsourcing relationships
"From the vendor's perspective: exploring the value proposition in information technology outsourcing" (Levina & Ross, 2003)	28 interviews from a single long-term client-vendor case study	Vendors' ability to deliver economic and management benefits to their clients	Vendor's efficiency is based on the economic benefits derived from the ability to develop a complementary set of core competencies. This ability, in turn, is based on the centralization of decision rights, and shared with clients through formal and informal relationship management structures.
"What will it take China to become a competitive force in offshore outsourcing? An analysis of the role of transaction costs in supplier selection" (Qu & Brocklehurst, 2003)	Conceptual, outlining a framework for analyzing transaction costs	Uses the framework for pinpointing where China is unable to compete in the supply of IT outsourcing	Transaction costs are almost as significant as production costs when it comes to offshore outsourcing. The paper concludes with a review of the policy implications for the Chinese Government.
"A transaction cost model for IT outsourcing" (Aubert, Rivard, & Patry, 2004)	Survey of 335 firms	Relying on transaction cost economics, the paper proposes and tests an explanatory model of IT outsourcing behavior.	Uncertainty is the major deterrent to outsourcing; firms seem to outsource more readily activities having low uncertainty. While the level of technical skills is the most important reason to outsource.

continued on following page

Table 2. continued

Title/ authors	Research method	Scope of the research	Key conclusions/ findings
"An empirical investigation of IT outsourcing versus quasi-outsourcing in France and Germany" (Barthélemy & Geyer, 2004)	Survey; 160 senior IT executives in Germany and France	Determinants of the outsourcing versus quasi-outsourcing decisions.	Quasi-outsourcing was introduced as firms setting up their own IT subsidiary. Findings shows that the decision to quasi-outsource is strongly influenced by IT activity asset-specificity, size of IT department, internal organization of IT, and institutional environment (e.g., *Mitbestimmung* in Germany).
"Perspectives on global outsourcing and the changing nature of work" (Clott, 2004)	Review of perspectives	Impact of global outsourcing	Most optimistic it will create good jobs in poor countries, shrink the gap between rich and poor nations, and create smaller, more highly innovative firms. In a different future we will see the development of far greater degree of protectionism and limits on globalization in the form of exclusive trade treaties, regional trade agreements, tariff and non-tariff barriers, and the increased power of "gatekeeping" organizations (e.g., ISO), to limit global outsourcing partners.
"Beyond offshoring: asses your company's global potential" (Farrell, 2004)	150 interviews	Globalization study at four major developing economies (China, India, Brazil, Mexico) and five industries (auto, consumer electronics, food, banking, IT/BPO)	Globalization can transform industries. Streamlining their production process and supply chains globally, companies can lower their cost and drop their prices to increase demand for their products, attract new customers, and enter new markets. Companies that read the landscape correctly will capture dramatic revenue growth.
"IT outsourcing success: a psychological contract perspective" (Koh et al., 2004)	Sequential qualitative-quantitative approach of IT outsourcing project managers in Singapore (15 interviews and sample of 370 project mangers)	Critical customer-supplier obligations in IT outsourcing relationships and the impact of fulfilling these obligations on outsourcing success	Results showed the existence of a psychological contract between customers and suppliers. Outsourcing success showed a significant positive relationship with five supplier and four customer obligations. Supplier obligations were: clear authority structures, taking charge, effective human capital management, effective knowledge management, effective knowledge transfer, and building effective inter-organizational teams. Customer obligations were: clear specifications, prompt payment, close project monitoring, and project ownership.
"Trust-building mechanisms utilized in outsourced IS development projects: a case study" (Lander, Purvis, McCray, & Leigh, 2004)	Single in-depth case study	Describe trust-building mechanisms used between different stakeholders over the course of an ERP implementation project.	The results indicate that the various stakeholders did not encounter previously identified stages of building trust. Significant differences were found in the use of trust-building mechanisms among top-level managers, project team members, users, and outsourcers.
"IT outsourcing strategies: universalistic, contingency, and configurational explanations of success" (Lee, Miranda, & Kim, 2004)	311 firms in South Korea	Exploring the effects of IT outsourcing strategies on outsourcing success	Findings indicate superiority of configurational approach over universalistic and contingency perspectives explaining outsourcing success.
"Transformational outsourcing" (Linder, 2004)	20 case studies	Outsourcing as a means of achieving radical organizational change	Four varieties of transformational outsourcing are rapid startup, pathway to growth, change catalyst, and radical renewal.

continued on following page

Table 2. continued

Title/ authors	Research method	Scope of the research	Key conclusions/ findings
"Preparing for utility computing: The role of IT architecture and relationship management" (Ross & Westerman, 2004)	Outsourcing experiences of eleven firms	Explore the potential impact of utility computing on firm's outsourcing practices	Utility computing will shift firm's objectives for outsourcing from a cost emphasis to an emphasis on strategic agility. Vendor relationship management and architecture design capabilities will continue to play key roles, as firms seek the benefits from utility computing.
"Offshoring without guilt" (Venkatraman, 2004)	-	Insight	Offshoring is defined as the practice among U.S. and European companies of migrating business overseas (..) to lower costs without significantly sacrificing quality. Offshoring represents the inevitable next generation of business practice.
"IT and business process outsourcing: the knowledge potential" (Willcocks, Hindle, Feeny, & Lacity, 2004)	Single enterprise partnership case study	What happens to knowledge when an organization outsources?	Both clients and suppliers need to be become much more aware of the role of knowledge assimilation, creation, and application in achieving improvements. Changes in management practices may well be the only real way of release the knowledge potential inherent in the practice of IT and BPO. The enterprise partnership model serves as a key benchmark as to what is possible.
"Taking the measure of outsourcing providers" (Feeny, Lacity, & Willcocks, 2005)	Multiple research bases; longitudinal studies of IT, business process, application, and off-shore outsourcing arrangements.	Develop a framework for helping client companies evaluate BPO suppliers	BPO suppliers possess delivery, transformation, and relationship competencies. Twelve supplier capabilities were identified. To ensure performance, client must identify which competencies to asses, evaluate supplier strengths, and remain involved in the business processes.
"Financial performance, CEO compensation, and large-scale information technology outsourcing decisions" (Hall & Liedtka, 2005)	Public available data for 51 firms outsourcing all or a large portion of their IT function during 1993 – 2001	The extent to which financial factors and managerial (CEO) self-interest influence the decision to outsource	CEOs make irreversible large-scale IT outsourcing decisions due to factors that include firm financial desperation, firm cash needs, and the desire to maximize personal compensation.
"The impact of IS sourcing type on service quality and maintenance efforts" (Park & Kim, 2005)	Survey; 107 responses from 28 organizations	Effects of IS sourcing on service quality and maintenance	Outsourced systems seemed to entail a higher level of service quality than insourced systems. The sourcing type did not influence the maintenance efforts. System type and age influenced the service quality and maintainers effort.
"IS outsourcing management competence dimensions: instrument development and relationship exploration" (Shi, Kunnathur, & Ragu-Nathan, 2005)	Large scale survey; 205 IS executives	Theoretical development and empirical testing of IS outsourcing management competence	Three second-order IS outsourcing management competence factors – informed buying, contract management, and relationship management – capture necessary organizational capabilities to plan and execute various IS outsourcing activities for both economic and intellectual benefits.
"Risk factors associated with offshore IT outsourcing" (Tafti, 2005)	Conceptual	Develop a framework for risk assessment of offshore IT outsourcing	Provides a general framework and a checklist of major risk factors related to offshore IT outsourcing – outsourcing contract, privacy and security, decision process, outsourcing scope, diminished technical returns, hidden costs, loss of IT expertise.

continued on following page

Table 2. continued

Title/ authors	Research method	Scope of the research	Key conclusions/ findings
"Information technology, production process outsourcing, and manufacturing plant performance" (Bardhan, Whitaker, & Mithas, 2006)	326 plants from IW/ MPI's database of manufacturing plants (secondary data source)	The role of IT and plant strategies as antecedents of production outsourcing, and the impact of production outsourcing and IT investments on plant cost and quality	Plants with greater IT investments are more likely to outsource their production processes. IT investments and production outsourcing are associated with lower plant costs and higher product quality improvement.
"Applying multiple perspectives to the BPO decision: a case study of call centres in Australia" (Borman, 2006)	Case study of outsourced call centers in Australia	Multi-perspective approach to BPO decision making	Nature and limits of BPO are: 1) BPO will be restricted to non-core activities, 2) organizations will seek to minimize supplier dependencies, 3) BPO is shaped by institutional context, and 4) organizations will ensure BPO doe not negatively impact their value system proposition.
"Smarter offshoring" (Farrell, 2006)	Analysis of offshore centers in 28 low-wage countries	Factors in choosing a location	To make the right offshoring decisions, companies should assemble detailed information on factors such as costs, availability of skills, environment, market potential, risk profile, quality of infrastructure. Comparing locations objectively: list possible locations, define criteria, collect data, assign weights to all criteria, and rank locations.
"Information systems outsourcing: A literature analysis" (Gonzales, Gasco, & Liopis, 2006)	Literature review – a total of 131 articles	Identifying the main topics and methodologies of IS research, and the main authors and countries contributed	Progressively increasing number of articles from 1988 until 2005. The articles are mainly empirical, a field study being the method preferred by researchers. Vendor perspective dominates research. Most prolific author is Willcocks (UK), but most authors come from US.
"Offshoring work: business hype or the onset of fundamental transformation?" (Lewin & Peeters, 2006)	Survey in 104 large and small US companies involved in offshoring	Adoption of offshoring	Offshore arrangements support companies' growth strategies.
"Transplants' role stress and work performance in IT outsourcing relationships" (Solli-Sæther, 2006)	Case study and survey	Individual level effects of IT outsourcing	Role stress was found as prevalent among transplants of IT outsourcing. In turn, perceived role stress was found to influence transplants' work outcome.

Note: The review included the following major IS journals from year 2000, to the most current volume available by March 2007; *European Journal of Information Systems, Information & Management, Information Systems Research, Journal of Information Technology, Journal of Management Information Systems, MIS Quarterly*, and *MIT Sloan Management Review*. Promising articles were followed back to their origin, whether based in articles, books, or dissertations.

& Straub, 2003; Koh, Ang, & Straub, 2004). Lately, research into global outsourcing has gained more attention.

CONCLUSION

From a theoretic point of view, IT outsourcing research has a basis in economic theories, organizational theories, and strategic management theories as well. For example, transaction cost theory and neo-classical economic theory are important elements in the outsourcing decision-making process. Resource-based theory of the firm, including the knowledge-based perspective of the firm, is another example of important scholarly value when applied to IT outsourcing models. Partnership and alliance theory is also applicable to understanding relationships between the two parties.

Based on the reviewed literature, eleven theories concerned with IT outsourcing were identified and recognized, and used to extend and strengthen our theoretical understanding of this complex field. The theories were compared in terms of what they recommend for outsourcing. Some theories are focused primarily on cost concerns (neo-classical economic theory, transaction cost theory, agency theory, contractual theory, theory of firm boundaries), and resource concerns (theory of core competencies and resource-based theory), while others have relational partnership concerns (partnership and alliance theory, relational exchange theory, social exchange theory, and stakeholder theory). In order to understand the inherent complexities and the underlying constructs of managing successful IT outsourcing relationships, these theories were presented and explored in this chapter.

REFERENCES

Adler, P. S. (2003). Making the HR Outsourcing Decision. *MIT Sloan Management Review*, *45*(1), 53–60.

Allen, D., Kern, T., & Mattison, D. (2002). Culture, power and politics in ICT outsourcing in higher education institutions. *European Journal of Information Systems*, *11*(2), 159–173. doi:10.1057/palgrave/ejis/3000425

Anderson, S. W., Glenn, D., & Sedatole, K. L. (2000). Sourcing parts of complex products: evidence on transactions costs, high-powered incentives and ex-post opportunism. *Accounting, Organizations and Society*, *25*(5), 723–749. doi:10.1016/S0361-3682(00)00015-5

Ang, S. (1993). *The etiology of information systems outsourcing.* Unpublished Doctor of Philosophy Thesis, University of Minnesota.

Ang, S., & Cummings, L. L. (1997). Strategic Response to Institutional Influence on Information Systems Outsourcing. *Organization Science*, *8*(3), 235–256. doi:10.1287/orsc.8.3.235

Ang, S., & Slaugther, S. A. (2001). Work Outcomes and Job Design for Contract Versus Permanent Information Systems Professionals on Software development Teams. *MIS Quarterly*, *25*(5), 321–350. doi:10.2307/3250920

Ang, S., & Straub, D. W. (1998). Production and Transaction Economics and IS Outsourcing: A study of the U.S. Banking Industry. *MIS Quarterly*, *22*(4), 535–552. doi:10.2307/249554

Artz, K. W., & Brush, T. H. (2000). Asset specificity, uncertainty and relational norms: an examination of coordination costs in collaborative strategic alliances. *Journal of Economic Behavior & Organization*, *41*(4), 337–362. doi:10.1016/S0167-2681(99)00080-3

Aubert, B. A., Rivard, S., & Patry, M. (2004). A transaction cost model of IT outsourcing. *Information & Management*, *41*(7), 921–932. doi:10.1016/j.im.2003.09.001

Bahli, B., & Rivard, S. (2003). The information technology outsourcing risk: a transaction cost and agency theory-based perspective. *Journal of Information Technology, 18*(3), 211–221. doi:10.1080/0268396032000130214

Baldwin, L. P., Irani, Z., & Love, P. E. D. (2001). Outsourcing information systems: drawing lessons from a banking case study. *European Journal of Information Systems, 10*(1), 15–24. doi:10.1057/palgrave.ejis.3000372

Bardhan, I., Whitaker, J., & Mithas, S. (2006). Information Technology, Production Process Outsourcing, and Manufacturing Plant Performance. *Journal of Management Information Systems, 23*(2), 13–40. doi:10.2753/MIS0742-1222230202

Barney, J. B. (2001). Is the resourced-based "view" a useful perspective for strategic management research? Yes. *Academy of Management Review, 26*(1), 41–56. doi:10.2307/259393

Barthélemy, J. (2001). The Hidden Costs of IT Outsourcing. *Sloan Management Review, 42*(3), 60–69.

Barthélemy, J. (2003a). The Hard and Soft Sides of IT Outsourcing Management. *European Management Journal, 21*(5), 539–548. doi:10.1016/S0263-2373(03)00103-8

Barthélemy, J. (2003b). The Seven Deadly Sins of Outsourcing. *The Academy of Management Executive, 17*(2), 87–100.

Barthélemy, J., & Geyer, D. (2004). An empirical investigation of IT outsourcing versus quasi-outsourcing in France and Germany. *Information & Management, 42*(4), 533–542. doi:10.1016/j.im.2004.02.005

Beamount, N., & Costa, C. (2002). Information Technology Outsourcing in Australia. *Information Resources Management Journal, 15*(3), 14–31.

Borman, M. M. B. (2006). Applying multiple perspectives to the BPO decision: a case study of call centres in Australia. *Journal of Information Technology, 21*(2), 99–115. doi:10.1057/palgrave.jit.2000057

Choudhury, V., & Sabherwal, R. (2003). Portfolios of Control in Outsourced Software Development Projects. *Information Systems Research, 14*(3), 291–314. doi:10.1287/isre.14.3.291.16563

Clott, C. B. (2004). Perspectives on Global Outsourcing and the Changing Nature of Work. *Business and Society Review, 109*(2), 153–170. doi:10.1111/j.0045-3609.2004.00189.x

Cross, J., Earl, M. J., & Sampler, J. L. (1997). Transformation of the IT Function at British Petroleum. *MIS Quarterly, 21*(4), 401–423. doi:10.2307/249721

Currie, W. L., & Seltsikas, P. (2001). Exploring the supply-side of IT-outsourcing: evaluating the emerging role of application service providers. *European Journal of Information Systems, 10*(3), 123–134. doi:10.1057/palgrave.ejis.3000393

Das, T. K., & Teng, B.-S. (2002a). Alliance Constellations: A Social Exchange Perspective. *Academy of Management Review, 27*(3), 445–456. doi:10.2307/4134389

Das, T. K., & Teng, B.-S. (2002b). The dynamics of alliance conditions in the alliance development process. *Journal of Management Studies, 39*(5), 725–746. doi:10.1111/1467-6486.00006

Das, T. K., & Teng, B.-S. (2003). Partner analysis and alliance performance. *Scandinavian Journal of Management, 19*(3), 279–308. doi:10.1016/S0956-5221(03)00003-4

Davis, K. J. (1996). *IT Outsourcing Relationships: An Exploratory Study of Interorganizational Control Mechanisms.* Unpublished DBA dissertation, Harvard University, Boston, MA.

Domberger, S., Fernandez, P., & Fiebig, D. G. (2000). Modelling the price, performance and contract characteristics of IT outsourcing. *Journal of Information Technology, 15*(2), 107–118. doi:10.1080/026839600344302

Earl, M. J. (1996). The Risks of Outsourcing IT. *Sloan Management Review, 37*(3), 26–32.

Earl, M. J. (2001). Knowledge Management Strategies: Toward a Taxonomy. *Journal of Management Information Systems, 18*(1), 215–233.

Eisenhardt, K. M. (1985). Control: organizational and economic approaches. *Management Science, 31*(2), 134–149. doi:10.1287/mnsc.31.2.134

Elitzur, R., & Wensley, A. (1998). Game Theory and IS Outsourcing Contracts. In L. P. Willcocks & M. C. Lacity (Eds.), *Strategic Sourcing of Information Systems. Perspectives and Practices.* Chichester: John Wiley & Sons, U.K.

Farrell, D. (2004). Beyond Offshoring: Assess Your Company's Global Potential. *Harvard Business Review, 82*(12), 82–90.

Farrell, D. (2006). Smarter Offshoring. *Harvard Business Review, 84*(6), 84–92.

Feeny, D. F., Lacity, M. C., & Willcocks, L. P. (2005). Taking the Measure of Outsourcing Providers. *MIT Sloan Management Review, 46*(3), 41–48.

Freeman, R. E. (1984). *Strategic Management: A Stakeholder Approach.* Boston: Pitman Publishing Inc.

Freeman, R. E., & Phillips, R. A. (2002). Stakeholder theory: A libertarian defense. *Business Ethics Quarterly, 12*(3), 331–349. doi:10.2307/3858020

Garicano, L., & Hubbard, T. N. (2003). Firms' Boundaries and the Division of Labor: Empirical Strategies. *Journal of the European Economic Association, 1*(2/3), 495–502. doi:10.1162/154247603322391134

Gilley, M. K., & Rasheed, A. (2000). Making More By Doing Less: An Analysis of Outsourcing and its Effects on Firm Performance. *Journal of Management, 26*(4), 763–790. doi:10.1016/S0149-2063(00)00055-6

Goles, T. (2001). *The Impact of the Client-Vendor Relationship on Information Systems Outsourcing Success.* Unpublished PhD Dissertation, University of Houston, Houston, TX.

Gonzales, R., Gasco, J., & Liopis, J. (2006). Information systems outsourcing: A literature analysis. *Information & Management, 43*(7), 821–834. doi:10.1016/j.im.2006.07.002

Gram, H. (2003). Openness versus Closedness in Classical and Neoclassical Economies. *Review of Political Economy, 15*(3), 419–425. doi:10.1080/09538250308433

Grover, V., Cheon, M. J., & Teng, J. T. C. (1996). The Effect of Service Quality and Partnership on the Outsourcing of Information Systems Functions. *Journal of Management Information Systems, 12*(4), 89–116.

Grover, V., Teng, T. C., & Cheon, M. J. (1998). Towards a Theoretically-Based Contingency Model of Information Systems Outsourcing. In L. P. Willcocks & M. C. Lacity (Eds.), *Strategic Sourcing of Information Systems. Perspectives and Practices* (pp. 79-101). Chichester, UK: John Wiley & Sons.

Hall, J. A., & Liedtka, S. L. (2005). Financial Performance, CEO Compensation, and Large-Scale Information Technology Outsourcing Decisions. *Journal of Management Information Systems, 22*(1), 193–221.

Hancox, M., & Hackney, R. (2000). IT outsourcing: frameworks for conceptualizing practice and perception. *Information Systems Journal, 10*(3), 217–237. doi:10.1046/j.1365-2575.2000.00082.x

Heide, J. B., & John, G. (1992). Do Norms Matter in Marketing Relationships? *Journal of Marketing, 56*(2), 32–44. doi:10.2307/1252040

Henisz, W. J., & Williamson, O. E. (1999). Comparative Economic Organization - Within and Between Countries. *Business and Politics, 1*(3), 261–277.

Hirschheim, R., & Lacity, M. C. (2000). The Myths and Realities of Information Technology Insourcing. *Communications of the ACM, 43*(2), 99–107. doi:10.1145/328236.328112

Hitt, M. A., Bierman, L., Shumizu, K., & Kochhar, R. (2001). Direct and moderating effects of human capital on strategy and performance in professional service firms: a resourced-based perspective. *Academy of Management Journal, 44*(1), 13–28. doi:10.2307/3069334

Ho, V. T., Ang, S., & Straub, D. (2003). When Subordinates Become IT Contractors: Persistent Managerial Expectations in IT Outsourcing. *Information Systems Research, 14*(1), 66–86. doi:10.1287/isre.14.1.66.14764

Hu, Q., Saunders, C., & Gebelt, M. (1997). Research Report: Diffusion of Information Systems Outsourcing: A Reevaluation of Influence Sources. *Information Systems Research, 8*(3), 288–301. doi:10.1287/isre.8.3.288

Jap, S. D. (2001). Perspectives on joint competitive advantages in buyer-supplier relationships. *International Journal of Research in Marketing, 18*(1-2), 19–35. doi:10.1016/S0167-8116(01)00028-3

Jensen, M. C., & Meckling, W. H. (1976). Theory of the firm: Managerial behavior, agency costs and ownership structures. *Journal of Financial Economics, 3*(4), 305–360. doi:10.1016/0304-405X(76)90026-X

Kern, T. (1999). *Relationships in IT Outsourcing: An Exploratory Research Study of a Conceptual Framework.* Unpublished Doctor of Philosophy, Christ Church College, University of Oxford, Oxford.

Kern, T., & Blois, K. (2002). Norm development in outsourcing relationship. *Journal of Information Technology, 17*(1), 32–42. doi:10.1080/02683960210137174

Kern, T., & Willcocks, L. P. (2000). Contract, Control and Presentiation in IT Outsourcing: Research in Thirteen UK Organizations. *Journal of Global Information Management, 8*(4), 15–29.

Kern, T., & Willcocks, L. P. (2002). Exploring relationship in information technology outsourcing: the interaction approach. *European Journal of Information Systems, 11*(1), 3–19. doi:10.1057/palgrave/ejis/3000415

Kern, T., Willcocks, L. P., & van Heck, E. (2002). The Winners Curse in IT Outsourcing: Strategies for Avoiding Relational Trauma. *California Management Review, 44*(2), 47–69.

King, W. R., & Malhotra, Y. (2000). Developing a framework for analyzing IS sourcing. *Information & Management, 37*(6), 323–334. doi:10.1016/S0378-7206(00)00046-X

Koh, C., Ang, S., & Straub, D. W. (2004). IT Outsourcing Success: A Psychological Contract Perspective. *Information Systems Research, 15*(4), 356–373. doi:10.1287/isre.1040.0035

Lacity, M. C., & Hirschheim, R. (1993). The Information Systems Outsourcing Bandwagon. *Sloan Management Review, 35*(1), 51–63.

Lacity, M. C., & Willcocks, L. P. (1998). An Empirical Investigation of Information Technology Sourcing Practices: Lessons from Experience. *MIS Quarterly, 22*(3), 363–408. doi:10.2307/249670

Lacity, M. C., & Willcocks, L. P. (2000a). Relationships in IT Outsourcing: A Stakeholder Perspective. In R. W. Zmud (Ed.), *Framing the Domains of IT Management: Projecting the Future Through the Past*. Cincinnati, OH: Pinnaflex Educational Resources.

Lacity, M. C., & Willcocks, L. P. (2000b). Survey of IT Outsourcing Experiences in US and UK Organizations. *Journal of Global Information Management, 8*(2), 5–23.

Lacity, M. C., & Willcocks, L. P. (2001). *Global Information Technology Outsourcing*. Chichester, UK: John Wiley & Sons, Ltd.

Lacity, M. C., Willcocks, L. P., & Feeny, D. F. (1996). The Value of Selective IT Sourcing. *Sloan Management Review, 37*(3), 13–25.

Lambe, C. J., Spekman, R. E., & Hunt, S. D. (2000). Interimistic Relational Exchange: Conceptualization and Propositional Development. *Journal of the Academy of Marketing Science, 28*(2), 212–225. doi:10.1177/0092070300282003

Lambe, C. J., Spekman, R. E., & Hunt, S. D. (2002). Alliance Competence, Resources, and Alliance Success: Conceptualization, Measurement, and Initial Test. *Journal of the Academy of Marketing Science, 30*(2), 141–158. doi:10.1177/03079459994399

Lambe, C. J., Wittmann, C. M., & Spekman, R. E. (2001). Social Exchange Theory and Research on Business-to-Business Relational Exchange. *Journal of Business-To-Business Marketing, 8*(3), 1–36. doi:10.1300/J033v08n03_01

Lander, M. C., Purvis, R. L., McCray, G. E., & Leigh, W. (2004). Trust-building mechanisms utliized in outsourced IS development project: a case study. *Information & Management, 41*(4), 509–528. doi:10.1016/j.im.2003.10.001

Langfield-Smith, K., & Smith, D. (2003). Management control systems and trust in outsourcing relationships. *Management Accounting Research*, *14*(3), 281–307. doi:10.1016/S1044-5005(03)00046-5

Lee, J.-N. (2001). The impact of knowledge sharing, organizational capability and partnership quality on IS outsourcing success. *Information & Management*, *38*(5), 323–335. doi:10.1016/S0378-7206(00)00074-4

Lee, J.-N., & Kim, Y.-G. (1999). Effect of Partnership Quality on IS Outsourcing Success: Conceptual Framework and Empirical Validation. *Journal of Management Information Systems*, *15*(4), 29–61.

Lee, J.-N., Miranda, S. M., & Kim, Y.-M. (2004). IT Outsourcing Strategies: Universalistic, Contingency, and Configurational Explanations of Success. *Information Systems Research*, *15*(2), 110–131. doi:10.1287/isre.1040.0013

Leiblein, M. J., Reuer, J. J., & Dalsace, F. (2002). Do make or buy decisions matter? The influence of organizational governance on technological performance. *Strategic Management Journal*, *23*(9), 817–833. doi:10.1002/smj.259

Levina, N., & Ross, J. W. (2003). From the Vendor's Perspective: Exploring the Value Proposition in Information Technology Outsourcing. *MIS Quarterly*, *27*(3), 331–364.

Lewin, A. Y., & Peeters, C. (2006). Offshoring Work: Business Hype or the Onset of Fundamental Transformation? *Long Range Planning*, *39*(3), 221–239. doi:10.1016/j.lrp.2006.07.009

Linder, J. (2004). Transformational Outsourcing. *MIT Sloan Management Review*, *45*(2), 52–58.

Loh, L., & Venkatraman, N. (1992a). Determinants of Information Technology Outsourcing: A Cross-Sectional Analysis. *Journal of Management Information Systems*, *9*(1), 7–24.

Loh, L., & Venkatraman, N. (1992b). Diffusion of Information Technology Outsourcing: Influence Sources and the Kodak Effect. *Information Systems Research*, *3*(4), 334–358. doi:10.1287/isre.3.4.334

Løwendahl, B. R. (2000). *Strategic Management of Professional Service Firms* (2nd ed.). Copenhagen: Copenhagen Business School Press.

Luo, Y. (2002). Contract, cooperation, and performance in international joint ventures. *Strategic Management Journal*, *23*(10), 903–919. doi:10.1002/smj.261

McFarlan, F. W., & Nolan, R. L. (1995). How to Manage an IT Outsourcing Alliance. *Sloan Management Review*, *36*(2), 9–23.

McLellan, K., Marcolin, B. L., & Beamish, P. W. (1995). Financial and strategic motivations behind IS outsourcing. *Journal of Information Technology*, *10*(4), 299–321. doi:10.1057/jit.1995.32

Park, J.-Y., & Kim, J.-O. (2005). The impact of IS sourcing type on quality and maintenance efforts. *Information & Management*, *42*(2), 261–274. doi:10.1016/j.im.2003.08.005

Phillips, R., Freeman, R. E., & Wicks, A. C. (2003). What stakeholder theory is not. *Business Ethics Quarterly*, *13*(4), 479–502.

Poppo, L., & Zenger, T. (2002). Do formal contracts and relational governance function as substitutes or compliments? *Strategic Management Journal*, *23*(8), 707–725. doi:10.1002/smj.249

Prahalad, C. K., & Hamel, G. (1990). The Core Competence of the Corporation. *Harvard Business Review*, *68*(3), 79–91.

Qu, Z., & Brocklehurst, M. (2003). What will it take china to become a competitive force in offshore outsourcing? An analysis of the role of transaction costs in supplier selection. *Journal of Information Technology*, *18*(1), 53–67. doi:10.1080/0268396031000077459

Quinn, J. B. (1999). Strategic Outsourcing: Leveraging Knowledge Capabilities. *Sloan Management Review*, *40*(4), 9–21.

Quinn, J. B. (2000). Outsourcing Innovation: The New Engine of Growth. *Sloan Management Review*, *41*(4), 13–28.

Quinn, J. B., & Hilmer, F. G. (1994). Strategic Outsourcing. *Sloan Management Review*, *35*(4), 43–55.

Ravichandran, R., & Ahmed, N. U. (1993). Offshore systems development. *Information & Management*, *24*(1), 33–40. doi:10.1016/0378-7206(93)90045-U

Rokkan, A. I., & Haugland, S. A. (2002). Developing relational exchange - Effectiveness and power. *European Journal of Marketing*, *36*(1), 211–230. doi:10.1108/03090560210412764

Ross, J. W., & Westerman, G. (2004). Preparing for utility computing: The role of IT architecture and relationship management. *IBM Systems Journal*, *43*(1), 5–19.

Saunders, C., Gebelt, M., & Hu, Q. (1997). Achieving Success in Information Systems Outsourcing. *California Management Review*, *39*(2), 63–79.

Schilling, M. A., & Steensma, H. K. (2002). Disentangling the Theories of firm Boundaries: A Path Model and Empirical Test. *Organization Science*, *13*(4), 387–401. doi:10.1287/orsc.13.4.387.2950

Schultze, U., & Boland, R. J. Jr. (2000). Place, space and knowledge work: a study of outsourced computer systems administrators. *Accounting . Management and Information Technologies*, *10*(3), 187–219. doi:10.1016/S0959-8022(00)00006-0

Shankman, N. A. (1999). Reframing the debate between agency and stakeholder theories of the firm. *Journal of Business Ethics*, *19*(4), 319–334. doi:10.1023/A:1005880031427

Shi, Z., Kunnathur, A. S., & Ragu-Nathan, T. S. (2005). IS outsourcing management competence dimensions: instrument development and relationship exploration. *Information & Management*, *42*(6), 901–919. doi:10.1016/j.im.2004.10.001

Smith, M. A., Mitra, S., & Narasimhan, S. (1996). Offshore outsourcing of software development and maintenance: A framework for issues. *Information & Management*, *31*(3), 165–175. doi:10.1016/S0378-7206(96)01077-4

Sobol, M. G., & Apte, U. (1995). Domestic and global outsourcing practices of America's most effective IS users. *Journal of Information Technology*, *10*(4), 269–280. doi:10.1057/jit.1995.30

Solli-Sæther, H. (2006). *Transplants' role stress and work performance in IT outsourcing relationships.* Unpublished PhD thesis, BI Norwegian School of Management, Oslo.

Steensma, H. K., & Corley, K. G. (2000). On the performance of technology-sourcing partnership: The interaction between partner interdependence and technology attributes. *Academy of Management Journal*, *43*(6), 1045–1067. doi:10.2307/1556334

Tafti, M. H. A. (2005). Risk factors associated with offshore IT outsourcing. *Industrial Management & Data Systems*, *105*(5), 549–560. doi:10.1108/02635570510599940

Teng, J. T. C., Cheon, M. J., & Grover, V. (1995). Decision to Outsource Information Systems Functions: Testing a Strategy-Theoretic Discrepancy Model. *Decision Sciences*, *26*(1), 75–103. doi:10.1111/j.1540-5915.1995.tb00838.x

Venkatraman, N. V. (2004). Offshoring Without Guilt. *MIT Sloan Management Review*, *45*(3), 14–16.

Willcocks, L. P., Hindle, J. L., Feeny, D. F., & Lacity, M. C. (2004). IT and Business Process Outsourcing: The Knowledge Potential. *Information Systems Management*, *21*(3), 7–15. doi:10.1201/1078/44432.21.3.20040601/82471.2

Willcocks, L. P., & Lacity, M. C. (1999). IT outsourcing in insurance services: risk, creative contracting and business advantage. *Information Systems Journal*, *9*(3), 163–180. doi:10.1046/j.1365-2575.1999.00061.x

Williamson, O. E. (1979). Transaction-Cost Economics: The Governance of Contractual Relations. *The Journal of Law & Economics*, *22*(2), 233–261. doi:10.1086/466942

Williamson, O. E. (1981). The Modern Corporation: Origins, Evolution, Attributes. *Journal of Economic Literature*, *19*(4), 1537–1568.

Williamson, O. E. (2000). The New Institutional Economics: Taking Stock, Looking Ahead. *Journal of Economic Literature*, *38*(3), 595–613.

Chapter 3
Critical Success Factors

We have identified a total of eleven theories that help explain why IT outsourcing is occurring worldwide. These theories were presented in the previous Chapter 2. Based on these theories, we develop eleven critical success factors in IT outsourcing, one for each theory. These factors are presented in the first section of this chapter. We developed the following research question: *How do practitioners rank critical success factors based on outsourcing theories?* To study this research question, we developed a survey instrument and conducted a survey among business organizations. Results from this survey and discussion of the findings are presented.

In the second section of this chapter, we conceptualize the outsourcing of IT services as an electronic business activity, where the vendor electronically provides IT services to the client. The idea is that the purchasing of IT services is a business-to-business (B2B) relationship, which leads to outsourcing implications in terms of services that the vendor has to provide to its customers. Thus, we will in the second section look at critical success factors in electronic business infrastructure as an example of issues that need to be addressed.

DOI: 10.4018/978-1-60566-796-6.ch003

Table 1. Possibilities and limitations in IT outsourcing based on theories

Theory	What should be outsourced?
Neo-classical economic theory	All IT functions which an external vendor can operate at lower costs than the company.
Transaction cost theory	All IT functions where benefits for the company are greater than the transaction costs. Benefits include increased revenues and reduced costs.
Contractual theory	Only IT functions where the company can expect and secure that vendor and customer will have the same contractual behavior. Common contract behavioral patterns include role integrity, reciprocity, implementation of planning, effectuation of consent, flexibility, contractual solidarity, reliance, restraint of power, proprietary of means and harmonization with the social environment.
Agency theory	Only IT functions where the agent (vendor) and the principal (client) have common goals and the same degree of risk willingness and aversion.
Theory of firm boundaries	All IT functions that satisfy several of the other theories, mainly resource-based theory and transaction cost theory.
Theory of core competencies	All IT functions, which are peripheral to the company's production of goods and services for the market.
Resource-based theory	All IT functions where the company does not have sufficient strategic resources to perform in a competitive way. Strategic resources are unique, valuable, difficult to imitate, exploitable and difficult to substitute.
Partnership and alliance theory	Only IT functions where the company can expect and secure a partnership and alliance with the vendor that imply interdependence between the partners based on trust, comfort, understanding, flexibility, co-operation, shared values, goals and problem solving, interpersonal relations and regular communication.
Relational exchange theory	Only IT functions where the company easily can develop and secure common norms with the vendor. Norms determine behavior in three main dimensions: flexibility, information exchange, and solidarity.
Stakeholder theory	Only IT functions where a balance can be achieved between stakeholders. Stakeholders relevant in IT outsourcing include business management, IT management, user management and key IT personnel at the client, and business management, customer account management and key service providers at the vendor.
Social exchange theory	Only IT functions where each of the parties can follow their own self-interest when transacting with the other self-interested actor to accomplish individual goals that they cannot achieve alone and without causing hazards to the other party.

THEORY-BASED CRITICAL SUCCESS FACTORS

Comparing organization and management theories, in terms of what they recommend for outsourcing, we found that some theories indicate possibilities for outsourcing (theory of core competencies, resource-based theory, transaction cost theory, neoclassical economic theory and theory of firm boundaries), while others indicate limitations (contractual theory, partnership and alliance theory, relational exchange theory, social exchange theory, agency theory and stakeholder theory).

According to neo-classical economic theory, all IT functions which an external vendor can operate at lower costs than the client company should be outsourced. Similarly and according to core competence theory, all IT functions which are peripheral to the client's production of goods and services for the market should be outsourced. Applying stakeholder theory as another example, only IT functions should be outsourced where a balance can be achieved between stakeholders. Stakeholders relevant in IT outsourcing include business management, IT management, user management and key IT personnel at the client, and business management, customer account management and key service providers at the vendor. An overview of possibilities and limitations in IT outsourcing based theories is shown in Table 1. From different theoretical perspectives, recommendations are made of what should be outsourced.

Based on organizational and management theories, we developed the following eleven critical success factors in IT outsourcing relationships (Gottschalk & Solli-Sæther, 2005):

1. *Production cost reduction.* The organization has to integrate and exploit IT services from the vendor in a cost effective way to produce competitive goods and services.
2. *Transaction cost reduction.* The organization has to minimize transaction costs by reducing the need for lasting specific IT assets, increase transaction frequency, reduce complexity and uncertainty in IT tasks, improve performance measurements, and reduce dependence on other transactions.
3. *Contract completeness.* The organization must have a complete IT outsourcing contract. The contract should prevent opportunistic behavior in an efficient collaborative environment with balance of power between client and vendor.
4. *Vendor behavior control.* The organization has to make it easy and inexpensive for itself to find out what the vendor is actually doing. In addition, both outcome-based and behavior-based incentives can be used to reduce and prevent opportunistic vendor behavior.
5. *Demarcation of labor.* The organization has to implement a strict and rigid division of labor between the vendor and itself.
6. *Core competence management.* The organization has to define its IT needs and manage IT services from the vendor.
7. *Vendor resource exploitation.* The organization has to integrate and exploit strategic IT resources from the vendor together with its own resources to produce competitive goods and services.
8. *Alliance exploitation.* The organization has to develop experience with alliances, develop alliance managers and develop the ability to identify potential vendors.
9. *Relationship exploitation.* The organization has to develop and secure common norms that are relevant to both parties.
10. *Stakeholder management.* The organization must create efficient and effective communication with and between stakeholders to secure continued support from all stakeholders, to balance their interests and to make the IT outsourcing arrangement so that all stakeholders achieve their goals.
11. *Social exchange exploitation.* The organization has to enable social and economic outcomes in the exchange between the vendor and itself such that these outcomes outperform those obtainable in alternative exchanges.

These critical success factors were empirically tested and investigated in three international-based outsourcing relationships (see Chapter 10 for a further description of these cases). The empirical research was carried out to provide further insight into the issue and to refine the developed factors. From each relationship studied, two-to-three interviewees were selected from both the client and the vendor organization. Interviewees were both asked question about managing IT outsourcing relationships. In addition, a survey instrument was developed. In the survey instrument, each of the critical success factors was defined and a 5-point Likert-scale was applied. All interviewees in the three international based case studies were asked to rate from 1 (low) to 5 (high) the importance of eleven individual factors. Ranking of critical success factors in IT outsourcing relationships is presented in Table 2. The score is based on the response from sixteen interviews.

Core competence management was found to be the most critical success factor in IT outsourcing relationships. Activities, which are not core competencies, should be considered for outsourcing with best-in-world suppliers. An organization may view IT itself as a core competence. It seems that most suc-

Table 2. Ranking of critical success factors in IT outsourcing relationships

Rank	Critical Success Factors	Score	Theory
1	Core competence management	4.67	Theory of core competencies
2	Stakeholder management	4.58	Stakeholder theory
3	Production cost reduction	3.92	Neoclassical economic theory
4	Social exchange exploitation	3.82	Social exchange theory
5	Transaction cost reduction	3.80	Transaction cost theory
6	Vendor resource exploitation	3.75	Resource-based theory
7	Contract completeness	3.75	Contractual theory
8	Relationship exploitation	3.50	Relational exchange theory
9	Vendor behavior control	3.33	Agency theory
10	Demarcation of labor	3.17	Theory of firm boundaries
11	Alliance exploitation	2.83	Partnership and alliance theory

cessful companies have a good understanding of IT's potential. However, some organizations outsource IT even though they see it as core and delivering competitive advantage. This may be because IT can be considered core at the corporate level, but some of its aspects, at lower levels, might be commodities. Thus the complexity of IT, and it's (at least in part) core nature, may make the contracting out of IT a particularly challenging exercise. Core competencies are the collective learning in the organization, especially how to coordinate diverse production skills and integrate multiple streams of technologies. One of the client companies were restructuring around two core business areas, and another admitted that information technology was not at the core of their business. Their outsourcing vendors had information technology as their core competence.

Next, *stakeholder management* was found important. A stakeholder is any group or individual who can affect, or is affected by, the achievement of a corporation's purpose. Following stakeholder theory recommendations for successful IT outsourcing relationships are to create efficient and effective communication with and between stakeholders to secure continued support from all stakeholders, to balance their interests and to make the IT outsourcing arrangement so that all stakeholders achieve their goals. During the case studies several stakeholder groups were identified – client senior managers, client business managers, client retained IT managers, transferred IT employees (transplants), vendor senior managers, vendor account managers, and vendor supplier IT staff – each group with their own expectations and goals. These findings are not very different from stakeholder groups defined by Lacity and Wollcocks (2000). An interesting observation was that the interviewees seemed to be aware of other stakeholders' expectations and goals. What was emphasized in the cases studied was the unique position of the transplants. Respecting and balancing stakeholders' interests were ranked as an important factor for successful relationship.

In all three cases studied, one important driver of outsourcing was *production costs reduction.* According to neo-classical economic theory, companies will justify their sourcing strategy based on evaluating possibilities for production cost savings. Thus, the question of whether or not to outsource, is a question whether the marketplace can produce product and services at a lower price than internal production. Client companies reported reduction of costs, better cost-performance, and economies of scale, compared to internal IT function.

Because production costs can be calculated by the accounting system, while transaction costs are assessed subjectively through indirect indicators, functional managers are likely to differ in the importance that they assign to reducing transaction costs. Consequently, the effect transaction costs have on a make-or-buy choice can partly reflect the influence exerted by the purchasing manager. Production cost differences seems more influential in sourcing decisions than transaction cost differences, and experience of the decision-maker is related to assessments of technological uncertainty. Perrons and Platts (2004) highlights the importance of industry clock speed and supplier relationships in make-or-buy decisions for new technologies. They suggest the "make" prescription may be more suited to either extremely fast or extremely slow rates of technological change, while the "buy" strategy might be more appropriate in market sectors where technologies evolve at a medium pace.

The ability to handle technological change was also reported as a major issue for outsourcing. According to the resource-based perspective, outsourcing is a strategic decision that can be used to fill gaps in the firm's IS resources and capabilities. In one case it was a difference between desired capabilities and actual capabilities. Vendor resources were used to innovate, which might be important for long-term survival of the client. In this specific case, the vendor's ability to do change management was an important criterion for vendor selection.

Based on the findings three managerial implications are suggested. Firstly, we argue that a holistic approach to IT outsourcing is needed, that recognizes and emphasizes the combination of several critical success factors. These factors have both divergent and convergent implications for management. Being aware of these factors, managers are enabled to recognize relationship problems as they occur and to handle them before they scrutinize the IT outsourcing success. Second, we emphasize the importance of both client and vendor success in an effective IT outsourcing relationship, as the two parties is mutually dependent on each other. Finally, we recognize the complexity of IT outsourcing. When contracts expire there is a need to have an exit strategy focusing not only on the economic success of the IT outsourcing, but also to question issues such as core competence management, access to resources, and the maturity of the relationship. Table 3 suggests some recommendations for managing successful IT outsourcing relationships and how to succeed in outsourcing arrangements.

The current research has several shortcomings that should be addressed in future research. Future research should (1) more carefully develop the motivation for such studies, elaborate on the specific research questions it addresses, and why these questions are important for research or practice; (2) more carefully develop and explain how critical success factors can be identified from the various theories; and (3) clarify the theoretical and empirical contributions this kind of research makes over and above the prior literature in the area. Perhaps future research should focus on one or two theories, explicitly laying out expectations with respect to the theories, and organizing rich data to test expectations. Furthermore, it would be interesting to observe theories where the predictions contradict each other, and using observational data to study conditions for one theory or another to dominate.

CRITICAL SUCCESS FACTORS IN E-BUSINESS INFRASTRUCTURE

Weill and Vitale (2001) define an e-business model as a description of the roles and relationships among a firm's consumers, customers, allies, and suppliers that identifies the major flows of product, information, and money, and the major benefits to participants. There are many different ways to describe and classify e-business models. There are a finite number of atomic e-business models; each captures a dif-

Table 3. Key success factors for client and vendor in managing successful IT outsourcing relationships based on theories

Theory	How to succeed as a client company in an outsourcing arrangement	How to succeed as a vendor company in an outsourcing arrangement
Theory of core competencies	We have to define our IT needs and manage IT services from the vendor.	We have to provide complementary core competencies, such as personnel, methodologies and services, to the client.
Resource-based theory	We have to integrate and exploit strategic IT resources from the vendor together with our own resources to produce competitive goods and services.	We have to enable the client to integrate and exploit strategic IT resources from us together with the clients' own resources to produce competitive goods and services.
Transaction cost theory	We have to minimize transaction costs by reducing the need for lasting specific IT assets; increase transaction frequency; reduce complexity and uncertainty in IT tasks; improve performance measurements; and reduce dependence on other transactions.	We have to minimize transaction costs by reducing the need for lasting specific IT assets; increase transaction frequency; reduce complexity and uncertainty in IT tasks; improve performance measurements; and reduce dependence on other transactions.
Contractual theory	We must have a complete IT contract based on information symmetry in a predictable environment with occurrence adaptation that prevents opportunistic behavior in an efficient collaborative environment with balance of power between client and vendor, where the contract is a management instrument that grants decision rights and action duties.	We must have a complete IT contract based on information symmetry in a predictable environment with occurrence adaptation that prevents opportunistic behavior in an efficient collaborative environment with balance of power between client and vendor, where the contract is a management instrument that grants decision rights and action duties.
Neoclassical economic theory	We have to integrate and exploit IT services from the vendor together with our own services to produce competitive goods and services.	We have to enable the client to integrate and exploit IT services from us together with own services to produce competitive goods and services.
Partnership and alliance theory	We have to develop experience with alliances, develop alliance managers and develop the ability to identify potential vendors.	We have to develop experience with alliances, develop alliance managers and develop the ability to identify potential clients.
Relational exchange theory	We have to develop and secure common norms that are relevant to both parties.	We have to develop and secure common norms that are relevant to both parties.
Social exchange theory	We have to enable social and economic outcomes in the exchange between the vendor and us such that these outcomes outperform those obtainable in alternative exchanges.	We have to enable social and economic outcomes in the exchange between the client and us such that these outcomes outperform those obtainable in alternative exchanges.
Agency theory	We have to make it easy and inexpensive for our self to find out what the vendor is actually doing. In addition, both outcome-based and behavior-based incentives can be used to reduce and prevent opportunistic vendor behavior.	It must be easy and inexpensive for the principal (client) to find out what the agent (vendor) is actually doing. In addition, both outcome-based and behavior-based incentives can be used to reduce and prevent opportunistic behavior.
Theory of firm boundaries	We have to implement a strict and rigid division of labor between the vendor and us.	We have to implement a strict and rigid division of labor between the client and us.
Stakeholder theory	We must create efficient and effective communication with and between stakeholders to secure continued support from all stakeholders, to balance their interests and to make the IT outsourcing arrangement so that all stakeholders achieve their goals.	We have to create efficient and effective communication with and between stakeholders to secure continued support from all stakeholders, to balance their interests and to make the IT outsourcing arrangement so that all stakeholders achieve their goals.

ferent way to conduct e-business. Firms can combine atomic e-business models as building blocks to create tailored e-business models and initiatives, using their competencies as their guide. They identified a small number of eight atomic e-business models, each of which describes the essence of conducting business electronically.

Model 1 – Direct to Customer

The distinguishing characteristic of this model is that buyer and seller communicate directly, rather than through an intermediary. The seller may be a retailer, a wholesaler or a manufacturer. The customer may be an individual or a business. Examples of the direct-to-customer model are Dell Computer Corporation www.dell.com and Gap, Inc. www.gap.com.

Infrastructure

The direct-to-customer model requires extensive electronic connection with the customer, including online payment systems. Many direct-to-customer implementations include an extranet to allow customized Web pages for major business-to-business (B2B) customers. Operating a direct-to-customer e-business requires significant investment in the equivalent of the store: the Web site. Direct-to-customer businesses spend millions of dollars developing easy-to-navigate and easy-to-use Web sites with the goal of improving the B2B or business-to-consumer (B2C) shopping experience online. For example, Lands End www.landsend.com has devised a feature by which women can build and store a three-dimensional model of themselves to "try on" clothes electronically.

In their field research, Weill and Vitale (2001) found that firms with e-business initiatives containing the direct-to-customer e-business model needed and were investing more heavily in three areas of infrastructure services: application infrastructure, communications, and IT management.

Direct-to-customer firms particularly needed payment transaction processing to process online customer payments, enterprise-wide resource planning (ERP) to process customer transactions, workflow infrastructure to optimize business process performance, communication network services linking all points in the enterprise to each other and the outside world (often using TCP/IP protocol), the installation and maintenance of workstations and local area networks supporting the large number of people required to operate a direct-to-customer model, and service-level agreements between the business and the IT group or outsourcer to ensure, monitor, and improve the systems necessary for the model.

Sources of Revenue

The main source of revenue in the direct-to-customer model is usually direct sales to customers. Supplemental revenues come from advertising, the sale of customer information, and product placement fees.

Critical Success Factors

Critical success factors are the things a firm must do well to flourish. The following list shows the critical success factors for the direct-to-customer model: create and maintain customer awareness, in order to build a critical mass of users to cover the fixed cost of building an electronic presence; reduce customer acquisition costs; strive to own the customer relationship and understand individual customer needs; increase repeat purchases and average transaction size; provide fast and efficient transaction processing, fulfillment, and payment; ensure adequate security for the organization and its customers; and provide interfaces that combine ease of use with richness of experience, integrating multiple channels.

Model 2 – Full-Service Provider

A firm using the full-service provider model provides total coverage of customer needs in a particular domain, consolidated via a single point of contact. The domain could be any major area of customer needs requiring multiple products and services, for example, financial services, health care or industrial chemicals. The full-service provider adds value by providing a full range of products, sourced both internally and externally, and consolidating them using the channel chosen by the customer. Examples of the full-service provider are the Prudential Advisor www.prusec.com and GE Supply Company www.gesupply.com.

Infrastructure

Virtually all businesses aspire to getting 100% of their customers' business, or at least to getting as much of that business as they can handle profitably. Yet the number of full-service providers remains small. Part of the reason for this is required infrastructure. The missing piece of infrastructure in many businesses is often a database containing information about the customer and the products that the customer owns. Without owning these data, a provider does not own the customer relationship, and therefore some of the customer's transactions are likely to take place directly with other providers. All of the important interactions with customers occurring across any channel or business unit must be recorded in the firm wide customer database.

Weill and Vitale (2001) identified in their field research databases and data warehouses as some of the most important infrastructure services associated with the full-service provider model. Other important infrastructure services included the following: the ability to evaluate proposals for new information systems initiatives to coordinate IT investments across a multi-business-unit firm with the goal of a single point of contact for the customer; centralized management of IT infrastructure capacity to integrate across multiple business units within the firm and third-party providers, the full-service provider model is not readily workable if each business unit optimizes its own IT needs; installation and maintenance of workstations and local area networks to operate the online business linking all the business units and third-party providers; electronic support for groups to coordinate the cross-functional teams required to implement this model; and the identification and testing of new technologies to find cost-effective ways to deliver this complex business model to the customer across multiple channels.

Sources of Revenue

A full-service provider gains revenues from selling its own products and those of others, and possibly also from annual membership fees, management fees, transaction fees, commissions on third-party products, advertising or listing fees from third-party providers, and fees for selling aggregated data about customers.

Critical Success Factors

One important critical success factor is the brand, credibility and trust necessary for a customer to look to the firm for its complete needs in an area. Another is owning the customer relationship in one domain and integrating and consolidating the offering of many third parties into a single channel or multiple channels. A third factor owns more of the customer data in the relevant domain than any other player. A final factor is enforcement of policies to protect the interests of internal and external suppliers, as well as customers.

Model 3 – Whole of Enterprise

The single point of contact for the e-business customer is the essence of the whole-of-enterprise atomic business model. Although many of this model's breakthrough innovations have occurred in public-sector organizations, the model is applicable in both the for-profit and the public sectors. An example of this model is the Australian state of Victoria with its Business Channel www.business.channel.vic.gov.au and Health Channel www.betterhealth.vic.gov.au.

Infrastructure

For the whole-of-enterprise model, infrastructure needs to link the different systems in the various business units and provide a firm wide perspective for management. The field research by Weill and Vitale (2001) revealed that the following infrastructure services are the most important for implementing this model: centralized management of infrastructure capacity to facilitate integration and capture economies of scale; identification and testing of new technologies to find new ways to integrate the often different systems in many business units into a single point of customer contact; management of key data independent of applications and the creation of a centralized repository for firm wide information; electronic means of summarizing data from different applications and platforms to manage the complexity arising from a single point of contact for multiple business units; development of an ERP service to process the transactions instigated by customers interacting with several different business units, often requiring consolidating or linking several ERPs in the firm; payment transaction processing, either on a firm wide basis or by linking several systems across the business units; large-scale data-processing facilities to process transactions from multiple business units, often centralized to achieve economies of scale; and integrated mobile computing applications, which provide another channel to the customer.

Sources of Revenue

In the for-profit sector, revenues are generated by provision of goods and services to the customer by the business units. There may also be the opportunity to charge an annual service or membership fee for this level of service. In the government sector, the motivation is usually twofold: improved service and reduced cost. Service to the community is improved through continuous, round-the-clock operation and faster service times. Sharing more infrastructures and eliminating the need to perform the same transaction in multiple agencies can potentially reduce government costs.

Critical Success Factors

The following list details the critical success factors for the whole-of-enterprise model: changing customer behavior to make use of the new model, as opposed to the customer continuing to interact directly with individual units; reducing costs in the individual business units as the direct demands on them fall, and managing the transfer pricing issues that will inevitably arise; altering the perspective of the business units to take an enterprise-wide view, which includes broad product awareness, training, and cross-selling; in the integrated implementation, reengineering the business processes to link into life events at the front end and existing legacy processes and systems at the back end; and finding compelling and practical life events that customers can use as triggers to access the enterprise.

Model 4 – Intermediaries

Intermediaries are such as portals, agents, auctions, aggregators, and others. E-business is often promoted as an ideal way for sellers and buyers to interact directly, shortening old-economy value chains by disintermediating some of their members. Yet some of the most popular sites on the Internet, both for consumers and for business users, are in fact intermediaries - sites that stand between the buyer and the seller. The services of intermediaries include search (to locate providers of products and services), specification (to identify important product attributes), price (to establish the price, including optional extras such as warranties), sale (to complete the sales transaction, including payment and settlement), fulfillment (to fulfill the purchase by delivering the product or service), surveillance (to conduct surveillance of the activities of buyers and sellers in order to report aggregate activity and prices and to inform and regulate the market), and enforcement (to enforce proper conduct by buyers and sellers). Examples of intermediaries are electronic malls, shopping agents, specialty auctions, electronic markets, electronic auctions and portals.

Infrastructure

Intermediaries generate value by concentrating information and bringing together buyers and sellers, operating entirely in space and thus relying on IT as the primary infrastructure. Weill and Vitale (2001) found in their field interviews that the most important infrastructure services for firms pursuing the intermediary atomic business model are the following: knowledge management, including knowledge databases and contact databases that enable the codification and sharing of knowledge in this highly information-intensive business; enforcing Internet and email policies to ensure proper and consistent use of electronic channels to buyers, sellers, and intermediaries; workstation networks to support the products and services of this all-electronic business model; centralized management of e-business applications, ensuring consistency and integration across product offerings; information systems planning to identify the most effective uses of IT in the business; and information systems project management to ensure that business value is achieved from IT investments.

Sources of Revenue

An intermediary may earn revenues from buyers, sellers, or both. Sellers may pay a listing fee, a transaction fee, a sales commission, or some combination. Similarly, buyers may pay a subscription fee, a success fee, or a sales commission.

Critical Success Factors

The chief requirement for survival as an intermediary is sufficient volume of usage to cover the fixed costs of establishing the business and the required infrastructure. Attracting and retaining a critical mass of customers is therefore the primary critical success factor. Another important critical success factor is building up infrastructure just quickly enough to meet demand as it increases.

Model 5 – Shared Infrastructure

The firm provides infrastructure shared by its owners. Other suppliers, who are users of the shared infrastructure, but not owners, can also be included. Customers who access the shared infrastructure directly are given a choice of suppliers and value propositions. The owner and the non-owner suppliers are generally represented objectively. In some situations, goods or services flow directly from the shared infrastructure to the customer. In other situations, a message is sent by the shared infrastructure to the supplier, who then completes the transaction by providing the goods or services to the customer.

An example illustrating the features of the shared-infrastructure business model is the system from 2000 by America's largest automakers, some of their dealers, and IBM, Motorola, and Intel. The initiative was named Covisint (collaboration vision integrity). General Motors, Ford and DaimlerChrysler see stronger potential benefits from cooperating on supply-chain logistics than from competing.

Infrastructure

The shared-infrastructure business model requires competitors to cooperate by sharing IT infrastructure and information. This level of cooperation requires agreement on high-level IT architectures as well as operational standards for applications, data communications, and technology. Effective implementation of the shared-infrastructure model also requires enforcement of these standards, and most shared-infrastructure models have a joint committee to set and enforce standards. Another role of these committees is to implement the policies of the shared infrastructure about what information, if any, is shared and what information is confidential to partner firms. Weill and Vitale (2001) found in their field research that the most important infrastructure services required by firms implementing the shared-infrastructure atomic business model all concerned architectures and standards: specification and enforcement of high-level architectures for data, technology, applications, communications, and work that are agreed to by alliance partners; and specification and enforcement of detailed standards for the high-level architectures.

Sources of Revenue

Revenues can be generated both from membership fees and from transaction fees. The alliance may be run on a nonprofit basis or on a profit-making basis. Not-for-profit shared infrastructures are typically open to all eligible organizations and distribute any excess revenues back to their members. The for-profit models are typically owned by a subset of the firms in a given segment, which split up any profits among themselves.

Critical Success Factors

Critical success factors for the shared-infrastructure model include the following: no dominant partner that gains more than any other partner; an unbiased channel and objective presentation of product and service information; critical mass of both alliance partners and customers; management of conflict among the ongoing e-business initiatives of the alliance partners; compilation and delivery of accurate and timely statements of the services and benefits provided to each member of the alliance; and interoperability of systems.

Model 6 – Virtual Community

Virtual communities deserve our attention, and not only because they are the clearest, and perhaps the last, surviving embodiment of the original intent of the Internet. By using IT to leverage the fundamental human desire for communication with peers, virtual communities can create significant value for their owners as well as for their members. Once established, a virtual community is less susceptible to competition by imitation than any of the other atomic business models. In this business model, the firm of interest – the sponsor of the virtual community – sits in the center, positioned between members of the community and suppliers. Fundamental to the success of this model is that members are able, and in fact are encouraged, to communicate with one another directly. Communication between members may be via email, bulletin boards, online chat, Web-based conferencing, or other computer-based media, and it is the distinguishing feature of this model. Examples of this model are Parent Soup www.parentsoup.com, a virtual community for parents, and Motley Fool www.motleyfool.com, a virtual community of investors.

Infrastructure

Virtual communities depend on IT to exist. In particular, the creation and continual enhancement of an Internet site is essential if a virtual community is to survive. Many virtual-community sites include not just static content and links, but also tools of interest to potential members. Weill and Vitale (2001) found in their field research that the infrastructure services most important for the virtual-community business model are the following: training in the use of IT for members of the community; application service provision (ASP) to provide specialized systems virtual communities need such as bulletin boards, email, and ISP access; IT research and development, including infrastructure services for identifying and testing new technologies and for evaluating proposals for new information systems initiatives; information systems planning to identify and prioritize potential investments in IT in this completely online business; and installation and maintenance of workstations and local area networks to support the electronic world of the virtual community.

Sources of Revenue

A sponsoring firm can gain revenue from membership fees, direct sales of goods and services, advertising, and click-through and sales commissions. A firm sponsoring a virtual community as an adjunct to its other activities may receive no direct revenue at all from the virtual community. Rather, the firm receives less tangible benefits, such as customer loyalty and increased knowledge about its customer base.

Critical Success Factors

The critical success factors for a virtual community include finding and retaining a critical mass of members; building and maintaining loyalty with an appropriate mix of content and features; maintaining privacy and security for member information; balancing commercial potential and members' interests;

leveraging member profile information with advertisers and merchants; and engendering a feeling of trust in the community by its members.

Model 7 – Value Net Integrator

Traditionally, most firms operate simultaneously in two worlds: the physical and the virtual. In the physical world, goods and services are created in a series of value-adding activities connecting the supply side (suppliers, procurement, and logistics) with the demand side (customers, marketing, and shipping). In the virtual world, information about the members of the physical value chain are gathered, synthesized, and distributed along the virtual value chain. E-business provides the opportunity to separate the physical and virtual value chains. Value net integrators take advantage of that split and attempt to control the virtual value chain in their industries by gathering, synthesizing, and distributing information. Value net integrators add value by improving the effectiveness of the value chain by coordinating information. A pure value net integrator operates exclusively in the virtual value chain, owning a few physical assets. To achieve the gathering, synthesizing, and distributing of information, the value net integrator receives and sends information to all other players in the model. The value net integrator coordinates product flows form suppliers to allies and customers. The product flows from the suppliers to customers may be direct or via allies. In some cases the value net integrator may sell information or other products to the customer. The value net integrator always strives to own the customer relationship with the other participants in the model, thus knowing more about their operations than any other player. Examples of value net integrators are Seven-Eleven Japan and Cisco Systems www.cisco.com.

Infrastructure

The value net integrator succeeds in its role by gathering, synthesizing, and distributing information. Thus, for a value net integrator, data and electronic connectivity with allies and other players are very important assets. Field research carried out by Weill and Vitale (2001) suggests that the most important infrastructure services required for a value net integrator include middleware, linking systems on different platforms across the many players in the value net; a centralized data warehouse that collects and summarizes key information for analysis from decentralized databases held by several players across the value net; specification and enforcement of high-level architectures and detailed standards for data, technology, applications, and communications to link together different technology platforms owned by different firms; call centers to provide advice and guidance for partners and allies in getting the most value from the information provided by the value net generator; and high-capacity communications network service to support the high volumes of information flowing across the value net.

Sources of Revenue

In this model, revenues are generally earned by fees or margins on the physical goods that pass through the industry value net. By using information about consumers, the value net integrator is able to increase prices by meeting consumer demand. By using information about suppliers, the value net integrator reduces costs by cutting inventories and lead times.

Critical Success Factors

The critical success factors for the value net integrator atomic business model are as follows: reducing ownership of physical assets while retaining ownership of data; owning or having access to the complete industry virtual value chain; establishing a trusted brand recognized at all places in the value chain; operating in markets where information can add significant value, such as those that are complex, fragmented, regulated, multi-layered, inefficient, and large with many sources of information; presenting the information to customers, allies, partners, and suppliers in clear and innovative ways that provide value; and helping other value chain participants capitalize on the information provided by the value net integrator.

Model 8 – Content Provider

Like many terms associated with e-business, content provider has different meanings to different people. We define content provider as a firm that creates and provides content (information, products, or services) in digital form to customers via third parties. The physical-world analogy of a content provider is a journalist, recording artist, or stock analyst. Digital products such as software, electronic travel guides, and digital music and video are examples of content. A virtual-world example of a content provider is weather forecasters such as Storm Weather Center www.storm.no.

Infrastructure

Content providers must excel at tailoring and manipulating their core content to meet the specific needs of customers. Content providers must categorize and store their content in well-indexed modules so it can be combined and customized to meet customer needs via a wide variety of channels. Customers and transactions tend to be relatively few, at least compared with the number of end consumers and their transactions. Often complex and unique IT infrastructures are needed to support the particular needs of the specialized professionals employed by the content provider. Field research by Weill and Vitale (2001) identified the most important infrastructure services: multimedia storage farms or storage area network infrastructures to deal with large amounts of information; a strong focus on architecture, including setting and enforcing standards particularly for work; detailed data architectures to structure, specify, link manipulate, and manage the core intellectual property; workstation network infrastructures to enable the fundamentally online business of a content provider; and a common systems development environment to provide compatible and integrated systems, ensuring the systems can provide content across multiple channels to their customers.

Sources of Revenue

The primary source of revenue for a content provider is fees from its third parties or allies. These fees may be based on a fixed price per month or year, or on the number of times the third party's own customers access the content. In some situations, the fees paid are lower for content branded by the provider, and higher for unbranded content, which then appears to the customer to have been generated by the third party itself.

Critical Success Factors

To succeed, a content provider must provide reliable, timely content in the right format and at the right price. The critical success factors for this model include the following: branding (the value of content is due in part to reputation), recognized as best in class (the business of content provision will be global and competitive), and network (establishing and maintaining a network of third parties through which content is distributed.

Information Technology Infrastructure

As firms integrate e-business into their existing business, they migrate from traditional physical business models to combined physical and virtual models. This shift increases the role of the information technology infrastructure because information and online transaction processing become more important. However, the large number of infrastructure investment options can easily overwhelm senior management. To help, Weill and Vitale (2002) classified e-business initiatives by the building blocks they use (which are called atomic e-business models), and they examined the main IT infrastructure services that these models need. The business models require surprisingly different IT infrastructure services, so categorization should help executives prioritize their IT infrastructure investments based on their business goals. At the heart of this prioritization process is the firm's IT governance process, which should ensure that IT knows of upcoming IT infrastructure needs early in the strategizing process.

Weill and Vitale (2002) define a firm's information technology portfolio as its total investment in computing and communications technology. The IT portfolio thus includes hardware, software, telecommunications, electronically stored data, devices to collect and represent data, and the people who provide IT services. The foundation of an IT portfolio is the firm's information technology infrastructure. This internal IT infrastructure is composed of four elements: IT components (the technologist's view of the infrastructure building blocks), human IT infrastructure (the intelligence used to translate the IT components into services that users can draw upon), shared IT services (the user's view of the infrastructure), and shared and standard applications (fairly stable uses of the services) (Weill & Vitale, 2001). The four elements are illustrated in Figure 1.

Information Technology Components

At the base of the internal infrastructure are the technical components, such as computers, printers, database software packages, operating systems, and scanners. These components are commodities and are readily available in the marketplace. Traditionally, IT infrastructures have been described in terms of these components. Unfortunately, while technologists understand the capabilities of these components, business people do not – components are not business language to them. Thus, technologists and business people have had difficulty discussing infrastructure needs and business models because they have not had a common language.

Human Information Technology Infrastructure

Describing IT components in business terms requires a translation. That translation is handled by people, and is performed in this layer, which builds on the IT components layer. The human IT infrastructure

Figure 1. The hierarchy of IT infrastructure

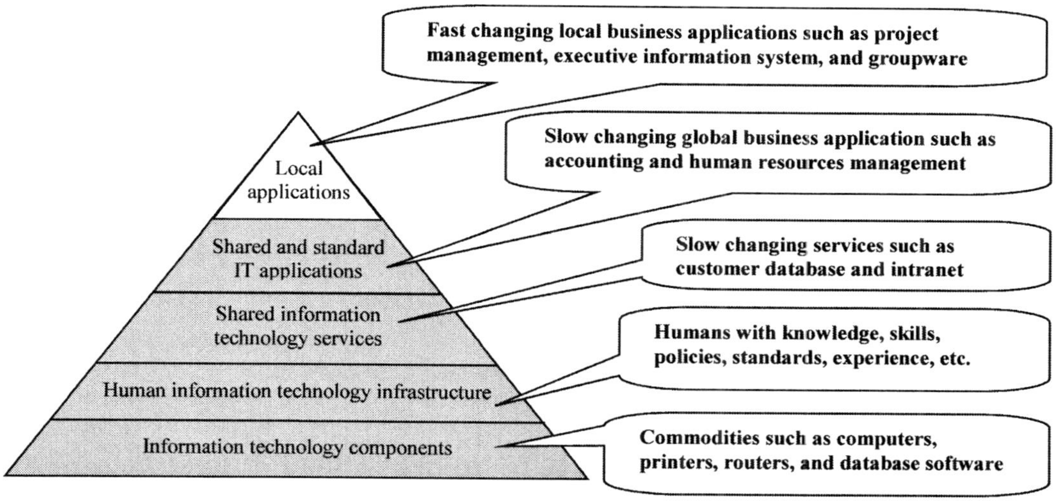

layer consists of knowledge, skills, standards, and experience. These tools are used to bind IT components into reliable services, which are services business people can understand.

Shared Information Technology Services

This layer views the infrastructure as a set of services that users can understand, draw upon, and share, to conduct their business. For example, to link with customers and partners, they can draw on channel management services. To manage data, they can draw on data management services. To handle security, they can draw on security and risk services. Nine service areas are needed by IT-enabled business models – with 70 services in all. Therefore describing IT infrastructure as a set of reliable services allows business people and technologists to discuss business models and their underlying infrastructure needs because the two parties speak the same language.

Shared and Standard Information Technology Applications

The top piece of the IT infrastructure consists of stable applications, such as human resource management, budgeting, and accounting. In the last five to seven years, there has been a significant trend by multi-business firms to standardize their common business processes and the associated IT applications. The driver for some firms was improving and reengineering their business processes; for others, it was implementation of large enterprise resource planning (ERP) systems. As a result, shared and standard applications have been added to the typical firm's IT infrastructure.

Based on these layers, a firm's IT infrastructure capability is its integrated set of reliable IT infrastructure services available to support both existing applications and new initiatives. The time required to implement a new e-business initiative depends in part on the firm's infrastructure capability. For example, in building a new web-based housing loan system, a large bank needed to use the following information technology infrastructure services: mainframe and server processing, customer databases, both local area and national communications networks, and security procedures and systems. Having most of these infrastructure services already in place significantly reduced the time and cost to build the loan system.

Infrastructure Services

Weill and Vitale (2001) identified nine service areas with 70 services needed by IT-enables e-business models. The service areas were (number of services in parenthesis): applications infrastructure (13), communications (7), data management (6), IT management (9), security (4), architecture and standards (20), IT research and development (2), and IT education (2), as listed in Table 4.

These 70 infrastructure services were identified by Weill and Vitale (2001) when they studied IT infrastructure services and e-business. They studied 50 e-business initiatives in 15 firms. Based on their study, they identified 8 atomic business models, 9 infrastructure areas with 70 infrastructure services. The nine infrastructure areas were defined as follows:

- **Applications infrastructure**. An application is a software program that resides on a computer for the purpose of translating electronic input into meaningful form. Applications management includes purchasing software, developing proprietary applications, modifying applications, providing installation and technical support, and other tasks related to ensuring that applications are meeting the needs of the organization.
- **Communications**. Technology that facilitates digital communication both within the organization and with the outside world is relevant here. It includes the management of hardware and software to facilitate communication via computer, telephone, facsimile, pagers, mobile phones, and other communication and messaging services. It includes the cabling and any other communication linkages required to create an effective communications network, in addition to the necessary hardware and applications to meet the needs of the organization.
- **Data management**. This refers to the way the organization structures and handles its information resources. Data may be sourced from internal or external databases. Data management includes data collection, database design, sorting and reporting information, creating links to external databases, assuring data compatibility, and other activities surrounding the effective management of electronic information.
- **IT management**. Information technology management includes many of the professional and strategic activities of the information technology group including negotiation, IS planning, project management, and other tasks. IS project management is defined as the coordination and control of all of the activities required to complete an information systems project.
- **Security**. To protect data, equipment, and processing time, organizations restrict access to certain data, and they protect data and applications from manipulation and contamination. Recovery refers to the need for a plan to maintain computer operations and information should a disaster occur.
- **Architecture and standards**. Information technology architecture is a set of policies and rules that govern the use of information technology and plot a migration path to the way business will be done in the future. In most firms it provides technical guidelines rather than rules for decision-making. Architecture has to cope with both business uncertainty and technological change, making it one of the most difficult tasks for a firm. A good architecture evolves over time and is documented and accessible to all managers in the firm. Each architecture decision needs a sound

Table 4. Infrastructure services

Applications infrastructure
1. Internet policies such as employee access
2. Enforce internet policies
3. Email policies such as inappropriate and personal mail, harassment policies, filtering policies
4. Enforce email policies
5. Centralized management of e-business applications such as common standards
6. Centralized management of infrastructure capacity such as server traffic
7. Integrated mobile computing applications such as access for internal users
8. ERP (enterprise resource planning) services
9. Middleware linking systems on different platforms
10. Wireless applications such as web applications for wireless devices
11. Application services provision to business units
12. Workflow applications such as groupware
13. Payment transaction processing such as EFT (electronic funds transfer)
Communications
14. Communications network services
15. Broadband communication services
16. Intranet capabilities to support publishing, directories, etc.
17. Extranet capabilities to support information and applications
18. Workstation networks
19. EDI (electronic data interchange) linkages to customers and suppliers
20. Electronic support to groups
Data management
21. Manage key data independent of applications
22. A centralized data warehouse that summarizes key information from decentralized databases
23. Data management advice and consultancy
24. Electronic provision of management information
25. Storage farms or storage area networks
26. Knowledge management in terms of contract database, information databases and communities of practice
IT management
27. Large scale data processing facilities
28. Server farms including mail server, web servers and printer servers
29. Installation and maintenance of workstations and LANs (local area networks)
30. Information systems planning for strategy
31. Information systems project management
32. Negotiate with suppliers and outsourcers
33. Service level agreements
34. Common systems development environment
35. Pilot e-business initiatives such as pilot web shop fronts
Security

continued on following page

Table 4. continued

36. Security policies for use of information systems
37. Enforce security policies for information systems
38. Disaster planning for business applications
39. Firewall on secure gateway services
Architecture and standards
40. Specify architectures for data by setting high level guidelines for data use and integration
41. Specify architectures for technology by setting high level guidelines for technology use and integration
42. Specify architectures for communications by setting high level guidelines for communications use and integration
43. Specify architectures for applications by setting high level guidelines for applications use and integration
44. Specify architectures for work by setting high level guidelines for the way work will be conducted
45. Enforce architectures for data
46. Enforce architectures for technology
47. Enforce architectures for communications
48. Enforce architectures for applications
49. Enforce architectures for work
50. Specify architecture standards for data
51. Specify architecture standards for technology
52. Specify architecture standards for communications
53. Specify architecture standards for applications
54. Specify architecture standards for work
55. Enforce architecture standards for data
56. Enforce architecture standards for technology
57. Enforce architecture standards for communications
58. Enforce architecture standards for applications
59. Enforce architecture standards for work
Channel management
60. Electronic file transfer protocols
61. Kiosks
62. Web sites
63. Call centers
64. IVRs
65. Mobile phones
66. Mobile computing
IT research and development
67. Identify and test new technologies for business purposes
68. Evaluate proposals for new information systems initiatives
IT education
69. Training and use of IT
70. Management education for generating value from IT use

business base to encourage voluntary agreement and compliance across the business. A standard is a detailed definition of the technical choices to implement architecture. Five elements of architectures and standards are important: data, technology, communications, applications, and work. It can be distinguished between specifying architecture or standards and enforcement.

- **Channel management.** New and emerging technologies allow direct connections or distribution channels to customers. Examples here are kiosks, call centers, mobile phones and other means of communications.
- **IT research and development.** The information systems market develops rapidly, particularly with the rise of new e-business technologies. It is thus necessary to continually test applications and hardware to assist with planning decisions. IT research and development includes identifying and testing new technologies for business purposes and evaluating proposals for new information systems initiatives.
- **IT education.** Training and education in the use of IT can be defined as formal classes, individual training, and technology-based self-training programs for users ensuring hands-on computer proficiency levels meeting corporate requirements. IS management education can be defined as education aimed at senior levels in the firm designed to generate value from IT use.

Successfully implementing e-business initiatives depends on having the necessary IT infrastructure in place. E-business initiatives can be decomposed into their underlying atomic e-business models, which can have quite different IT infrastructure requirements. It is important for outsourcing vendors providing IT infrastructure services to understand which atomic e-business models are represented in the firm's anticipated e-business initiative. Senior customer management has to design a process to involve vendor management in e-business strategizing, both to get IT input into business strategy and to provide the vendor with an early warning of what infrastructure services will be critical.

CONCLUSION

Although cost savings still seem to be the overriding motivation for and cause of IT outsourcing, the success of outsourcing relationships depends on other factors as well. Both core competence management and stakeholder management, as identified in this chapter, are primarily non-cost factors. This chapter demonstrates that a holistic approach to IT outsourcing is needed that recognizes and emphasizes the combination of several critical success factors. The theory-based factors have both divergent and convergent implications for management, which require a contingent approach to outsourcing decision-making.

We looked at critical success factors in electronic business infrastructure, where the extent of IT outsourcing can be determined by expanding from a list of 70 infrastructure services. The actual number of infrastructure services needed by a company depends on the company's e-business model as well as the e-business intensity in the outsourcing relationship. Some e-business models require many services, while others require few. For a client company to provide a total of 70 infrastructure services in case they are all needed by the client, seems to be difficult and too costly. For a vendor, providing all 70 infrastructure services may be feasible, as clients will draw on different infrastructure services as they may apply different e-business models. E-business has a double role here, as an outsourced IT function more and more will be handled electronically. This means that the transactions between vendor and client after outsourcing will be conducted as electronic business.

REFERENCES

Gottschalk, P., & Solli-Sæther, H. (2005). Critical success factors from IT outsourcing theories: an empirical study. *Industrial Management & Data Systems*, *105*(5), 685–702. doi:10.1108/02635570510606941

Lacity, M. C., & Willcocks, L. P. (2000). Relationships in IT Outsourcing: A Stakeholder Perspective. In R. W. Zmud (Ed.), *Framing the Domains of IT Management: Projecting the Future Through the Past*. Cincinnati, OH: Pinnaflex Educational Resources.

Perrons, R. K., & Platts, K. (2004). The role of clockspeed in outsourcing decisions for new technologies: insights from the prisoner's dilemma. *Industrial Management & Data Systems*, *104*(7), 624–632. doi:10.1108/02635570410550287

Weill, P., & Vitale, M. R. (2001). *Place to Space. Migrating to eBusiness Models*. Boston, MA: Harvard Business School Press.

Weill, P., & Vitale, M. R. (2002). What IT Infrastructure Capabilities Are Needed To Implement E-Business Models? *MIS Quarterly Executive*, *1*(1), 17–34.

Chapter 4
Value Configurations

Understanding how firms differ is a central challenge for both theory and practice of management. For a long time, Porter's (1985) value chain was the only value configuration known to managers. Stabell and Fjeldstad (1998) identified two alternative value configurations. First, a value shop schedules activities and applies resources in a fashion that is dimensioned and appropriate to the needs of client problems, while a value chain performs a fixed set of activities that enables it to produce a standard product in large numbers. Examples of value shops are professional service firms, as found in medicine, law, architecture and engineering. Next, a value network links clients or customers who are or wish to be interdependent. Examples of value networks are logistic companies, telephone companies, retail banks and insurance companies.

In this chapter, we apply the contingent approach to systems outsourcing by making the outsourcing decision dependent on the value configuration of the enterprise. We present the three different value configurations – the value chain, the value shop, and the value network. Next, the three different value configurations are compared according to key characteristics, e.g. use of information systems. Then, we take a look at interfirm relations to be able to identify areas for outsourcing, and value configuration as a determinant and predictor for the extent of outsourcing. Finally, we discuss levels of strategy and we introduce the Y-model for IS/IT strategy work.

DOI: 10.4018/978-1-60566-796-6.ch004

Figure 1. Examples of IS/IT in the value chain

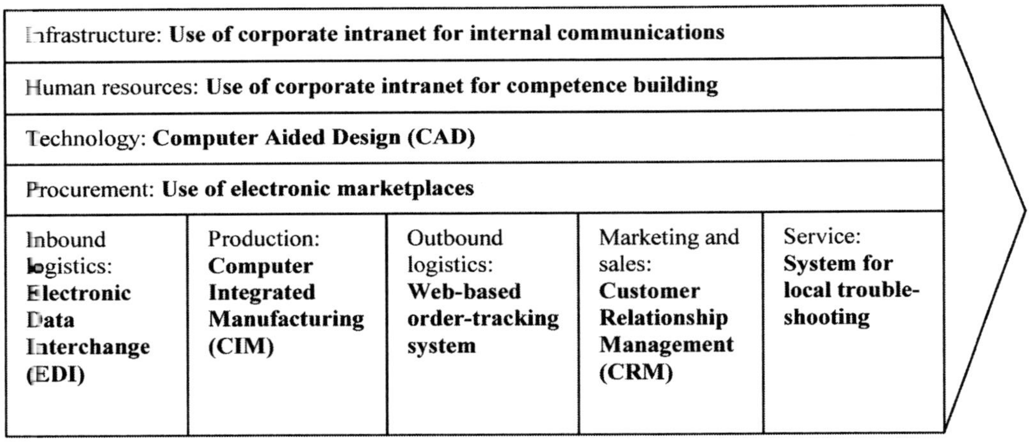

VALUE CHAIN CONFIGURATION

The best-known value configuration is the value chain. In the value chain, value is created through efficient production of goods and services based on a variety of resources. The company is perceived as a series or chain of activities. Primary activities in the value chain include inbound logistics, production, outbound logistics, marketing and sales, and service. Support activities include infrastructure, human resources, technology development and procurement. Attention is on performing these activities in the chain in efficient and effective ways. In Figure 1, examples of IS/IT are assigned to primary and support activities. This figure can be used to describe the current IS/IT situation in the organization as it illustrates the extent of coverage of IS/IT for each activity.

To deliver low-cost or differentiated products, a firm must perform a series of activities. The different activities are called the firm's value chain. The typical assembler/manufacturer's value chain can be illustrated using the example of a manufacturer of computer hardware, such as a personal computer. The inbound logistics stage involves raw materials handling, such as computer CPU chips, memory modules, disk drives, fans, and so forth. A manager would also have to worry about an inspection of the materials, selection of parts, and delivery issues. The production stage involves the production of in-house components, assembly of the computer, testing and tuning, maintenance of equipment, and operation of the plant. The outbound logistics stage involves order processing and shipping. The marketing and sales stage is concerned with advertising, pricing, promotion, and management of the sales force. Finally, the service stage involves managing technical support and service representatives and replacement and repair of computers. In performing the activities of its value chain, a firm must interact with suppliers, customers, and firms in related industries. The other firms also have value chains of their own. A system of value chains is called a value chain system (Afuah & Tucci, 2003).

The value chain is more about efficiency than about new product development. It is about process more than product. And it is about low cost more than differentiation. The value chain describes the necessary activities once a product and its features have been conceived, and it is not necessarily concerned with developing a continual stream of innovations. However, marketing does have two roles in the value chain. The first was implied above: to stimulate demand for the product. The second role, however, is

Figure 2. Examples of IS/IT in the value shop

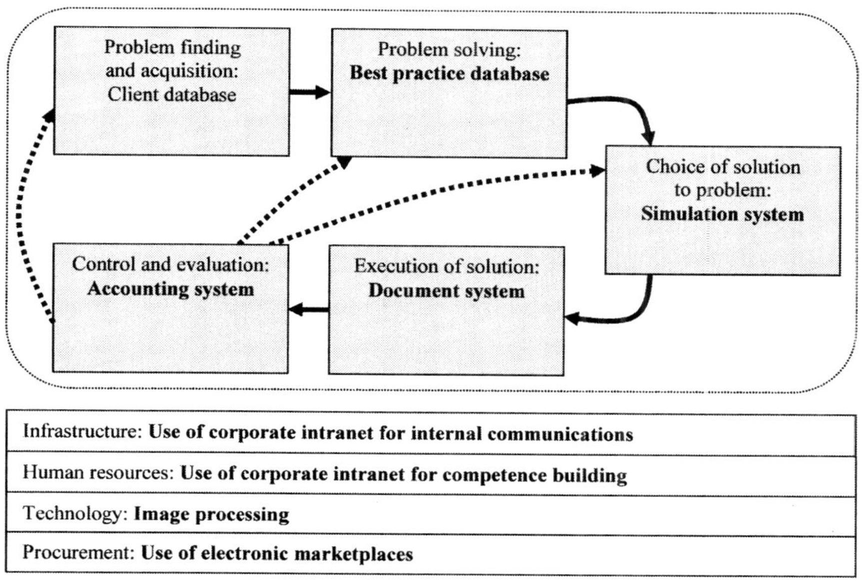

to provide input into the product specifications themselves, along with estimates of expected volume. This allows for limited differentiation.

VALUE SHOP CONFIGURATION

Value cannot only be created in value chains. Value can also be created in two alternative value configurations: value shop and value network (Stabell & Fjeldstad, 1998). In the value shop, activities are scheduled and resources are applied in a fashion that is dimensioned and appropriate to the needs of the client's problem, while a value chain performs a fixed set of activities that enables it to produce a standard product in large numbers. The value shop is a company that creates value by solving unique problems for customers and clients. Knowledge is the most important resource, and reputation is critical to firm success. The value shop is illustrated in Figure 2.

While typical examples of value chains are manufacturing industries such as paper and car production, typical examples of value shops are law firms and medical hospitals. Often, such companies are called professional service firms or knowledge-intensive service firms. Like the medical hospital as a way to practice medicine, the law firm provides a standard format for delivering complex legal services. Many features of its style – specialization, teamwork, continuous monitoring on behalf of clients (patients), and representation in many forums – have been emulated in other vehicles for delivering professional services.

Knowledge-intensive service firms are typical value shops. Sheehan (2002) defines knowledge-intensive service firms as entities that sell problem-solving services, where the solution chosen by the expert is based on real-time feedback from the client. Clients retain knowledge intensive service firms to reduce their uncertainty. Clients hire knowledge-intensive service firms precisely because the client believes the firm knows something that the client does not and believes it is necessary to solve their problems (Gottschalk & Berg, 2007). While expertise plays a role in all firms, its role is distinctive in knowledge-intensive service firms. Expert, often professional, knowledge is at the core of the service provided by the type of firm.

Knowledge-intensive service firms not only sell a problem-solving service, but equally a problem-finding, problem-defining, solution-execution, and monitoring service. Problem finding is often a key for acquiring new clients. Once the client is acquired and their problem is defined, not all problems will be solved by the firm. Rather the firm may only clarify that there is no problem (i.e. the patient does not have a heart condition) or that the problem should be referred to another specialist (i.e. the patient needs a heart specialist). If a problem is treated within the firm, then the firm needs to follow up the implementation to assure that the problem in fact has been solved (i.e. is the patient's heart now working properly?). This follows from the fact that there is often uncertainty in both problem diagnosis and problem resolution.

Sheehan (2002) has created a typology of knowledge-intensive service firms consisting of the following three types. First, knowledge-intensive search firms search for opportunities. The amount of value they create depends on the size of the finding or discovery, where size is measured by quality rather than quantity. Examples of search firms include petroleum and mineral exploration, drug discovery in the pharmaceutical industry, and research in the biotechnology industry. Second, knowledge-intensive diagnosis firms create value by clarifying problems. Once the problem has been identified, the suggested remedy usually follows directly. Examples of diagnosis firms include doctors, surgeons, psychotherapists, veterinarians, lawyers, auditors and tax accountants, and software support. Finally, knowledge-intensive design firms create value by conceiving new ways of constructing material or immaterial artifacts. Examples of design firms include architecture, advertising, research and development, engineering design, and strategy consulting.

Knowledge-intensive service firms create value through problem acquisition and definition, alternative generation and selection, implementation of an alternative, and follow up to see if the solution selected resolves the problem. To reflect this process, Stabell and Fjeldstad (1998) have outlined the value configuration of a value shop. A value shop is characterized by five primary activities: problem finding and acquisition, problem solving, choice, execution, and control and evaluation, as illustrated in Figure 2. Problem finding and acquisition involves working with the customer to determine the exact nature of the problem or need. It involves deciding on the overall plan of approaching the problem. Problem solving is the actual generation of ideas and action (or treatment) plans.

Choice represents the decision of choosing between alternatives. While the least important primary activity of the value shop in terms of time and effort, it is also the most important in terms of customer value. Execution represents communicating, organizing, and implementing the decision, or performing the treatment. Control and evaluation activities involve monitoring and measurement of how well the solution solved the original problem or met the original need. This may feed back into the first activity, problem finding and acquisition, for two reasons. First, if the proposed solution is inadequate or did not work, it feeds back into learning why it was inadequate and begins the problem-solving phase anew. Second, if the problem solution was successful, the firm might enlarge the scope of the problem-solving process to solve a bigger problem related to or dependent upon the first problem being solved.

Figure 2 can be used to identify current IS/IT in the organization. We let a law firm serve as example in Table 1. Within each of the five activities there are many tasks in a law firm. For each task, there may be IS/IT support. For example, problem solving may consist of the two tasks of case analysis and reference search. Lawyers will be eager to discuss the case and to search more information on similar

Table 1. Examples of IS/IT in the value shop

Activities	Tasks	IS/IT
Problem finding and acquisition	Register client information Register case information	Financial system Case database
Problem solving	Do case analysis Do reference search	Case-based reasoning Library search engine
Choice	Evaluate alternatives Make recommendation to client	Case-based reasoning Office systems
Execution	Participate at meetings Revise recommendation	Office systems Office systems
Control and evaluation	Register recommendation Check client satisfaction	Case database Financial system

cases. A system for case-based reasoning may be installed, where the current case can be compared to similar cases handled by the law firm. Also, intelligent search engines with thesaurus may be available in the law firm to find relevant information on the Internet and in legal databases.

Knowledge-intensive service firms are typical value shops, and such firms depend on reputation for success, as reputation is a key driver of firm value creation. Reputation is a relational concept, in the sense that firms are judged by their stakeholders relative to their competitors. Reputation is what is generally said or believed about an entity by someone, it is the net perception of a firm held by stakeholders judged relative to other firms. According to Sheehan (2002), there are four conditions, which must be present for reputation to work. Firstly, rents earned from maintaining a good reputation must be greater than not. Secondly, there must be a minimum of contact among stakeholders to allow for the changes in reputation to be communicated. Thirdly, there needs to be a possibility of repeat business. And lastly, there must be some uncertainty regarding the firm's type and/or behavior.

Reputation is related to the asymmetry of information, which is a typical feature of knowledge intensive service firms. Asymmetry is present when clients believe the firm knows something that the clients do not and believe it is necessary to know to solve their problems. Reputation can be classified as a strategic resource in knowledge-intensive firms. To be a strategic resource, it has to be valuable, rare, and costly to imitate, and possible to organize. Reputation is valuable as it increases the value received by the client. Reputation is rare, as by definition only a few firms can be considered best in the industry. Reputation is costly to imitate, as it is difficult to build a reputation in the short run. Reputation is possible to organize in the general sense of controllability, which implies that a firm can be organized to take advantage of reputation as a resource.

VALUE NETWORK CONFIGURATION

The third and final value configuration is the value network. A value network is a company that creates value by connecting clients and customers that are, or want to be, dependent on each other. These companies distribute information, money, products and services. While activities in both value chains and value shops are done sequentially, activities in value networks occur in parallel. The number and combination of customers and access points in the network are important value drivers in the value network. More customers and more connections create higher value to customers as illustrated in Figure 3.

Figure 3. Examples of IS/IT in the value network

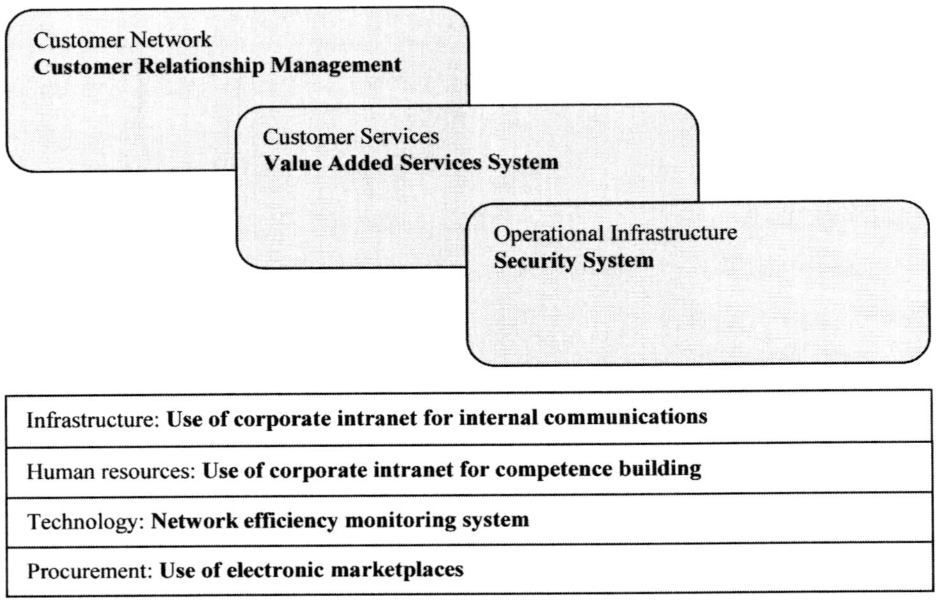

Stabell and Fjeldstad (1998) suggest that managing a value network can be compared to managing a club. The mediating firm admits members that complement each other, and in some cases exclude those that don't. The firm establishes, monitors, and terminates direct or indirect relationships among members. Supplier-customer relationships may exist between the members of the club, but to the mediating firm they are all customers. Examples of of value networks include telecommunication companies, postal services, financial institutions such as banks and insurance companies, and stockbrokers. As illustrated in Figure 3, value networks perform three activities:

- *Development of customer network through marketing and recruiting of new customers, to enable increased value for both existing customers and new customers.* This activity involves promoting and building the network, acquiring customers, and managing contracts for service provision. The management of contracts involves the initiation, maintenance, and termination of contracts to provide whatever service the intermediary proposes to furnish. This activity is distinguished from sales and marketing in the value chain by its active selection of customers to join the network. As the level of commitment rises, the complexity of the contracting process and of the contracts themselves rises.
- *Development of new services and improvement in existing services.* Service provisioning involves linking people in the network and then collecting payment from them for making the connection. Specifically, it involves setting up contracts – directly, as in real-time chat telephone service, or indirectly, as in banking or electronic mail – seeing that the contacts are maintained for the appropriate amount of time, and ending the contact at the appropriate moment. Collecting payment is about tracking the usage (both volume and time) and billing for direct contact or, in the case of indirect contacts, collecting a commission for putting the two parties together. Upon receiving a service request, the intermediary needs to check the feasibility of making the connection as well as the eligibility of the requestor.

- *Development of infrastructure so that customer services can be provided more efficiently and effectively.* Infrastructure operations are activities that allow the infrastructure to operate efficiently and remain in a state of readiness to provide service to the next customer. Stabell and Fjeldstad (1998) provided examples of different types of infrastructure activities that vary with the type of network: For telecommunications providers, the main infrastructure is embedded in switches and distribution centers; for postal services, it is collecting, sorting, and delivery of mail and package services, for financial services companies, it is embedded in the branch offices, financial assets, or connections to trading floors.

The value network is an extensive connector, a machine for establishing connections and providing services to support the exchanges customers want to make across them. The managerial trade-off is between reach (network size) and richness (capacity and services) between whom you can connect and what you can do for them. Large network size increases connectivity measured in nodes (frequently customers) that can be reached. Capacity increases speed of change. The major costs are associated with attracting customers to increase the value of membership and building the infrastructure and services to carry customer exchanges. Costs are predominantly fixed (Fjellstad & Andersen, 2003).

The current IS/IT situation in a value network will mainly be described through the infrastructure that typically will consist of information technology. In addition, many of the new services may be information systems that will be used by customers in their communication and business transactions with other customers. The knowledge component will mainly be found in the services of a value network, as information systems are made available to customers to exchange relevant information.

According to Andersen and Fjeldstad (2003), the mediating technology is extensive. It is used to connect customers that are or wish to be interdependent. The quality of mediation services depends on the nodes between which exchange can take place and on what type of objects can be exchanged. Therefore, nodes and links covered by the service are primary resources of mediators. Control of nodes and links enable mediators to perform activities that convey the objects of interest. Service quality depends on properties of the links between the nodes. Links properties, e.g. bandwidth or security, determine what objects can be exchanged as well as the speed, capacity, reliability, and security exchanges. Higher-level specialization services, e.g. exchange of payment transactions, and depend on use of general lower level services as a medium. The mediation networks made available by these lower levels services are necessary resources in the provisioning of higher-level services. Conversely, the higher-level mediation networks are also resources for the lower level networks; they provide uses of the latter.

THE ROLE OF IT IN DIFFERENT VALUE CONFIGURATIONS

The strategic impact of technology and IT are different in the three value configurations. While the value chain has cost orientation, the value shop is oriented towards value, and the value network needs to balance cost and value, as scale and capacity utilization are drivers of both. Andersen and Fjeldstad (2003) suggest that much use of information technology today is counterproductive, because of a lack of understanding of the underlying business logic in different value configurations. In particular, they suggest that companies and organizations in the network and shop configuration have implemented information technology to pursue economic goals derived from a model of the company or organiza-

Table 2. Characteristics of the three value configurations

	Chain	Shop	Network
Value creation logic	Transformation of input into output	Solving customer problems	Linking customers
Primary technology	Long-linked	Intensive	Mediating
Work characteristic	Sequential production	Integrated and cyclical problem solving	Monitored and simultaneous connections
Primary activities	Inbound logistics, operations, outbound logistics, marketing, service	Problem-finding, problem solving, choice, execution, control/evaluation	Network promotion, service provisioning, infrastructure operation
Role of IT	Improve product and process	Co-performed with primary activities	Part of basic infrastructure
Contribution from IS	Making production more efficient and effective	Adding value to knowledge work	Adding value to infrastructure services
Examples	Pulp and paper industry, car manufacturing, and IT hardware industry	Law firms, hospitals, consulting, police, and government authorities	Telecom industry, postal services, banking, finance, and insurance

tion as a chain. It is important to be aware of the different value configurations when developing and implementing new information technology.

Value chain, value shop and value network are alternative value configurations that impact the use of information technology in the company as illustrated in Table 2. While the role of IT is to make production more efficient in a value chain, IT creates added value in the value shop, while IT in the form of infrastructure is the main value in the value network. Some companies have more than one value configuration, but most companies have one dominating configuration. In the long term, business organizations can choose to change their value configurations. A bank, for example can be a value shop when it focuses on converting inputs to outputs. The value resides in the output and once you have the output, you can remove the production organization. This removal does not impact on the value of the output. The value shop is a solution provider. It is somebody that solves problems. The input is a problem. The output is a solution to the problem. A bank that does this would view itself as a financial service operator, a financial advisor that also has the ability to provide the money. But what it would do is identify client problems, it would address those problems, it would select a solution together with the client and help to implement it. It would have stringent quality controls. As part of it's offering, it would probably supply the client with some cash as a loan or accept some of the clients' cash for investment. Or, the bank can be a value network, which is basically the logic of the marketplace. The bank would define its role as a conduit between people that do not have money and those people that do have money. What the bank does is to arrange the flow of cash between them. The bank will attract people with money to make deposits and investments. The bank will also attract people without money to make loans. As a value network, the bank will connect people with opposite financial needs. The network consists of people with different financial needs. Over time, persons in the network may change status from money needier to money provider and vice versa (Chatzkel, 2002).

Both as a value shop and as a value network, the business organization can be identified as a bank. But it would have completely different consequences for what it will focus on doing well, what it will focus on doing itself, versus what it would not want to do itself. This provides a kind of strategic systems logic. It asks, "Which strategic system in terms of value configuration are we going to operate in?" Choosing an appropriate value configuration is a long-term decision with long-term consequences.

Figure 4. An example of interfirm relations in value networks

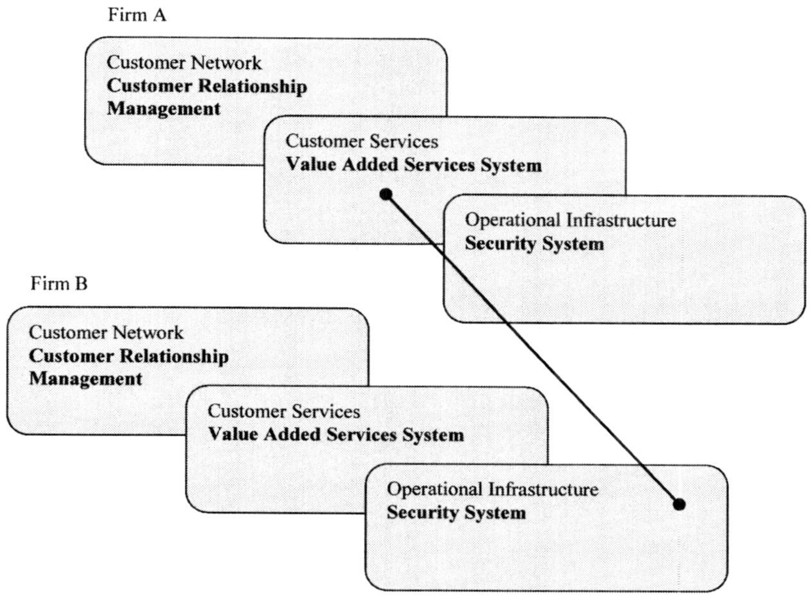

INTERFIRM RELATIONS IN VALUE SYSTEMS

To be able to identify potential areas for outsourcing in the firm, it is important to understand firm boundaries and firm relations. Interfirm relations and institutional arrangements that parties deploy to support exchange exist within the context of value systems. A value system consists of all the activities and firms that create and deliver value to the end customer (Andersen & Fjeldstad, 2003).

In our outsourcing perspective, interfirm relations are a challenge, as it may not be obvious who is the outsourcer; is it firm A or firm B, or both, as illustrated in Figure 4. Firm A uses the operational infrastructure of firm B to provide customer services. For example, a telecom firm may use the physical infrastructure such as antennas of a competing telecom firm to provide its services, so that a forest of antennas from competing firms does not cover a country.

A value system describes the division of labor among firms and defines exchanges relevant for integration of end value. Value system properties are potentially important determinants of interfirm relations because the organization of exchanges is likely to depend on the properties of the objects exchanged. For example, the exchange of knowledge or skills is more likely to occur in networks, whereas the transfer of tangible items more commonly occurs through a market transaction. Firms that perform similar or substitutionable activities in a value system compete. Firms that perform complementing activities in a value system may cooperate to maximize their joint value creation (Andersen & Fjeldstad, 2003).

In our outsourcing context, the vendor and the client can be understood as a value system as illustrated in Figure 5. In this example, the outsourcing vendor is defined as a value shop that solves client problems. The outsourcing client might be a telecom firm that buys problem-solving services from the vendor.

Figure 5. An example of outsourcing vendor as value shop and outsourcing client as value network

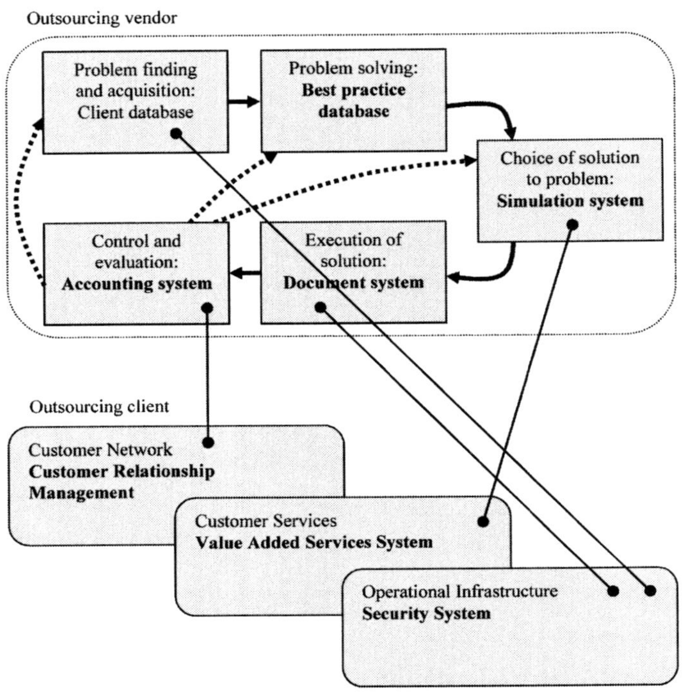

VALUE CONFIGURATION AS DETERMINANT OF OUTSOURCING

The decision to outsource is influenced by a number of factors. Gottschalk and Solli-Sæther (2005) discuss factors such as production economies, transaction economies, technological uncertainty, functional complexity, transaction specific investments, supplier presence, slack resources and criticality of business functions. Such factors are based on agency theory, resource-based theory, core competency theory, transaction cost theory, alliance theory, stakeholder theory, and other theories, as discussed in Chapter 2.

According to the core competency theory, for example, tasks that are not core competencies of the organization are candidates for being contracted out. However, Lankford and Parsa (1999) argue that any skill or knowledge that allows you to serve your customer base better, that deals directly with the product or service you are trying to put out of the door, is one that must remain in-house. Today, they argue, the outsourcing of selected organizational activities is an integral part of corporate strategy. Today, outsourcing decision-making is important, as it explicitly determines firm boundaries.

As the role of information technology in an organization is dependent on value configuration, the extent of outsourcing of operating IT systems is expected to be dependent on value configuration as well (Gottschalk & Solli-Sæther, 2009). In developing research hypotheses linking configuration to outsourcing, we will argue that knowledge-intensive value configurations will be less inclined to outsource their operating IT systems, as information is the raw material of knowledge work.

While information systems make production more efficient in value chains, information systems are adding value to the knowledge work in value shops, while their main value lies in the use of IT infrastructure in value networks. In this perspective, we are able to rank the knowledge-closeness in value configurations as follows. First, value shops experience the highest knowledge intensity in IT systems (King, 2006), which suggests that value shops will have the relatively lowest extent of outsourcing. Next, value chains have some knowledge-intensive activities, which suggest that value chains will have the second lowest extent of outsourcing. Finally, the IT infrastructure in value networks is relatively independent of knowledge work, which suggests that value networks will have the greatest extent of outsourcing. Thus, the following hypotheses were formulated:

Hypothesis 1: The extent of outsourcing will be lower in a value shop as compared to a value chain.

Hypothesis 2: The extent of outsourcing will be lower in a value shop as compared to a value network.

Hypothesis 3: The extent of outsourcing will be lower in a value chain as compared to a value network.

A questionnaire survey of senior financial executives was used to gather information pertaining to outsourcing of functions. The 657 largest Norwegian companies were selected as sample for a survey. Usable responses were returned by 116 firm (17.6%). Respondents came from a wide range of industries with most from manufacturing firms (value creation logic as chain). While 62.1% of the companies were value chains, 25.0% were value shops, and only 12.9% were value networks. Average extent of outsourcing among responding firms was 35%. The three different types of companies were measured in terms of value configurations when asking outsourcing questions. The extent of outsourcing was 32% for value chains, 36% for value shops, and 55% for value networks respectively.

Companies having the value configuration of a value network are more likely to outsource business functions. When we look at various functions in a business, and to what extent they were outsourced by responding enterprises we get results as listed in Figure 6. For example, operating IT systems was outsourced by 52% of the responding organizations. When applying statistical t-tests (Hair, Black, Babin, Anderson, & Tatham, 2006), we receive results as listed in Table 3. When applying the most demanding statistical requirement of 0.01 (or 0.05 significance), we find no support of the research hypotheses in our empirical data. When relaxing this requirement to an acceptable level, the second hypothesis finds support in this research. The extent of outsourcing will be lower in a value shop as compared to a value network. As there were only 19 value networks in our sample, it comes as no surprise that significant differences were hard to find. We believe that a larger sample would provide support for more hypotheses. (Table 4)

While the number of respondents was satisfactory in this research, the distribution among configurations was not. Future research will have to target first and foremost value networks to collect sufficient empirical data. The extent to which companies with the value configuration of a value network are outsourcing functions is substantial higher than the alternative configurations of value chain and value shop. Future research might investigate reasons in terms of causal relationships.

Figure 6. The extent to which functions are outsourced

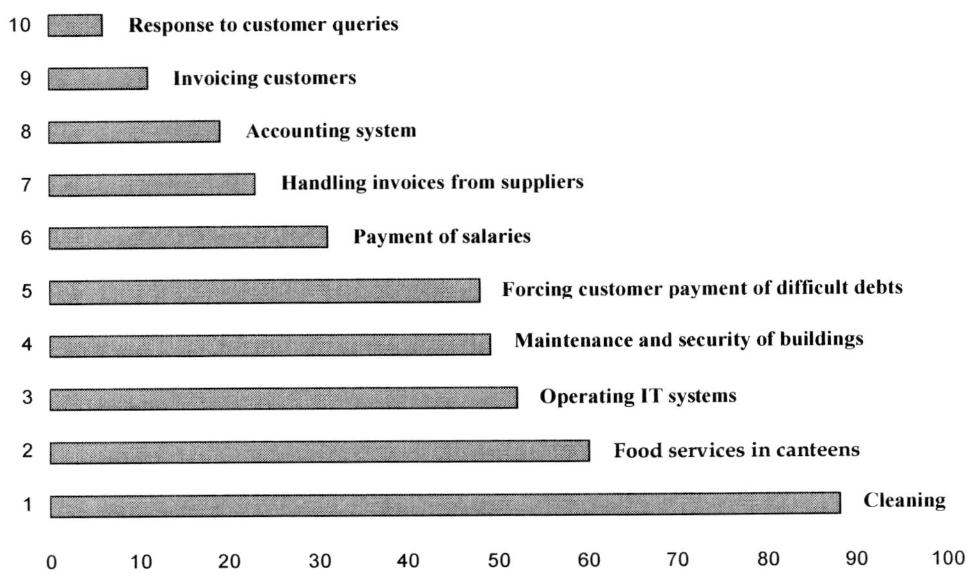

STRATEGIC IT PLANNING

Strategy is both a plan for the future and pattern from the past, it is the match an organization makes between its internal resources and skills (sometimes collectively called competencies) and the opportunities and risks created by its external environment. Strategy is the long-term direction of an organization. Strategy is the course of action for achieving an organization's purpose. Strategy is the direction and scope of an organization over the long term, which achieves advantage for the organization through its configuration of resources within a changing environment and to fulfill stakeholders' expectations (Johnson & Scholes, 2002).

Business strategy is concerned with achieving the mission, vision and objectives of an organization, while IS strategy is concerned with use of IS/IT applications, and IT strategy is concerned with the technical infrastructure as illustrated in Figure 7. An organization has typically several intra-organizational as well as inter-organizational IS/IT applications. The connection between them is also of great interest,

Table 4. Testing of research hypotheses using t-tests

Research hypothesis	T-statistic	Significance
Hypothesis 1: The extent of outsourcing will be lower in a value shop as compared to a value chain.	0.928	0.358
Hypothesis 2: The extent of outsourcing will be lower in a value shop as compared to a value network.	0.912	0.065
Hypothesis 3: The extent of outsourcing will be lower in a value chain as compared to a value network.	1.411	0.122

Figure 7. Relationships between strategies at three levels

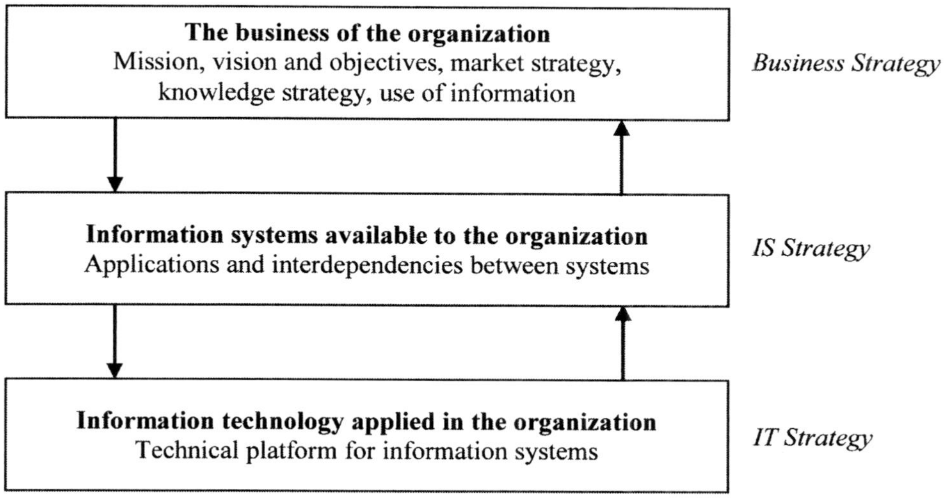

as interdependencies should prevent applications from being separate islands. Furthermore, the arrows in the illustration in the figure are of importance. Arrows from business strategy to IS strategy, and from IS to IT strategy represent the alignment perspective, they illustrate *what* before *how*. What do we want to achieve? How might we achieve it? Arrows from IT to IS strategy, and from IS to business strategy represent the extension from *what* to *how* to *what*. This is the impact perspective, representing the potential impacts of modern information technology on future business options. Necessary elements of a business strategy include mission, vision, objectives, market strategy, knowledge strategy, and our general approach to the use of information, information systems and information technology.

Mission describes the reason for firm existence. For example, the reason for law firm existence is client's needs for legal advice. The mission addresses the organization's basic question of 'What business are we in?' This single, essential, sentence should include no quantification, but must unambiguously state the purpose of the organization and should, just as carefully define what the organization does not do. According to Ward and Peppard (2002, p. 189), the mission is an unambiguous statement of what the organization does and its long-term, overall purpose:

Its primary role is to set a direction for everyone to follow. It may be short, succinct and inspirational, or contain broad philosophical statements that tie an organization to certain activities and to economic, social, ethical or political ends. Values are also frequently stated alongside the mission. Three widely-differing examples of missions are:

- To be the world's mobile communications leader, enriching the lives of individuals and business customers in the networked society (large global telecommunication company)
- To eradicate all communicable diseases worldwide (World Health Organization)
- The company engages in the retail marketing on a national basis of petroleum products and the equitable distribution of the fruits of continuously increasing productivity of management, capital and labor amongst stockholders, employees and the public (a large public company).

Figure 8. IS/IT strategy elements and interdependencies

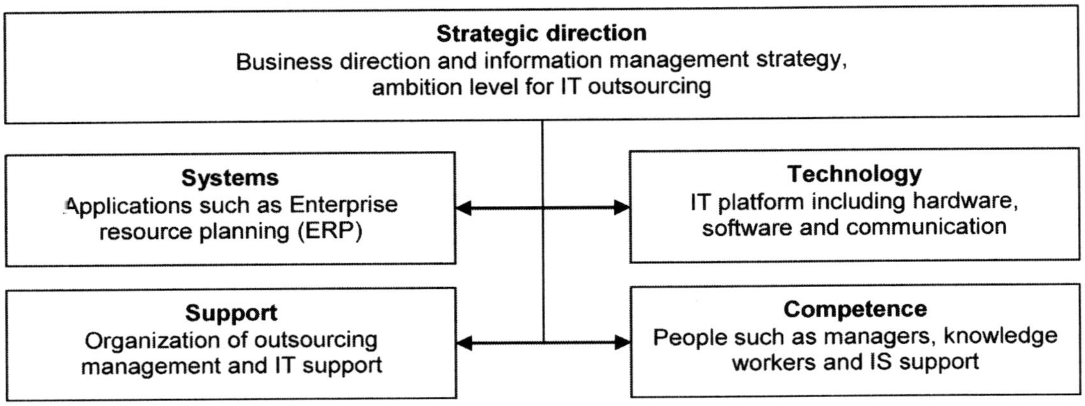

Vision describes what the firm wants to achieve. For example, the law firm wants to become the leading law firm in Norway. The vision represents the view that senior managers have for the future of the organization; so it is what they want it to become. This view gives a way to judge the appropriateness of all potential activities that the organization might engage in. According to Ward and Peppard (2002), the vision gives a picture, frequently covering many aspects, that everyone can identify with, of what the business will be in the future, and how it will operate. It exists to bring objectives to life, and to give the whole organization a destination that it can visualize, so that every stakeholder has a shared picture of the future aim.

Objectives describe where the business is heading. For example, the law firm can choose to merge with another law firm to become the leading law firm in Norway. Objectives are the set of major achievements that will accomplish the vision. These are usually small in number, but embody the most important aspects of the vision, such as financial returns, customer service, manufacturing excellence, staff morale, and social and environmental obligations.

Necessary elements of an *IS strategy* include future IS/IT applications, future competence of human resources (IS/IT professionals), and future IS/IT organizational structure, and control of the IS/IT function. An important application area is knowledge management strategy. The future applications are planned according to priorities, how they are to be developed or acquired (make or buy), how they meet user requirements, and how security is achieved. The future competence is planned by types of resources needed, motivation and skills needed (managers, users, IS/IT professionals), salaries, and other benefits. The future IS/IT organization defines tasks, roles, management and possibly outsourcing.

Necessary elements of an *IT strategy* include selection of IT hardware, basic software, and networks, as well as how these components should interact as a technological platform, and how required security level is maintained. The IT platform consists of hardware, systems software, networks and communications, standards and support form selected vendors.

An *IS/IT strategy* is a combined strategy including business context, the IS in a narrow sense and the technological platform. Necessary elements of an IS/IT strategy include business direction and strategy (mission, vision, objectives, outsourcing strategy), applications (such ERP), people (future competence of human resources), organization (future organization and control of IT function), and IT platform (future technical infrastructure). Hence, IS/IT is quite a broad term. The term is broad to take care of all connections and interdependencies in a strategy, as changes in one element will have effect on all other elements, as illustrated in Figure 8.

Why is strategic IS/IT planning undertaken within business organizations? Hann and Weber (1996) see IS/IT planning as a set of activities directed toward achieving the following objectives:

1. Recognizing organizational opportunities and problems where IS/IT might be applied successfully
2. Identifying the resources needed to allow IS/IT to be applied successfully to these opportunities and problems
3. Developing strategies and procedures to allow IS/IT to be applied successfully to these opportunities and problems
4. Establishing a basis for monitoring and bonding IT managers so their actions are more likely to be congruent with the goals of their superiors
5. Resolving how the gains and losses from unforeseen circumstances will be distributed among senior management and the IT manager
6. Determining the level of decision rights to be delegated to the IT manager.

IT outsourcing strategy should be embedded in IS/IT strategy. Developing an IS/IT strategy is taken to mean thinking strategically and planning for the effective long-term application and optimal impact of electronic information to support and influence business performance in the organization. Strategy can simply be defined as principles, a broad based formula, to be applied in order to achieve a purpose. These principles are general guidelines guiding the daily work to reach business goals. Strategy is the pattern of resource development and application decisions made throughout the organization. These encapsulate both desired goals and beliefs about what are acceptable and, most critically, unacceptable means for achieving them.

The Y-Model for IS/IT Strategy Work

Empirical studies of information systems/information technology planning practices in organizations indicate that wide variations exist. Hann and Weber (1996) found that organizations differ in terms of how much IS/IT planning they do, the planning methodologies they use, the personnel involved in planning, the strength of the linkage between IS/IT plans and corporate plans, the focus of IS/IT plans (e.g., strategic systems versus resource needs), and the way in which IS/IT plans are implemented. It has been argued that the Internet renders strategic planning obsolete. In reality, it is more important than ever for companies to do strategic planning (Porter, 2001, p. 63):

Many have argued that the Internet renders strategy obsolete. In reality, the opposite is true. Because the Internet tends to weaken industry profitability without providing proprietary operational advantages, it is more important than ever for companies to distinguish themselves through strategy. The winners will be those that view the Internet as a complement to, not a cannibal of, traditional ways of competing.

In all kinds of strategy work, there are three steps. The first step is concerned with analysis. The second step is concerned with choice (selection and decision), while the final step is concerned with

Figure 9. The Y-model for IS/IT strategy work

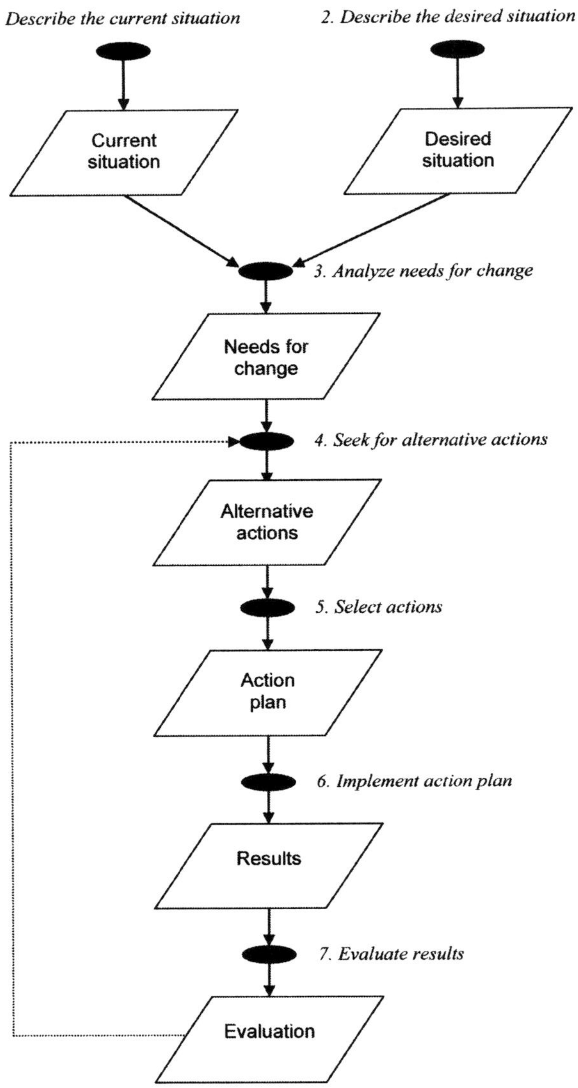

implementation. The model consists of seven stages covering analysis, choice and implementation. As illustrated in Figure 9 the stages are as follows:

1. *Describe current situation.* The current IS/IT situation in the business can be described using several methods. The benefits method identifies benefits from use of IS/IT in the business. Distinctions are made between rationalization benefits, control benefits, organizational benefits and market benefits. Other methods include the three-era model, management activities, and stages of growth.
2. *Describe desired situation.* The desired business situation can be described using several methods described in this book, such as value configurations, maturity levels, knowledge management, the Internet and electronic business, and information technology benefits.

3. *Analyze and prioritize needs for change*. After descriptions of the current situation and the desired situation, the needs for change can be identified. The gap between desired and current situation is called needs for change. Analysis is to provide details on needs, what change is needed, and how changes can take place. *What*-analysis will create an understanding of vision and goals, knowledge strategy, market strategy, and corporate problems and opportunities. *How*-analysis will create an understanding of technology trends and applications. These analyses should result in proposals for new IS/IT in the organization.
4. *Seek for alternative actions*. When needs for change have been identified and proposals for filling gaps have been developed, alternative actions for improving the current situation can be developed. New IS/IT can be developed, acquired, and implemented in alternative ways. For example, an information system can be developed in-house by company staff, it can be purchased as a standard application from a vendor, or it can be leased from an application systems provider (ASP).
5. *Select actions and make an action plan*. When needs for change and alternative actions have been identified, several choices have to be made and documented in an action plan. Important issues here include development process, user involvement, time frame and financial budget for IS/IT projects.
6. *Implement plan and describe results*. This is the stage of action. Technical equipment such as servers, PCs, printers and cables are installed. Operating systems are installed. Application packages, software programs, programming tools, end user tools and database systems are installed. Development projects are organized. Management and user training takes place. Document results over time.
7. *Evaluate results*. Implementation results are compared with needs for change. It is determined to what extent gaps between desired and current situation have been closed. This is the beginning of the IS/IT strategy revision process, where a new process through the Y-model takes place. Typically, a new IS/IT strategy process should take place every other year in business organizations.

While stages 1 to 3 cover *analysis*, 4 and 5 cover *choice*, and 6 and 7 cover *implementation*. In some strategy models, stage 2 is listed as the first stage. It is here recommended to do stage 1 before stage 2. It is easier to describe the ideal situation when you know the current situation. If you start out with stage 2, it often feels difficult and abstract to describe what you would like to achieve. Having done stage 1 first makes the work more relevant. Stage 3 is a so-called gap analysis, looking at the difference between the desired and actual situation. This stage also includes prioritizing. Stage 4 is a creative session as it calls for ideas and proposals for alternative actions. Stages 5 and 6 are typical planning stages. The final stage 7 is important because we can learn from performing an evaluation.

Describing the Current IS/IT Situation

The Y-model starts with a description of the current situation. We focus on the IS/IT situation, as this will be the subject of change later in the model. First of all we have to understand in what ways the company is using IS/IT. Many approaches can help us gain an understanding of the present IS/IT situation. Some methods are listed in the following:

1. *Benefits of IS/IT*. IS/IT is applied in business organizations to achieve benefits. We can study current IS/IT in the organization to understand what benefits have been achieved so far. Here we can

determine what main benefit categories is currently the case. We will make distinctions between rationalization benefits, control benefits, organizational benefits, and market benefits.

2. *Stages of IS/IT growth.* IS/IT in business organizations change over time. New hardware and software, new areas of applications, and new IS/IT support functions emerge. Most business organizations develop through stages over time. Here we can determine at what stage the business organization is for the time being. These stages are classified into three eras: data processing, information systems and information networks.
3. *IS/IT in management activities.* Management activities can be studied in a hierarchical perspective of operational, tactical and strategic management. Current IS/IT in the organizations can be assigned to these levels to determine the extent of support at each level.
4. *IS/IT in business processes.* In a company, many business processes take place at the same time. Some of the processes may rely heavily on IS/IT, while others are mainly manual at the current point in time.
5. *IS/IT support for value configuration.* We make distinctions between value chain, value shop and value network. In each of these value configurations, IS/IT can support activities. The current IS/IT situation is described by identifying activities in the value configuration depending on the extent of technology support.
6. *Strategic integration.* Business strategy and IT strategy have for a long time suffered from lack of coordination and integration in many organizations. Here we measure the current IS/IT situation by use of ten integration mechanisms to determine integration stage in an organization.
7. *IS/IT in e-business.* For most firms, becoming an e-business is an evolutionary journey. We introduce six stages to describe the evolving e-business: external communications, internal communications, e-commerce, e-business, e-enterprise, and transformation.
8. *IS/IT enabled business transformation.* IT-enabled transformation can include business direction change, but more often we find examples at lower levels, such as business design change and business process change.
9. *IS/IT support for knowledge management.* The stages of growth model for knowledge management technology can be applied, where the current IS/IT situation is described by the stage at which the firm currently is performing.

Description of the current situation assumes that we have been able to define borders for our study. Borders exist for both breath and depth. Breath is a question of whether the whole company or only one division should be studied. Depth is a question of whether all aspects such as technology, marketing, management and finance should be included in the study. We recommend both extensive breath and thorough depth to ensure that a wide range of alternative solutions and alternative actions can be identified in later stages of the Y-model. In the case of breath, this may imply that both suppliers and customers are included because there may be electronic market places used by our suppliers and customers. In the case of depth, this may imply that analysis of top management is included because management competence in the area of IS/IT can influence both management attitudes and ambitions concerning future applications of IS/IT.

Description of the current IS/IT situation should focus on issues of importance in technology and knowledge management. Less emphasis should be put on technology itself, such as drawings of company networks and servers. Technology management is focused on the management of information technology, while knowledge management is focused on knowledge strategy and knowledge management systems.

Describing the Current and Desired Business Situation

We have used some of the nine methods to describe the current situation of IS/IT. Now we have to consider whether the current IS/IT applications are what the company needs or if there might be changes needed. We use the Y-model as our guiding approach. We compare the present business situation (with its support from IS/IT) with the desired business situation. If the current IS/IT applications are not able to serve the needs of the future desired business, then there are needs for change in IS/IT applications and the way we do business. At this point we are moving into stage 2 of the Y-model.

There are many techniques for business analysis. Some are general, while others are more specific. General analysis techniques include SWOT analysis and the X-model. Specific analysis techniques include business direction (mission, vision, and objectives), market strategy, value system, competitive forces and product life cycle. Some of these analytical tools are listed in the following:

1. *SWOT analysis* is an analytical tool for assessing the present and future situation focusing on strengths (S), weaknesses (W), opportunities (O) and threats (T). The whole company may be the object of analysis, but also a department in a company or a project in a company may be the study object. How can IS/IT exploit our strengths, compensate our weaknesses, use opportunities and avoid threats? How can IS/IT help make it happen?
2. *X-model.* The X-model is a tool for description and analysis of both the current and a desired situation. It is a method for assessing the situation within a company, a project, or a department. The situation consists of a time period in which work is done. In the beginning of the time period, there are both factual and personal inputs, and at the end of the period, there are both factual and personal outputs. How can IS/IT improve factual and personal outputs? How can IS/IT help make it happen?
3. *Business direction.* Important business concepts are mission, vision and objectives. How can IS/IT make the firm achieve its vision? How can IS/IT make the firm reach its objectives? How can IS/IT help make it happen?
4. *Market strategy.* The market strategy shows our position and ambition in the market place. We can either have the same product as our competitors, or we can have a different product. If we have the same product as everyone else, it has to be sold at the same price as all the others (as in a vegetable market or through the Internet). It is not possible for an Internet bookstore to sell at a higher price than others, when there is perfect information and information searching is associated with no costs. This is called the law of indifference. In order to survive, the company must have a cost advantage that will give higher profits and result in higher earnings for the owners. How can IS/IT cause a cost advantage? How can IS/IT help make it happen? If we are selling a product that our customers perceive to be different from our competitors' product, then we have differentiation. A service may in its basic form be the same for all companies, like an airline travel, in the sense that all airlines are supposed to bring you safely to your destination. The product is differentiated by supplementary services. How can IS/IT make our customers perceive our products and services to be different from our competitor's? How can IS/IT help make it happen?

5. *Competitive forces*. The basis of this method is that a company exists within an industry and to succeed, it must effectively deal with the competitive forces that exist within the particular industry. For example, the forces in an emerging industry such as mobile communication are considerably different from those of established industries such as financial services. The company interacts with its customers, suppliers and competitors. In addition, there are potential new entrants into the particular competitive marketplace and potential substitute products and services. To survive and succeed in this environment, it is important to understand these interactions and the implications in terms of what opportunities or competitive advantage can occur. How can IS/IT reduce the threat of new entrants, reduce the bargaining power of suppliers, reduce the bargaining power of buyers, reduce the threat of substitute products and services, and reduce the rivalry among existing competitors? How can IS/IT help make it happen?
6. *Product portfolio analysis*. There are a number of approaches that aim to relate the competitive position of an organization to the maturity of its product. The models assume there is a basic S-shaped curve description to the growth phenomenon of products. Four stages in the life cycle of any product can be identified as introduction, growth, maturity, and decline. When we look at the life cycle of all products in the firm, we can apply product portfolio analysis. This method shows the relationship between a product's current or future revenue potential and the appropriate management stance. The two by two matrix names the products in order to chart symptoms into a diagnosis so that effective management behavior can be adopted. The matrix classifies products according to the present market share and the future growth of that market. A successful product that lasts from emergent to mature market goes around the matrix. This strategy is simply to milk the cows, divest the dogs, invest in the stars and examine the wild cats. How can IS/IT get more milk for a longer period of time from the cows? How can IS/IT explore and exploit the stars? How can IS/IT eliminate the dogs? How can IS/IT develop the wild cats into stars? How can IS/IT help make it happen?
7. *Environmental analysis*. Environmental analysis is concerned with the external corporate environment. An analysis of the environment is important because it increases the quality of the strategic decision making by considering a range of the relevant features. The organization identifies a threats and opportunities facing it, and those factors that might assist in achieving objectives and those that might act as a barrier. The strategy of the organization should be directed at exploiting the environmental opportunities and blocking environmental threats in a way that is consistent with internal capabilities. This is a matter of environmental fit that allows the organization to maximize its competitive position. An external analysis can investigate politics, the economy, the society and the technology. This is sometimes called PEST analysis. If we include the study of legal and environmental matters, we call it PESTLE. The analytical work that has to be done in the company when doing environmental analysis is concerned with questions such as: What are the implications of the trends (changes in the environment)? What can the company do in order to meet the opportunities and threats that follow? How can knowledge management meet the opportunities and threats that follow? How can IS/IT help make it happen? For example, how can IS/IT help in global competition (politics)? How can IS/IT help in alliances and partnerships (economy)? How can IS/IT help serve an increasing number of older people (society)?
8. *External knowledge analysis*. Distinctions can be made between core knowledge, advanced knowledge and innovative knowledge. While core knowledge is required to stay in business, advanced knowledge makes the firm competitively visible, and innovative knowledge allows the firm to lead

its entire industry. The knowledge map can be applied to identify firm position. The map in terms of the strategic knowledge framework illustrates firm knowledge levels compared with competitors' knowledge levels.

9. *Internal knowledge analysis*. While the knowledge map represents an external analysis of the firm's current knowledge situation, the knowledge gap represents an internal analysis of the firm's current knowledge situation. The knowledge gap is dependent on business strategy. What the company does is different from what the company will do, creating a strategy gap. What the company knows is different from what the company has to know, creating a knowledge gap. Two important links emerge: the strategy-knowledge-link and the knowledge-strategy-link.

Strategic Alignment

IT is recognized as a critical business discipline because it is central to all business activities of modern enterprises in the creation of organizational and customer value. To create business value from IT, business needs to understand the role IT plays, not only in supporting the running of the business in such back-office functions as HR, finance, inventory control, but more importantly the special and competitively differentiated ways that IT plays in delivering products and services to the cooperating agencies and citizens. The integral role that IT has enmeshed into all business functions today means that IT has become a central nervous system of the business. In particular, information *is* the blood stream of business, which flows through all business functions (processes) supported by the IT nervous system. Business value is created by each business function or process through dynamic consumption (processing) of input information and creation of new output information, which in turn will be 'consumed' by another business function (process) as defined by the value configuration of the business.

The fundamental principle of all the critical success factors of IT strategy is therefore IT and business acting as one. This requires each IT task to be aligned with and 'justified' by the business function it is designed to contribute, for and based on which its business value is measured.

IT and business acting as one is easier said than done, however. In reality not many enterprises have yet fully mastered the practice of the fundamental principle of IT and business acting as one. This is because of the bad old tradition of IT in the past (and even today for some enterprises) working (either being treated or wanted to be treated) as the 'back-office techie guys' who seemed to do as they were told (or requested) by the business without having any concern for the end-customers or indeed the business purpose of the tasks being requested. In the past, IT saw themselves as the technical guys who would do whatever technical task is requested of them by the business. There was no need to understand the business, let alone the business strategy or points of differentiation. The 'us-versus-them' working relationship or company culture permeates between IT and business in most enterprises in the past, and indeed even till today.

While this scenario may be an extreme example for today's enterprises, it is nonetheless still a common issue for most enterprises today that some degree of misalignment still exists between business and IT. The varying degrees of organizational misalignment and functional disconnect between business and IT have been the key inhibitor of value creation by IT in all enterprises, past and present. Despite rigorous and diligent attempts by researchers and practitioners alike, in the past twenty years, various surveys have shown that business-IT alignment remains a strategically critical priority for business and IT leaders to manage and achieve.

CONCLUSION

To comprehend the value that resources provide to organizations, we must first understand the way a particular organization conducts business and how resources such as information systems affect the performance of various component activities within the organization. In our outsourcing perspective, impacts of various sourcing strategies on value creation processes have to be understood. We have applied Stabell and Fjeldstad's (1998), set of three alternative value configurations for an enterprise. The most well-known value configuration is the value chain. Less well known are the value shop and the value network. A value configuration describes how value is created in a company and shows how the most important business processes function to create value for customers. A value configuration represents the way a particular organization conducts business.

This chapter was also concerned with what types of companies are more likely to outsource business functions. We defined types of companies in terms of value configurations. Furthermore we identified what business functions are being outsourced. This is important, as it introduces value configurations to the contingent outsourcing approach. An interesting finding from our research is that the extent of outsourcing will be lower in a value shop as compared to a value network. While value networks (banks, insurance companies, stock brokers) are connecting individuals on a mutual technology infrastructure, value shops (law firms, hospitals, consulting firms) are solving problems for their clients in various ways. Value network success is determined by efficiency and effectiveness, while value shop success is determined by knowledge and creativity. Based on our research results we may argue that outsourcing tends to contribute more to efficiency and effectiveness and less to knowledge and creativity from the outsourcee to the outsourcer.

Resource-based strategy is concerned with development and application of resources. While the business strategy is the broadest pattern of resource decisions, more specific decisions are related to (the outsourcing of) information systems and information technology. IS must be seen both in a business and an IT context. IS is in the middle because IS supports the business while using IT. As part of a resource-based strategy, both IS and IT represent capabilities and resources that have to be developed. The Y-model is presented as a tool for development of an IS/IT strategy. The model consists of seven stages covering analysis, choice and implementation. The stages are describe current solution, describe desired solution, analyze and prioritize needs for change, seek for alternative actions, select actions and make an action plan, implement plan and describe results, evaluate results.

REFERENCES

Afuah, A., & Tucci, C. L. (2003). *Internet Business Models and Strategies* (2nd Ed.). New York: McGraw-Hill.

Andersen, E., & Fjeldstad, Ø. (2003). Understanding interfirm relations in mediation industries with special reference to the Nordic mobile communication industry. *Industrial Marketing Management*, *32*(5), 397–408. doi:10.1016/S0019-8501(03)00013-0

Chatzkel, J. (2002). A conversation with Göran Roos. *Journal of Intellectual Capital*, *3*(2), 96–117. doi:10.1108/14691930210424716

Fjellstad, Ø., & Andersen, E. (2003). Casting off the chains. *European Business Journal,* (14), 47-53.

Gottschalk, P., & Berg, M. E. (2007). Information systems in the value shop business of police investigations. *International Journal of Business and Systems Research, 1*(1), 47–60. doi:10.1504/IJBSR.2007.014768

Gottschalk, P., & Solli-Sæther, H. (2005). Critical success factors from IT outsourcing theories: an empirical study. *Industrial Management & Data Systems, 105*(5), 685–702. doi:10.1108/02635570510606941

Gottschalk, P., & Solli-Sæther, H. (2009). Value configuration as determinant of IT operating systems outsourcing. *International Journal of Business and Systems Research, 3*(2). doi:10.1504/IJBSR.2009.024858

Hair, J. F., Black, C. W., Babin, B. J., Anderson, R. E., & Tatham, R. L. (2006). *Multivariate Data Analysis*. Upper Saddle River, NJ: Prentice-Hall.

Hann, J., & Weber, R. (1996). Information systems planning: a modern and empirical test. *Management Science, 42*(7), 1043–1063. doi:10.1287/mnsc.42.7.1043

Johnson, G., & Scholes, K. (2002). *Exploring Corporate Strategy*. Harlow, UK: Pearson Education, Prentice Hall.

King, W. R. (2006). The critical role of information processing in creating an effective knowledge organization. *Journal of Database Management, 17*(1), 1–15.

Lankford, W. M., & Parsa, F. (1999). Outsourcing: a primer. *Management Decision, 37*(4), 310–316. doi:10.1108/00251749910269357

Porter, M. E. (1985). *Competitive Advantage: Creating and Sustaining Competitive Performance*. The Free Press.

Porter, M. E. (2001). Strategy and the Internet. *Harvard Business Review, 79*(3), 62–78.

Sheehan, N. T. (2002). *Reputation as a Driver in Knowledge-Intensive Service Firms.* Unpublished Doctoral Thesis, Norwegian School of Management, Sandvika.

Stabell, C. B., & Fjeldstad, Ø. D. (1998). Configuring Value for Competitive Advantage: On Chains, Shops and Networks. *Strategic Management Journal, 19*(5), 413–437. doi:10.1002/(SICI)1097-0266(199805)19:5<413::AID-SMJ946>3.0.CO;2-C

Ward, J., & Peppard, J. (2002). *Strategic planning for information systems*. Chichester, UK: Wiley.

Chapter 5
Maturity in Outsourcing Relationships

Stages of growth models have been used widely in both organizational research and information technology management research. According to King and Teo (1997), these models describe a wide variety of phenomena – the organizational life cycle, product life cycle, biological growth, stages of growth in information systems, growth model for integration between business planning and information systems planning, electronic commerce evolution, stages of knowledge management technology, and a number of other interesting developments in time perspectives. These models assume that predictable patterns (conceptualized in terms of stages or levels) exist in the growth of organizations and organizational parts, the sales levels of products, and the growth of living organisms. These stages are (1) sequential in nature, (2) occur as a hierarchical progression that is not easily reversed, and (3) evolve a broad range of organizational activities and structures.

This chapter starts with an introduction to stages of growth models. In the following sections we present the three-stage model for the evolution of IT outsourcing relationships (Gottschalk & Solli-Sæther, 2006). The three stages are labelled cost stage, resource stage, and partnership stage respectively. Theory-based benchmark variables for measuring maturity in IT outsourcing relationships are presented, followed by the stage hypothesis and a description of how benchmark variables are used to indicate characteristics at each stage of growth. Finally in this chapter, we present results from an exploratory study testing the

DOI: 10.4018/978-1-60566-796-6.ch005

stage model. The purpose of this chapter is to develop a framework for improved understanding of the current situation in an IT outsourcing relationship in terms of a specific stage, to develop strategies for moving to a higher stage in the future, and to learn from earlier stage experience.

STAGES OF GROWTH MODELS

Various multistage models have been proposed for organizational evolution over time. For example, Nolan (1979) introduced a model with six stages for information technology maturity in organizations, which later was expanded to nine stages. Earl (2000) suggested a stages of growth model for evolving the e-business, consisting of the following six stages: external communication, internal communication, e-commerce, e-business, e-enterprise, and transformation, while Rao and Metts (2003) describe a stage model for electronic commerce development in small and medium sized enterprises. In the area of knowledge management, Housel and Bell (2001) developed a five level model. In the area of knowledge management systems, Gottschalk (2007) developed a four-stage model applied to knowledge management in law enforcement. Gottschalk and Tolloczko (2007) developed a maturity model for mapping crime in law enforcement, while Gottschalk and Solli-Sæther (2008) developed a maturity model for e-government interoperability. Each of these models identifies certain characteristics that typify firms in different stages of growth.

The concept of stages of growth has been widely employed for many years. Already two decades ago, Kazanjian and Drazin (1989) found that a number of multistage models have been proposed, which assume that predictable patterns exist in the growth of organizations, and that these patterns unfold as discrete time periods best thought of as stages. These models have different distinguishing characteristics. Stages can be driven by the search for new growth opportunities or as a response to internal crises. Some models suggest that organizations progress through stages while others argue that there may be multiple paths through the stages. Kazanjian (1988) applied dominant problems to stages of growth. Dominant problems imply that there is a pattern of primary concerns that firms face for each theorized stage. In criminal organizations, for example, dominant problems can shift from lack of skills to lack of resources to lack of strategy associated with different stages of growth.

Kazanjian and Drazin (1989) argue that either implicitly or explicitly, stages of growth models share a common underlying logic. Organizations undergo transformations in their design characteristics, which enable them to face the new tasks or problems that growth elicits. The problems, tasks or environments may differ from model to model, but almost all suggest that stages emerge in a well-defined sequence, so that the solution of one set of problems or tasks leads to the emergence of a new set of problems and tasks, that the organization must address.

In IT outsourcing relationships it is often a requirement in the contracts that a relatively intimate relationship should be established between the outsourcing company and the outsourcing vendor (Kern & Blois, 2002). The existence of such a relationship may reduce the need for detailed monitoring of the performance of the outsourcing vendor by the outsourcing company. Ongoing relationships may lead to the establishment of trust and perceptions of common interest. The more the outsourcing vendor interacts with the outsourcing company the more comfortable they are likely to feel with each other (Elitzur & Wensley, 1998). As most outsourcing relationships last for several years, it is not unlikely that they develop or transform from one stage to another as time passes by.

This chapter applies cumulative theory that suggests stages of growth over time in organizational development (Frankfort-Nachmias & Nachmias, 2002; Nunnally & Bernstein, 1994). The research methodology applied in is content analysis (Weber, 1990) of outsourcing theories. This chapter uses IT outsourcing related literature and research to develop stages of growth model for IT outsourcing relationships. The model presented in the following sections might serve as a conceptual basis for further studies of this kind of relationship.

STAGE 1: COST STAGE

Initially, IT outsourcing is driven by cost concerns. According to neoclassical economic theory, firms outsource IT to attain cost advantages from assumed economies of scale and scope possessed by vendors (Ang & Straub, 1998). Neoclassical economic theory regards every business organization as a production function (Williamson, 2000), and where their motivation is driven by profit maximization. This means that companies offer products and services to the market where they have a cost or production advantage. They rely on the marketplace where they have disadvantages. According to neoclassical economic theory, companies will justify their sourcing strategy based on evaluating possibilities for production cost savings. Thus, the question whether to outsource, is a question whether the marketplace can produce products and services at a lower price than internal production. In the context of IT outsourcing, a company will keep its IT function internally if this has production cost advantages, and it will outsource when the marketplace can offer production cost savings.

However, IT outsourcing causes additional costs occur that are labeled transaction costs. Transaction costs occur in the exchange between client and vendor. According to transaction cost theory, transaction costs are positively associated with (1) the necessity of investments in durable, specific assets, (2) infrequency of transacting, (3) task complexity and uncertainty, (4) difficulty in measuring task performance; and (5) independencies with other transactions. Hancox and Hackney (2000) interviewed IT managers to find support for the transaction cost theory in IT outsourcing. Many of the features of transaction cost economics could be identified in the outsourcing arrangements.

When entering an IT outsourcing arrangement, vendor and client sign a contract. An outsourcing contract provides a legally bound, institutional framework in which each party's rights, duties, and responsibilities are codified and the goals, policies, and strategies underlying the arrangement are specified. Every outsourcing contract has the purpose of facilitating exchange and preventing opportunism. Luo (2002) examined how contract, cooperation, and performance are associated with each other. He argues that contract and cooperation are not substitutes but complements in relation to performance. A contract alone is insufficient to guide outsourcing evolution and performance. Since outsourcing involves repeated inter-organizational exchanges that become socially embedded over time, cooperation is an important safeguard mechanism mitigating external and internal hazards and overcoming adaptive limits of contracts, as we will see at higher levels of relationship maturity.

In an outsourcing relationship, the cooperating parties engage in an agency relationship defined as a contract under which one organization (the principal) engage another organization (the agent) to perform some service on its behalf which involves delegating some decision-making authority to the agent. Agency theory describes the relationship between the two parties. According to Eisenhardt (1985), agency theory is concerned with resolving two problems that can occur in agency relationships. The first is the agency problem that arises when the desires or goals of the principal and agent conflict, and it is difficult or expensive for the principal to verify what the agent is actually doing. The second is the problem of risk sharing that arises when the principal and agent have different risk preferences (Gonzales, Gasco, & Liopis, 2005). These problems are well known in IT outsourcing. An example might be that the client organization wants to reduce its costs, while the vendor organization wants to maximize profits.

A final theory for the cost stage is the theory of firm boundaries. Firm boundaries – defined as the scope of revenue-sharing arrangements across individuals – reflect trade-offs associated with referral problems, which are problems of matching economic opportunities to individuals' efficiency (Garicano & Hubbard, 2003). A large theoretical literature focuses on the question, 'What determines firms' boundaries?' In our case of IT outsourcing, firms' boundaries are determined by the extent to which there are large markets for specialization. If there are large markets for IT services available from vendors, then a client company will tend to outsource more of its internal IT function.

When an outsourcing relationship has solved all problems at the cost stage, the parties are ready for resource stage. Solving all problems implies that the client achieves intended cost savings, transaction costs are at acceptable level, the contract is successful in preventing opportunistic behavior, principal and agent avoids conflicts and the division of labor between client and vendor works satisfactorily.

STAGE 2: RESOURCE STAGE

The central tenet in resource-based theory is that unique organizational resources of both tangible and intangible nature are the real source of competitive advantage. With resource-based theory, organizations are viewed as a collection of resources that are heterogeneously distributed within and across industries. Outsourcing gives a client organization access to resources in the vendor organization as the vendor handles IT functions for the client. Vendor resources can produce innovation, which is essential for long-term survival of the client. Quinn (2000) argues that the time is right for outsourcing innovation, because demand is growing fast in the global economy, creating a host of new specialist markets sufficiently large to attract innovation.

The value generation potential of an outsourcing relationship consists of three factors: client characteristics, the vendor-client relationship, and vendor characteristics. A key client characteristic is an understanding of how to manage resources that a firm does not own. A key in the vendor-client relationship is formal (contractual) aspect of the relationship. The third factor shaping the outsourcing value proposition is the vendor's own capabilities. From an outsourcing vendor's perspective, there are many potential opportunities and benefits for the client. These opportunities and benefits can be derived from the IT outsourcing vendor's value proposition. Important vendor characteristics include capabilities such as technical competence, understanding the customer's business, and relationship management.

Levina and Ross (2003) stressed the importance of vendor characteristics in terms of the vendor value proposition. The concepts of complementarities and competencies explain that outsourcing vendors can increase productivity and reduce costs on client projects by applying a set of complementary application management competencies. They identified three complementary vendor competencies: IT personnel development, methodology development and dissemination, and customer relationship management.

The value generation potential from vendor resources can be significant for the client. If the vendor has strategic resources, applications of these resources for the client can provide the client organization with sustained competitive advantage. Strategic resources are characterized by being valuable, rare, non-imitable, non-transferable, non-substitutable, combinable, and exploitable (Barney, 2002).

The resource stage is not only characterized by access to vendor resources. Also, the client will focus on internal resources at this stage. Those resources are typically concerned with core competencies. After outsourcing, the client organization will typically focus on and strengthen its core competencies. Core competencies can be defined as the skills that are the determinant resources for a firm's competitive advantage. Quinn (1999) argues that core competencies are not products or 'those things we do relatively well'. They are those activities – usually intellectually based service activities or systems – that the company performs better than any other enterprise. They are the set of skills and systems that a company does at best-in-the-world levels and through which a company creates uniquely high value for customers. According to the theory of core competencies, developing best-in-the-world capabilities is crucial in designing a core competency strategy. Long-term advantage will depend on identifying the next unique combination no one else is exploiting in the marketplace; however, sustainable competitive advantage is strongest if tied to firm-specific capabilities.

When the vendor value proposition is working in terms of successful application of vendor resources for the client organization, and when the client organization is able to work on its core competencies, then the relationship is ready to move from the resource stage to the partnership stage.

STAGE 3: PARTNERSHIP STAGE

Partnership appears to be a less rigorously defined analytical framework than other theories such as transaction costs, agency and core competencies. Indeed, the very word 'partnership' has a more everyday ring to it and is associated with the readily understood characteristics, which may be found in a relationship between two or more parties in a particular context. Partnership's treatment in the IS literature seems largely non-theoretical, perhaps reflecting a wide diversity of practical arrangements and the absence of a single commonly recognized theory. Although the sharing of risk and reward is sometimes mentioned in the IS literature (Tafti, 2005), often the emphasis is on intangibles, such as trust, comfort, understanding, flexibility, cooperation, shared values, goals, and problem solving, good interpersonal relation, and regular communication (Hancox & Hackney, 2000).

Partnership, often referred to as an alliance, has frequently been noted as a major feature of IT outsourcing. Alliances are broadly defined as collaborative efforts between two or more firms in which the firms cooperate in an effort to achieve mutually compatible goals that they could not achieve easily alone (Koh, Ang, & Straub, 2004).

According to relational exchange theory, a partnership is dependent on relational norms. Norms are expectations about behavior that are at least partially shared by a group of decision makers. Norms are important in relational exchange because they provide the governance rules of the game. Relational norms are based on the expectation of mutuality of interest, essentially prescribing stewardship behavior, and are designed to enhance the wellbeing of the relationship as a whole (Lambe, Spekman, & Hunt, 2000). Kern and Blois (2002) have studied norm development in a major IT outsourcing relationship. Their findings suggests: 1) where unusual organizational structure is proposed, management must recognize the possibility that norms dominant within the constituent organizations will not necessarily be compatible, 2) where norms are not compatible the action must be taken through changing management schemes in order to develop appropriate norms, and 3) the development and initialization of new norms takes time. Norm development becomes more salient as the relationship matures.

Figure 1. Critical issues in each stage of maturity in outsourcing relationships

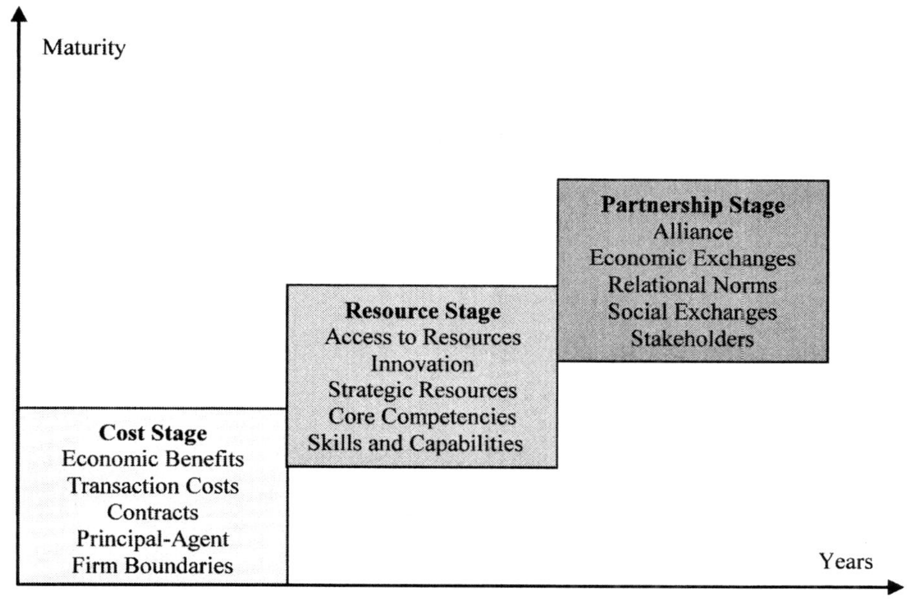

Social exchange theory suggests that each party in an exchange relationship compares the social and economic outcomes from these interactions to those that are available from exchange alternatives, which determines their dependence on the exchange relationship. Positive economic and social outcomes over time increase the partners' trust of each other and commitment to maintaining the exchange relationship (Lambe, Wittmann, & Spekman, 2001).

A final theory that can illustrate the partnership stage is stakeholder theory. Stakeholder theory is concerned with balancing the interests of the stakeholders in an outsourcing relationship. According to Lacity and Willcocks (2000), there are four distinct client IT stakeholder groups and three distinct supplier IT stakeholder groups. The groups identified are customer senior business managers, customer senior IT managers, customer IT staff, customer IT users, and supplier senior managers, supplier account managers, and supplier IT staff. Upholding four principles: 1) honoring agreements, 2) avoiding lying, 3) respecting the autonomy of others, and 4) avoiding harm to other, are necessary precondition for efficient working. And thus, stakeholder theories of the firm establish economic relationships within a general context of moral management.

MODEL STAGES

As illustrated in Figure 1, the cost stage is concerned with high economic benefits, low transaction costs, effective contracts, good principal-agent cooperation, and efficient division of labor from firm boundaries. The resource stage is concerned with access to vendor resources, resources for innovation, strategic resources, and development of core competencies in the client organization in terms of skills and

Table 1. Characteristics of each stage of maturity of IT outsourcing relationships

Stage Characteristics	Cost Stage	Resource Stage	Partnership Stage
BMK1: Economic benefits	**Cost minimization and operational efficiency**	**Business productivity Technology innovation**	**Business benefits Mutual goals**
BMK2: Primary transactions	**Infrastructure**	**Applications**	**Joint investments**
BMK3: Contractual completeness	**Specified obligations Service level agreements**	**Key competence Critical projects Access to resources**	**Profit sharing Personnel exchanges**
BMK4: Vendor behavior control	**Service level agreement Costs**	**Project performance Service quality**	**Strategy implementation**
BMK5: Demarcation of labor	**Procurement**	**Innovation projects**	**Continuous innovation**
BMK6: Core competence management	**Client defines technology requirements and business needs**	**Vendor is regarded as a strategic resource**	**Co-developing business processes**
BMK7: Vendor resource exploitation	**Excellent operations**	**Technology initiatives**	**Complementary capabilities, skills, competences, and methods**
BMK8: Alliance exploitation	**Account manager IT manager**	**Operations manager Division manager**	**Business manager**
BMK9: Relationship exploitation	**Interfirm information sharing**	**Joint planning**	**Relational norms**
BMK10: Social exchange exploitation	**Low**	**Medium**	**High**
BMK11: Stakeholder management	**Economic interests has priority**	**Recognizing a number of stakeholder groups**	**Balancing interests**

capabilities. The third and final partnership stage is concerned with alliance work, economic exchanges, mutual relational norms, social exchanges, and balancing stakeholder interests.

As an outsourcing relationship matures, the maturity model suggests that performance measures develop beyond cost minimization and operational efficiency into business productivity and technology innovation, and further into business benefits and achievement of mutual goals for client and vendor. The outsourcing contract changes focus from specified obligations and service level agreements, to availability of strategic resources, management of key competence and critical projects, to arrangements for profit sharing and personnel exchanges between vendor and client. As suggested by King and Teo (1997), the stages of growth are sequential in nature, occur as a hierarchical progression that is not easily reversed, and involve a broad range of organizational activities and structures.

BENCHMARK VALUES

Benchmark variables in Table 1 indicate theoretical characteristics of each stage of maturity of the IT outsourcing relationship. For example, relationships at Stage 1 can theoretically be expected to conform to values of benchmark variables listed under Stage 1. It is possible for relationships at Stage 1 to have values of benchmark variables applicable to other stages. However, the values of benchmark variables indicate the most likely theoretical characteristics of each stage of integration. The benchmark variables are adapted from Gottschalk and Solli-Sæther (2005). Based on extensive literature review of outsourcing theories, they identified and empirically tested eleven critical success factors for IT outsourcing relationships. These factors are used as the basis for development of benchmark variables. The values of each benchmark variable in each of the three stages are discussed below.

BMK1: Economic Benefit

As shown in Table 1, for Benchmark variable 1 (BMK1), the economic benefit from the relationship varies at the different stages. At stage 1, the outsourcing relationship focuses primarily on cost minimization and operational efficiency. This gradually changes as the relationship matures and vendor resources are leveraged towards increased client business productivity and technology innovation (Stage 2). At Stage 3, there is a joint focus on business benefits and mutual goals.

BMK2: Primary Transactions

Table 1 shows how the primary transactions of the relationship (BMK2). In Stage 1 primary transactions are related to infrastructure operations. Typically better-cost performance can be obtained when vendor take care of IT infrastructure operations. In Stage 2, the vendor is regarded as a resource and is likely to take care of business applications. As client and vendor do joint investments in infrastructure and business applications, they mature into the partnership stage (Stage 3).

BMK3: Contractual Completeness

Key IT outsourcing contractual issues are such as service levels, transfer of assets, staffing, pricing and payment, warranty and liability, dispute resolution mechanisms, termination, intellectual property matters, and information security (Lee, 1996). The focus on contractual issues changes as the relationship matures (BMK3). In Stage 1 the two parties focus heavily on specified obligations and service levels. As agreed-upon operational performance is established the relationship move towards the resource stage, where project performance and overall service quality is the main focus (Stage 2). As the relationship matures cooperation becomes more prominent overcoming adaptive limits of contract. In Stage 3 contract and cooperation are associated with profit sharing and personnel exchange.

BMK4: Vendor Behavior Control

As the outsourcing relationship matures, the mechanisms for vendor behavior control changes (BMK4) from a structured focus on operational efficiency to a more unstructured concern for the relationship's impact on strategic direction. In Stage 1 this means a strong focus on measurement of service levels and performance criteria. The emphasis gradually shifts to overall service quality (Stage 2). Ultimately, the performance criteria should be on the long-term impact on the organization (Stage 3).

BMK5: Demarcation of Labor

Theorists have proposed that firms' boundaries reflect the division of labor across individuals (Garicano & Hubbard, 2003). Whether a set of task is organized within one or multiple firms depends on the extent to which individuals specialize. Demarcation of labor changes as the relationship matures (BMK5). In Stage 1, the division of labor between the two contractual parties is specialized following the scope of the contract. To secure economic opportunities of the deal, the guiding principle is following that of procurement In Stage 2, specialization is no longer a hindrance to work together in innovative project. Finally, the parties work close together doing continuous innovation (Stage 3), but with different specialization and job design.

BMK6: Core Competence Management

Core competence management is the sixth benchmark variable (BMK6) in Table 1. Outsourcing place responsibilities for the IT function in the hands of the constituent most capable of performing these successfully. At Stage 1 in the relationship the client defines business needs, whereas the vendor is regarded as a contractual partner necessary to fulfill them. In IT outsourcing client companies transfer IT assets and employees to vendor companies. These employees formally leave their organization and get transplanted into the vendor company, which employs them and offers their services back to the original employer for a service fee. As these employees previously worked for client organization they have developed competencies and skills about client core competence (Sommer, 2003). When this competence is recognized as valuable, rare, and appropriable for client organization, they become a strategic resource (Stage 2). As relationship maturity continues to grow client and vendor are co-developing business processes (Stage 3).

BMK7: Vendor Resource Exploitation

Outsourcing is a strategic decision (Perrons & Platts, 2004), which can be used to fill gaps in the firm's resources and capabilities (Grover, Cheon, & Teng, 1996). The level of exploiting vendor resources is the basis for the seventh benchmark variable (BMK7) in Table 2 In the first stage, the obligation of vendor resources is to secure excellent operations (Stage 1). As the relationship matures in Stage 2, vendor resources make technology initiatives to the client. In resource-based theory firms are considered to be highly heterogeneous, and the bundles of resources available to each firm are different. At Stage 3, the vendor represents a set of complementary capabilities, skills, competences, and methods.

BMK8: Alliance Exploitation

Alliances are broadly defined as collaborative efforts between two or more firms in which the firm pool their resources in an effort to achieve mutually compatible goals that they cold not achieve easily alone (Lambe, Spekman, & Hunt, 2002). IT outsourcing relationships are collaborative in nature, and can be classified as a partnership or alliance. This benchmark variable (BMK8) identifies the level of partnership manager. At Stage 1, the managers involved are typically vendor account managers and client IT managers. The objective of these managers is most likely focused around services deliveries and costs. As the relationship matures, vendor operation managers and client division mangers get involved to make sure business needs are fulfilled (Stage 2). Finally at Stage 3, business managers get involved to ensure that any tangible or intangible resource is available for use.

Table 2. Characteristics of respondents (n = 116)

Measure	Items	Frequencies	Percent
Value creation logic	Value chain	72	62.1%
	Value shop	29	25.0%
	Value network	15	12.9%
Annual sales ($ Million)	Below 100	19	16.4%
	100 – 199	31	26.7%
	200 – 299	15	12.9%
	300 – 399	10	8.6%
	400 – 499	8	6.9%
	500 – 999	9	7.7%
	Above 1000	8	6.9%
	Missing data	16	13.8%
Number of employees	Less than 200	45	38.8%
	200 – 499	35	30.2%
	500 – 999	13	11.2%
	1,000 – 1,999	10	8.6%
	2,000 – 2,999	7	6.0%
	Above 3,000	6	5.2%
Respondents hierarchical level	Vice President/CFO	10	8.6%
	Director (of Finance)	53	45.7%
	Manager (of Finance)	38	32.8%
	Controller/Accountant	8	6.9%
	Others	7	6.0%

BMK9: Relationship Exploitation

A key to determine how efficiently the relationship is carried out lies in the relational norms between the client and vendor (BMK9). At Stage 1, interfirm information sharing is established. Then, at Stage 2 the parties engage in joint planning. And finally in a mature relationship the parties have developed and use relational norms that can simplify and smooth processes and activities between them (Stage 3).

BMK10: Social Exchange Exploitation

Social exchange exploitation is the tenth benchmark variable (BMK10) in Table 1 The need for social exchange is created by the scarcity of resources, prompting actors to engage one another to obtain valuable input. This is voluntary action of individuals that are motivated by return they are expected to bring and typically in fact bring from others (Das & Teng, 2002). In the first stage of the relationship, social exchange is generally low (Stage 1). Interpersonal exchanges that are not purely economic, is not carried out. However, as the relationship matures resources individuals recognize the value of non-economic exchange (Stage 2). At Stage 3 social exchange is high, and is recognized as one important factor not to misperceive each other.

BMK11: Stakeholder Management

Firms have responsibilities to stakeholders for moral reasons, and there is no priority of one set of interests over another (BMK11). All stakeholder groups are presumed to have significant differences in expectations and goals regarding IT outsourcing. At Stage 1, economic interests override other interests. As the maturity increases, different stakeholder groups are recognized (Stage 2). In Stage 3, the relationship is upholding the interest of different stakeholder groups with the principles of moral management.

The benchmark variables in Table 1 indicate theoretical characteristics of each stage of maturity of the IT outsourcing relationship. If the eleven benchmark variables are to be successful in classifying maturity of IT outsourcing relationship, empirical evidence should conform closely to the proposed conceptual formulations in Table 1. For example, in terms of economic benefits (BMK1), parties in stage 1 should generally describe their relationship as focused on 'cost minimization and operational efficiency', and parties in stage 2 should generally describe their relationship as focused on 'technology innovation', and parties in stage 3 should generally describe their relationships as focused on 'business benefits and mutual goals', according to the patterns for BMK1 in Table 1.

THE STAGE HYPOTHESIS

In the literature models have been labeled maturity models, development models and stage models. The basic idea is the same: An evolution in terms of aggregation and accumulation. What we are suggesting here by means of the levels of growth model with benchmark variables is a stage hypothesis. A stage model is based on a number of assumptions and that is why it is called a stage hypothesis. It assumes that predictable patterns (conceptualized in terms of stages) exist in the growth of a phenomenon such as maturity in an IT outsourcing relationship. It assumes that stages are sequential in nature, occur as a hierarchical progression that is not easily reversed, and evolve a broad range of organizational activities and structures (King & Teo, 1997).

The following level in the maturity model does not only represent a progression and an improvement when compared to the previous level. The next level also involves new kinds of challenges for the organization. The kinds of problems to be solved at the next level are different from those problems solved at the previous level. Problems, challenges and solutions change as an organization moves from one level to the next in Figure 1.

Benchmark variables should involve activities and structures that are characteristic for each stage of maturity. Relationships at Stage 1 can theoretically be expected to conform to values of benchmark variables listed under Stage 1. It is possible for relationships at Stage 1 to have values of benchmark variables applicable to other stages. However, the values of benchmark variables indicate the most likely theoretical characteristics of each stage of maturity in IT outsourcing relationships.

The stage hypothesis suggested here might be formulated in two parts:

- *Hypothesis 1:* Values of benchmark variables for maturity in IT outsourcing relationships will significantly correspond with their conceptual stage formulations given (in Table 1).
- *Hypothesis 2:* The stages of maturity in IT outsourcing relationships show predictable patterns of growth from cost stage, to resource stage, and into partnership stage.

Figure 2. Benchmark variables are used to indicate characteristics at each stage level

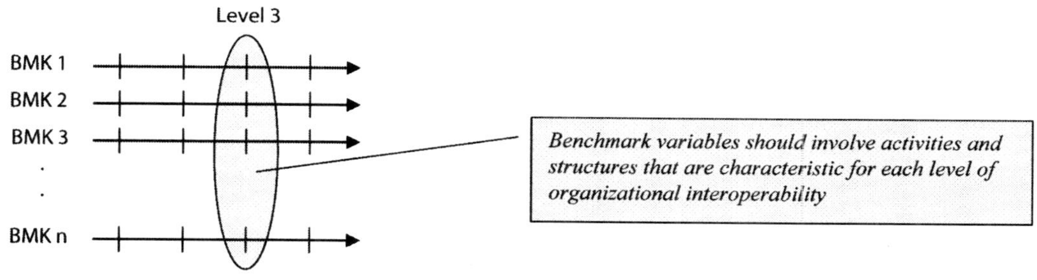

The stage hypothesis is based on the following implications when moving from one stage to the next stage. Stating that organizations suffer under lack of maturity in IT outsourcing relationships means that maturity research efforts should be spent in finding out which level of maturity an organization might strive for. To guide developmental energies at lower levels of orientation, which provide additional understanding of the transitional events, individuals and organizations have to accumulate experience in order to move and grow from one stage of development to the next. The stages of growth are sequential in nature, occur as a hierarchical progression that is not easily reversed, and involve a broad range of organizational activities and structures.

The evolving maturity model of IT outsourcing relationships assumes predictable patterns of growth. When an outsourcing relationship has solved all problems at the cost stage, the parties are ready for resource stage. Solving all problems in the cost stage implies that the client achieves intended cost savings, transaction costs are at acceptable level, the contract is successful in preventing opportunistic behavior, principal and agent avoids conflicts and the division of labor between client and vendor works satisfactorily. When the vendor value proposition is working in terms of successful application of vendor resources for the client organization, and when the client organization is able to work on its core competencies, then the relationship is ready to move from the resource stage to the partnership stage.

Benchmark variables are used to indicate characteristics at each stage of growth as illustrated in Figure 2. Measurement is carried out using Guttman scales. The purpose is to identify the average level at which the organization is currently. A wide distribution of answers might indicate that the organization has a very unclear understanding of what and why efforts currently are underway in their relationship with other organizations. Two co-operating parties might compare their results in terms of level and benchmark values.

For many outsourcing relationships, it is crucial and critical to be moving from one level to the next level:

- Efforts should be spent finding out which level of maturity the organization should strive for.
- Individuals and organizations have to accumulate experience in order to move and grow from one level of development to the next.
- The levels of maturity are sequential in nature, they occur as a hierarchical progression that is not easily reversed, and involve a broad range of organizational activities and structures.

EXPLORATORY STUDY OF CLIENT COMPANIES

In the following, results from an empirical test of the three stage maturity model for IT outsourcing relationships is presented (Solli-Sæther & Gottschalk, 2008). Although past research has identified key elements in customer-supplier outsourcing relationships (Lacity & Willcocks, 2000), and considered the role of norms in outsourcing relationships (Kern & Blois, 2002), empirical research focusing specifically on the level of maturity is relatively sparse. This study extends existing research by validating the maturity model for IT outsourcing relationships. The underlying logic of most stages of growth models is that organizations undergo transformations in their characteristics when moving from one stage to the next, enabling them to face new tasks or problems that growth elicits (Kazanjian & Drazin, 1989).

Research Methodology

The sample of this survey comprised the 657 largest Norwegian firms, all of them with turnover of more than 500 MNOK (about $80 million) in year 2005. The sample was selected because firms listed as medium and large in size are likely to have more experience with outsourcing relationships than smaller firms. A letter was sent to the companies' senior financial executive, asking them to participate in the survey by following a link to an electronic questionnaire prepared using the web-based tool ConfirmIt. A follow-up letter was sent about one month after the initial letter. Useable responses were returned by 116 firms (17.6%). A summary of the characteristics of respondents is shown in Table 2. Respondents came from a wide range of industries with most coming from manufacturing firms (value creation logic as chain). The annual sales revenue was widely distributed, from anticipated $80 million to above $10 billion. The number of employees in each firm varied. There was a predominance of firms below 1,000 employees. Around 54.3% of the respondents were senior executives at the director level or higher.

In the data collection instrument, the stages of maturity of the IT outsourcing relationship that are presented in Figure 1 were described. Respondents were asked to indicate their firm's path of evolution as well as the stage that best described their firm's current level of maturity. This type of self-typing paragraph approach has been used in organizational research before (e.g., King & Teo, 1997). In addition, for each benchmark variable, three levels of maturity were described corresponding to the values for that benchmark variable for the three stages. Respondents were asked to select the characteristic that most closely described their companies' present situation. A similar methodology has been used by King & Teo (1997) in their empirical testing of benchmark variables for integration of business planning and information systems planning.

The current maturity model was measured by asking respondents to place a check mark beside one of the three descriptions of maturity level. We tried to make the descriptions and conceptual representations as clear and concise as possible. We evaluated the descriptions through discussions with outsourcing practitioners in two companies. None of our discussion partners had difficulties understanding or distinguishing between phases of maturity.

Table 3 shows the number of responding organizations currently operating at each stage of maturity. Generally, cost stage occurs most often (52.6%), followed by resource stage (39.7%) and partnership stage (7.8%). This was not unexpected as the model assumes predictable patterns of growth, where organizations are likely to start solving problems in the cost stage before moving on to the resource stage and the partnership stage. Very few companies indicated that they had reached full integration. Note that in stage 3 the sample size is relatively small.

Table 3. Distribution of stages of maturity

Maturity	Number	Percent
Cost stage (stage 1)	61	52.6%
Resource stage (stage 2)	46	39.7%
Partnership stage (stage 3)	9	7.8%
Total	116	100%

Validating the Benchmark Variables

When testing hypotheses, values of benchmark variables are expected to correspond statistically with conceptual formulations. In this approach, the Kruskal-Wallis test for 3 or more independent samples (Kruskal & Wallis, 1952) was applied. As a reminder, the assumptions of the one-way ANOVA for independent samples are: that the scale on which the dependent variable is measured has the properties of an equal interval scale; that the k samples are independently and randomly drawn from the source population(s); that the source population(s) can be reasonably supposed to have a normal distribution; and that the k samples have approximately equal variances. Unlike the parametric independent group ANOVA, the Kruskal-Wallis test is non-parametric making no assumptions about the distribution of the data (e.g., normality) (Sidney & Castellan, 1988).

To assess the effects of the eleven benchmark variables, companies where subdivided into 3 groups based on scores from a textual description of their outsourcing relationship maturity. These three groups were presented in Table 3. As we expect maturity level to grow as companies gain experience with outsourcing, it is not reasonable to assume the underlying source population to be normally distributed. In this case, an appropriate non-parametric alternative to the one-way independent-samples ANOVA can be found in the Kruskal-Wallis test. The null hypothesis for the comparison of three independent groups is that the samples come from identical populations. Notice that the hypothesis makes no assumptions about the distribution of the populations. The test statistics for the Kruskal-Wallis test is H. If H exceeds the critical value for H at some significance level it means that there is evidence to reject the null hypothesis in favor of the alternative hypothesis.

For benchmark variables 1, 2, 4, 6 and 7, we found significant differences between group means (Kruskal-Wallis test, P is less than 0.05). The samples of benchmark variable economic benefit (BMK1) come from different population (H=15.178, 2 d.f., P=0.001), and it has increasing group mean for the three samples. This fits well with our hypothesis of increasing maturity from cost minimization and operational efficiency (stage 1), through business productivity and technology innovation (stage 2), and finally business benefits and mutual goals (stage 3).

The samples of benchmark variable vendor behavior control (BMK4) comes from different samples (H=10.169, 2 d.f., P=0.006), and we see an increasing group mean from service level agreement (stage 1), through project performance (stage 2), and finally strategy implementation (stage 3). Likewise, the samples of benchmark variable vendor resource exploitation (BMK7) comes from different samples (H=9.067, 2 d.f., P=0.011), with increasing group mean from excellent operations (stage 1), through technology initiatives (stage 2), and finally complementarities (stage 3).

For benchmark variable primary transactions (BMK2) we find three samples (H=10.762, 2 d.f., P=0.005). Looking at group means, we can see the path of growth is not according to our hypothesis.

Group mean of application (stage 2) has higher value than joint investments (stage 3). For benchmark variable core competence management (BMK6) we also find three different samples (H=6.330, 2 d.f., P=0.042). We found co-developing business processes (stage 3) as the group mean with lowest value.

Thus, our set of benchmark variables was not successful. They were all derived from outsourcing theories as listed by Gottschalk and Solli-Sæther (2006). Only 3 out of 11 benchmark variables were found to support our hypothesis. First, in terms of economic benefits (BMK1), cost minimization and operational efficiency belonged to stage 1, while business productivity and technology innovation belonged to stage 2, and business benefits and mutual goals belonged to stage 3. Second, vendor behavior control (BMK4) was statistically significant by cost stage being associated with service level agreement and cost, resource stage being associated with project performance and service quality, and partnership being associated with strategy implementation. Finally, vendor resource exploitation (BMK7) was characterized by excellent operations at the cost stage, technology initiatives at the resource stage, and complementary capabilities, skills, competencies, and methods at the partnership stage.

For benchmark variable primary transactions (BMK2) and benchmark variable core competence management (BMK6) we found three different samples. Looking at group means the path of growth was not according to our hypothesis. Explanations for this counter-intuitive result can be found in construct, formulation, as well as measurement errors. Hence, our first research hypothesis found only support in 3 out of 11 benchmark variables, making it important in future research to identify alternative benchmark variables that might supplement the three variables confirmed in this research.

Analyzing hypothesis two, where the maturity model suggests predictable patterns of growth, we asked respondents to indicate (textually) the development of the relationship in terms of duration at each stage and the reason for changing from previous stage. Findings from this question were somewhat difficult to analyze, as very few respondents had a clear statement regarding duration of each stage. Companies at the cost stage reported they were still focusing on costs, and they will continue to do so for a long time. Reasons for change from previous stage were not applicable to these companies. Companies at the resource stage reported availability of resources and competence as the most important reason for change. Other reasons for change included more complex IT, exploiting vendor resources, and strategic decision to focus on internal core competencies. Although companies had changed their main focus after a few years at cost stage, costs were still important as they moved into the resource stage. Only a few companies reported they were at partnership stage (see Table 3). The reasons for change were reported as convenience, natural progression in a long lasting relationship, and vendor experience.

Overall, statements supplied by responding companies provided limited support for the stages of growth model. Reasons may be found in both reality and our research design. Future empirical research might rephrase some of our questions into measuring more closely intentions and perceptions.

Despite limited support for the stage model, some policy implications can be derived from our research. First, economic benefits should always be visible and achieved in outsourcing relationships. It will not be acceptable for partners to argue that a relationship is "strategic" or "long-term" to avoid the topic of how much it actually costs. Next, an outsourcing relationship should always strive to have a content of more than accounting and service level agreements. The ambition should be to explore resources available to the IT service provision, before entering the stage of "marriage" in terms of mutual long-term dependency. In this evolution, leadership will be of critical importance (Andresen, Ekker, & Gottschalk, 2007), as well as creativity (Dean, Fashing, Gottschalk, & Solli-Sæther, 2008) and culture (Glomseth & Gottschalk, 2008).

Managerial and Research Implications

The conceptual framework of the maturity model for IT outsourcing relationships (Gottschalk & Solli-Sæther, 2006) has been proposed for organizational evolution over time. According to Lavoie and Culbert (1978), organization development, to be effective, should link with the progressively mature reasoning processes which characterize managers working within increasingly higher stages in the evolution of an organization. To guide developmental energies at lower levels of orientation, which provide additional understanding of the transitional events, individuals and organizations have to accumulate experience in order to move and grow from one stage of development to the next. As suggested by King and Teo (1997), the stages of growth are sequential in nature, occur as a hierarchical progression that is not easily reversed, and involve a broad range of organizational activities and structures.

When client and vendor companies enter an outsourcing relationship, client companies tend to focus on economic benefits. Economic benefits are initially measured in terms of cost minimization and operational efficiency, evolving into business productivity and technology innovation, and ending in business benefits and mutual goals. Accordingly, companies move from the cost stage, via the resource stage to the partnership stage. This result was empirically supported in the reported research.

Three benchmark variables found support in our empirical study. First in terms of economic benefits, cost minimization and operational efficiency belonged to stage 1, while business productivity and technology innovation belonged to stage 2, and business benefits and mutual goals belonged to stage 3. Second, vendor behavior control was statistically significant by cost stage being associated with service level agreement and cost, resource stage being associated with project performance and service quality, and partnership being associated with strategy implementation. Finally, vendor resource exploitation was characterized by excellent operations at the cost stage, technology initiatives at the resource stage, and complementary capabilities, skills, competencies, and methods at the partnership stage.

However, most of the benchmark variables in this research as well as the progression model suggested, found limited support in our empirical material. Future research will have to carefully evaluate the stage model, benchmark variables as well as measurement issues concerned with stages of growth.

CONCLUSION

Based on interpretations of relevant organizational and managerial theories as discussed in Chapter 2, a three-stage maturity model for IT outsourcing relationships was developed. The purpose of the model is both to understand the current situation in the relationship in terms of a specific stage and to develop strategies for moving to a higher stage in the future. The first stage is the cost stage. This stage is based on transaction cost theory, neoclassical economic theory, contractual theory, theory of firm boundaries, and agency theory. The second stage is the resource stage. This stage is based on core competencies theory and resource-based theory. The third and final stage is the partnership stage, which is based on partnership and alliance theory, relational exchange theory, stakeholder theory, and social exchange theory.

Managing successful IT outsourcing relationships depends on an understanding of the relationship state and development. The proposed maturity model for IT outsourcing relationship can help both clients and vendors in outsourcing relationships understand both current state and future direction of development in their relationship. If the relationship is at the cost stage, both parties must accept a cost focus. It will be damaging to the relationship if the client is still cost focused, while the vendor is appealing to alliance and partnership attention. To be successful, both parties must agree to move on to higher relationship stages. If the client has economic problems and continues paying main attention to costs, the vendor has no other choice but to respond to cost issues. If the vendor invites the client into a partnership with mutual new gains, the client has no other choice but to respond to this invitation.

REFERENCES

Andresen, R., Ekker, K., & Gottschalk, P. (2007). Critical success factors from outsourcing theories as determinants of leadership roles in IT outsourcing projects. *International Journal of Management and Enterprise Development*, *4*(4), 477–487. doi:10.1504/IJMED.2007.013158

Ang, S., & Straub, D. W. (1998). Production and Transaction Economics and IS Outsourcing: A study of the U.S. Banking Industry. *MIS Quarterly*, *22*(4), 535–552. doi:10.2307/249554

Barney, J. B. (2002). *Gaining and Sustaining Competitive Advantage*. Upper Saddle River, NJ: Prentice Hall.

Das, T. K., & Teng, B.-S. (2002). Alliance Constellations: A Social Exchange Perspective. *Academy of Management Review*, *27*(3), 445–456. doi:10.2307/4134389

Dean, G., Fashing, I. A., Gottschalk, P., & Solli-Sæther, H. (2008). Investigative thinking and creativity: an empirical study of police detectives in Norway. *International Journal of Innovation and Learning*, *5*(2), 170–185. doi:10.1504/IJIL.2008.016763

Earl, M. J. (2000). Evolving the E-business. *Business Strategy Review*, *11*(2), 33–38. doi:10.1111/1467-8616.00135

Eisenhardt, K. M. (1985). Control: organizational and economic approaches. *Management Science*, *31*(2), 134–149. doi:10.1287/mnsc.31.2.134

Elitzur, R., & Wensley, A. (1998). Game Theory and IS Outsourcing Contracts. In L. P. Willcocks & M. C. Lacity (Eds.), *Strategic Sourcing of Information Systems. Perspectives and Practices*. Chichester, UK: John Wiley & Sons.

Frankfort-Nachmias, C., & Nachmias, D. (2002). *Research Methods in the Social Sciences* (Fifth Ed.). London: Arnold.

Garicano, L., & Hubbard, T. N. (2003). Firms' Boundaries and the Division of Labor: Empirical Strategies. *Journal of the European Economic Association*, *1*(2/3), 495–502. doi:10.1162/154247603322391134

Glomseth, R., & Gottschalk, P. (2008). Predictors of police officers' involvement: an empirical study of occupational culture in the Norwegian antiterror police. *International Journal of Management and Enterprise Development*, *5*(2), 251–263. doi:10.1504/IJMED.2008.016975

Gonzales, R., Gasco, J., & Liopis, J. (2005). Information systems outsourcing risks: a study of large firms. *Industrial Management & Data Systems*, *105*(1), 45–61. doi:10.1108/02635570510575180

Gottschalk, P. (2007). *Knowledge Management in Law Enforcement: Technologies and Techniques*. Hershey, PA: Idea Group Publishing.

Gottschalk, P., & Solli-Sæther, H. (2005). Critical success factors from IT outsourcing theories: an empirical study. *Industrial Management & Data Systems, 105*(5), 685–702. doi:10.1108/02635570510606941

Gottschalk, P., & Solli-Sæther, H. (2006). Maturity model for IT outsourcing relationships. *Industrial Management & Data Systems, 106*(2), 200–212. doi:10.1108/02635570610649853

Gottschalk, P., & Solli-Sæther, H. (2008). Stages of e-government interoperability. *Electronic Government, an International Journal, 5*(3), 310-320.

Gottschalk, P., & Tolloczko, P. (2007). Maturity model for mapping crime in law enforcement. *Electronic Government, an International Journal, 4*(1), 59-67.

Grover, V., Cheon, M. J., & Teng, J. T. C. (1996). The Effect of Service Quality and Partnership on the Outsourcing of Information Systems Functions. *Journal of Management Information Systems, 12*(4), 89–116.

Hancox, M., & Hackney, R. (2000). IT outsourcing: frameworks for conceptualizing practice and perception. *Information Systems Journal, 10*(3), 217–237. doi:10.1046/j.1365-2575.2000.00082.x

Housel, T., & Bell, A. H. (2001). *Measuring and managing knowledge*. Boston: MacGraw-Hill Irwin.

Kazanjian, R. K. (1988). Relation of dominant problems to stages of growth in technology-based new ventures. *Academy of Management Journal, 31*(2), 257–279. doi:10.2307/256548

Kazanjian, R. K., & Drazin, R. (1989). An empirical test of a stage of growth progression model. *Management Science, 35*(12), 1489–1503. doi:10.1287/mnsc.35.12.1489

Kern, T., & Blois, K. (2002). Norm development in outsourcing relationship. *Journal of Information Technology, 17*(1), 32–42. doi:10.1080/02683960210137174

Kern, T., & Willcocks, L. P. (2002). Exploring relationship in information technology outsourcing: the interaction approach. *European Journal of Information Systems, 11*(1), 3–19. doi:10.1057/palgrave/ejis/3000415

King, W. R., & Teo, T. S. H. (1997). Integration Between Business Planning and Information Systems Planning: Validating a Stage Hypothesis. *Decision Sciences, 28*(2), 279–308. doi:10.1111/j.1540-5915.1997.tb01312.x

Koh, C., Ang, S., & Straub, D. W. (2004). IT Outsourcing Success: A Psychological Contract Perspective. *Information Systems Research, 15*(4), 356–373. doi:10.1287/isre.1040.0035

Kruskal, W., & Wallis, A. (1952). Use of ranks in one-criterion variance analysis. *Journal of the American Statistical Association, 47*(260), 583–621. doi:10.2307/2280779

Lacity, M. C., & Willcocks, L. P. (2000). Relationships in IT Outsourcing: A Stakeholder Perspective. In R. W. Zmud (Ed.), *Framing the Domains of IT Management: Projecting the Future Through the Past*. Cincinnati, OH: Pinnaflex Educational Resources.

Lambe, C. J., Spekman, R. E., & Hunt, S. D. (2000). Interimistic Relational Exchange: Conceptualization and Propositional Development. *Journal of the Academy of Marketing Science*, *28*(2), 212–225. doi:10.1177/0092070300282003

Lambe, C. J., Spekman, R. E., & Hunt, S. D. (2002). Alliance Competence, Resources, and Alliance Success: Conceptualization, Measurement, and Initial Test. *Journal of the Academy of Marketing Science*, *30*(2), 141–158. doi:10.1177/03079459994399

Lambe, C. J., Wittmann, C. M., & Spekman, R. E. (2001). Social Exchange Theory and Research on Business-to-Business Relational Exchange. *Journal of Business-To-Business Marketing*, *8*(3), 1–36. doi:10.1300/J033v08n03_01

Lavoie, D., & Culbert, S. A. (1978). Stages in organization and development. *Human Relations*, *31*(5), 417–438. doi:10.1177/001872677803100503

Lee, M. K. O. (1996). IT outsourcing contracts: practical issues for management. *Industrial Management & Data Systems*, *96*(1), 15–20. doi:10.1108/02635579610107684

Levina, N., & Ross, J. W. (2003). From the Vendor's Perspective: Exploring the Value Proposition in Information Technology Outsourcing. *MIS Quarterly*, *27*(3), 331–364.

Luo, Y. (2002). Contract, cooperation, and performance in international joint ventures. *Strategic Management Journal*, *23*(10), 903–919. doi:10.1002/smj.261

Nolan, R. L. (1979). Managing the crisis in data processing. *Harvard Business Review*, *57*(2), 115–116.

Nunnally, J. C., & Bernstein, I. H. (1994). *Psychometric theory* (Third Ed.). New York: McGraw-Hill.

Perrons, R. K., & Platts, K. (2004). The role of clockspeed in outsourcing decisions for new technologies: insights from the prisoner's dilemma. *Industrial Management & Data Systems*, *104*(7), 624–632. doi:10.1108/02635570410550287

Quinn, J. B. (1999). Strategic Outsourcing: Leveraging Knowledge Capabilities. *Sloan Management Review*, *40*(4), 9–21.

Quinn, J. B. (2000). Outsourcing Innovation: The New Engine of Growth. *Sloan Management Review*, *41*(4), 13–28.

Rao, S. S., & Metts, G. (2003). Electronic commerce development in small and medium sized enterprises: A stage model and its implications. *Business Process Management*, *9*(1), 11–32. doi:10.1108/14637150310461378

Sidney, S., & Castellan, N. J. J. (1988). *Nonparametric Statistics for the Behavioral Sciences*. New York: McGraw-Hill.

Solli-Sæther, H., & Gottschalk, P. (2008). Maturity in IT outsourcing relationships: an exploratory study of client companies. *Industrial Management & Data Systems*, *108*(5), 635–649. doi:10.1108/02635570810876769

Sommer, R. (2003). Business process flexibility: a driver for outsourcing. *Industrial Management & Data Systems*, *105*(5), 549–560.

Tafti, M. H. A. (2005). Risk factors associated with offshore IT outsourcing. *Industrial Management & Data Systems*, *105*(5), 549–560. doi:10.1108/02635570510599940

Weber, R. P. (1990). *Basic Content Analysis* (2nd Ed.). Newbury Park, NY: Sage Publications.

Williamson, O. E. (2000). The New Institutional Economics: Taking Stock, Looking Ahead. *Journal of Economic Literature*, *38*(3), 595–613.

Chapter 6
Costs, Benefits, and Risks

Managing costs successfully requires more than traditional cost accounting. It requires an understanding of cost-influencing factors based on cost-explaining theories, such as production and transaction economics, hidden costs, and contract termination costs. Managing IT outsourcing successfully implies that costs are not judged in isolation. Rather costs are compared to benefits, before judgments on cost level and development occur. In this chapter, we discuss production and transaction economics, hidden costs and contract termination costs, and we will also take a look at benefits and risk behavior.

PRODUCTION AND TRANSACTION ECONOMIES

The neo-classical economic perspective of a firm regards an organization as a production function motivated by profit-maximization. The choice of alternative IT sourcing arrangements is thus treated as a traditional make-or-buy decision, hinging on efficiency considerations of production costs savings or operational advantage. Seeking economic efficiency, firms will attempt to obtain all factors of production at the lowest possible price to achieve the least costly methods of operations. From this theoretical standpoint of production economic efficiency, the decision to outsource IS services are determined by the

DOI: 10.4018/978-1-60566-796-6.ch006

relative production costs of market versus internal operations. Since IT providers may reap economics of scale via specialization or possess special skills, knowledge or technology in managing and operating IT, we would expect that the greater the production cost advantage of IT service-providers, the more likely the firm will outsource its IS services (Ang, 1993).

Transaction cost economics extends the neo-classical economic perspective of the firm by contending that market transactions are not frictionless. Transaction costs are those costs incurred to ensure proper execution of the contracting process. Transaction costs include the costs of creating and maintaining an exchange relationship, that is, the effort in negotiating, writing, monitoring, and enforcing contracts between buyers and their suppliers. Although outsourcing may yield production cost savings by exploiting scale economies in outsourcing, additional costs in the form of transaction costs are incurred when a firm enters into an outsourcing relationship with a service provider. Accordingly, transaction cost economics posit that, in addition to production cost efficiencies, transaction cost efficiencies must be considered in evaluating alternative organization schemes. From the transaction cost perspective, economic activities are governed by the market, hierarchies, or a hybrid form. Transaction cost economics posits that sourcing decisions for IS services are based on transaction costs. For example, even if a particular external IT service-provider can provide IT operational services at the most competitive price, if the same provider requires a great deal of supervision and monitoring during the course of the contract, the advantages of a cheaper price may be eroded by the excessive monitoring costs incurred by the firm. Here, excessive transaction costs can cause market failure. Thus, as market exchanges and firms lose their production cost advantage to transaction diseconomies, firms would turn to internal sourcing to meet their needs. Therefore, we would expect that the higher the transaction costs with IT service-providers, the less likely the firm will outsource its IS services (Ang, 1993).

Transaction cost theory maintains that the organization of economic activity depends on balancing production economics, such as scale, against the cost of transacting. Transactions are here the exchanges of goods and services between economic actors, who are technologically separate units, inside and/or outside the organization (Williamson, 1981). The analysis of transactions focuses on achieving efficiency in their administration. In this perspective, organizational success depends on managing transactions efficiently. Organizations exist to mediate the economic transactions among members inside and/or outside the organization. The transaction cost approach offers a method of evaluating the relative advantages of the different internal and external organization forms for handling transactions. This theory also provides an excellent framework for analyzing the outsourcing options, since the essential choice here is between using an outsourcing service provider (a market mechanism) and providing in-house services (an organizational hierarchy). First, the theory seems to be very useful for investigating the outsourcing option as an economic reorganization of IT departments. Second, the theory appears to be useful for formulating an action plan to reduce transaction cost and thereby improves the benefit one can realize through outsourcing (Grover, Teng, & Cheon, 1998).

A focus on comparative economic theories and models can improve our ability to explain outsourcing within the larger context of business strategy and environment. Specifically, productions cost, transaction cost and financial slack often influence the outsourcing decision (Ang & Straub, 1998):

- *Production cost advantage.* Neo-classical economics regards any business organization as a production function motivated by profit maximization. Organizations provide goods and services to markets where they have cost advantages and rely on the marketplace for goods and services in which they have comparative cost disadvantages. Neo-classical economics predicts that firms justify sourcing options based on production economies. In terms of production economies, acquiring goods and services is treated as an economic make-or-buy decision – a decision that compares production costs of internal operations with the price offered in the marketplace. In the context of IS, a firm will choose to outsource or insource based on the comparative costs of internalizing IS versus the price it has to pay vendors for the same IS services. Production economies suggest that the higher the comparative production cost advantage offered through IT outsourcing, the greater is the degree of IT outsourcing.

- *Transaction cost advantage*. Transaction cost economics extends the neo-classical economic perspective of the firm by recognizing the significance of transaction costs in any market exchange. Transaction costs refer to the effort, time, and costs incurred in searching, creating, negotiating, monitoring, and enforcing a service contract between buyers and suppliers. Transaction costs can erode comparative advantages in production costs of vendors. When a firm has to incur substantial effort and costs in supervising, coordinating, and monitoring the activities of the vendor, it may decide that external sourcing is too costly. Accordingly, firms may opt for internal sourcing when they perceive transaction diseconomies to override any production cost advantages in market exchanges. Transaction economies suggest that the less the transaction costs involved in hiring outsourcee, the greater is the degree of IT outsourcing.
- *Financial slack advantage*. The sourcing conundrum may also be explained by a firm's discretionary use of financial slack. Financial slack refers to financial resources in excess of what is required to maintain the organization. Slack can be defined as the difference between total financial resources and necessary payments or as a cushion of excess resources available in an organization that will either solve many organization problems or facilitate the pursuit of goals outside the realm of those dictated by optimization principles. When organizations possess slack resources, firms may enlarge the scale and scope of their operations by deploying slack resources toward building up internal IT resources in the form of hardware, software, and IS human resources. Conversely, when slack resources are low, firms are likely to resist internalizing in response to the anxiety provoked by loss of financial resources. Thus, when slack resources are low, firms can be expected to downsize internal IS services by selling off IT assets and reducing IS personnel expenses. Financial economies suggest that the less financial slack, the greater the degree of IT outsourcing.

To empirically test these relationships between economies and outsourcing, Ang and Straub (1998) gathered information from senior IT managers in 243 US banks. Results from the study show that IS outsourcing was strongly influenced by production cost advantages offered by vendors. Transaction costs played a role in the outsourcing decision, but they were much smaller than production costs. Finally, financial slack was not found to be a significant control factor.

Ang and Cummings (1997) conducted a similar test on the same information gathered from senior IT managers in 243 US banks. Commercial banks in the United States operate in highly institutionalized environments. Historically, stringent banking legislation restricted operations and suppressed competition. In recent years, regulation that formerly had fended off competition from other financial institutions weakened. As banks search for ways to grow and maintain their competitive edge, outsourcing emerged as a dominant organizational strategy for achieving those goals. In their empirical study, Ang and Cummings suggest relationships between institutional influence and IS outsourcing from external production cost advantage, level of slack resources in a bank, and specificity of IS assets. Institutional influences on IS outsourcing come from both peer banks and federal regulators. Peer banks exert considerable influence on each other because of tight professional networks formalized by memberships in regional and national bank associations. Federal regulators exert substantial influence on bank practices and operations.

Ang and Cummings (1997) found that the greater the external production cost advantage, the stronger the relationship between institutional influence and IS outsourcing. This finding suggests that the effect of external production cost advantage on the relationship of peer influence to outsourcing is different between large and small banks. Subsequent analysis showed that the cost advantage significantly strengthened conformity to peer influence for IS outsourcing in large banks and not in small banks. Ang and Cummings also found that the lower the level of slack resources in a bank, the stronger the relationship between institutional influences and IS outsourcing. Conversely, the higher the level of slack resources in a bank, the weaker the relationship between institutional influences and IS outsourcing. Subsequent analysis showed that, regardless of bank size, conformity to peer influence for IS outsourcing was weakened with increasing perceived slack resources. Ang and Cummings' third finding was that the greater the specificity of IS assets, the weaker the relationship between institutional influences and IS outsourcing. This finding suggests that the effect of specific assets on the relationship of peer influence to outsourcing is significantly different between large and small banks. Subsequent analysis for large and small banks showed that specificity of IS assets significantly weakened conformity to influence for peer outsourcing in large banks and not in small banks. Several implications can be derived from this study. From a managerial perspective, recognition of strategic economic considerations is important. Hence, organizations should be cautious when imitating strategies or when learning vicariously from the experience of peers. Especially for small organizations, which tend to exhibit substantial follower behavior, more proactive evaluation of the efficiencies and effectiveness of alternative organizational arrangements is warranted to ensure a timely strategic response to the environment (Ang & Cummings, 1997).

Production and transaction economies through supply and demand forces place in perspective the interesting conflict of a reluctant organization striving to maintain its independence from others while knowing that it must assent to interorganizational ties to procure the resources needed. Outsourcing poses challenges to both user organizations and service providers: in estimating the "true" costs and saving of outsourcing; in managing power dependencies in the exchange; and in balancing the opportunities offered by open boundaries and free-flowing information against the need to protect the organization's unique capabilities. The study by Ang and Straub (1998) was an attempt to compare the relative effects of production and transaction costs on managerial outsourcing decisions in the IT context. Both production costs and transaction costs can and, it is argued, should have a major impact on decisions to outsource. Managers need to be especially vigilant to see that estimates of both kinds of costs figure into their calculations of returns on investments.

Aubert, Rivard, and Patry (2004) applied transaction cost theory to formulate four hypotheses about the level of outsourcing of IT operation activities. The first pertains to asset specificity. Transactions requiring specific assets will bear higher transaction costs; hence they will be more likely to be retained in-house. Hence, the degree of asset specificity will have a negative effect on the level of outsourcing of IT operation activities (hypothesis 1).

The second hypothesis assumed that uncertainty would be a deterrent for organizations trying to outsource IT operation activities. The difficulties associated with writing contracts or with measurement will

Figure 1. Results of causal statistical analysis to explain outsourcing level

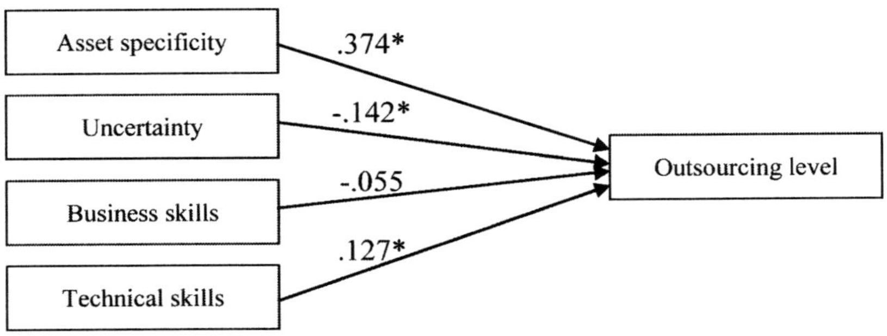

induce them to prefer internal governance for highly uncertain activities. Hence, the level of uncertainty will have a negative effect on the level of outsourcing of IT operation activities (hypothesis 2).

Finally, the last two hypotheses are related to the origin of the investments. Two types of skills are required to carry any given activity. Business skills refer to the knowledge of the business environment of the firm, while technical skills are more related to the generic components of a given activity. Activities presenting a high level of business content should be kept in-house, because the members of the organization are more likely to master the content. Conversely, highly technical activities should be outsourced, since suppliers can nurture the critical technical skills. Hence, the amount of business skills required to perform IT operation activities will have a negative effect on their level of outsourcing (hypothesis 3). And, the amount of technical skills required to perform IT operation activities will have a positive effect on their level of outsourcing (hypothesis 4).

Aubert et al. (2004) collected data from three sources and conducted a statistical analysis to test relationships as illustrated in Figure 1. The most surprising finding is the link between asset specificity and the outsourcing level. It was anticipated that the presence of specific assets would deter companies from outsourcing IT activities. The result obtained suggests the opposite. The link between asset specificity and outsourcing level is strong and significant. As anticipated, increased technical skills tend to favor outsourcing. Similarly, the presence of uncertainty and measurement problems seems to preclude outsourcing of IT activities. Overall, 19.4% (R squared) of the variance was explained.

The objective of the study by Aubert et al. (2004) was to test an explanatory model of IT outsourcing behavior. Based on transaction costs and incomplete contract theories, the model embedded hypotheses that constitute the foundations of these theoretical domains. The results obtained support, at least in part, the transaction cost model. From the results, it was clear that uncertainty and measurement problems play a role in the IT outsourcing decision. Firms outsource more readily activities having low uncertainty. These results support the transaction cost hypothesis. The market is seen as less efficient to ensure the execution of transactions prone to high uncertainty or severe measurement problems. The internal governance is a more efficient alternative. The presence of technical skills was positively related to the outsourcing decision. It supports the idea from incomplete contract theory stating that activities should be under the control of the party making the critical investment for the transaction. However, business skills did not seem to play a significant role in the decision to outsource. It may be attributed to the rather low level of business skills required to perform IT operations. Asset specificity showed conflicting results, suggesting that more specific assets lead to more outsourcing. This contradicted the transaction cost hypothesis.

HIDDEN COSTS

The hidden management costs in outsourcing relationships were identified in research conducted by Kern and Willcocks (2002). Three areas of hidden costs were identified, which received little attention at the outset by client companies. Firstly, the significant costs involved in post-contract management are not planned for. The findings suggested that management resorting to develop and maintain relations is generally higher than initially anticipated and expected. The split of management time on relationship management and the rest, i.e., contract management is 70-30. Secondly, ongoing monitoring costs generally are not considered. These arise due to the client's management agenda of assuring not only that the vendor keeps its commitment to deliver the agreed services, but also to control the costs of the deal. Finally, the renegotiation or update costs involved in ensuring the contract always reflects the current statutes of the IT outsourcing arrangement. This is essential to ensure, for example, that in the event of termination all service levels, technological assets, and staffing is listed to simplify insourcing or vendor switch. Planning a contract that caters for every contingency is generally impossible in long-term business deals. Hence, outsourcing contracts, like so many other long-term business contracts, suffer from an inherent incompleteness and hence necessitate updating.

Overlooking hidden costs of outsourcing was listed as the sixth deadly sin of outsourcing by Barthélemy (2003). In a separate research article, Barthélemy (2001) discussed the various hidden costs of IT outsourcing. Most companies outsourcing IT for the first time are not aware of those costs. Companies say they entered an outsourcing agreement believing that they understood all major costs. They agree that some amount was needed for activities such as finding a vendor, drafting the contract and managing the effort, but they think the amount would be negligible – in some cases, they halved or even canceled out the company's potential savings from outsourcing. Only those companies who have a bad experience take preventive measures. Barthélemy (2001) identified four categories of hidden costs:

1. *Vendor search and contracting*. Many enterprises underestimate the expense to identify and evaluate suitable IT vendors, select a finalist, and negotiate and draft the contract. Companies incur such costs before spending the first dollar on the actual work. Thus it costs something just to think about IT outsourcing. Companies may not want to reduce their spending for search and contracting, because it can significantly lower the other hidden costs. Additional time and expense early on helps avoid problems later, such as having to renegotiate the contract or constantly monitor the vendor to get the needed performance.
2. *Transition to the vendor*. Switching in-house IT activities to a vendor presents probably the most elusive hidden cost. Most companies do not realize how much they have spent until the transition is complete. It can take months before the vendor knows as much as the internal IT department, and it is hard to say exactly when the vendor has taken over. Most managers are unable to analyze transition cost. The best they can do is report transition time; a measure offering only limited insight into what drives transition cost. The average transition period – when the organization actually incurred a cost – was about a year. Transition costs are elusive: A company incurs them as long as the vendor has not completely taken over from the internal IT department. The time that internal employees spend helping the vendor is transition costs. Costs that stem from disruption – and from the vendor's inability to react as quickly and appropriately as the internal department did at the beginning of the contract – are transition costs. The characteristics of the outsourced activity greatly influence transition cost. The more idiosyncratic the activity (the more tailored for

the specific company), the higher the cost to pass it to a vendor that must take time to learn the activity. Outsourcing commodities such as PC procurement and maintenance entail lower transition costs. Also, the more complex the outsourced activity, the harder the transition. Furthermore, outsourcing activities that require transferring many people to the vendor also increase transition costs. The transferred employees often feel betrayed. They can resist outsourcing initiatives either directly (e.g., strike) or indirectly (e.g., slow motion).

3. *Managing the effort*. Managing the effort probably represents the largest category of hidden costs because it covers three areas: monitoring to see that IT vendors fulfill their contractual obligations, bargaining with IT vendors (and sanctioning them if necessary), and negotiating any needed contract changes. Unlike outsourcing fees, vendor-management costs for IT outsourcing are not readily apparent. A company knows what it pays to the vendor. Indeed, many businesses outsource to find out how much they pay for IT. Management costs, in contrast, are purely internal. Because of the costs' relative obscurity, many companies do not take them into account until they become visible – usually when the overall outsourcing cost has noticeably escalated.
4. *Transitioning after outsourcing*. The fourth hidden cost comes from switching vendors or reintegrating IT activities internally. When activities must be redirected to a new vendor, the cost involves finding that vendor, drafting a new contract and transitioning resources. When activities must be reintegrated, the cost involves building a new internal IT activity from scratch. The time needed is roughly the same regardless of the kind of transition. Such hidden costs represent expenses that managers find hard to quantify. Most managers are reluctant to think about the end of the contract. Outsourcing IT to focus on a company's core business or to cut costs is generally meant to be permanent. Companies do not plan to reintegrate IT. Even switching vendors is a move they prefer to avoid. Thus, regardless of how the contract ends, the end signifies a failed outsourcing effort. Most managers find it hard to consider that possibility.

All too often, companies neglect the hidden costs of IT outsourcing. Overlooking hidden costs is unwise. A better approach is to manage the four costs proactively and holistically and to spend extra time and resources in the early stages of the outsourcing effort. Knowing what the company wants and spending time on the contract can help curb the cost of managing the initiative and of transitioning outsourced activities when the contract ends (Barthélemy, 2001).

CONTRACT TERMINATION COSTS

An emerging area for debate between customers and suppliers is which of them bears the risk of prospective redundancy costs at the end of a contract where there is no transfer of an undertaking, and therefore no transfer of the supplier's staff assigned to the undertaking. This is an issue of real commercial significance as customers become more prepared to change suppliers, and since the sums involved can be quite significant (Foster, 2003).

When a supplier bids for an outsourcing contract, it should take into account all costs connected with the take-on of the contract, and also those costs arising from expiry or termination. It will probably assume that it is able to cease paying sums (e.g. license fees, lease rentals, maintenance costs) to third party suppliers for goods and services connected with the contract at the point, when, at the end of the contract, it ceases to receive revenue from the customer to cover this expenditure. But this still leaves one major area of cost to the supplier where the costs cannot be turned off quite so easily – the costs related to the ongoing employment or termination of employment of the staff that have hitherto delivered the service to the customer. At the end of the outsourcing contract, there are three possible scenarios in relation to these assigned staff (Foster, 2003):

1. The staff transfers their employment automatically from the outgoing supplier to the incoming supplier, and this has the effect of removing from the outgoing supplier all future costs of employment connected with such staff.
2. The outgoing supplier redeploys the staff elsewhere in its business.
3. The staff does not transfer their employment from the outgoing supplier, and since no suitable redeployment opportunities are available, their posts are redundant at the point of contract termination/expiry. The outgoing supplier will be liable for the redundancy costs unless they are recoverable from the customer under the terms of the outsourcing contract.

Generally, either point 1 or 2 will apply. The difficulty arises where one of the parties does not want one of these scenarios to occur but is also unable or unwilling to allow the alternative scenario to be implemented. This situation will normally occur where the customer takes the view that it is not in its commercial interests for them to be a transfer. The incoming supplier may have proposed a different way of delivering the service at a lower charge on the assumption that not all, or none of, the staff transfer their employment. In such a situation, there is no instrument for facilitating the transfer of staff from an outgoing to an incoming supplier.

For these reasons, the outgoing supplier will probably concentrate its efforts on redeployment of the staff affected, but this will not always be available, particularly where the make-up of its work is geographically and technically disparate. When redeployment is not available for an employee, then when the contract terminates, his/her post is redundant and the outgoing supplier will be responsible for the redundancy payment due to the employee (Foster, 2003).

BENEFITS

Let us look at an evaluation example. We assume that the company now has implemented an outsourcing solution. The outsourcing contract may have been implemented to achieve results such as:

- Both organizational (cost reduction) and market (revenue increase) benefits
- IT function solving systems integration
- Improved communication and combination of information for decision-making
- Improved business processes
- Improved efficiency and effectiveness in value shop activities
- Knowledge management systems supporting knowledge sharing and creation
- Enable use of Internet at the level of e-business
- Develop supplementary services to take advantage of opportunities
- Improve working procedures in accordance with firm vision
- Create different product according to market strategy
- Create entry barriers according to competitive forces model

Figure 2. Evaluating effects from IS/IT

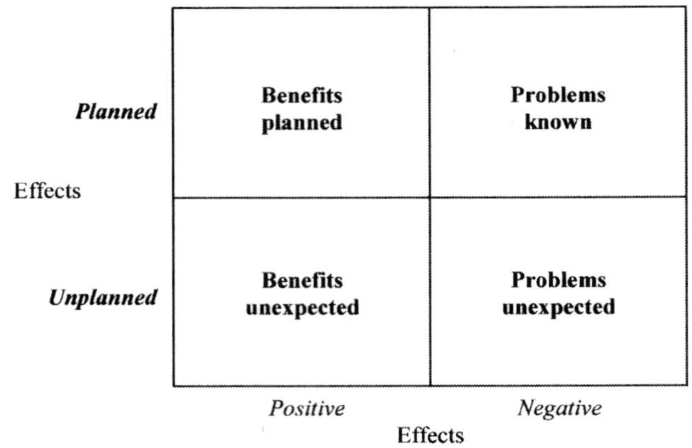

- Extend the life of products classified as stars
- Attract knowledgeable people in the labor market
- Knowledge management technology enabling knowledge competitor role

As this list illustrates, there may have been a variety of reasons for implementing an outsourcing solution. When we do the evaluation of results, we will evaluate to what extent such results have been achieved. But the evaluation should not be limited to such planned, positive effects of a new service provision. The evaluation should investigate all kinds of effects as illustrated in Figure 2. All planned, positive effects listed above belong in the upper-left quadrant for planned benefits. Here we evaluate to what extent we have achieved results in accordance with the IS/IT strategy. However, we will also have achieved other benefits from outsourcing implementation that we did not think of when the IS/IT strategy was developed. These benefits may be just as valuable as the results that we aimed for. Hence, results are both planned and unplanned results.

At the other side of Figure 2, there are negative effects of implementing the IS/IT strategy. Some problems were known, and these problems have been dealt with. However, we will also experience new problems from systems implementation that we did not think of when the IS/IT strategy was developed. These new problems cause an increase in negative effects from implementing the IS/IT strategy.

STRATEGIC RISK BEHAVIOR

IT outsourcing represents strategic decision-making involving risk. Risk behavior of client managers will influence outsourcing decisions, governance decisions and termination decisions. Risk can be defined as a condition in which decision makers know the possible consequences of the decisions as well as their associated probabilities. In strategic management, it is seldom that all consequences and their probabilities are known. Thus, risk is often used as if it is the same as uncertainty, or unpredictable consequences and/or probabilities. In this sense, strategic management scholars refer to risk as variance in performance beyond the control of decision makers. In recent years, recognition has been growing in the strategy literature that managers conceive of risk only as downside possibilities. That is, managers are more concerned with negative variations in performance, not performance variances as a whole. For our purposes here, we define risk broadly as the unpredictability in decision outcomes. Thus, risk taking would be to consciously undertake tasks, which are associated with uncertain consequences (Das & Teng, 2001a).

Strategic risk behavior constitutes an essential perspective in analyzing strategic behavior. Broadly defined, strategic risk taking refers to corporate strategic moves that cause returns to vary, that involve venturing into the unknown, and that may result in corporate ruin. Considering that risk is a problematic aspect in the management of business organizations, it is important to understand the reasons that lead strategists to engage in risky decision-making behavior. Extensive research on risk taking carried out by psychologists over the years has resulted in two competing paradigms concerning the attributes of risk taking behavior – one suggested by the personality psychologists who focus on individual differences in risk taking behavior, and the other by the experimental psychologists who deal with risk taking in such terms as subjective expected utility.

The view of the personality psychologists focuses on individual differences in risk taking, so that it ascribes risk behavior mostly to the general traits and dispositional tendencies of decision makers. Scholars have observed that individuals are fairly consistent in their attitudes towards risk – some people seem more comfortable with risk taking than others. Based on such stable individual attribute, researchers differentiate decision makers in terms of their risk propensity – namely, as being either risk averters or risk seekers. Some researchers also believe that a dispositional risk propensity can help explain, to a large extent, the risk behavior of individuals.

In contrast, the experimental psychologists challenge the consistency of such dispositional traits and argue that situational factors have a greater influence on risk taking behavior. Unlike other psychological attributes, the risk propensity of decision makers seems to lack constancy across decision situations. Since this view attempts to understand Everyman's risk taking behavior, it regards the external stimulus as more important. Many empirical studies suggest that situational factors such as outcome history and decision framing are salient in determining the riskiness of strategic decisions. Hence, the view of the experimental psychologists – which treats risk taking as situation-contingent – seems to command substantial support. Since both views have their virtues and considerable empirical support, efforts have been made to integrate them. These studies suggest that the dispositional risk propensity interacts with situational factors in determining risk-taking behavior. In their article, Das and Teng (2001a) present an alternative framework for reconciling the two views on the determinants of strategic risk behavior. Their framework is illustrated in Figure 3.

Figure 3 illustrates the interplay of two factors – risk propensity and decision context. This framework suggests that decision makers will exhibit high-risk behavior in short-range risk horizons, if the decision context is perceived as a loss position (negative context). The framework further suggests that decision makers will exhibit low-risk behavior in short-range risk horizons, if the decision context is perceived as a gain position (positive context). Furthermore, decision makers who are risk averters will exhibit low-risk behavior in long-range risk horizons. Finally, decision makers who are risk seekers will exhibit high-risk behavior in long-range risk horizons.

In another study, Das and Teng (2001b) developed an integrated framework for trust, control and risk in strategic alliances, as illustrated in Figure 4. Trust and control are inextricably interlinked with risk in strategic alliances such as outsourcing relationships. To understand how partner firms can effectively reduce and manage this risk, we need to examine the inter-relationships between trust, control, and risk. Based on this framework, they developed the following propositions:

Figure 3. Strategic risk behaviors based on risk propensity, decision context, and risk horizon (adapted from Das & Teng, 2001a)

		Decision context	
		Positive	Negative
Risk propensity	Risk avert	*Cell A* Short-range low-risk behavior Long-range low-risk behavior	*Cell B* Short-range high-risk behavior Long-range low-risk behavior
	Risk seeker	*Cell C* Short-range low-risk behavior Long-range high-risk behavior	*Cell D* Short-range high-risk behavior Long-range high-risk behavior

1. A firm's goodwill trust in its partner firm will reduce its perceived relational risk in an alliance, but not it's perceived performance risk.
2. A firm's competence trust in its partner firm will reduce its perceived performance risk in an alliance, but not it's perceived relational risk.
3. Perceived relational risk in an alliance will be reduced more effectively by behavior control than by output control.
4. Perceived performance risk in an alliance will be reduced more effectively by output control than by behavior control.
5. Social control in an alliance will reduce both perceived relational risk and perceived performance risk.
6. Both output control and behavior control will undermine goodwill trust and competence trust in an alliance.

Figure 4. Integrated framework of trust, control, and risk in strategic alliances (adapted from Das & Teng, 2001b)

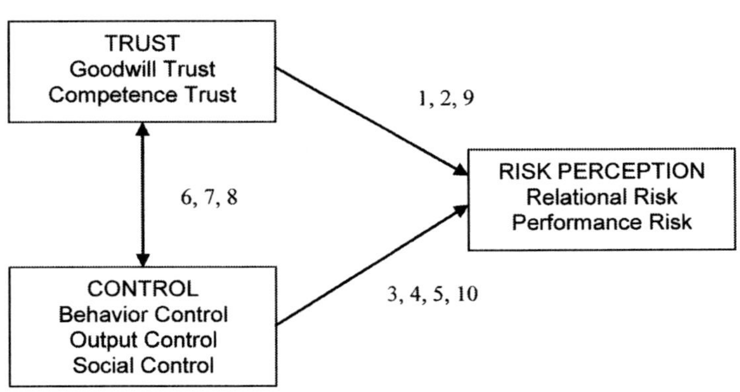

7. Social control will enhance both goodwill trust and competence trust in an alliance.
8. Goodwill trust and competence trust will enhance the effectiveness of all control modes (behavior, output, and social) in an alliance.
9. Control levels remaining the same, the lower the acceptable relational risk level, the higher the needed goodwill trust level in an alliance. Control levels remaining the same, the lower the acceptable performance risk level, the higher the needed competence trust level in an alliance.
10. Goodwill trust remaining the same, the lower the acceptable relational risk level, the more will be the use of behavior control and social control in an alliance. Competence trust remaining the same, the lower the acceptable performance risk level, the more will be the use of output control and social control in an alliance.

Das and Teng's (2001b) proposed an integrated framework of trust, control, and risk leading to these ten propositions. Overall, the framework suggests that trust and control are two separate routes to risk reduction in alliances. While trust can be seen as a more intrinsic source for lowering the perception of risk, control may be viewed as a more overt and active way of reducing risk.

Managing IT outsourcing performance is concerned with avoiding outsourcing risks. We should remind our self of some of the *outsourcing risks* suggested by Earl (1996) to reduce them and possibly avoid them. Possibility of weak management can be avoided by replacing and strengthening existing IT management after outsourcing. Inexperienced staff can be avoided by interviewing and testing vendor staff. Risks from business uncertainty can be reduced through flexible contracts that are both flexible in scope and time. Outdated technology skills can be avoided by interviewing and testing vendor staff on a regular basis, which is specified in the contract. Endemic uncertainty can be reduced by regular measurements in terms of user surveys and other research instruments. Hidden costs, again, can be avoided by identifying search and contracting costs, vendor management costs and other potentially hidden costs. Lack of organizational learning can be reduced by project-based systems development and operations, where both client and vendor personnel participate in the projects. Loss of innovative capacity can be reduced by slack resources, organic and fluid organizational processes, and experimental and entrepreneurial competencies. Dangers of an external triangle should be avoided by direct contact between problem owner and solution provider. Technological indivisibility can be reduced by modular design, flexible application architecture, common data architecture and modular infrastructure. Fuzzy focus can be avoided by always answering the "what" question (what does the business want to achieve?) before the how question (how can information technology support the business in achieving what it wants?).

Finally, let us look at another set of *outsourcing risks* as suggested by Bahli and Rivard (2003). Lock-in can be reduced by low asset specificity, large number of suppliers, and the client's high degree of expertise in outsourcing contracts. Costly contractual amendments can be reduced by systematic forecasting of changes in the business environment and in the internal environment. We can make distinctions between dynamic and turbulent environments. An environment perceived as dynamic, is changing fast, but we do understand what is going on. An environment perceived as turbulent, is changing fast, and we do not know what is going on. In the latter circumstances, not only outsourcing, but also the whole business, is at stake, as management does not understand what is going on. Change of management is probably needed. Unexpected transition and management costs can be reduced by improved understanding of the future and improved expertise in IT operations. Disputes and litigation can be reduced by frequent measurements, IT expertise and professional relationships.

CONCLUSION

Production and transaction economies have a major impact on decisions to outsource. Not all companies benefit from outsourcing, and the disadvantages of outsourcing can create serious problems for organizations if they are not well understood and managed. Many firms underestimate costs for identifying and evaluating vendors of information technology services, for transitioning to a new vendor, and for monitoring vendors to make sure they are fulfilling their contractual obligations as well as the underlying expectations after contract negotiations. Hidden costs can easily undermine anticipated benefits from outsourcing. When a firm allocates the responsibility for developing and operating its information systems to another organization, the firm can loose control over its information systems function. If the organization lacks the expertise to negotiate a sound contract, the firm's dependency on the vendor might result in high costs or loss of control over technological direction. Firms should be especially cautious when using an outsourcer to develop or to operate applications that give it some type of competitive advantage. A firm is most likely to benefit from outsourcing if it understands exactly how the outsourcing vendor will provide value and can manage the vendor relationship with an advantageous benefit/cost ratio both on contract paper and in reality.

REFERENCES

Ang, S. (1993). *The etiology of information systems outsourcing.* Unpublished Doctor of Philosophy Thesis, University of Minnesota.

Ang, S., & Cummings, L. L. (1997). Strategic Response to Institutional Influence on Information Systems Outsourcing. *Organization Science*, *8*(3), 235–256. doi:10.1287/orsc.8.3.235

Ang, S., & Straub, D. W. (1998). Production and Transaction Economics and IS Outsourcing: A study of the U.S. Banking Industry. *MIS Quarterly*, *22*(4), 535–552. doi:10.2307/249554

Aubert, B. A., Rivard, S., & Patry, M. (2004). A transaction cost model of IT outsourcing. *Information & Management*, *41*(7), 921–932. doi:10.1016/j.im.2003.09.001

Bahli, B., & Rivard, S. (2003). The information technology outsourcing risk: a transaction cost and agency theory-based perspective. *Journal of Information Technology*, *18*(3), 211–221. doi:10.1080/0268396032000130214

Barthélemy, J. (2001). The Hidden Costs of IT Outsourcing. *Sloan Management Review*, *42*(3), 60–69.

Barthélemy, J. (2003). The Seven Deadly Sins of Outsourcing. *The Academy of Management Executive*, *17*(2), 87–100.

Das, T. K., & Teng, B.-S. (2001a). Strategic risk behaviour and its temporalities: between risk propensity and decision context. *Journal of Management Studies*, *38*(4), 515–534. doi:10.1111/1467-6486.00247

Das, T. K., & Teng, B.-S. (2001b). Trust, Control, and Risk in Strategic Alliances: An Integrated Framework. *Organization Studies*, *22*(2), 251–283. doi:10.1177/0170840601222004

Earl, M. J. (1996). The Risks of Outsourcing IT. *Sloan Management Review, 37*(3), 26–32.

Foster, A. (2003). The procurement and bidding process. In J. Angel (Ed.), *Technology Outsourcing* (pp. 6-65). London: The Law Society.

Grover, V., Teng, T. C., & Cheon, M. J. (1998). Towards a Theoretically-Based Contingency Model of Information Systems Outsourcing. In L. P. Willcocks & M. C. Lacity (Eds.), *Strategic Sourcing of Information Systems. Perspectives and Practices* (pp. 79-101). Chichester, UK: John Wiley & Sons.

Kern, T., & Willcocks, L. P. (2002). Exploring relationship in information technology outsourcing: the interaction approach. *European Journal of Information Systems, 11*(1), 3–19. doi:10.1057/palgrave/ejis/3000415

Williamson, O. E. (1981). The Modern Corporation: Origins, Evolution, Attributes. *Journal of Economic Literature, 19*(4), 1537–1568.

Chapter 7
Knowledge Transfer

In an outsourcing setting we find that knowledge, which earlier existed internally in an organization, is moved to and exchanged with an external organization (Bahli & Rivard, 2005). Therefore, changes in the knowledge transfer requirements are viewed as the single most important challenge to knowledge management and knowledge management systems in an outsourcing arrangement. A relevant approach to outsourcing relationships from the knowledge management literature includes intellectual capital management, as presented in the beginning of this chapter. Then, we continue presenting how knowledge transfer might influence outsourcing success. Finally, clients' and vendors' need for knowledge transfer and knowledge exchange in IT outsourcing relationships is discussed.

INTELLECTUAL CAPITAL MANAGEMENT

In an outsourcing relationship, the vendor will need to manage its intellectual capital so that clients experience efficient and effective knowledge transfers. One of the key authors in the area of intellectual capital is Sveiby (2001) who has developed a knowledge-based theory of the firm to guide in strategy formulation. He distinguished between three families of intangible assets with the outsourcing vendor.

DOI: 10.4018/978-1-60566-796-6.ch007

The *external structure* family consists of relationships with customers and suppliers and the reputation (image) of the firm. Some of these relationships can be converted into legal property such as trademarks and brand names. The value of such assets in primarily influenced by how well the company solves its customers' problems, and there is always an element of uncertainty here. The *internal structure* family consists of patents, concepts, models, and computer and administrative systems. These are created by the employees and are thus generally owned by the organization. The structure is partly independent of individuals and some of it remains even if a large number of the employees leave. *The individual competence* family consists of the competence of the professional staff, the experts, the research and development people, the factory workers, sales and marketing – in short, all those that have a direct contact with customers and whose work are within the business idea.

Competence is a term introduced here. Competence can be defined as the sum of knowledge, skills and abilities at the individual level. With this definition, we say that knowledge is part of competence, and competence is part of intellectual capital.

These three families of intangible resources have slightly different definitions when compared to the capital elements. The external structure seems similar to relational capital; the internal structure seems similar to structural capital, while the individual competence seems similar to human capital. Given three families of intangible assets, it is possible to identify nine knowledge transfers, within a family and between families, as explained by Sveiby (2001):

1. *Knowledge transfers between individuals* concern how to best enable the communication between employees within the organization. The strategic question is: how can we improve the transfer of competence between people in the organization? Activities for intellectual capital management focus on trust building, enabling team activities, induction programs, job rotation and master/apprentice scheme.
2. *Knowledge transfers from individuals to external structure* concern how the organization's employees transfer their knowledge to the outer world. The strategic question is: how can the organization's employees improve the competence of customers, suppliers and other stakeholders? Activities for intellectual capital management focus on enabling the employees to help customers learn about the products, getting rid of red tape, enabling job rotation with customers, holding product seminars and providing customer education.
3. *Knowledge transfers from external structure to individuals* occur when employees learn from customers, suppliers and community feedback trough ideas, new experiences and new technical knowledge. The strategic question is: how can the organization's customers, suppliers and other stakeholders improve the competence of the employees? Activities for intellectual capital management focus on creating and maintaining good personal relationships between the organizations own people and the people outside the organization.
4. *Knowledge transfers from competence to internal structure* concern the transformation of human capital into more permanent structural capital through documented work routines, intranets and data repositories. The strategic question is: how can we improve the conversion individually held competence to systems, tools and templates? Activities for intellectual capital management focus on tools, templates, process and systems so they can be shared more easily and efficiently.
5. *Knowledge transfers from internal structure to individual competence* is the counterpart of the above. Once competence is captured in a system it needs to be made available to other individuals in such a way that they improve their capacity to act. The strategic question is: how can we improve

individuals' competence by using systems, tools and templates? Activities for intellectual capital management focus on improving human-computer interface of systems, action-based learning processes, simulations and interactive e-learning environments.

6. *Knowledge transfers within the external structure* concern what customers and others tell each other about the services of an organization. The strategic question is: how can we enable the conversations among the customers, suppliers and other stakeholders so they improve their competence? Activities for intellectual capital management focus on partnering and alliances, improving the image of the organization and the brand equity of its products and services, improving the quality of the offering, conducting product seminars and alumni programs.
7. *Knowledge transfers from external to internal structure* concern what knowledge the organization can gain from the external world and how the learning can be converted into action. The strategic question is: how can competence from the customers, suppliers and other stakeholders improve the organization's systems, tools and processes and products? Activities for intellectual capital management focus on empowering call centers to interpret customer complaints, creating alliances to generate ideas for new products and research and development alliances.
8. *Knowledge transfers from internal to external structure* is the counterpart of the above. The strategic question is: how can the organization's systems, tools and processes and products improve the competence of the customers, suppliers and other stakeholders? Activities for intellectual capital management focus on making the organization's systems, tools and processes effective in servicing the customer, extranets, product tracking, help desks and e-business.
9. *Knowledge transfers within the internal structure* where the internal structure is the backbone of the organization. The strategic question is: how can the organization's systems, tools and processes and products be effectively integrated? Activities for intellectual capital management focus on streamlining databases, building integrated information technology systems and improving the office layout.

The outsourcing promise is to leverage the supplier's superior technical know-how (human capital), superior management practices (structural capital), economies of scale, and increasingly, access to strategic and business advice. This should enable the client to refocus on strategic, core capability and knowledge areas. But Willcocks, Hindle, Feeny, and Lacity's (2004) research into IT outsourcing has shown consistently over the past decade that the prospects have been disappointing for meaningful knowledge management, and value creation. Most clients report their frustration with endless cost-service debates, and sometimes significant loss of control over their IT destiny and knowledge base. Most vendors find it difficult to deliver on their promises of innovation and value added, because of their lack of knowledge about the client's long-term business strategy.

Typically, even on the very big, long-term deals considered to be strategic vendor relationships, the supplier offers technical know-how for routine solutions, with high performers in short supply. There is little influx of new technical/managerial talent, and disappointing access to the supplier's global capacity and knowledge base. Meanwhile, the client does not thoroughly think through the issues of core capability and retained knowledge. As a result, the client spends much time fire fighting and experiences little value-added or technical/business innovation. Over time, the client loses control over its IT destiny or business process destiny, as knowledge asymmetries develop in favor of the vendor.

The loss of information and knowledge can be traumatic for both outsourcing parties unless specific and purposeful steps are undertaken to develop and sustain new information pathways and capabilities.

That is why the nine knowledge transfer mechanisms are so important for success. In addition, the client has to retain several core capabilities. These ensure the elicitation and delivery of business requirements, the development of technical/business architecture, the managing of external supply, and the coordination and governance of these tasks. In practice, Willcocks et al. (2004) have found all too many client organizations inadequately making these critical, initial knowledge investments.

The traditional IT outsourcing approach restricts creation and leveraging of knowledge concerns only to one specialist area – IT operations. However, much bigger knowledge gains can arise if whole functions or processes that include IT are outsourced. This is the premise of the dramatic growth in business process outsourcing. The knowledge contract of BPO is to outsource IT functions to suppliers that have superior structural and human capital in the areas of business process and specific expertise. Some deals also recognize the need for closer partnering to get closer to the customer: to create and leverage relational capital to both parties' advantage.

KNOWLEDGE TRANSFER IN IT OUTSOURCING RELATIONSHIPS

According to Alavi and Leidner (2001), organizations have four knowledge processes: creation, storage and retrieval, transfer and application. A knowledge management system (KMS) is an IT-based system developed to support and enhance these organizational processes of knowledge. In an IT outsourcing relationship, the requirements on a KMS to support creation, storage and retrieval, and application of knowledge will not change dramatically. However, the requirements concerning support for knowledge transfer will change significantly.

The problem of knowledge transfer is often faced by individuals or groups once an appropriate source of knowledge is located (Sambamurthy & Subramani, 2005). The new challenge lies mostly in how to transfer knowledge between the vendor and the client. The environment for communication in certain areas of a company will be drastically altered as a consequence of an outsourcing decision. Knowledge, which earlier could be transferred between people in the same organization, now has to be transferred across two different organizations. Consequently, the channels for transferring knowledge will be more formal and impersonal. A KMS has to find a way to transfer all relevant information through more formal and impersonal channels or to find a new creative way of making the communication channel less formal and/or impersonal.

According to (Ko, Kirsch, & King, 2005), some researchers have defined knowledge transfer as dyadic exchanges of organizational knowledge between a source and a recipient unit in which the identity of the recipient matters. Others also focus on the resulting changes to the recipient. For example, knowledge transfer can be seen as the process through which one unit (e.g., group, department, or division) is affected by the experience of another. Other researchers go further by arguing that knowledge transfer occurs when a contributor shares knowledge that is used by an adopter.

Knowledge is in the heads of individuals. Therefore, we have to understand knowledge transfer in terms of individual behavior (Liebowitz, 2004; Liu & Chen, 2005; Wong, 2005). Wasko and Faraj (2005) examined social capital and knowledge contribution in electronic networks of practice. They found that reputation, centrality and tenure were significant factors influencing the extent to which individuals are motivated to make knowledge contributions. Reputation is an important asset that an individual can leverage to achieve and maintain status within a collective. Centrality is the extent to which the individual is in regular contact with others; the more individuals are in regular contact with one another, the more likely they are to develop a habit of cooperation and act collectively. Individuals with longer tenure in the shared practice are likely to better understand how their expertise is relevant, and are thus better able to share knowledge with others.

Given the multiple objectives of knowledge transfer in IT outsourcing relationships, only a sophisticated operationalization of the concept will suffice here. Since the literature suggests that key aspects of knowledge transfer are knowledge movement and the application of knowledge, Ko et al. (2005) captured both of these ideas by defining knowledge transfer as the communication of knowledge from a source so that it is learned and applied by a recipient. Knowledge is taken to be transferred when learning takes place and when the recipient understands the intricacies and implications associated with that knowledge so that he or she can apply it. For example, the vendor may transfer knowledge about testing procedures to the client who learns and applies this knowledge, as evidenced by clients developing test scripts, conducting tests of individual modules, and running integration tests to ascertain whether data are correctly passed between two or more modules. Similarly, Inkpen and Tsang (2005) define knowledge transfer as a process through which one relationship partner is affected by the experience of another. Knowledge transfer manifests itself through changes in knowledge or performance of the recipient unit.

Partnerships can create a competitive advantage through the strategic sharing of organizations' key information and knowledge. Close relationships result from more frequent and more relevant information and knowledge transferred between high performance partners. By transferring knowledge between the client and vendor, they are able to sustain a more effective outsourcing relationship over time. Lee (2001) found that the association between the degree of knowledge sharing and outsourcing success is mediated by the quality of the partnership. According to Lee and Kim (1999), there is a significant positive relationship between partnership quality and outsourcing success. In their research, they identified five factors that make up partnership quality: trust, business understanding, benefit-risk share, conflict avoidance, and commitment. A successful partnership enables participants to achieve organizational objectives and build a competitive advantage that each organization could not easily attain by itself.

The links and causalities are presented in Figure 1. First, the use of knowledge management systems to support knowledge transfer in IT outsourcing relationships has effects on the relationships. Next, these effects are determinants of partnership quality. Finally, partnership quality influences outsourcing effects. For example, participation is important in a partnership. From a social perspective, participation is prescribed as a remedy when there is conflict, frustration and vacillation in the group. Active participation of the partnership members plays a major part in enhancing the sustainability of their partnership over time (Lee & Kim, 1999). Knowledge transfer using knowledge management systems can be an enabler of easier and more comprehensive participation. Hence, participation is influenced by knowledge transfer, and participation influences partnership quality, as illustrated in Figure 1.

CLIENT'S NEED FOR KNOWLEDGE TRANSFER

In order to understand the knowledge transfer in IT outsourcing relationship we studied three international cases (Gottschalk & Solli-Sæther, 2007), as described in more detail in Chapter 10. For the purpose of knowledge transfer we studied the areas as listed in Table 1. The table illustrates that there is a need for knowledge transfer to the client, to the vendor, and between client and vendor.

All three case studies demonstrate that both vendor and client discovered the importance of knowledge transfer after implementation of the IT outsourcing arrangement. With changing business environments,

Figure 1. Knowledge transfer influencing outsourcing success

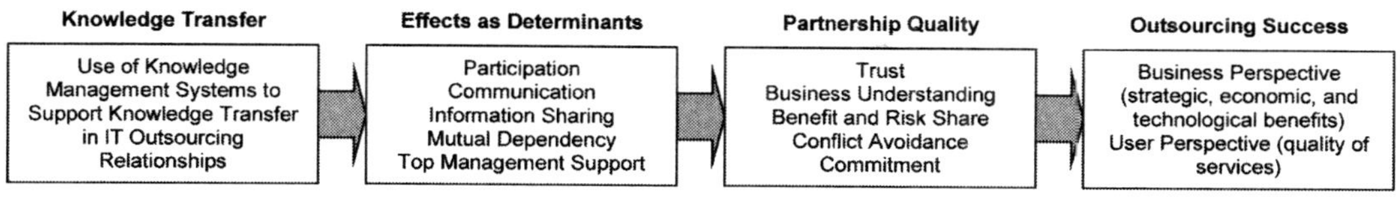

the locus of value creation is no longer within the boundaries of a single firm, but occurs instead at the nexus of relationships between parties. With the growing importance of pooling knowledge resources, knowledge management will have to transcend organizational boundaries. An IT outsourcing relationship is an inter-organizational arrangement for the exchange of IT services after the transfer of IT assets from the client to the vendor. In an outsourcing setting knowledge, which earlier existed internally in an organization, is moved to an external organization. Accordingly, changes in the knowledge transfer requirements are viewed as the single most important challenge to knowledge management systems in an outsourcing arrangement.

When the initial outsourcing took place, one client organization kept very little skills in-house. They realized that was unhelpful, because it created naivety on client's side and created a degree of frustration on the outsourcer side. Client had to rebuild their retained IT management team with two very experienced IT outsourcing managers. One of them was managing the services and the projects (Gottschalk & Karlsen, 2005), and the other was managing the procurement activities. Teams were built around them. The client found that the best way arriving at a strong relationship with the outsourcer was to have people that deeply understood the business. Meaning, you need to be an intelligent buyer, and you need to understand your own business.

We gave away all our IT components and all of our knowledge. All we had left was the contract managers. (Client ICT director).

Another client organization had gradually built management capacity, contract management, and service level management. When they sold out their IT department, there had been frame agreements between CIO's staff and the IT department for several years, being more professional and market oriented year by year. They had the necessary resources to manage and follow-up services, analyze new requirements, and to purchase from the outsourcer.

A third client organization was pretty clear of their responsibilities for the agreements, and they kept resources to take care of operations management, contract management, and of their business applications, which was not outsourced.

Table 1. Needs for knowledge transfer in an IT outsourcing relationship

	Need for knowledge transfer
Client	Know how to set up retained IT management to manage an outsourcer Know how to use new technologies/innovations
Vendor	Know how to support client businesses process
Relationship	Know how to create and maintain a good working relationship

Failure to set up retained IT management is probably one of 2 or 3 key success crusher. We have a lot of problems with it, and the outsourcer does not feel that it is on their span of influence, because you cannot tell the client how you should be managed. It requires a lot of trust to do that. (Outsourcer senior account manager)

One of the client companies was looking for an outsourcer they might discuss as a change agent, a company somewhat different from themselves. They were not looking for a traditional outsourcer, but a very service oriented company. A major transformation seemed to be a part of the plan, a transformation of the client from a manufacturing oriented company to a service oriented company. The culture that the outsourcer was bringing was part of what the client was looking for; a service oriented, global, and people oriented company.

Vendor organizations have knowledge of how to set up retained IT management teams, but none of them seems to transfer this knowledge to client organizations. Through years of experience outsourcers have been supporting clients with business and technology transformation. To succeed in the relationship knowledge transfer from vendor to client is essential.

VENDOR'S NEED FOR KNOWLEDGE TRANSFER

Outsourcers cannot give all business and IT strategies on where client companies want to go in the future. Outsourcers do not know the clients' business well enough. Client companies realized that they needed to keep knowledge about the business processes (the applications), and how it was built up, which included the architecture. They had to keep that knowledge in-house – overall architecture skills, solution architecture skill, contract management skills, strategic management skills, and skills to manage top-down governance.

They [outsourcers] haven't got the overall picture. They [outsourcers] do not really know what is happening at your company. You have got the big issue of giving all the knowledge to them. Because they do not have the experience, it is just you that have the experience. (Client ICT director)

To enhance the value of the outsourcing arrangement one client – vendor relationship put in place an alignment project. The objective of the relationship alignment project was (among others) to create a framework to manage the natural tension between both parties, find an agreement on a vision of how the parties need to work together, build a strong working relationship between the teams in the various countries, build and commit to an appropriate strategic relationship structure and enabling mechanisms, support a group wide collaborative approach, review and refine roles & responsibilities. These things relay on the extent to which the relationship work together rather than against one another. As long as the parties transfer knowledge between each other, they should be capable of sustaining a successful relationship.

Findings from case studies support the importance of knowledge transfer in IT outsourcing relationships. With the growing importance of pooling knowledge resources, knowledge management will have to transcend organizational boundaries to include sourcing partners. However, the focus of previous research studies has mainly been on intra-organizational knowledge management (e.g., Biloslavo, 2005).

In this study, we have attempted to direct the attention of knowledge management researchers toward inter-organizational interfaces (e.g., Kodama, 2005; Kodama & Ohira, 2005).

In a different empirical setting, Malhotra et al. (2005) attempted to direct the attention of knowledge management researchers toward inter-organizational interfaces. They studied absorptive capacity configurations in supply chains. Their study indicates that enterprises have to build requisite absorptive capacity to prepare for collaborative knowledge creation with their supply chain partners. Absorptive capacity in this context is the ability of enterprises to acquire and assimilate information from their supply chain partners and to transform and exploit this information to achieve superior operational and strategic outcomes.

Similarly, Allard and Holsapple (2002) attempted to direct the attention of knowledge management researchers toward inter-organizational interfaces. They studied knowledge management as a key for e-business competitiveness (Gottschalk, 2006). In their knowledge chain model, knowledge externalization describes the embedding of knowledge into organizational outputs that are then released into the external environment.

The extent of inter-organizational knowledge transfer between vendor and client in an IT outsourcing relationship will depend on the extent of outsourcing. Total IT outsourcing will typically require a greater extent of inter-organizational knowledge transfer (Barthélemy & Geyer, 2004). This can be explored in future research, as outsourcing choices represent alternate ways for organizations to leverage available resources to increase the value of IT in meeting corporate objectives (Lee, Miranda, & Kim, 2004).

CONCLUSION

In an outsourcing relationship, the vendor and the client need to transfer, exchange and develop knowledge on a continuous basis. All services delivered, received and evaluated are based on an exchange of knowledge between vendor personnel and client personnel. If this knowledge exchange is poorly structured or completely unstructured, then misunderstandings leading to poor service quality will occur. In an outsourcing relationship, the vendor and the client need to transfer, exchange and develop knowledge on a continuous basis. All services delivered, received and evaluated are based on an exchange of knowledge between vendor personnel and client personnel. If this knowledge exchange is poorly structured or completely unstructured, then misunderstandings leading to poor service quality will occur. Opposite, success might be created and sustained if knowledge is freely exchanged.

An open exchange and creation of knowledge requires more than mechanisms, systems and leadership. It requires knowledge workers who are willing and able to explore and exploit their knowledge with others. A prerequisite for knowledge workers to be open is self-confidence in the sense that they trust their own knowledge as well as trust their own exposure of not knowing. Another prerequisite is the demand-side of knowledge sharing, where both vendor knowledge workers and client knowledge workers ask questions when in need of knowledge. This is so because knowledge always resides in the heads of individuals.

REFERENCES

Allard, S., & Holsapple, C. W. (2002). Knowledge management as a key for e-business competitiveness: from the knowledge chain to KM audits. *Journal of Computer Information Systems*, *42*(5), 19–25.

Bahli, B., & Rivard, S. (2005). Validating measures of information technology outsourcing risk factors. *Omega*, *22*(2), 175–187. doi:10.1016/j.omega.2004.04.003

Barthélemy, J., & Geyer, D. (2004). The determinants of total IT outsourcing: An empirical investigation of French and German firms. *Journal of Computer Information Systems*, *44*(4), 91–97.

Biloslavo, R. (2005). Use of knowledge management framework as a tool for innovation capability audit. *International Journal of Innovation and Learning*, *2*(4), 402–424. doi:10.1504/IJIL.2005.006663

Gottschalk, P. (2006). Research propositions for knowledge management systems supporting electronic business. *International Journal of Innovation and Learning*, *3*(6), 593–606.

Gottschalk, P., & Karlsen, J. T. (2005). A comparison of leadership roles in internal IT projects versus outsourcing projects. *Industrial Management & Data Systems*, *105*(9), 1137–1149. doi:10.1108/02635570510633220

Gottschalk, P., & Solli-Sæther, H. (2007). Knowledge transfer in IT outsourcing relationships: three international case studies. *International Journal of Innovation and Learning*, *4*(2), 103–111. doi:10.1504/IJIL.2007.011687

Inkpen, A. C., & Tsang, E. W. K. (2005). Social capital, networks, and knowledge transfer. *Academy of Management Review*, *30*(1), 146–165.

Ko, D. G, Kirsch, L. J., & King, W. R. (2005). Antecedents of Knowledge Transfer from Consultants to Clients in Enterprise System Implementations. *MIS Quarterly*, *29*(1), 59–85.

Kodama, M. (2005). Customer value creation through knowledge transfer fwith customers: case studies of IT and multimedia businesses in Japan. *International Journal of Innovation and Learning*, *2*(4), 357–385. doi:10.1504/IJIL.2005.006661

Kodama, M., & Ohira, H. (2005). Customer value creation through customer-as-innovator approach: a case study of video processing LSI development. *International Journal of Innovation and Learning*, *2*(4), 434–445. doi:10.1504/IJIL.2005.006661

Lee, J.-N (2001). The impact of knowledge sharing, organizational capability and partnership quality on IS outsourcing success. *Information & Management*, *38*(5), 323–335. doi:10.1016/S0378-7206(00)00074-4

Lee, J.-N., & Kim, Y.-G. (1999). Effect of Partnership Quality on IS Outsourcing Success: Conceptual Framework and Empirical Validation. *Journal of Management Information Systems*, *15*(4), 29–61.

Lee, J.-N., Miranda, S. M., & Kim, Y.-M. (2004). IT Outsourcing Strategies: Universalistic, Contingency, and Configurational Explanations of Success. *Information Systems Research*, *15*(2), 110–131. doi:10.1287/isre.1040.0013

Liebowitz, J. (2004). Will knowledge management work in the government? *Electronic Government, an International Journal, 1*(1), 1-7.

Liu, C. C., & Chen, S. Y. (2005). Determinants of knowledge sharing of e-learners. *International Journal of Innovation and Learning, 2*(4), 434–445. doi:10.1504/IJIL.2005.006665

Malhotra, A., Gosain, S., & El Sawy, O. A. (2005). Absorptive Capacity Configurations in Supply Chains: Gearing for Partner-Enabeld Market Knowledge Creation. *MIS Quarterly, 29*(1), 145–187.

Sambamurthy, V., & Subramani, M. (2005). Special Issue on Information Technologies and Knowledge Management. *MIS Quarterly, 29*(1), 1–7.

Sveiby, K. E. (2001). A knowledge-based theory of the firm to guide in strategy formulation. *Journal of Intellectual Capital, 2*(4), 344–358. doi:10.1108/14691930110409651

Wasko, M. M., & Faraj, S. (2005). Why Should I Share? Examining Social Capital and Knowledge Contribution in Electronic Networks of Practice. *MIS Quarterly, 29*(1), 35–57.

Willcocks, L. P., Hindle, J. L., Feeny, D. F., & Lacity, M. C. (2004). IT and Business Process Outsourcing: The Knowledge Potential. *Information Systems Management, 21*(3), 7–15. doi:10.1201/1078/44432.21.3.20040601/82471.2

Wong, K. Y. (2005). Critical success factors for implementing knowledge management in small and medium enterprises. *Industrial Management & Data Systems, 105*(3), 261–279. doi:10.1108/02635570510590101

Chapter 8
Outsourcing Performance

For the vendor an IT outsourcing relationship is successful if it generates profit for the company and if it strengthens the company's value proposition in terms of complementary competencies such as IT personnel development, methodology development and dissemination, and customer relationship management (Levina & Ross, 2003). For the client an IT outsourcing relationship is successful if it generates profit for the company and if it contributes to achievement of outsourcing objectives as exemplified by Lee and Kim (1999). Managing successful IT outsourcing relationships means to us that source firm and sourcing firm both achieve their objectives in a joint effort. Achieving objectives is a matter of outsourcing outcome.

In this chapter we start by presenting the vendor's value proposition because outsourcing outcomes are dependent on the vendor's ability to create value for both parties in the relationship. Satisfaction based on successful exploration and exploitation of the vendor value proposition plays an important role in building other important assets for the client company. The following two sections in this chapter discuss outsourcing opportunities and threats in a client perspective. Next, we present a method for developing quantitative performance measurements. Although decisions to outsource should be a part of the overall business strategy, control and objective measurement of service quality is important for

DOI: 10.4018/978-1-60566-796-6.ch008

any company as this may influence the overall relationship. At the end of this chapter, we take a look at how to measure the success of IT outsourcing relationships.

VENDOR VALUE PROPOSITION

The value generation potential of an outsourcing relationship consists of three factors: client characteristics, the vendor-client relationship, and vendor characteristics. A key client characteristic is an understanding of how to manage resources that a firm does not own. A key in the vendor-client relationship is formal (contractual) aspect of the relationship. The third factor shaping the outsourcing value proposition is the vendor's own capabilities. From an outsourcing vendor's perspective, there are many potential opportunities and benefits for the client. These opportunities and benefits can be derived from the IT outsourcing vendor's value proposition. Important vendor characteristics include capabilities such as technical competence, understanding of the customer's business, and relationship management. Our presentation and discussion in the following text of this third factor in terms of vendor value proposition is based on a research article by Levina and Ross (2003).

To date, most research on information technology outsourcing concludes that firms decide to outsource IT services because they believe that outside vendors possess production cost advantages. Yet it is not clear whether vendors can provide production cost advantages, particularly to large firms who may be able to replicate vendors' production cost advantages in-house. Mixed outsourcing success in the past decade calls for a closer examination of the IT outsourcing vendor's value proposition. The concepts of *complementarities* and *competencies* explain that outsourcing vendors can increase productivity and reduce costs on client projects by applying a set of complementary application management competencies. This is the vendor value proposition.

The concept of complementarity posits that firms can improve productivity by engaging in complementary activities where benefits from doing more of one activity increase if the firm is also doing more of the other activity. This concept of complementarity has been used in studies of manufacturing to show that modern manufacturing approaches work as a system, rather than as a set of independent factors. Those firms that invest simultaneously in several complementary activities perform better than those firms that increase the level of some of these activities, but not others. In fact, literature on complementarity argues that firms that increase one factor without also increasing complementary factors may be worse off than firms that keep the factors at the same lower level.

An outsourcing vendor may develop different competencies. In the case study by Levina and Ross (2003), the vendor developed a set of three competencies to respond to client needs and market demands: personnel development, methodology development and dissemination, and customer relationship management:

- *IT personnel development* addressed existing IT labor market constraints by the vendor in ways that the client had not. The vendor replaced experienced, high-cost client staff with mostly lower-cost, junior programmers and then developed their skills through training, mentoring, and team-based project work. Junior staff valued the professional growth while their mentors often relished opportunities to watch somebody take off. As a professional services firm, the vendor viewed maintenance work as a first step in a career development path, which involved rotating professionals within engagements, assigning personnel development managers, and creating both technical and management hierarchies.

- *Methodology development and dissemination* was necessary for consistent delivery of best of breed solutions to client problems. Whereas the client's staff focused on addressing users' immediate needs, the vendor introduced methodologies that focused on overall operational improvements on projects. The vendor had a long history of methodology development. The methodologies not only specified processes, they also standardized project documentation through forms and templates such as change request forms, lost time logs, and weekly status report forms, to closely monitor project status.
- *Customer relationship management* was formalized through level of service agreements. Each agreement set a fixed price for agreed-upon services. The major philosophy of outsourcing was that the vendor is taking a risk. The vendor is responsible for whatever is defined in that client interface document as being the vendor's responsibility. While agreements might not lead to greater user satisfaction with the level of IT services, it did reduce uncertainty, thereby creating clearer expectations and an acceptance of limits. As users accepted these limits, they recognized and appreciated services that exceeded contract requirements.

These three competencies turned out to be complementary by being mutually reinforcing. Management practices targeted at one competency tended to enhance the other competencies as well. This reinforcing pattern was apparent in all three pairings of the competencies:

- *Personnel development and methodology development and dissemination are complementary competencies.* The methodology competency reinforced personnel development by helping junior staff learn quickly what they were expected to do. While methodologies were sometimes viewed as constraining individual initiative, one junior consultant argued that the methodology empowered her and others to challenge management directives that might be inconsistent with documented practices. In addition, standardization of practices around methodology facilitated staff rotations and scheduling. In the same way, personnel development practices, such as skill development, rotations, and promotion policies, provided training, encouragement, and incentives that led to consistent use and improvement of methodologies across the organization.
- *Methodology development and dissemination and customer relationship are complementary competencies.* When methodology delivered operational improvements, the vendor could sometimes increase service levels with no added cost to the client. In some cases, the vendor had been able to pull people off a project and had elected to share the savings with the client. These very visible improvements in IT service levels reinforced the customer relationship. Methodological approaches also improved customer relationship management practices by defining and standardizing best practices for creating and managing level of service agreements. The customer relationship management competence similarly reinforced the methodology competence. The vendor regularly communicated with the client to discuss issues and expectations, and one outcome was to help the client managers understand the methodologies so that they could facilitate, rather than hinder, the vendor's ability to meet expectations. Thus, client managers shared their knowledge of systems with the vendor and provided early warnings, where possible, when business or corporate IT changes might have an impact on the vendor's responsibilities.

- *Personnel development and customer relationship are complimentary competencies.* Personnel development practices reinforced customer relationships by ensuring that staff understood and accepted accountability for meeting contractual obligations. Personnel development practices also developed communication skills to help staff establish customer expectations and build trust. At the same time, strong customer relationships led to better buy-in, on the customer's part, to personnel development policies that required release time or movement of personnel, such as training programs, mentoring, and job rotations.

The concepts of complementarities and core competencies explain that the vendor can increase productivity and reduce costs on client projects by applying this set of complementary application management competencies. Levina and Ross (2003) examined how the vendor delivers value to clients as a result of its ability to develop complementary competencies. First, they went beyond neoclassical economics theory to explain why potential clients are unlikely to develop these complementary competencies internally. They then explored the mechanisms that ensure that the benefits of the vendor's competencies are, in part, passed on to clients.

Why Clients do not Replicate and Apply Vendors' Competencies

Typically, clients have a different set of market structures and resource constraints than the IT services industry. Accordingly, clients have a different organization and different business processes. Clients have hired personnel to address the market conditions and customer demands of their industry. Clients can attempt to build IT application competencies rather than outsource to vendors, but, unlike vendors, they may find that optimizing the development and application of IT competencies will conflict with optimizing core business activities. Vendors, on the other hand, can shield themselves from these conflicts through the structure provided by contracts, which specify deliverables rather than levels of investment in competencies.

For example, to address labor market constraints, clients could increase the compensation of technical specialists, but non-IT workers might perceive the inflated IT salaries as unfair. Similarly, clients are typically not as well positioned as vendors to institute an IT personnel career development office or a practice of IT personnel rotation and promotion.

Why Vendors Share Productivity Gains with Clients

From the client perspective, the vendor's value proposition would not exist if the benefits of complementary competencies accrued solely to the vendor. Contract-based, interpersonal, and reputation-based mechanisms encourage vendors to share advantages with clients. Clients may deploy some contract-based mechanisms including pilot projects, multiphase contracting with penalties, interpersonal relationship building, carrot and stick incentives and short-term contracts, and competent contract monitoring. All of these mechanisms increase client control and motivate vendors to demonstrate value to the client. Since the value of outsourcing to the client is very hard to measure, most researchers have focused on client satisfaction.

Reputation-based mechanisms provide vendors with a strong incentive to share productivity gains with clients. IT service vendors' focus on reputation building in their relationships with clients. In addition to their current contracting structure, vendors care about their long-term market position. Thus, the vendor is inclined to share benefits with the client so that the information about the vendor's contribution enables it to win future contracts. Developing a solid industry reputation helps a vendor win new, and extend existing, engagements, which lead to the acquisition of, and control over, more projects.

Knowledge-intensive service firms like outsourcing vendors are typical value shops (Gottschalk, 2005), and such firms depend on reputation for success, as reputation is a key driver of firm value creation. Reputation is a relational concept, in the sense that firms are judged by their stakeholders relative to their competitors. Reputation is what is generally said or believed about an entity by someone, it is the net perception of a firm held by stakeholders judged relative to other firms. According to Sheehan (2002), there are four conditions, which must be present for reputation to work. Firstly, rents earned from maintaining a good reputation must be greater than not. Secondly, there must be a minimum of contact among stakeholders to allow for the changes in reputation to be communicated. Thirdly, there needs to be a possibility of repeat business. And lastly, there must be some uncertainty regarding the firm's type and/or behavior.

Reputation is related to the asymmetry of information, which is a typical feature of knowledge-intensive service firms. Asymmetry is present when clients believe the firm knows something that the clients do not and believe it is necessary to know to solve their problems. Reputation can be classified as a strategic resource in knowledge-intensive firms. To be a strategic resource, it has to be valuable, rare, and costly to imitate, and possible to organize. Reputation is valuable as it increases the value received by the client. Reputation is rare, as by definition only a few firms can be considered best in the industry. Reputation is costly to imitate, as it is difficult to build a reputation in the short run. Reputation is possible to organize in the general sense of controllability, which implies that a firm can be organized to take advantage of reputation as a resource.

The vendor's strategy and practices are depicted in Figure 1. This model of the IT vendor's value proposition suggests that client needs, as shaped by market constraints, specify the requirements for client satisfaction. Client satisfaction results from services provided by vendors through the application

Figure 1. Vendor's value proposition (adapted from Levina & Ross, 2003)

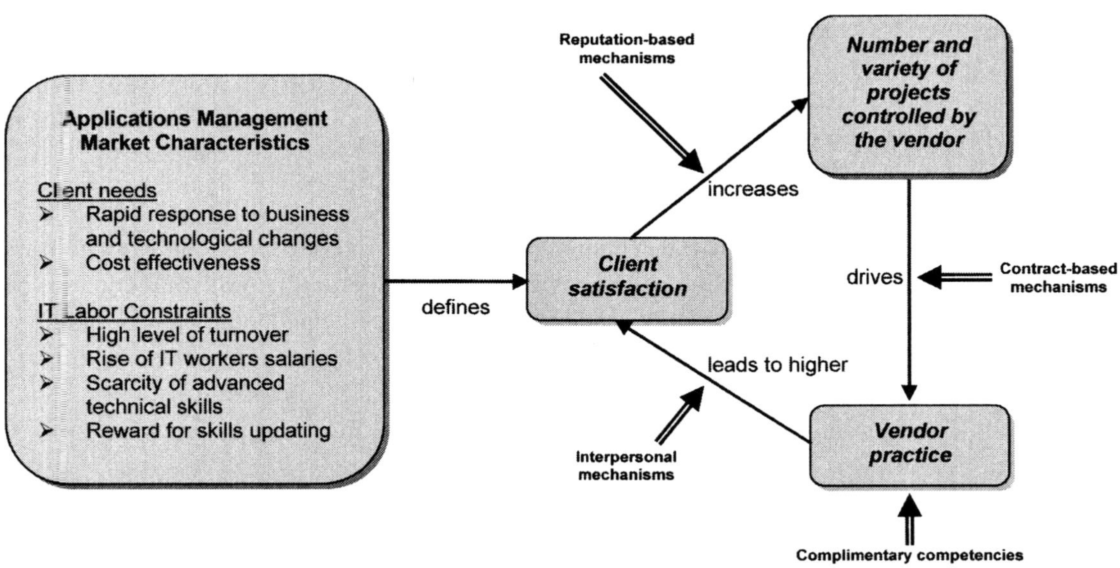

of a complementary set of core competencies targeted at delivering higher service at a lower marginal cost.

Client satisfaction is achieved in Figure 1 when the application of core competencies to projects is enabled by healthy client-vendor relationship, which is in part influenced by the vendor's expertise in managing client relationships. Competencies, in turn, grow through the vendor's firm-wide experience gained from controlling a large number and variety of projects, which, in turn, grow due to the reputation the vendor, develops through its ability to satisfy customers. The model represents a set of positive feedback loops, which will result in negative outcomes if, for example, the competencies do not match client needs.

OUTSOURCING OPPORTUNITIES

An empirical study of information technology sourcing in US and UK organizations identified indicators of success. The objective of the study was to develop indicators of success based on participants' perceptions of whether the outcome of their IT sourcing decisions met their expectations. Participants cited a variety of expectations (anticipated and hoped-for outcomes) and reasons (justifications and explanations) for their sourcing decisions. Fifteen categories of expectations/reasons for sourcing were identified (Lacity & Willcocks, 1998). Each participant's expectations/reasons were mapped into the 15 chosen categories. In many instances, participants stated more than one expectation/reason. The ranking from 1 to 15 was based on total responses from participants.

1. Reduce IT costs
2. Improve technology or technical service
3. Jump on the bandwagon; outsourcing perceived as a viable, irreversible trend within their industry
4. Focus business on core competencies; IT perceived as non-core
5. Restructure IT budgets from capital budgets to fixed operating budgets
6. Play good corporate citizen; IT managers perceive an outsourcing evaluation demonstrates their willingness to subordinate the good of IT department for the good of the overall business
7. Focus internal IT staff on critical IT activities, such as development, while outsourcing more stable and predictable IT activities, such as data center operations
8. Prove efficiency; invite bids to receive a free benchmark
9. Eliminate an IT burden; assume a vendor will solve problematic IT function(s)
10. Downsizing – the entire company is pressured to reduce headcount
11. Preemptive move by IT managers to expose exaggerated claims made to senior executives by consultants or vendors
12. Improve cost controls
13. Forced market testing by the government
14. Justify new IT resources by bundling capital budget requests with a kind of proof that vendors cannot do it cheaper
15. Facilitate mergers and acquisitions – vendors are perceived as experts in merging data centers quickly.

Global outsourcing's defenders list a number of arguments in favor of outsourcing. Arguments in favor of outsourcing can be broken down to five areas: concentration on core business development by firms, cost control, access to state of the art technology, market discipline through greater transparency, and added flexibility to respond to demand changes (Clott, 2004). The motivations for outsourcing are evolving from a primary focus on cost reduction to an emerging emphasis on improving business performance. The traditional rationale of vendor economies of scale and specialization is becoming less convincing as companies with well-run, innovative IS departments that are large enough to accrue the same scale and specialization benefits as a vendor, are nevertheless engaged in significant outsourcing deals.

DiRomualdo and Gurbaxani (1998) discovered in their research that while the academic literature and business press discuss IT outsourcing as if it were always driven by a singular focus on reducing the costs and enhancing the efficiency of IT resources, this is in fact only one of three kinds of strategic intent for IT outsourcing. They called this well-established intent IS Improvement. The other two have more recently emerged as significant factors in many companies' decision to outsource. Outsourcing for business impact focuses on improving IT's contribution to company performance within the existing lines of business. The third category of intent, commercial exploitation, focuses on leveraging technology-related assets in the marketplace:

- *IS Improvement.* Companies that want better performance from their core IS resources – the hardware, software, networks, people, and processes involved in managing and operating the technology and supporting users – have the strategic intent of IS improvement. Their objective typically includes cost reduction, service quality improvement, and acquisition of new technical skills and management competencies. They believe that outside specialists who are better able to keep pace with new technologies and skills, and who use superior processes and management methods, should manage some, if not all, of their IT services.
- *Business Impact.* Many IS organizations are struggling to develop the right mix of technical and business skills to exploit technology. As a result, many companies are looking to the IT outsourcing market for help, on the premise that outsourcing vendors' state-of-the-art skills, capabilities, and proficiency at recruiting and managing technologists make them better than internal IS organizations at using IT to improve business results. The strategic intent is deploying IT to significantly improve critical aspects of business performance.
- *Commercial Exploitation.* Outsourcing information technology with the strategic intent of commercial exploitation aims to improve the return on IT investment by generating new revenue and profit or by offsetting costs. The means by which IT assets can be leveraged commercially range from licensing systems and technologies developed initially for internal use, through selling IS products and services to other firms, to launching new IT-based businesses. Our study discovered that companies pursuing commercial exploitation were often those with innovative information systems. Many come from technology-intensive industries, such as air transport and financial services, and have mission-critical systems that are expensive to maintain and enhance.

OUTSOURCING THREATS

While literature on outsourcing has often sought to draw lessons from highly visible companies that have been successful in outsourcing, Barthélemy (2003) in his article on "The seven deadly sins of outsourcing" sheds light on failed efforts. Failed outsourcing endeavors are rarely reported because firms are reluctant to publicize them. Firms do not like to report their failures because such information can damage their reputation. His study was based on in-depth analysis of 91 outsourcing efforts carried out by European and North American firms. Through his survey, he found that the same mistakes underlie most failed outsourcing efforts. These mistakes have been termed the seven deadly sins of outsourcing:

1. *Outsourcing activities that should not be outsourced.* Determining which activities can be best performed by outside vendors requires a good understanding of where the firm's competitive advantage comes from. Resources and capabilities that are valuable, rare, difficult to imitate, and difficult to substitute can be employed to create superior performance. Activities that are based on such resources and capabilities (i.e., core activities) should not be outsourced because firms risk loosing competitive advantage and becoming hollow corporations.
2. *Selecting the wrong vendor.* Selecting a good vendor is crucial for successful outsourcing. The literature has identified numerous criteria for successful provider choice. A useful distinction can be made between hard and soft qualifications. Hard qualifications are tangible and can be easily verified by due diligence. They refer to the ability of vendors to provide low-cost and state-of-the-art solutions. Important criteria also include business experience and financial strength. Soft qualifications are attitudinal. They may be non-verifiable and may change depending on circumstances. Important soft criteria include a good cultural fit, a commitment to continuous improvement, flexibility, and a commitment to develop long-term relationships.
3. *Writing a poor contract.* Since the 1980s, vendor partnerships have emerged as a model of purchasing excellence. Partnerships replace market competition by close and trust-based relationships with a few selected vendors. The notion that outsourcing vendors are partners and that contracts play a minor role was popularized by early outsourcing deals. However, there are pitfalls in partnership management. A good contract is essential to outsourcing success because the contract helps establish a balance of power between the client and the vendor. Spending too little time negotiating the contract and pretending that the partnership relationship with the vendor will take care of everything is a mistake. Drafting a good contract is always important because it allows partners to set expectations and to commit themselves to short-term goals.
4. *Overlooking personnel issues.* The efficient management of personnel issues is crucial because employees generally view outsourcing as an underestimation of their skills. This may result in a massive exodus even before an actual outsourcing decision has been made. Firms that contemplate outsourcing must face two interrelated personnel issues. First, key employees must be retained and motivated. Second, the commitment of employees transferred to the vendor must also be secured.
5. *Loosing control over the outsourced activity.* When the performance quality of an activity is low, managers are often tempted to outsource it. If poor performance is attributable to factors such as insufficient scale economies or a lack of expertise, outsourcing makes sense. If poor performance is attributable to poor management, outsourcing is not necessarily the right solution. For an outsourcing client, it is particularly important to avoid losing control over an outsourced activity. It is critical to keep the outsourced activity in alignment with the overall corporate strategy. While vendor management skills are very important, they must also be complemented with technical skills. If no one in the company is able to assess technological developments, outsourcing is bound to fail.

6. *Overlooking hidden costs of outsourcing*. Outsourcing clients are generally confident that they can assess whether or not outsourcing results in cost savings. However, they often overlook costs that can seriously threaten the viability of outsourcing efforts. Transaction cost economics suggests two main types of outsourcing hidden costs. First, outsourcing vendor search and contracting costs are costs of gathering information to identify and assess suitable vendors and costs of negotiating and writing the outsourcing contract. Second, outsourcing vendor management costs include monitoring the agreement to ensure that vendors fulfill their contractual obligations, bargaining with vendors and sanctioning them when they do not perform according to the contract, and negotiating changes to the contract when unforeseen circumstances arise.
7. *Failing to plan an exit strategy*. Many managers are reluctant to anticipate the end of an outsourcing contract. Therefore, they often fail to plan an exit strategy (i.e., vendor switch or reintegration of an outsourced activity). Outsourcing relationships can be viewed on a continuum. At one end are long-term relationships where one or both partners have made investments specific to the relationship. There is a considerable advantage in recontracting with the same vendor because switching vendors or reintegrating the outsourced activity is very difficult. At the other end are market relationships where the client has a choice of many vendors and the ability to switch vendors with little cost and inconvenience. In this case, there is no real advantage in recontracting with the same vendor.

Today, outsourcing has extended to more crucial activities such as IT, telecommunications, finance, and logistics. Increasingly, complex types of outsourcing have developed. Based on his survey of 91 outsourcing efforts, Barthélemy (2003) found that there are seven deadly sins of outsourcing, as summarized in Table 1. Historically, outsourcing was restricted to basic support activities such as janitorial services. Some sins were "deadlier" than others. "Writing a poor contract" and "losing control over the outsourced activity" had the largest impact on the outcome of outsourcing efforts. On the other hand, "failing to plan an exit strategy" was not a good differentiator between success and failure, perhaps because planning an exit strategy only becomes necessary in the case of vendor switch or reintegration of an outsourced activity.

Table 1. The seven deadly sins of outsourcing and lessons learned

Timetable	#	Deadly sin	Lesson learned
Original idea to outsource	1	Outsourcing activities that should not be outsourced	Only non-core business activities
↓	2	Selecting the wrong vendor	State-of-the art and trustworthy vendors
↓	3	Writing a poor contract	Precise, complete, balanced, and flexible contract
Beginning of the relationship	4	Overlooking personnel issues	Good communication and ethical behavior towards employees
↓	5	Losing control over the outsourced activity	Active management of the vendor
↓	6	Overlooking the hidden costs of outsourcing	Search, contracting and managing costs
Vendor switch or reintegration of the outsourced activity	7	Failing to plan an exit strategy	Building reversibility clauses into the contract

Several years before Barthélemy, Earl (1996) identified risks of outsourcing. According to him, there are many risks that, in practice, indicate limits to outsourcing. Those who have outsourced have more regrets than they acknowledge and more anxieties about vendors than they care to confront. Chief Information Officers (CIO) in firms that are currently on the cusp of deciding to outsource have confided apparently sound cautionary instincts, but momentum can be difficult to stop. Earl argues that the IT sourcing question should be rephrased to, "Why should we not insource IT services?" instead of, "Why should we outsource IT services?" by considering the following eleven risks of outsourcing:

1. *Possibility of weak management.* If an IT service scores low on operational performance, a company will clearly be tempted to outsource it to a third party. This is true whether poor performance is real or imagined, or whether top management's views are rational or emotional. If the IT activity has been badly managed in the first place, will the IT managers be any better at managing an external provider? Indeed, does executive management want to give the benefits of improving an inefficient management to the marketplace? Once outsourcing has been initiated, managing IT services on the outside is far from easy. If the third party is not necessarily better, a company has to enhance its management of vendor skills and placate users. Hence, to reduce initial risks in outsourcing, a company must first be capable of managing the IT service.
2. *Inexperienced staff.* One argument for outsourcing is that specialist IT companies is likely to have better IT specialists. While this might be true, relatively new IT services businesses do not necessarily have either the best expertise or solid experience. What is worse is that in facilities management contracts with even the most established IT service businesses, the customer's staff may go work with the vendor. Transferring internal weak staff and then having to deal with them all over again as contractor staff will not solve the problems. Since some of the largest outsourcing contracts were initiated to transform a resistant and slack IS function, the risk becomes even starker. The biggest risk, however, may occur when a large outsourcing contract is awarded to a major vendor. Headhunters call their network of contacts with a frantic request for someone who can manage a large facility that has just been outsourced or anyone who has experience in managing contracts and can head up a rapidly growing outsourcing division. If the candidate is someone working for the company that has just decided to outsource, the chances are that he or she will be retained by the original company anyway, or will prefer to work for another user company where his or her experience is better suited. Shrewd personnel policies can help mitigate some of the risks at the time an outsourcing contract is signed. However, capable IT staff people are rare, and there is a chance that the customer company will want to keep them or that they will decide to go elsewhere.
3. *Business uncertainty.* If a firm decides to outsource IT services because of costs or focus, it is assuming that its future direction and needs are clear. However, when cost is the driver of outsourcing, or converting fixed costs to variable costs is the declared aim, it is likely that the company will sacrifice crucial competencies or capabilities. The IT marketplace may offer more variety in services and suppliers than any corporation can. Thus, unknown future business needs may, in principle, be satisfied when they arise.
4. *Outdated technology skills.* When a company outsources an IT service to a third party, how can the company be sure that the vendors' skills stay current? If cost reduction is the objective in an outsourcing deal, the hope is that the current cost case is reduced and that, over time, there are further cost reductions due to learning and technological change. Indeed, a company can force these improvements into the contract at the outset or negotiate them at annual reviews. However,

if the vendors' skills do not advance, the cost-reduction potential is lessened, and unless further market testing is done, target setting is sub optimal.

5. *Endemic uncertainty*. IT operations and development have always been inherently uncertain. Users are not sure of their needs, new technology is risky, business requirements change, and implementation is full of surprises. A systems project management regime that demands no changes to specifications and rigid time and budget controls can produce applications that do not achieve their full potential or can create user-specialist conflicts. Companies should avoid outsourcing contracts that are set in concrete. At the same time, contracts should be precise, complete, incentive based, balanced and flexible, according to Barthélemy (2003a). However, being willing to pay for flexibility may be better than specifying tight performance contracts with penalty clauses, followed by litigation.
6. *Hidden costs*. When cost reduction is the objective of outsourcing, there is typically a promise of early cash flow benefits and long-term cost savings. There are two tendencies, however, that are of concern. First, companies underestimate the setup costs, including redeployment costs, relocation costs, and longer-than-expected handoff or parallel running costs. Second, companies may underestimate management costs. Some companies never anticipated the management resources and time - and thus cost - that has to be put in. Companies rarely record the costs of management.
7. *Lack of organizational learning*. Much learning about the capability of IT is experiential. Organizations tend to learn to manage IT by doing; they do not appreciate the challenges until they have experienced them. Management tends to learn the value of IT applications (or of infrastructure) by using them and seeing further opportunities for development. Many strategic information systems were discovered in an evolutionary fashion. Thus the strategic scope of systems often emerges as users learn what is possible and as the business context and needs change. Of course, there is no reason that a third party cannot operate, enhance, or rebuild an application that has been reclassified as strategic. However, in other areas of business, responsibility for strategic assets is not so easily delegated to the marketplace.
8. *Loss of innovative capacity*. In the long run, a company wants to maintain innovative capacity in IT because there will be new ways of providing IT services and of exploiting IT for business. If the company has outsourced IT services and downsized as well, its ability to innovate may be impaired. Innovation needs slack resources, organic and fluid organizational processes, and experimental and entrepreneurial competencies - all attributes that external sourcing does not guarantee.
9. *Dangers of an external triangle*. Some years ago when IT specialists and users could not understand each other, a few companies created a new role for intermediaries or interpreters between the two parties. Often called business analysts, client managers, or systems liaison officers, they sought in theory to understand user needs and convey them to the specialists, while representing the specialists' concerns to the users. Similarly after outsourcing, the remaining IT people may act as conduits or consultants between the line managers and the vendors. In practice, the liaison roles often only succeed in keeping two communities apart and in creating more confusion.
10. *Technological indivisibility*. Much of IT is not divisible or capable of separation. Current information systems are increasingly integrated or interconnected, and problems can occur at the interface of responsibility between different vendors or between the vendor's domains and the customer's domain.
11. *Fuzzy focus*. Outsourcing is essentially concerned with the supply side of IT. The marketplace in principle can provide IT operations, development, service, and training. It is not so able to provide

acceptable, innovative application ideas, the challenging effort and commitment required in systems implementation, and the harvesting and delivery of IT benefits. A real problem, then, with outsourcing is that it concentrates on the how of IT, not on the what. It focuses on the supply side, not the demand side. And because it occupies substantial management resources and executive time, it can unwittingly become another form of denominator management rather than revenue creation - not a prescription for long-term success.

Also Bahli and Rivard (2003) identified information technology outsourcing risks. They define risks as factors that influence the occurrence of undesirable outcomes. The degree to which each factor is present in IT outsourcing will contribute to the increased likelihood of a given outcome. Once this list of factors is drawn, risk management methods will consist of devising and using mechanisms that will either diminish the loss related to the outcome or decrease the likelihood of its occurrence by reducing the level of the risk factors. Four undesirable outcomes can be identified in IT outsourcing, and associated risk factors and consequences can be defined as follows:

1. *Lock-in* is an undesirable outcome based on risk factors such as high asset specificity, small number of suppliers, and the client's low degree of expertise in outsourcing contracts. Consequences are cost escalation and service debasement. Suggested mitigation mechanisms are mutual hostaging and dual sourcing.
2. *Costly contractual amendments* are an undesirable outcome based on risk factors such as high uncertainty and unanticipated changes. Consequences are cost escalation and service debasement. Suggested mitigation mechanisms are sequential contracting and contract flexibility.
3. *Unexpected transition and management costs* is an undesirable outcome based on risk factors such as high uncertainty, the client's low degree of expertise in IT operations, and the client's low degree of expertise in outsourcing contracts. Consequences are cost escalation and service debasement. Suggested mitigation mechanisms are clan mechanisms and use of external expertise.
4. *Disputes and litigation* is an undesirable outcome based on risk factors such as measurement problems, the supplier's degree of expertise in IT operations, and the supplier's degree of expertise in outsourcing contracts. Consequences are cost escalation and service debasement. Suggested mitigation mechanisms are alternative methods of dispute resolution, clan mechanisms, and use of external expertise.

As global outsourcing or offshoring arises, companies must also be aware of the pitfalls of migrating business process overseas to India, the Philippines, Ireland, China, and elsewhere to lower their costs. Meta Group reports offshoring saves 20 percent in the first year, and creates a 20-percent loss in productivity. In other words, actual savings are oftentimes misperceived. Other offshoring pitfalls to consider are: security, scope creep, culture, and knowledge transfer. Risks are raised when working internationally and companies must address privacy concerns. Many projects grow during the development cycle. Scoop creep is not only a phenomenon of offshoring, but might increase as language and cultural differences increase. Differences in customs must be taken into account, as the differences are often more significant than anticipated. Time and effort to educate and train the vendor is a cost rarely accounted for by the IT client organization (InfoWorld, 2004).

PERFORMANCE MEASUREMENT

The rapidly increasing use of outsourcing for IT services, both in the public and private sectors, has attracted much interest from researchers and practitioners alike. While early studies of IT outsourcing were largely qualitative in nature, more recent studies have attempted to analyze the outcomes achieved in quantitative terms. Domberger, Fernandez, and Fiebig (2000) are consistent with the latter, but goes further by modeling the price, performance and contract characteristics that are relevant to IT outsourcing. A two-equation recursive regression model was used to analyze 48 contracts for IT support and maintenance. The results did not reveal any quantitatively significant price-performance trade-off, but did suggest that first-term contracts (i.e., the first ever contract awarded by a client for the provision of a particular IT service) were more expensive than repeat contracts. Although competitive tendering did not result in lower prices than directly negotiated contracts, it was associated with comparatively better performance. Well-defined expectations of an organization's IT requirements were also likely to lead to improved performance when the service was outsourced.

Service Attributes

Domberger et al. (2000) measured IT outsourcing performance by both desired performance and realized performance. Clients typically have an expectation of service quality prior to awarding a contract. This can be referred to as desired performance. A necessary part of contract management involves an assessment of the realized performance of the contract. The clients responding to the study were asked to rate the desired performance and realized performance of the contracts for each of the following eight service attributes:

1. Service availability and timeliness
2. Out-of-hours availability
3. Response in emergencies
4. Provision at expected cost
5. Delivery to expected quality
6. Accuracy of advise
7. Correctness of error fixes
8. Minimization of system downtime

The original scale for the desired and realized performance ratings was from 1 to 4. A rating of 1 corresponded to not important for the former and unsatisfactory for the latter, while 4 corresponded to very important and excellent, respectively. Ratings which were not reported were filled with zeros to preserve the continuity of the scale on the assumption that they were considered irrelevant or very low in terms of desired or realized performance.

The eight service attributes listed were taken to represent measures of quality. For the purposes of analysis and estimation, a single quality/performance variable was sought. Here there were a number of choices. One possibility was to construct what is called principal components. The first principal component, which explained approximately 50% of the variation in the attributes, is essentially a simple average of the realized ratings. It turned out that the responses were all positively and highly correlated.

Thus, the simple average of the ratings attached to the eight attributes represented a simple and readily interpretable choice for a single performance variable.

A second possibility was to consider the realized performance relative to the base, as represented by the desired performance ratings. Constructing a new set of attributes by subtracting the desired from the realized rating for each attribute and contract results in data that has as its first principal component a variable which is essentially the simple average. Once again this accounted for approximately 50% of the variation in the data. Thus, a second possible proxy for the performance variable is the average of the eight realized minus desired attributes. Rather than choose between these alternative proxies, the results for both realized and differences were reported (Domberger et al., 2000). Mean of the eight realized performance ratings was 2.97. This result can be interpreted as satisfactory, but not excellent, indicating that the average response by the 48 firms was that they found realized performance to be satisfactory. Mean of the realized minus desired performance ratings was -0.49. The negative mean for this performance variable indicates a slight tendency to under-perform relative to the desired levels of service quality.

Method for Development of Quantitative Performance Measurements

As with any control or performance measure, it is vitally necessary to develop an objective performance standard for measuring the success of an outsourcing program. This leads to four main questions surrounding the development of a standard for measuring an outsourcing program (Milgate, 2000):

1. What was your purpose in setting up an outsourcing program? What did you want to gain?
2. Who was this outsourcing program supposed to benefit directly? Customers? Suppliers? Employees?
3. Given the above, what should we measure?
4. What can we measure? Moreover, how can we measure it accurately?

Any decision to outsource should be part of an overall business strategy. Ultimately, what will determine your measures will be your overall aims for your outsourcing program. If, for example, you wanted to outsource your logistics system, your purpose may be decrease delivery times of goods to your customers. If this is the case, then your performance measures would be focused on the issues of meeting delivery schedules and getting goods to customers within a certain guaranteed time frame.

Customer Satisfaction

Customer attitudes and feelings of satisfaction are vitally important for any company. Attitudes are of general interest because attitudes are tied closely to behavior. Using satisfaction surveys to measure attitudes is often required. Many vendors do regular *surveys* of customers to measure customer satisfaction. High score in terms of agreement is achieved for the statement that the vendor has a breath of product portfolio, while low score is achieved for the statement that the vendor is living up to the expectations. There are two curves, one for the local market and one for all Nordic markets.

While there are a variety of techniques for reporting customer attitudes, self-reporting is the most common, probably the cheapest, and perhaps the most objective. Attitudes are usually measured using a variety of scales, such as Likert scales that attempt to quantify concepts by assigning numbers to them

Figure 2. Results from a customer satisfaction survey by an outsourcing vendor

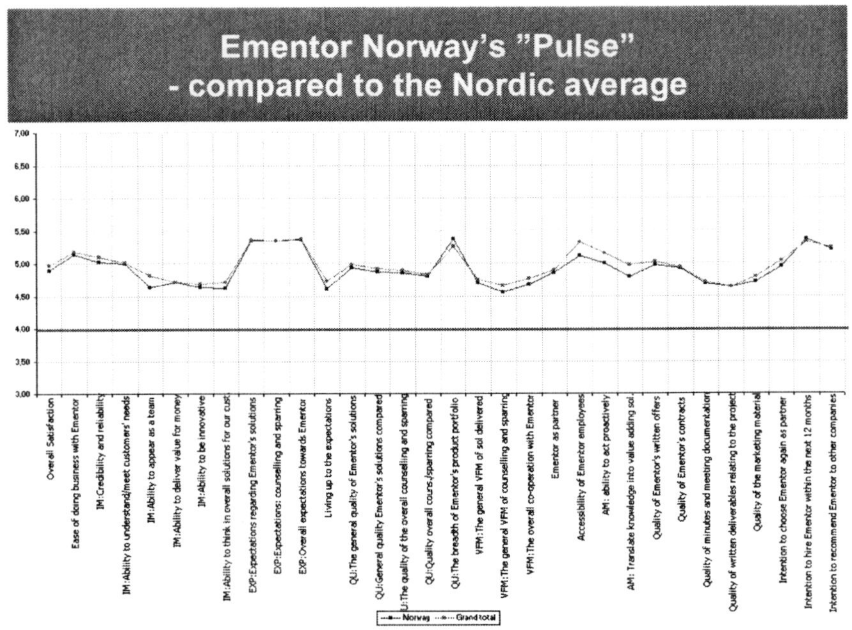

as illustrated in the Ementor example. With these numbers, we can count different responses, prepare frequency tabulations of multiple-choice questions, and calculate percentages (Milgate, 2000). (Figure 2)

However, it is important to note that two errors can occur when we attempt to use attitude scales to understand customer satisfaction. First, merely attaching a number to a concept in no way guarantees increased accuracy. For example, if on a five-point scale, you attach five to very satisfied, the meaning of very satisfied to the customer is still unknown to you. While the ability to count percentages of fives is useful in analysis, it in no way gives you the level of understanding you really need. Second, to gain any accuracy out of attitude scales you must be sure that the questions you are asking are the right ones. This goes for any research in general, but is more important for quantitative research. Typically, to ensure increased accuracy of your instrument, you should either pre-test the instrument on a selected sample of customers or construct the questions from qualitative data suggested by customers or salespersons that deal with customers. Techniques such as focus groups, telephone surveys and experience surveys are useful for this. The basic rule to follow is that if you want to increase the accuracy of your satisfaction surveys, you need to have a concerted approach to research that involves the end-user, a series of different measures and methods, and a constant review of your approach and questions.

Using satisfaction surveys and involving the end user in this process is implicit in benchmarking. However, in the context of an outsourcing agreement, what happens if a major technological change enables the service provider to meet customer needs more cheaply? Alternatively, what happens if a major new player comes into the market and offers far better service than your service-level agreement requires? Essentially, how do you set absolute standards for performance in an environment of continual change and high competition in which people's self-interest is in finding better ways to meet customers' needs? The answer is *benchmarking*. Setting benchmark allows taking into account changes in technology and monitor whether the provider is keeping up with any changes. One should make sure that any potential supplier is innovative by constantly initiating best practice and by investing in its plant, staff, and any other essential business functions (Milgate, 2000).

A benchmark is essentially a minimum industry-based standard that you stipulate must be met by your service provider. It allows you to at least keep in touch with your competitors and, if constantly updated, can enable you to monitor the performance systems. However, they do not cover all aspects of work. IT organizations provide user support, help desks, and may use technologies for which functional points do not apply. This measure also will not pick up maintenance and technological changes. In short, one measure is not enough. In addition, quantitative measures may not provide all the answers to the questions asked nor the depth of data needed to give the IT manager a sense of what is going on.

Qualitative measures may be useful in several areas. Quality has to do with nuance, with detail, with the subtle and unique things that make a difference beyond the points on a standardized scale. Quality is what separates and falls between those points on a standardized scale. Qualitative descriptions provide the detail to explain the difference between two people who responded on a scale of five points with a "highly" satisfactory experience and someone who responded that she had an "extremely" satisfactory experience. This is not a question of interval versus ordinal scaling, but one of meaning.

Qualitative data can provide insights into whether the promises made by the service provider actually are occurring. Satisfaction surveys represent an attempt at quantifying attitudes, or feelings. Since these factors are generally more qualitative in nature, ringing up or interviewing some customers or questioning staff that receive service from the provider can give a great deal of insight into quality issues in relation to outsourcing and can often give a much truer picture of the level of quality than a quantitative measure can, especially when dealing with intangible items like service.

It is important to know the extent to which an IT outsourcing program is effective after it is fully implemented. But to answer that question it is first necessary to know how and the extent to which the program was actually implemented. One company that outsourced was less than impressed with the mid-term results. They bemoaned the fact that outsourcing had not produced the results they had hoped for. However, the program had not been fully implemented. They had decided to outsource in stages so as to not to create antagonism amongst their staff (Milgate, 2000).

SUCCESSFUL RELATIONSHIPS

Increasing attention is paid to building successful partnerships in information technology outsourcing. Lee and Kim (1999) have studied the effect of partnership quality on IS outsourcing success. They define partnership as an interorganizational relationship to achieve the participants' shared goals. Partnership is not a new concept in the management area. Marketing and interorganization systems research has explored relationships between customer and vendor, buyer and seller, manufacturer and distributor, or auditor and client, and so on. A number of different views emerged concerning interorganizational relationships.

Research has classified the relationship between organizations into two types: transactional style and partnership style. A transactional style relationship develops through the formal contract in which rules of the game are well specified and the failure to deliver on commitments by either party should be resolved through litigation or penalty clauses in the contract. In contrast, the requirements of a partnership style relationship include risk and benefit sharing, the need to view the relationship as a series of exchanges without a definite endpoint, and the need to establish a range of mechanisms to monitor and execute its operations.

In traditional IS management, the role of a service provider was limited in terms of the size of the contract and the type of service. Maintenance of hardware or program subcontracting has traditionally been the typical IS service provider. However, the type of relationship in outsourcing is changing from such buyer-seller relationships to the more strategic partnership relationship. Therefore, a necessary condition to move away from self-interest is a belief that the exchange relationship is a win-win situation for organizations to gain competitive advantages.

Relevant theories to analyze the interorganizational relationship include the resource-dependency theory, transaction-cost theory, agent-cost theory from the economic viewpoint, and social exchange theory and power-political theory from the social viewpoint. Economic theories aim at explaining the characteristics of governance or contract. They treat each sourcing decision as an independent event regardless of prior relationships that affect the ongoing sourcing decision. This treatment may be inappropriate where organizations repeatedly enter transactions with each other. Explaining the relationship between organizations from a purely economic point of view is unjustifiable because interorganizational relationships form from the social learning experiences based on specific sequential interactions (Lee & Kim, 1999).

Social theorists assume that processes evolve over time as participants mutually and sequentially demonstrate their trustworthiness, whereas, in the economic perspective, the organization's exchange activities are enforceable. Social theorists understand relationship as a dynamic process through specific sequential interactions in which two participants carry out activities toward one another. However, a good relationship does not always bring about the participants' desired results. According to social theories, two mechanisms – trust and power – can explain the relationship between organizations. Trust, a feature of relationship quality, has been conceptualized as the firm's belief that the other company will perform actions that will result in positive outcome for the firm, and will not take unexpected actions that would result in negative outcomes for the firm. Power is determined by the relative dependence between two actors in an exchange relationship, and the concept of power is only meaningful when compared with another organization. While social exchange theory uses the concept of trust to explain interactions between participants, power-political theory relies on the power derived from offering valuable resources that few other sources can provide (Lee & Kim, 1999).

Partnership Quality

Partnership is an effective way to improve economies of scale and scope provided by the traditional modes of organization. However, partnership does not guarantee a desired outcome. Therefore, careful attention needs to be paid to the partnership problems that may lead to an unstable and conflicting relationship. Partnership quality is an important concept in this respect. Quality is treated as having two dimensions: (1) fitness of use – Does the product or service does what it is supposed to do? Does it possess the features that meet the customer's needs? and (2) reliability – To what extent is the product free from deficiencies? If we apply the first dimension to partnership, partnership quality may be expressed as how well the outcome of a partnership delivered matches the participants' expectations (Lee & Kim, 1999).

From this outset, partnership quality can be viewed as an antecedent of the outsourcing success. High partnership quality may be a necessary condition for outsourcing success, but not a sufficient condition. For instance, if the main objective of the outsourcing was cost reduction but the outsourcing vendor failed to meet the objective, such an outsourcing project would be a failure regardless of the partnership quality between the service receiver and provider. Thus, Lee and Kim (1999) distinguish the concept of partnership quality from that of outsourcing success, and empirically tested whether outsourcing is successful when high-quality partnership exists. They identified the following five factors that make up partnership quality: trust (degree of confidence and willingness between partners), business understanding (degree of understanding of behaviors, goals, and policies between partners), benefit/risk share (degree of articulation and agreement on benefit and risk between partners), conflict (degree of incompatibility of activities, resource share and goals between partners), and commitment (degree of the pledge of relationship continuity between partners).

Partnership quality is affected by organizational, human, and environmental factors. However, most literature does not explicitly distinguish the components of partnership quality from the factors that affect it. Lee and Kim (1999) introduced the factors from previous literature as potential determinants of partnership quality and presented the hypotheses related to each factor. They expected to find a positive relationship between each of the hypothesized determinants of partnership quality and trust, business understanding, benefit/risk share, and commitment among the components of partnership quality, and a negative relationship between each of the hypothesized determinants of partnership quality and conflict.

Figure 3 illustrates their findings. Participation was found to be significantly related to partnership quality. From a social perspective, participation is prescribed as a remedy when there is conflict, frustration, and vacillation in the group. Active participation of the partnership members plays a major part in enhancing the sustainability of their partnerships over time. When one partner's actions influence the ability of the other to compete effectively, the need for participation in specifying roles, responsibilities, and expectations increases. Accordingly, the higher the degree of participation, the higher the quality of partnership. Communication quality was found to be significantly related to partnership quality. According to the social exchange literature, effective communication between partners is essential in order to achieve the intended objectives. Intensive communication should lead to better informed parties, which in turn should make each party more confident in the relationship and more willing to keep it alive. Communication quality is treated as an antecedent of trust in the research literature. Accordingly, higher communication quality is believed to enhance the quality of partnership. Information sharing is the third significant determinant in Figure 3. Information sharing is the extent to which critical or proprietary information is communicated to one's partner. Partnerships can create a competitive advantage through the strategic sharing of organizations' key information. Closer relationships result from more frequent and relevant information exchanges among high-performance partners. Participants are expected to sustain more effective relationships over time by sharing information and by being knowledgeable about each other's organization.

Age of relationship had a significant negative effect on the partnership quality. Among the components of partnership quality, conflict and commitment were significantly associated with age of relationship. However, contrary to many expectations, age of relationship had a positive effect on conflict and a negative effect on commitment. Interestingly, mutual dependency was also negatively associated with partnership quality. This means that the degree of partnership quality was lower when mutual dependency was higher. Although mutual dependency had a significant effect on business understanding, benefit

Figure 3. Partnership quality affected by determinants and effecting outsourcing success

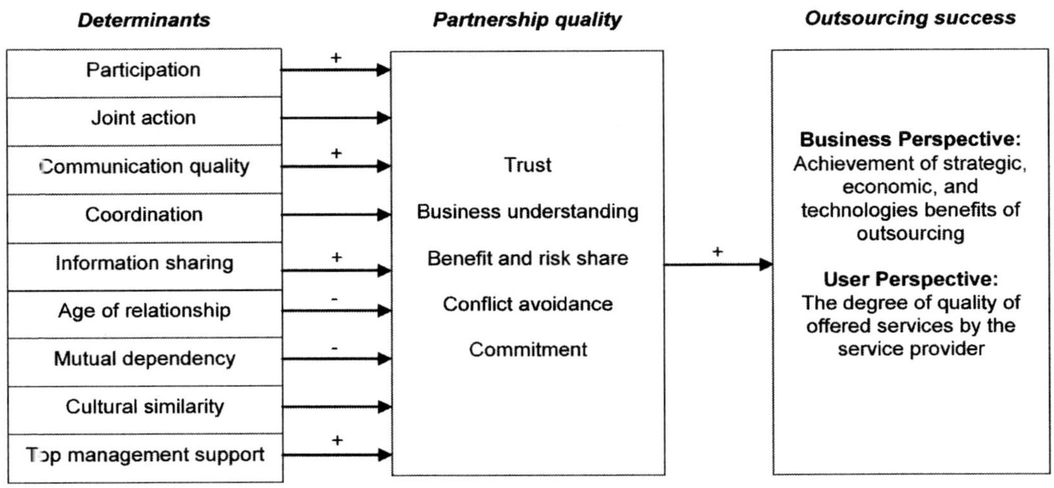

and risk share, and conflict, these results were contrary to the researchers' expectation. The relationship between top management support and partnership quality was significant. Top management support also was significantly associated with trust and business understanding, while it was not related to benefit and risk share, conflict, or commitment.

In Figure 3, there is a causal relationship between partnership quality and outsourcing success. Successful partnership enables participants to achieve organizational objectives and to build a competitive advantage that each organization could not easily attain by itself. To gain these advantages of partnership, participants should try to enhance their partnership quality to reflect the extent of intimacy between partners. Therefore, a higher quality of partnership is likely to lead to a successful outsourcing relationship.

Outsourcing Success

In their statistical analysis, Lee and Kim (1999) found that the quality of outsourcing partnership had a strong positive relationship with both business satisfaction and user satisfaction, as well as with overall outsourcing success. Trust showed a strong positive relationship with business satisfaction, while it had no effect on user satisfaction. This indicates that trust is a critical predictor of outsourcing success in terms of the business perspective, as opposed to the user perspective. Unlike the result with trust, business understanding was not a good predictor of business satisfaction while it significantly influenced user satisfaction. This means that the outsourcing outcome matched the users' requirements as understanding of its partner's business increased. Benefit and risk share showed a strong positive relationship with both business satisfaction and user satisfaction, as well as with overall outsourcing success. Although conflict was a predictor of business satisfaction, it had no effect on the overall outsourcing success and user satisfaction. Lee and Kim's (1999) finding for the conflict variable indicated that outsourcing success was not affected by the degree of conflict between the service receiver and provider. Their study also indicated that commitment was significantly associated with outsourcing success in terms of both the business and the user perspective. In summary, all partnership quality variables except conflict were significantly related to outsourcing success.

In the study by Lee and Kim (1999), success was measured on two variables. The first variable, business perspective, had the following items: (i) we have been able to refocus on core business, (ii) we have enhanced our IT competence, (iii) we have increased access to skilled personnel, (iv) we have enhanced economies of scale in human resources, (v) we have enhances economies of scale in technological resources, (vi) we have increased control of IS expenses, (vii) we have reduced the risk of technological obsolescence, (viii) we have increased access to key information technologies, and (ix) we are satisfied with our overall benefits from outsourcing. The second variable, user perspective, had the following items: (i) reliability of information, (ii) relevancy of information, (iii) accuracy of information, (iv) currency of information, (v) completeness of information, and (vi) timeliness of information. Most of the other reviewed literature that touch on success, apply the client perspective. However, successful IT outsourcing relationships require success for both client and vendor.

In a study conducted among 80 Norwegian large companies the authors examined organizational change-related factors that impact outsourcing success (Solli-Sæther, Gottschalk, & Kierulf, 2008). The idea was to investigate how firm readiness for change influenced its performance. Outsourcing was considered as a change initiative for the purpose of achieving competitive advantage. The independent variable outsourcing readiness was defined as a condition that describes how complete a company is to begin outsourcing. The dependent variable outsourcing success was defined as the degree to which service receivers was satisfied (first defined by Grover, Cheon, & Teng, 1996; and later used by Lee & Kim, 1999). The linear influence of organizational readiness on outsourcing success was examined, suggesting that understanding of business situation has significant positive effect on outsourcing success. As expected, higher levels of understanding business situation increased perception of outsourcing success.

CONCLUSION

The provider of outsourcing services benefits from economies of scale and complementary core competencies that would be difficult for a firm that does not specialize in information technology services to replicate. The vendor's specialized knowledge and skills can be shared with many different customers, and the experience of working with so many information systems projects further enhances the vendor's expertise. To succeed in an IT outsourcing relationship clients cannot replicate and apply vendor's competencies, and vendors must share productivity gains with clients.

Outsourcing success can be viewed as the level of fitness between the customer's requirements and the outsourcing outcomes. In a business perspective, outsourcing is motivated by the promise of strategic, economic, and technological benefits. The success of outsourcing, then, should be assessed in terms of attainment of these benefits. Strategic benefits refer to the ability of a firm to focus on its core business by outsourcing routine information technology activities. Economic benefits refer to the ability of a firm to use expertise and economies of scale in human and technological resources of the service provider and to manage its cost structure through unambiguous contractual arrangements. Technological benefits refer to the ability of a firm to gain access to leading edge IT and to avoid the risk of technological obsolescence that results from dynamic changes in IT. From a user perspective, outsourcing success may also be the level of quality of offered services.

A decision to outsource on the basis of saving costs without analysis of the quality of service frequently leads to higher costs and lower user satisfaction. Therefore, it is imperative to conduct a proper analysis of the service quality before building a relationship with a service provider for a successful outsourcing project (Lee & Kim, 1999). This chapter provided examples of how to measure the quality of IT services outsourced, client outsourcing satisfaction, partnership quality, and the success of outsourcing relationships. Some of these measures are objective and some are subjective in nature.

Managing IT outsourcing performance is not only about benefits and service quality that can be expected and realized. Managing performance is also about benefits and service quality that can be created by entrepreneurial vision and insight. Where others see problems, entrepreneurs see opportunities (Markowski & Hall, 2007). Thus, entrepreneurial management will enhance outsourcing performance.

REFERENCES

Bahli, B., & Rivard, S. (2003). The information technology outsourcing risk: a transaction cost and agency theory-based perspective. *Journal of Information Technology*, *18*(3), 211–221. doi:10.1080/0268396032000130214

Barthélemy, J. (2003). The Seven Deadly Sins of Outsourcing. *The Academy of Management Executive*, *17*(2), 87–100.

Clott, C. B. (2004). Perspectives on Global Outsourcing and the Changing Nature of Work. *Business and Society Review*, *109*(2), 153–170. doi:10.1111/j.0045-3609.2004.00189.x

DiRomualdo, A., & Gurbaxani, V. (1998). Strategic Intent for IT Outsourcing. *Sloan Management Review*, *39*(4), 67–80.

Domberger, S., Fernandez, P., & Fiebig, D. G. (2000). Modelling the price, performance and contract characteristics of IT outsourcing. *Journal of Information Technology*, *15*(2), 107–118. doi:10.1080/026839600344302

Earl, M. J. (1996). The Risks of Outsourcing IT. *Sloan Management Review*, *37*(3), 26–32.

Gottschalk, P. (2005). *Strategic Knowledge Management*. Hershey, PA: Idea Group Publishing.

Grover, V., Cheon, M. J., & Teng, J. T. C. (1996). The Effect of Service Quality and Partnership on the Outsourcing of Information Systems Functions. *Journal of Management Information Systems*, *12*(4), 89–116.

InfoWorld. (2004). Five Risks of Outsourcing. from www.infoworld.com

Lacity, M. C., & Willcocks, L. P. (1998). An Empirical Investigation of Information Technology Sourcing Practices: Lessons from Experience. *MIS Quarterly*, *22*(3), 363–408. doi:10.2307/249670

Lee, J.-N., & Kim, Y.-G. (1999). Effect of Partnership Quality on IS Outsourcing Success: Conceptual Framework and Empirical Validation. *Journal of Management Information Systems*, *15*(4), 29–61.

Levina, N., & Ross, J. W. (2003). From the Vendor's Perspective: Exploring the Value Proposition in Information Technology Outsourcing. *MIS Quarterly*, *27*(3), 331–364.

Markowski, S., & Hall, P. (2007). Public sector entrepreneurialism and the production of defense. *Public Finance and Management, 7*(3), 260–294.

Milgate, M. (2000). Effective Outsourcing through Performance Measurement. *Contract Management,* (July), 32-46.

Sheehan, N. T. (2002). *Reputation as a Driver in Knowledge-Intensive Service Firms.* Unpublished Doctoral Thesis, Norwegian School of Management, Sandvika.

Solli-Sæther, H., Gottschalk, P., & Kierulf, K. (2008, December, 12-14). *Organizational Readiness for Successful Outsourcing.* Paper presented at the Strategic Management Society India Special Conference, Hyderabad, India.

Chapter 9
Outsourcing Governance

The overall objective of this chapter is to concentrate on the important issues of strategy, structure, and management of IT outsourcing arrangements. First, we take a look at the broader issue of governance. Learning that IT outsourcing governance includes not only information and IT assets, but also such aspects as human, financial, physical, intellectual property, and relationship assets, we present in the next section the interaction approach as a model that focuses both on short-term episodes and general long-term relationships in dyadic buyer-supplier ventures. Then we discuss how appropriate governance structures – including management control systems and the development of trust – may work to reduce risk and decrease failure. We continue by presenting the important partnering process, where management can take actions when building and sustaining outsourcing relationships. Important stakeholder groups are presented as they may have distinct expectations and goals in outsourcing and for outsourcing relationships. Hard and soft sides of outsourcing management are presented, as both sides are keys to success. Finally, using theoretical perspectives described earlier and experience earned from several business case studies, we present a governance model for successful management of IT outsourcing relationships.

DOI: 10.4018/978-1-60566-796-6.ch009

PERSPECTIVES ON GOVERNANCE

IT governance can be defined as *a firm's overall process for sharing decision rights about IT and monitoring the performance of IT investments*. Weill and Ross (2004) define IT governance as specifying the decision rights and accountability framework to encourage desirable behavior in using IT. IT governance is not about making specific IT decisions – management does that – but rather determines who systematically makes and contributes to those decisions. IT governance reflects broader corporate governance principles while focusing on the management and use of IT to achieve corporate performance goals. Effective IT governance encourages and leverages the ingenuity of the enterprise's people in IT usage and ensures compliance with the enterprise's overall vision and values.

All enterprises have IT governance. Those with effective governance have actively designed a set of IT governance mechanisms (committees, budgeting processes, approvals, and so on) that encourage behavior consistent with the organization's mission, strategy, values, norms and culture. In these enterprises, IT can factor significantly into competitive strategy. In contrast, enterprises that govern IT by default more often find that IT can sabotage business strategy. Before we dive into IT outsourcing governance, we must look at the broader issue of corporate governance in enterprises. Corporate governance is concerned with governing key assets, such as (Weill & Ross, 2004):

- *Human assets*: People, skills, career paths, training, reporting, mentoring, competencies and so on.
- *Financial assets*: Cash, investments, liabilities, cash flow, receivables and so on.
- *Physical assets*: Buildings, plant, equipment, maintenance, security, utilization, and so on.
- *IP assets*: Intellectual property (IP), including product, services, and process know-how formally patented, copyrighted, or embedded in the enterprises' people and systems.
- *Information and IT assets*: Digitized data, information, and knowledge about customers, processes performance, finances, information systems, and so on.
- *Relationship assets*: Relationships within the enterprise as well as relationships, brand, and reputation with customers, suppliers, business units, regulators, competitors, channel partners, and so on.

As we can see from this list, IT outsourcing governance includes not only information and IT assets. IT outsourcing governance is concerned with several of these assets, sometimes even all of these assets. In this perspective, IT outsourcing governance may be as comprehensive in scope as corporate governance.

In governing IT outsourcing, we can learn from good financial and corporate governance. For example, the CFO (chief financial officer) does not sign every check or authorize every payment. Instead, he or she sets up financial governance specifying who can make the decisions and how. The CFO then oversees the enterprise's portfolio of investments and manages the required cash flow and risk exposure. The CFO tracks a series of financial metrics to manage the enterprise's financial assets, intervening only if there are problems or unforeseen opportunities. Similar principles apply to who can commit the enterprise to a contract or a partnership. Exactly the same approach should be applied to IT governance (Weill & Ross, 2004).

The dichotomy market or hierarchy has exercised a dominant influence on the study of forms of governance and their operation for some time. However, in the past two decades there have been large numbers of investigations of intermediate forms of governance. Subsequently it has been recognized that the behavior that occurs within exchanges is not necessarily determined by the forms of governance used, and this points to a need to understand behavior within a variety of exchanges. Blois (2002) defines governance as the institutional framework in which contracts are initiated, monitored, adapted, and terminated. An exchange occurs between two organizations when resources are transferred from one party to the other in return for resources controlled by the other party.

The organization of interfirm exchanges has become of critical importance in today's business environment. Many scholars have criticized the inadequacies of legal contracts as mechanisms for governing exchange, especially in the face of uncertainty and dependence. Other scholars argue that it is not the contracts per se but the social contexts in which they are embedded that determine their effectiveness. Cannon, Achrol, and Gundlach (2000) investigated the performance implications of governance structures involving contractual agreements and relational social norms, individually and in combination (plural form) under varying conditions and forms of transactional uncertainty and relationship-specific adaptation. Hypotheses were developed and tested on a sample of buyer-seller relationships. The results provide support for the plural form thesis – increasing the relational content of a governance structure containing contractual agreements enhanced performance when transactional uncertainty was high, but not when it was low.

Cannon et al. (2000) applied the term legal bonds to refer to the extent to which detailed and binding contractual agreements were used to specify the roles and obligations of the parties. To the extent contracts were characterized in this way, they were less flexible and therefore more constrained in their adaptive properties. Highly detailed contracts were also less likely to possess the kinds of general safeguards that are more effective in thwarting self-interest-seeking behavior under circumstances of ambiguity.

Various perspectives on the nature of contracts as a mechanism of governance may be found in the literature. According to the original transaction cost framework (Williamson, 1979), formal contingent claims contracts (i.e. classical contracts) are inefficient mechanisms of governance in the face of uncertainty because organizations are bounded in their rationality and find it impossible to contemplate all possible future contingencies. For exchanges involving high levels of idiosyncratic investments and characterized by uncertainty, internal organization or hierarchy is predicted to be a more efficient form of governance than the market (Cannon et al., 2000).

However, neo-classical contract law argues that contracts can provide useful governance in exchange relationships even in the face of uncertainty and risk. This tradition of contract law is marked by doctrine and rules that attempt to overcome the difficulties posed by the classical tradition's emphasis on discreteness and presentation of exchange. The new doctrines enable parties to respond to unforeseen contingencies by making adjustments to ongoing exchange and ensuring continuity in their relationships. For example, concepts such as "good faith" and "reasonable commercial standards of fair dealing in the trade" are recognized under the Uniform Commercial Code (UCC) of 1978 in the US as general provisions for contracting behavior that also help to ensure continuity in exchange relationships. Similarly, "gap filler" provisions of the UCC rely on "prior dealings" between parties and "customary practices" across an industry or trading area for completing contract terms intentionally left open or omitted, thus allowing for adjustments to contingencies (Cannon et al., 2000).

However, neo-classical contracts are not indefinitely elastic (Williamson, 1991). Many scholars remain skeptical of how effective even the most carefully crafted contracts can be. It is argued that the scope for drafting rules in contracts to address changing or ambiguous conditions, or the ability to rely on general legal safeguards for controlling commercial conduct, is limited by both practicality and the law itself.

Drawing on these views, Cannon et al. (2000) argue that when a transaction involves relationship-specific adaptations and is (1) subject to dynamic forces and future contingencies that cannot be foreseen or (2) involves ambiguous circumstances where tasks are ill-defined and prone to exploitation, the difficulty of writing, monitoring, and enforcing contracts is increased, and their overall governance effectiveness weakened. In each case, efforts to govern the relationship on the basis of detailed and formal contracts – without the benefit of some additional apparatus – are not likely to enhance performance. Social or relational norms are defined generally as shared expectations regarding behavior. The norms reflect expectations about attitudes and behaviors parties have in working cooperatively together to achieve mutual and individual goals. The spirit of such sentiments is captured by many overlapping types of relational contracting norms. These can be reduced to a core set of five (Cannon et al., 2000):

- *Flexibility*. The attitude among parties that an agreement is but a starting point to be modified as the market, the exchange relationship, and the fortunes of the parties evolve.
- *Solidarity*. The extent to which parties believe that success comes from working cooperatively together versus competing against one another. It dictates that parties stand by one another in the face of adversity and the ups and downs of marketplace competition.
- *Mutuality*. The attitude that each party's success is a function of everyone's success and that one cannot prosper at the expense of one's partner. It expresses the sentiment of joint responsibility.
- *Harmonization of conflict*. The extent to which a spirit of mutual accommodation toward cooperative ends exists.
- *Restraint in the use of power*. Forbearance from taking advantage of one's bargaining position in an exchange. It reflects the view that the use of power not only exacerbates conflict over time but also undermines mutuality and solidarity, opening the door to opportunism.

Together, these cooperative norms define relational properties that are important in affecting adaptations to dynamic market conditions and safeguarding the continuity of exchanges subject to task ambiguity. Norms represent important social and organizational vehicles of control in exchange where goals are ill defined or involve open-ended performance. They provide a general frame of reference, order, and standards against which to guide and assess appropriate behavior in uncertain and ambiguous situations. In such situations contracts are often incomplete, and legal remedies can undermine relationship continuity. In contrast, norms motivate performance through focusing attention on the shared values of the partners to safeguard and rely on peer pressure and social sanctions to mitigate the risk of shirking and opportunistic expropriation. Because they involve expectations rather than rigid requirements of behavior, they create a cooperative as opposed to a confrontational environment for negotiating adaptations, thus promoting continuity in exchange.

The plural form thesis contends that exchange is best understood as embedded in a complex matrix of economic, social, and political structures and that the governance of exchange relations more often relies on combinations of market, social or authority-based mechanisms than on any one category exclusively. While the plural form thesis is that the various mechanisms in fact work together to reinforce or complement one another in some way, little attention has focused on exactly how these mechanisms actually complement one another (Cannon et al., 2000).

Figure 1. Model explaining how supplier effect customer costs (adapted from Cannon & Homburg, 2001)

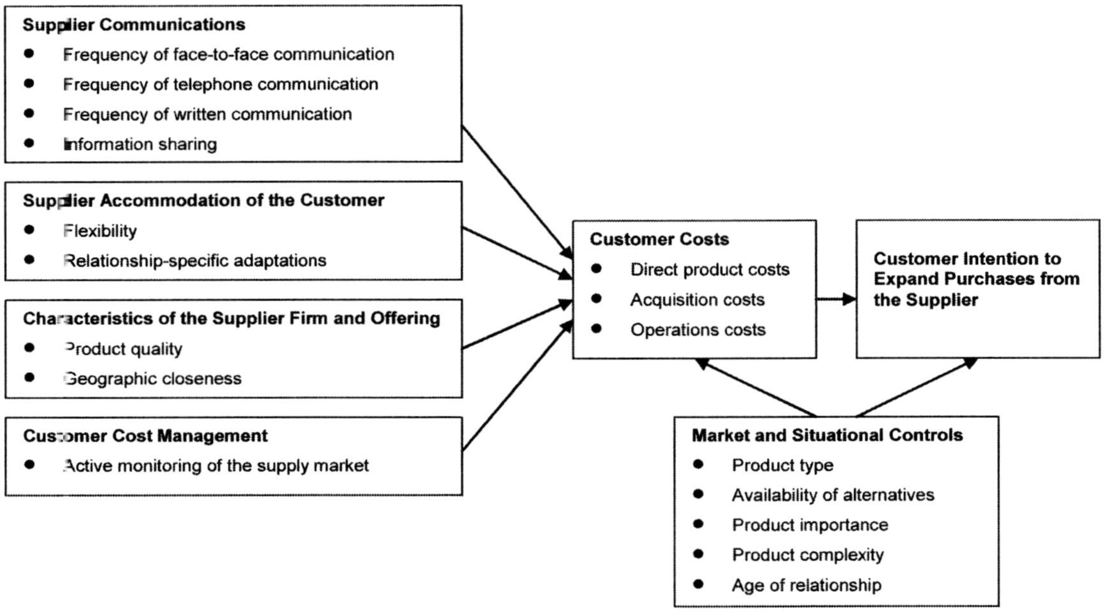

Academic literature and business practice are directing increased attention to the importance of creating value in buyer-supplier relationships. One method for creating value is to reduce costs in commercial exchange. Cannon and Homburg (2001) developed at model that explains how supplier behaviors and the management of suppliers affect a customer firm's direct product, acquisition, and operations costs. The model proposes that these costs mediate the relationship between buyer-supplier relationship behaviors and the customer firm's intentions to expand future purchases from the supplier, as illustrated in Figure 1.

Cannon and Homburg (2001) empirically tested all relationships in their model. Their findings provide support for the expectation that more complex operational issues at times may require the richer interaction provided in face-to-face communications but at other times may benefit from simpler written exchanges. As expected, the more standardized issues typical of product acquisition benefit from more efficient written/electronic communication. In contrast, open information sharing by suppliers was not found to be related to a customer firm's costs. The lack of support for these hypotheses may be caused by buying firms' failure to use the information received from suppliers effectively. For example, customer firms may suffer from information overload and be unable to process and act on such information effectively. Further hypotheses in Figure 1 predict the effects supplier accommodation would have on customer costs. The empirical results support the prediction that greater supplier flexibility results in lower acquisition and operations costs. Contrary to the researchers' predictions, higher levels of relationships-specific adaptation did not lead to lower acquisition or operations costs. This may be because many of these adaptations are targeted at enhancing value through increasing the benefits a customer receives, not through cost reduction.

Whereas Cannon and Homburg (2001) developed a hypothesis that higher direct product costs would be associated with greater supplier adaptation, the result was statistically significant in the opposite direction. Several factors may explain this unanticipated finding. First, relationship-specific adaptations may evolve into regular business practices with all customers, which may subsequently lower the cost of accommodation. Second, buying organizations may effectively bargain away the premium prices a supplier must initially charge for customized products. Finally, at a more general level, buyers may compensate suppliers through long-term commitments and/or promises of higher sales volume. Typically, such agreements also involve lower prices over time.

As predicted in the model in Figure 1, geographic proximity of the supplier's facilities helped lower acquisition costs. The expected effects of quality in lowering the customer's acquisition costs and operations costs were found, but Cannon and Homburg (2001) were surprised to find that higher-quality products had lower direct product costs. Possible explanations for the unexpected finding for the product quality-direct product costs relationship can be drawn from the quality literature. It may be that quality operates as an order qualifier and high quality is necessary just to be considered as a supplier but does not allow a supplier to charge higher prices.

Another hypothesis in Figure 1 predicts the effects of actively monitoring the supply market on each cost. More active monitoring of the supply market was found to be associated with higher operations costs but not with higher acquisition costs. A final hypothesis in Figure 1 was supported in the empirical data. It predicts that lowering the customer firm's direct product, acquisition, and operations costs leads the customer to expand its business with the supplier. These findings suggest that a supplier's efforts to lower a customer firm's costs can have long-term benefits to suppliers as well.

As IT outsourcing becomes more commonplace, new organizational forms are emerging to facilitate these relationships. Chase Bank has created "shared services" units that compete with outside vendors to furnish services to the bank's own operating units. Delta Airlines has established a "business partners" unit to oversee its relations with vendors. Microsoft outsources almost everything – from the manufacturing of its computer software to the distribution of its software products, thereby focusing the organization on its primary area of competitive advantage: the writing of software code. Still other firms are creating "strategic services" divisions in which activities formerly decentralized into autonomous business units are now being recentralized for outside contracting. As these various approaches suggest, the best ways to structure outsourcing remain the subject of ongoing management debate and media coverage (Useem & Harder, 2000).

As companies devise new forms of organization to assure that outsourcing works as intended, those responsible require a new blend of talents. Rather than issuing orders, managers must concentrate on negotiating results, replacing a skill for sending work downward with a talent for arranging work outward. Thus, the outsourcing of services necessitates lateral leadership. Useem and Harder (2000) reached this conclusion about leadership capabilities required for outsourcing through interviews conducted with several companies. What emerged from the interviews and a broader survey was a picture of more demanding leadership environment, even as day-to-day management tasks are streamlined by outsourcing. They found that four individual capabilities encompass much of what is required of managers as outsourcing becomes commonplace:

- *Strategic thinking.* Within the outsourcing framework, managers must understand whether and how to outsource in ways that improve competitive advantage.
- *Deal making.* Outsource process managers must broker deals in two directions simultaneously - securing the right services from external providers and ensuring their use by internal managers.
- *Partnership governing.* After identifying areas suitable for outsourcing through strategic

Figure 2. Economics of institutions

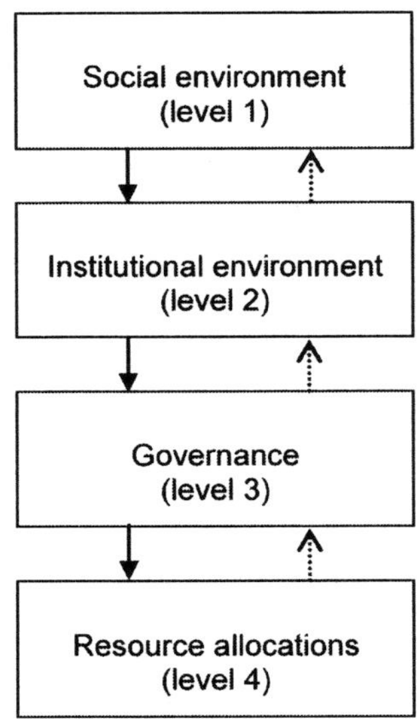

assessment and upon clinching a deal, effectively overseeing the relationship is essential.

- *Managing change*. Forcefully spearhead change is critical because companies are certain to encounter employee resistance.

These four capabilities emerged repeatedly when Useem and Harder (2000) were discussing the essential skills of those responsible for outsourcing decisions, contracting, and oversight. None of these qualities taken singly were found to be unique to outsourcing, but their combination is critical to leading laterally.

Williamson (2000) argues that governance is at level 3 in the new institutional economics as illustrated in Figure 2. He defines governance as play of the game – especially contract by aligning governance structures with transactions. At level 1 we find the social environment, consisting of norms, customs, mores, traditions, and religion. Level 2 is the institutional environment consisting of laws, bureaucracy and politics. Level 4 is resource allocation and employment, where we also find prices and quantities for resources and incentive alignment for employees. It is useful for the purposes of perspectives on IT governance to study the hierarchy of Figure 2. The solid arrows that connect a higher with a lower level signify that the higher level imposes constraints on the level immediately below. The reverse arrows that connect lower with higher levels are dashed and signal feedback.

In the models of corporate governance literature one can organize the variety of variables and concepts used to describe the complexity of corporate governance mechanisms into two main categories: capital-related and related-related. The capital related aspects contain, among others, variables like ownership structure, corporate voting, the identity of owners, and the role of institutional owners. The related-related aspects refer mainly to the stakeholdning position of related in corporate governance. Here one could mention employee involvement schemes, participatory management, and co-determination (Cernat, 2004).

Figure 3. Interaction approach to governance structure for outsourcing customer and outsourcing vendor

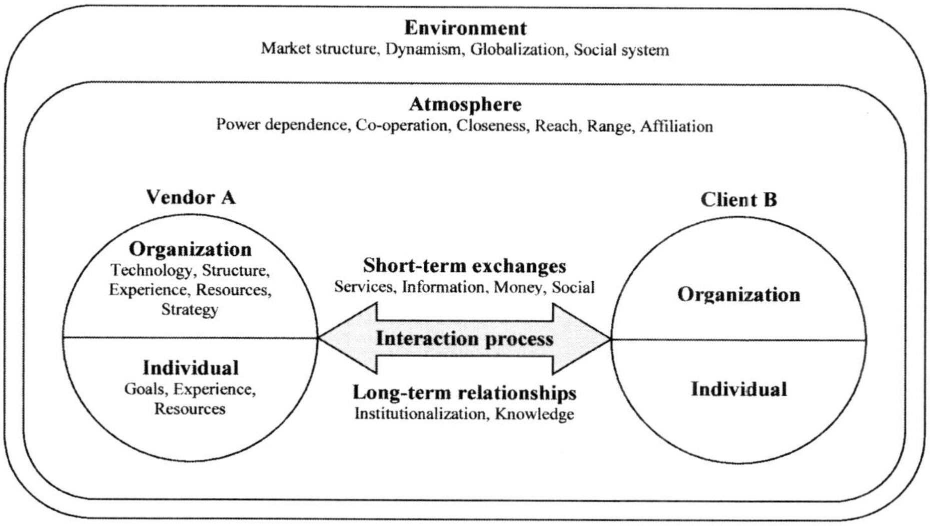

INTERACTION APPROACH

The interaction approach draws upon inter-organizational theory, the marketing and purchasing literature, and on transaction cost theory to substantiate its different constructs and dimensions. Figure 3 reproduces the basic interaction model, which Kern and Willcocks (2002) adopted from Håkansson (1982). The model focuses both on short-term episodes and general long-term relationships in dyadic buyer-supplier ventures. The model recognizes that participants are commonly confronted with a complex pattern of interactions between and within organizations, and that the interactions become institutionalized into a set of roles that each organization's stakeholder expects the others to perform. This process may involve different degrees of both conflict and co-operation. As illustrated in Figure 3, the interaction model suggests that the environment, in which the interaction takes place, and the atmosphere affecting and affected by the interaction, are important variables. The interaction process is influenced by both short-term exchange episodes and long-term relationships.

Environment of organizations can be described in terms of market structure determining the rate of change, the concentration of suppliers and buyers, and the number of alternative relationships available for the participants; the degree of dynamism influencing either party's ability to predict and forecast changes in the market that in turn may affect the relationship; and social system defining the real barriers to interacting between organizations. Such aspects as protocols, procedures, experiences and ways of behaving when dealing with particular industries and organizations influence relations.

Atmosphere of working relations between organizations can best be described in terms of power dependence, the degree of conflict or co-operation, and the overall social distance between the contributing organizations. In the age of electronic business, the important dimensions of reach, affiliation and richness have to be included in the atmosphere construct (Evans & Wurster, 1999). Reach is about willingness to provide access and connection, affiliation is about whose interests the business represents, and richness is the depth and detail of information that the business can and will give the other organization.

Short-term exchanges are the core part of the model. The goods and services bought and sold may entail a number of risks, depending on their complexity. Information exchanges are essential and are constituted by content in technical and financial areas, media of communication, and the degree of formality. Financial exchanges reveal the importance of the relationship. Social exchanges help to reduce uncertainty, especially in situations of cultural or spatial disparity. Formalization, trust, understanding, flexibility and integrity are important aspects of social exchange.

Long-term relationships are concerned with institutionalization and knowledge transfer. Institutional theory seeks to explain homogeneity of organizational forms and practices. The role of institutional influence is particularly powerful in explaining organizational phenomena in industries where well laid-out rules, structures, external regulation and practices govern organizational exchanges and operations (Ang & Cummings, 1997). Knowledge transfer concerns how an organization's individuals and internal structure transfer their knowledge to another organization. Knowledge transfer has the purpose of improving the competence of customer and supplier (Sveiby, 2001).

Informed by this interaction approach as a guiding framework, Kern and Willcocks (2002) searched for insights into the nuances of relationship practice in IT outsourcing. They found several contributions the interaction approach can make to increase clarity and improved management:

- *Four exchange episodes.* Practitioners have tended to become over-focused on the financial and service exchanges. All too often they complain of little manifest development, and business optimization, of the relationship, but do all too little on the informational and social exchange fronts. Clearly, all four exchange episodes need to be managed interactively and for the length of the contract.
- *Beyond transaction or relationship-based exchanges.* Relatedly, practitioners tend to see IT outsourcing in terms of a dichotomy – that is, as a transaction-based or relationship-based exchange. However, applying the interaction approach shows that there is always a complex relationship dimension that needs to be managed if IT outsourcing is going to be effective for all parties.
- *How to mitigate risks.* A major risk that materializes often in IT outsourcing is a client's loss of control of the arrangements and, eventually, its IT destiny. The focus in the interaction approach on power-dependency, commitment, cooperation and on exchange theory shows to practitioners that dealing with certain issues beyond contract monitoring form fundamental ground for achieving or failing in their managerial objectives.
- *Being realistic about trust.* Given that there are a lot of IT outsourcing arrangements self-defined variously as strategic alliances, strategic partnerships or strategic relationships, the interaction approach brings home to practitioners the naivety of the earlier notions of trust on which these seemed to be founded, resulting in contracts of insufficient detail and clarity, and an over-belief in the suppliers' good offices. The interaction approach offers a more complex, realistic positioning of the role of trust amongst other influential factors, and provides the tools to show how trust needs to be earned over time, through experiences, and cannot be assumed to be in place at any time, let alone on day one.

Outsourcing research and experience recurrently emphasizes the importance of the contract. Contracting needs careful consideration, as it is traditionally seen as the beginning and foundation of the outsourcing relationship. Kern and Willcocks (2002) find that the interaction approach largely neglects it. Although the outsourcing relationship is contractually governed to ensure opportunistic behavior can be regulated at any point by termination, Kern and Willcocks' study underlines that the contract is no panacea nor does it ensure successful relations. Instead, the contract provides a sub-stratum, it is about getting the foundations right. Careful contract – management is fundamental, and entails careful monitoring of services, payments and other requirements and regular revisiting of the contract for updates.

Kern and Willcocks (2002) found that IT outsourcing requires active management involvement beyond what most expect when they contract out. Traditionally, clients expect that the supplier takes over and delivers the service while the client stands back and monitors. However, this is a misperception. In fact, 70% of client managers' time in post-contract management is spent on managing relations. This suggests two considerations. Firstly, it is critical for the client to establish an appropriately skilled management infrastructure prior to outsourcing, which it can implement during post-contract management. Secondly, the supplier needs to formalize an account team that mirrors the customer's management group. In other words, the overall contract structure should be formalized and both parties should be aware who their respective counterpart is.

It should be a key goal of client companies to move together with the supplier towards standardization of interactions and routine operations. Achieving what others have termed the state of embeddedness holds the true benefits of outsourcing ventures for both parties. For the client, it provides potential areas of where the supplier can add true value by applying its specific technological expertise, which in a number of client organizations can result in reengineering programs and new technology investments. For the supplier, it entails potential opportunities for new business and hence increased profits. Some refer to this level of client-supplier integration as a win-win situation, where both parties benefit in their ways from the relationship. Others have explained it as the result of embeddedness, where economic actions become embedded in ongoing social ties that facilitate further exchange relations.

The interaction approach has both potential and limitations in explaining IT outsourcing relationships. It represents an interesting starting point for further research into identifying IT outsourcing relationship practice. The interaction approach's focus on exchange issues is highly pertinent to the study of IT outsourcing relationships, but it further needs to be combined with contract and transaction cost perspectives (Kern & Willcocks, 2002).

MANAGEMENT CONTROL SYSTEMS

Outsourcing is a form of strategic alliance that has increased in popularity over the past decade. However, there is a growing body of evidence of a high failure rate in such arrangements. One cause of this is the high level of risk associated with alliances, compared to in-house activities. Aspects that cause high risk include the difficulties inherent in gaining cooperation with partners who have different objectives, and the potential for opportunistic exploitation of the dependence relationship that exists between partners. Appropriate governance structures, including management control systems and the development of trust, may work to reduce risk and decrease failure (Langfield-Smith & Smith, 2003).

There are several, well-established models or frameworks for studying the design of management control systems. However, these frameworks typically focus on control systems within organizations. It is only recently that researchers have begun to consider the design of governance structures in situations that span traditional organizational boundaries, including strategic alliances with suppliers, or outsourcing. These alliances involve the sharing of joint decision making in areas such as strategic planning, and new product and process development. They may also entail joint investments in relation-specific assets.

Compared to arms-length relationships, which are often well defined and contractually based, outsourcing relationships may encompass a great deal of uncertainty or risk for both parties. The nature of the contract between the two parties can be complex and cover many areas of interest that extend beyond the mere actions of supply and receipt of goods and services. The complexity of such arrangements may preclude the complete ex ante specification of detailed contracts. In addition, the need for flexibility and adaptation in those partnerships may imply that control systems rely less on formal mechanisms. However, in some outsourcing situations the institution of a formal control system may enable greater control and transparency, which not only may impact on the interorganizational relationship, but also may have implications for strengthening control and increasing insights within the outsourcing firm.

Almost every control system involves some degree of trust that the individuals of concern will do what is best for the organization without any, or with only incomplete, monitoring of actions or results. Trust in governance relationships may develop over time through processes of learning and adaptation, which are essential to the strengthening of the relationship between partners, making the relationship more durable in the face of conflict and encouraging interactions between partners involving knowledge exchange and promotion of each other's interests (Langfield-Smith & Smith, 2003).

A common framework for viewing the choice of governance structures in inter-firm relationships is transaction cost economics. Transaction cost economics is based on the notion that firms choose efficient organizational forms and governance structures based on transactional issues, such as firm-specific investments, and external and internal uncertainty. Governance structures can be characterized as one of three forms: markets, hybrids (including strategic alliances) and hierarchies (Williamson, 1991). Transaction cost economics is based on the idea that three aspects of transactions determine the appropriate mode of governance: the frequency of the transaction, the uncertainty encompassed in those transactions, and the asset specificity of the transactions (Williamson, 1979). Asset specificity, in particular, is said to be of particular significance in explaining the choice of governance structure (Langfield-Smith & Smith, 2003). Asset specificity is the degree to which an asset can be redeployed to alternative use without sacrifice of productive value. It is the opportunity loss associated with the early termination of a relationship. High level of asset specificity creates dependency between the parties in a relationship, increases switching costs and leads to difficult governance situations.

Three broad types of governance structures have been suggested by Williamson (1979): non-transaction-specific, semi-specific and highly specific. The market is the classic nonspecific governance structure within which faceless buyers and sellers meet for an instant to exchange standardized goods at equilibrium prices. By contrast, highly specific structures are tailored to the special needs of the transaction. Identity here clearly matters. Semi-specific structures, naturally, fall in between. Several propositions are suggested immediately. (1) Highly standardized transactions are not apt to require specialized governance structure. (2) Only recurrent transactions will support a highly specialized governance structure. (3) Although occasional transactions of a nonstandardized kind will not support a transaction-specific governance structure, they require special attention nonetheless.

For outsourcing relationships, management control systems will, according to transaction cost economics theory, depend on three dimensions: task programmability, ex post information impactedness (output measurability) and asset specificity. Two control archetypes for outsourcing relationships can be specified hybrid arms-length control and hybrid exploratory control. Langfield-Smith and Smith (2003) developed three different outsourcing control patterns labeled market based pattern, bureaucracy based pattern and trust based pattern:

- The *market-based pattern* suits transactions characterized by high task programmability, high measurability of output, low asset specificity and high task repetition. Many suppliers will compete for the contract, and market prices will be directly linked to the quality of the output of the outsourcer's activities. Detailed contracts are not required, and the possibility of returning to the market for competing bids provides discipline for the current outsourcer to provide an efficient and effective output. In the face of effective market mechanisms, no specific control instruments are needed to manage the relationship. The institutional environment is not relevant, and nor is supplier reputation, prior history of cooperation, or risk attitude. If one party to the relationship behaves opportunistically, another party can be chosen without high switching costs, as there are no specific investments. The transaction environment is characterized by low uncertainty and many available alternative suppliers.
- The *bureaucracy based pattern*, or *hybrid arms-length control*, suits transactions that have high task programmability, high output measurability, moderate asset specificity and low to medium repetitiveness. The transaction environment has relatively low uncertainty, and the future is fairly predictable. Controls will be prescriptive and include detailed rules of behavior and rigid performance targets. These will be captured in detailed contracts, which are used to monitor performance. Comprehensive selection criteria are set up and formal bidding is used to select a partner. So-called hostage arrangements can be used to ensure compliance to contractual provisions, and arbitration may be used to resolve contract disputes and to counter opportunistic behavior in an environment of moderate asset specificity. Contracts are specific and long-term, and the autonomy of the two parties is preserved. In this situation, a combination of behavior and outcome controls will be used, which is consistent with prescriptions for control systems in the face of high task programmability and high output measurability. Trust plays a limited role in the bureaucracy based pattern, but is important in the early stages of a relationship. Where human knowledge and skills are critical to the quality of the work, the outsourcing firm must perceive that the outsourcer has high levels of competence trust and contractual trust in order to select the outsourcer and to proceed with the contract.
- The *trust-based pattern* is characterized by low levels of task programmability, low levels of output measurability and high asset specificity. Transactions are not highly repetitive. The environment is highly uncertain and risky, so trust becomes the dominant mechanism for achieving control in this form of relationship, and this mitigates the risks associated with high asset specificity. The initial selection of the outsourcer is based on perceptions of competence trust, contractual trust and goodwill trust, which arise through friendships, former contractual relationships and reputation. Initially, contracts are merely broad frameworks, which then develop further over time. A series of control devices, such as personal consultations and intense communications, are put in place to develop competence trust and goodwill trust. In addition, the institutional environment can stimulate the development of competence trust and contractual trust, through certification of the firm's activities and legal regulations. Goodwill trust becomes the solution to overcoming information asymmetry, and regular personal contacts and an attitude of commitment can lead to its development. Control systems, in general, are more informal under these forms of relationships, and often take the form of social controls. Behavior controls are not suited in these situations of low task programmability, and when controls are formalized they tend to emphasize outcome controls, and these develop over time through the sharing of private information and the alignment of the parties' performance expectations. Trust is necessary to achieve control, as activities and output cannot be measured with any certainty.

The transaction characteristics of *hybrid exploratory control* are similar to those of trust-based control, except that asset specificity is moderate rather than high. High asset specificity (as found under a trust based pattern) cannot be tolerated under an outsourcing situation as it increases the potential for opportunistic behavior and information leakage, requiring outsourced function to be taken back in-house. However, firms do continue to engage in outsourcing in situations of high asset specificity. The trust-based pattern demonstrates that the development of goodwill trust and contractual trust can mitigate opportunistic behavior and the abuse of unequal bargaining power. Similarly, under hybrid exploratory control, exclusive contacts with suppliers are considered unacceptable, as they increase asset specificity, dependence and risk, in light of incomplete contracts. However, organizations do enter into exclusive contracts with outsourcers. Again, goodwill trust and contractual trust will counter the potential opportunistic behavior.

Table 1 contains a summary of the characteristics of the transaction, transaction environment and parties for the three patterns of control, as well as the form of control mechanisms and the role of trust in achieved control. Thus, depending on the characteristics of the transaction, the transaction environment and the parties, we would expect the management control system of outsourced operations to follow one of these patterns.

PARTNERING RELATIONSHIPS

Partnering is not new to the information systems literature, and the development of partnering has been studied elsewhere in the management literature as well, particularly in marketing, and a number of models have been proposed for the building and sustaining of these relationships. Social exchange theory

Table 1. Control mechanisms and trust (adapted from Langfield-Smith & Smith, 2003)

	Market based pattern	Bureaucratic based pattern	Trust based pattern
Transaction	High task programmability High output measurability Low asset specificity High repetition	High task programmability High output measurability Moderate asset specificity Low repetition	Low task programmability Low output measurability High asset specificity Low repetition
Transaction environment	Many potential parties All market information Social not relevant	Future known High market risks Institutional factors	Future unknown High market risks Social embeddedness Institutional factors
Parties	Not important	Competence reputation Medium risk sharing Asymmetry in bargaining	Competence reputation Experience in networks Experience with parties Risk sharing attitude No asymmetry
Control mechanisms	No specific instruments Competitive bidding No detailed contracts Market prices	Outcome control Rigid performance targets Detailed rules Detailed contracts Comprehensive selection Hostage arrangements	Social controls Non-specific contracts Performance assessed High levels of information
Role of trust	Not relevant	In selecting the outsourcer	Perceptions of competence trust, contractual trust and goodwill trust

underlies many of the contributions. In partnering relationships, five processes occur, where customer management can take action (Klepper, 1998):

- *Attraction.* This process involves rewards provided directly to the client by the vendor and rewards inherent in the characteristics of the vendor. Direct rewards are the benefits the client receives from work done for it by the vendor in the past and present. Vendors that carry out high quality work within time and budget constraints offer higher direct rewards than vendors who do not. Vendors whose personnel work easily and co-operatively with personnel of the client firm offer higher direct rewards than vendors who do not. Customer management action is to systematically gather and centralize the information on rewards of the vendor and characteristics of the vendor.
- *Communication and bargaining.* This process involves open revelation of needs and resources related to the future of the relationship. Bargaining arises as part of contract negotiations with every project undertaken by a vendor, and often arises again when unforeseen mid-project circumstances require an adjustment of requirements and performance. Customer management action is to rate vendors in terms of communication skills and bargaining results.
- *Expectations development.* This process involves actions that are beneficial to the other party in expectation that the second party will reciprocate. These expectations and the actions that stem from them are based on trust. Expectations that are fulfilled build trust, and trust allows expectations to rise. Customer management action is to develop sets of expectations to which it will hold any partner-vendor, and by providing incentives for vendors who meet these expectations.
- *Norm development.* This fourth process has to do with expected patterns of behavior in a relationship. Norms guide the actions of the client and vendor and set the stage for further interaction. Customer management can strengthen and promote norm development by identifying positive vendor actions as the basis for possible norms as they occur and communicating these expectations to the vendor.
- *Power and justice.* This is the final process. One party has power over a second party if the second is dependent on the first for valued resources, and this power is enhanced if there are limited alternative sources available to the second party. Exercise of power can be classified as just or unjust. It is unjust if the first uses its power for its sole benefit, without the second party's consent or understanding. It is just if both parties benefit jointly from, or if the second party is adequately compensated for, the exercise of the first party's power. Customer management can exercise power in information technology outsourcing relationships through investment in knowledge, practices and assets that are specialized to the relationship between client and vendor.

Klepper (1998) presents four stages of partnership development: awareness, exploration, expansion and commitment. Management processes listed above are found particularly important in the exploration stage. The five processes continue to operate in the expansion and commitment stages. Management can work through the processes to speed the movement toward full partnering relationship in the final stage of commitment and to maintain the partnership, once it is established.

STAKEHOLDERS

An IT stakeholder group consists of people tending to have the same expectations, perceptions, and goals for IT and outsourcing. Rather than merely categorizing people as either customers or suppliers, Lacity and Willcocks (2000) identified eight types of IT stakeholders: customer senior business managers, customer senior IT managers, customer IT staff, customer IT users, supplier senior managers, supplier account managers, supplier IT staff, and subcontractors. There are four distinct customer IT stakeholders, three distinct supplier stakeholders and one subcontractor role:

- *Customer senior business managers* are responsible for achieving business results from IT expenditures, but they often lack the tools to assess whether the IT function is adding value. They often ask senior managers for evidence of business value.
- *Customer senior IT managers* are typically centralized and responsible for balancing the costs of IT with the services provided to ensure value for money. In general, senior IT managers are often frustrated by their charge. Users often demand service excellence while their bosses often demand cost containment.
- *Customer IT staff* is responsible for IT service delivery. Although they are expected to meet budgets and deadlines, IT professionals are generally technology enthusiasts who also seek to please users. The internal IT staff is often the stakeholder groups most profoundly affected by outsourcing.
- *IT users* typically focus on IT service excellence, expecting systems to be up and running, to provide business functionality, and to facilitate the execution of their business responsibilities. IT users rarely resist outsourcing, although they frequently have questions about confidentiality and integrity of data.
- *Supplier senior managers* are responsible for sales and negotiations. They must balance the need to satisfy their customers with the need to generate a profit for their organization. A tremendous amount of judgment, typically based on years of experience, is often needed to assess what can be delivered at what price while still generating profit.
- *Supplier account managers* are responsible for profitability and customer satisfaction on a given IT contract. Again, supplier account managers must strike a delicate balance between the often-conflicting goals of service excellence and cost containment.
- *Supplier IT staff* are concerned with providing good customer service. Like customer IT staff, supplier IT staff is generally technology enthusiasts who are anxious to please users. Sometimes their enthusiasm for customer service has to be harnessed by their management to protect profit margins.
- *Subcontractors* are hired by prime suppliers to deliver part of the service to customers. Prime contractors often hire subcontractors to access scarce technical skills.

These eight types of stakeholders generally hold different IT expectations and goals in outsourcing. Some stakeholders primarily focus on IT costs because they are the ones paying for IT. Other stakeholders focus on service excellence because they are the ones using the IT service or providing the IT service. Such diverse goals and orientations amongst stakeholders can have a profound impact on the types of relationships that can develop.

HARD AND SOFT SIDES

Barthélemy (2003) contends that IT outsourcing management has two sides. While the hard side refers to the contract, the soft side refers to trust. Both sides are keys to success. The hard side and the soft side are often used separately. The greater the contractual hazards that characterize an IT outsourcing operation, the more likely the soft side will be preferred over the hard side. However, the hard side and the soft side can also be used simultaneously. In that case, the interplay between these two techniques can lead to a virtuous circle. Finally, IT outsourcing that are managed neither through the hard side nor through the soft side are doomed to fail.

The hard side of IT outsourcing management refers to the development and enforcement of a good contract. Contractual quality has huge impact on the outcome of IT outsourcing efforts as it helps protect the client from the potential opportunism of the vendor. When clients sign bad contracts, there is a risk that vendors may not provide the expected level of service or charge excess fees for services that are not included in the contract. A good contract is essential because it helps establish a balance of power between the client and the vendor. The contract also provides incentives for value creation. Drafting a good contract also helps organize the relationship because it allows partners to set expectations and to commit themselves to short and medium-term goals the literature suggests a good contract must have the following characteristics (Barthélemy, 2003):

- *Preciseness.* Ill-defined contracts generally result in high IT costs and poor IT service levels. Hence, cost and performance requirements should be established from the outset and clearly specified in the contract.
- *Completeness.* Writing a contract, which is as complete as possible, has important benefits. Basically, the more complete the contract, the smaller the exposure to the potential opportunism of the vendor and the smaller the probability that costly renegotiations will be needed.
- *Balance.* In general, one-sided contracts do not last long. Even a contract that is weighted against the vendor is not necessarily beneficial for the client. Indeed, the vendor will try to win back some value by imposing extra fees.

The actual content of a good contract will vary according to the level of contractual hazards. In IT outsourcing, the main sources of contractual hazards typically are asset specificity and technological uncertainty. Asset specificity refers to the uniqueness of the firm's hardware and software and the specialized know-how of IT employees. The soft side of IT outsourcing management refers to the development of relationships based on trust. Trust can be defined as the expectation that the vendor will not take advantage of the client or vice versa, even when the opportunity is available. Trust implies that both partners will subordinate their own interests to the joint-interest of the IT-outsourcing relationship.

Management of IT outsourcing through the soft side is associated with success for several reasons. First, trust provides a context in which partners can achieve individual and joint goals. When an IT outsourcing relationship is characterized by trust, partners are aware that joint efforts lead to superior outcomes. Second, trust lowers transaction costs. The mechanisms through which the soft side mitigates contractual hazards are both economic and sociological. Economists emphasize the rational and calculative origin of trust. For economists, expectations of future exchange lead to cooperation in the present. For sociologists, trust is embedded in relationships between people.

There is agreement that trust will develop only when there is some kind of risk and interdependence between partners. When contractual hazards are low, the hard side is sufficient to manage IT outsourcing relationships. Requirements can be totally specified up-front and included in the contract. As it is easy to switch to another vendor there is no advantage for the incumbent vendor to behave opportunistically. When contractual hazards are high, managing through the contract becomes increasingly difficult. The client is often captive to the relationship and not every future contingency can be known at the time the contract is signed. The vendor may then seize these opportunities to levy additional fees for servicing new needs. In that case, the soft side becomes crucial.

Barthélemy (2003) studied IT outsourcing management practice. He found that 44% of the studied companies had hard and soft sides, 16% had hard side only, and 10% had soft side only, while 30% had neither hard nor soft side. These four management types were compared with the level of contractual hazards. The study showed that 62% of the IT outsourcing operations management through the hard side only were surrounded by low contractual hazards, while 60% of the IT outsourcing operations management through the soft side only were surrounded by high contractual hazards. This is quite consistent with the contingency view that was advocated above.

THE IT OUTSOURCING GOVERNANCE MODEL

The IT outsourcing governance model consists of five elements (contracts, principles, resources, activities and managers), two main links (terms-exchanges link between contracts and resources, and norms-relationships link between principles and activities), and four local links (roles between contracts and principles, capabilities between principles and resources, efficiencies between resources and activities, and outcomes between activities and contracts). Our governance model is illustrated in Figure 4.

Contracts provide a legally bound, institutional framework in which each party's rights, duties, and responsibilities are codified and the goals, policies, and strategies underlying the arrangement are specified. *Principles* define decision rights concerning general IT principles, IT infrastructure, IT architecture, business application needs and IT investments. *Resources* define decision rights concerning human assets, financial assets, physical assets, IP assets, information and IT assets, and relationship assets. *Activities* define decision rights concerning transactions, projects, and problem solving and reporting. *Managers* are classified into stakeholder groups of client business management, client IT management, vendor business management, and vendor account management.

Exchanges of resources occur through transactions based on contracts. *Terms* for use of resources are defined in contracts. *Norms* create expectations of behavior and imply a certain action and are shared by the actors. Norms are based on principles and they occur in activities. Norms are concerned with flexibility, solidarity, mutuality, harmonization, and power. *Relationships* frame activities based on principles and norms.

Roles are defined by contracts and carried out when making decisions about principles. Management roles include spokesperson, entrepreneur, personnel leader, resource allocator, monitor, and liaison roles. *Capabilities* enable the use of resources based on principles. *Efficiencies* are determined by the use of resources in activities. *Outcomes* occur in activities that are performance results from contracts.

Table 2 illustrates how managers and principles are related through decision rights. *General principles* are high-level statements about how IT is used in the business. *IT infrastructure* are strategies for the base foundation of budgeted-for IT capability (technical and human), shared throughout the firm as reliable

Figure 4. IT Outsourcing Governance Model

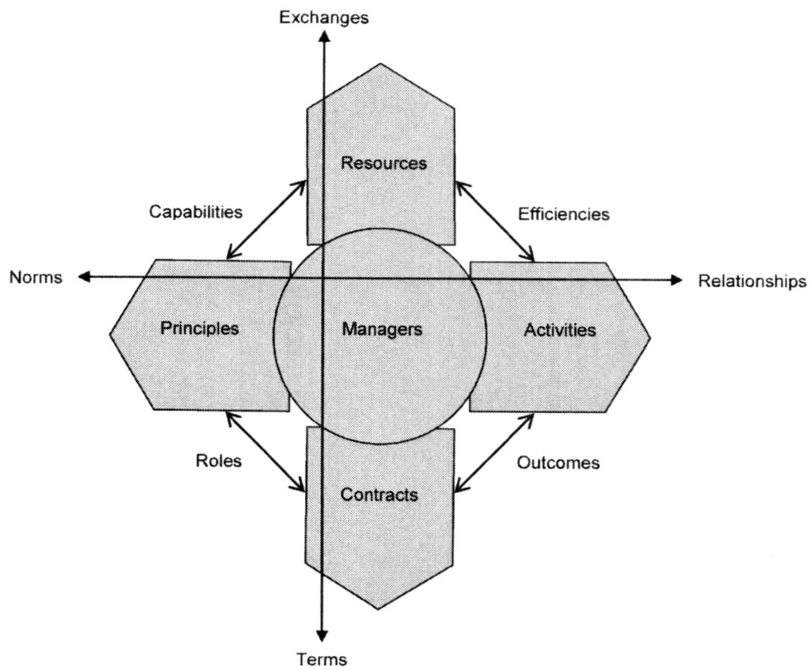

services, and centrally coordinated such as network, help desk and shared data. *IT architecture* is an integrated set of technical choices to guide the organization in satisfying business needs. The architecture is a set of policies and rules that govern the use of IT and plot a migration path to the way business will be done (includes data, technology and applications). *Business application needs* are concerned with business applications to be acquired and built. *IT investment* and prioritization are decisions about how much and where to invest in IT, including project approvals and justification techniques (Weill & Ross, 2004).

Table 3 illustrates how managers and resources are related through decision rights. *Human assets* are people, skills, career paths, training, reporting, mentoring, competencies, and so on. *Financial assets* are cash, investments, liabilities, cash flow, receivables, and so on. *Physical assets* are buildings, plant, equipment, maintenance, security, utilization, and so on. *IP assets* are intellectual property (IP), including product, services, and process know-how formally patented, copyrighted, or embedded in the enterprises' people and systems. *Information and IT assets* are digitized data, information, and knowledge about customers, processes performance, finances, information systems, and so on. *Relationship assets* are relationships within the enterprises as well as relationships between client and vendor at all levels (Weill & Ross, 2004).

IT outsourcing governance consists of five elements as illustrated in Figure 4. Four of these elements are really dimensions of governance, while the remaining element is management, which integrates the four dimensions of governance. In Figure 5, the four dimensions of governance are illustrated along the time dimension, defined as the formation stage (vision, evaluation, negotiation), the operation stage (transition, improvement) and the outcome stage (performance, results, goals, objectives).

Table 2. The governance model defines decision rights concerning principles

Principles Stakeholders	**General principles**	**IT infrastructure**	**IT architecture**	**Business application needs**	**IT investments**
Client business management	Strategic information systems planning decisions	Infrastructure capabilities decisions	Architecture performance decisions	Strategic information systems planning decisions	Financial investments decisions
Client IT management	Technology business alignment decisions	Infrastructure functions decisions	Architecture structure decisions	Information systems decisions	Investment analysis contents decisions
Vendor business management	Service level decisions	Service organization decisions	Service organization decisions	Information systems organization decisions	Financial investments decisions
Vendor account management	Technology decisions	Infrastructure integration decisions	Architecture integration decisions	Technology decisions for information systems	Investment analysis contents decisions

Table 3. The governance model defines decision rights concerning resources

Resources Stakeholders	**Human assets**	**Financial assets**	**Physical assets**	**IP assets**	**Information and IT assets**	**Relationship assets**
Client business management	Knowledge management decisions	User investment decisions	Tangible assets policy	Intangible assets policy	Strategic information systems planning decisions	Information sharing policy
Client IT management	Internal IT personnel decisions	User technology investment decision	Tangible assets management	Intangible assets management	Technology business alignment decision	Project sharing policy
Vendor business management	Knowledge management decisions	Vendor investment decisions	Tangible assets governance	Intangible assets governance	Service level decisions	Competence sharing policy
Vendor account management	Internal IT personnel decisions	Vendor technology investment decisions	Tangible assets governance	Intangible assets governance	Technology decisions	Knowledge transfer policy

In the formation stage, contracts are concerned with transactions in the outsourcing arrangement. Later, as relationships and norms develop between vendor and client, contracts will be renegotiated, shifting focus from transactions to relationships and partnerships. While the first contracts will be transactional contracts, later contracts will be relational contracts. Contract work is characterized by progressive contractual work, where focus slowly shifts from transactions to relationships as contract outcomes start to materialize.

It is important to design effective IT outsourcing governance. We defined governance as specifying the decision rights and accountability framework to encourage desirable behavior in an IT outsourcing relationship. Governance performance must then be how well the governance arrangements encourage desirable behaviors and ultimately how well both firms achieve their desired performance goals as vendor and client.

Early on in this book we presented several IT outsourcing theories. Each theory implies suggestions for managing successful IT outsourcing relationships. As a total set of suggestions and ideas from all theories, these guidelines represent critical success factors after outsourcing, as illustrated in Chapter

Figure 5. Stages of Growth in IT outsourcing

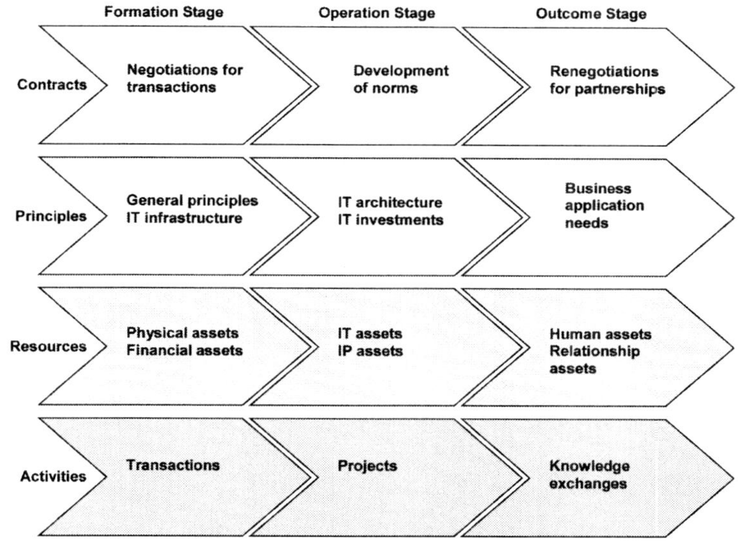

Figure 6. Managing successful IT outsourcing relationships through the governance model based on IT outsourcing theories

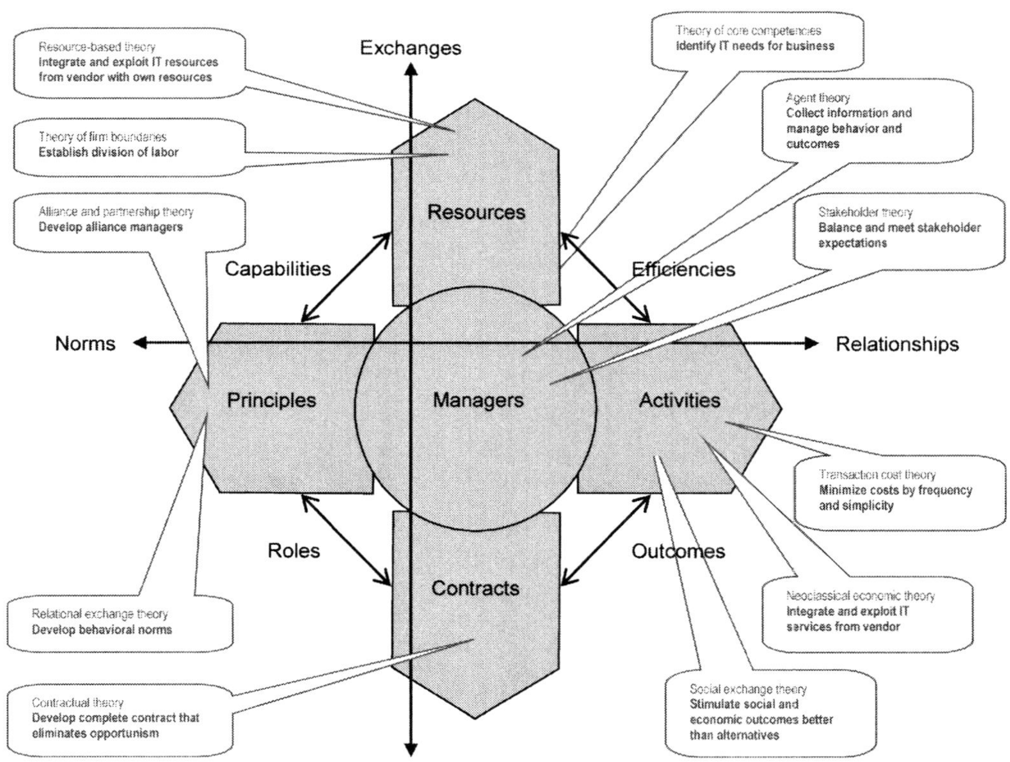

3. The guidelines can be implemented in the governance model as illustrated in Figure 6. We see that resource-based theory and theory of firm boundaries both provide guidelines for resource management. Alliance and partnership theory and relational exchange theory both provide guidelines for principles management. Transaction cost theory, neo-classical economic theory and social exchange theory all provide guidelines for activity management, while contractual theory provide guidelines for contract management. Theory of core competencies, agency theory and stakeholder theory provide guidelines directly to managers in charge of the outsourcing arrangement.

Based on outsourcing theories and practice presented in Chapter 2, recommendations for managing successful IT outsourcing relationships and how to succeed in outsourcing arrangements are listed in Table 4. The interaction approach to outsourcing governance focuses both on short-term episodes and general long-term relationships in dyadic buyer-supplier ventures. In addition to understand and applying

Table 4. Recommendations for managing successful IT outsourcing relationships based on theories

Theory	How to succeed in an outsourcing arrangement
Neo-classical economic theory	Capability to integrate and exploit IT services from the vendor together with own services to produce competitive goods and services. An example of such a service is the vendor's operation of the client's communication network.
Transaction cost theory	Minimize transaction costs by reducing the need for lasting specific IT assets; increase transaction frequency; reduce complexity and uncertainty in IT tasks; improve performance measurements; and reduce dependence on other transactions.
Contractual theory	A complete IT contract based on information symmetry in a predictable environment with occurrence adaptation that prevents opportunistic behavior in an efficient collaborative environment with balance of power between client and vendor, where the contract is a management instrument that grants decision rights and action duties.
Agency theory	It must be easy and inexpensive for the principal (client) to find out what the agent (vendor) is actually doing. In addition, both outcome-based and behavior-based incentives can be used to reduce and prevent opportunistic behavior.
Theory of firm boundaries	The supply of IT services from the organization's environment should change firm boundaries between the firm that desires the competence (sourcing firm) and the firm having the technology (source firm) in a clear and unambiguous manner. This can be achieved in a strict and rigid division of labor between client and vendor.
Theory of core competencies	Capability to define IT needs and ability to manage IT services from the vendor represent the core competence within IT needed in the client organization to succeed in an IT outsourcing arrangement.
Resource-based theory	Capability to integrate and exploit strategic IT resources from the vendor together with own resources to produce competitive goods and services. An example of such a resource is the vendor's competence in an IT application area where the client has limited experience.
Partnership and alliance theory	Develop experience with alliances, develop alliance managers and develop the ability to identify potential partners.
Relational exchange theory	Develop and secure common norms that are relevant to both parties. Norms determine behavior and are mainly concerned with flexibility, information exchange and solidarity. Norms shall secure integration in the relation, which takes place through involvement. Involvement occurs by coordination of activities, adaptation of resources and interaction between individuals. The degree of involvement in these three dimensions is called activity link, resource link and actor link.
Stakeholder theory	Create efficient and effective communication with and between stakeholders to secure continued support from all stakeholders, to balance their interests and to make the IT outsourcing arrangement so that all stakeholders achieve their goals.
Social exchange theory	Enable social and economic outcomes in the exchange between client and vendor such that these outcomes outperform those obtainable in alternative exchanges. Positive economic and social outcomes over time increase the partners' trust of each other and commitment to maintaining the exchange relationship. Commitment is important, as it is an exchange partner's belief that an ongoing relationship with another is so important as to warrant maximum efforts at maintaining it.

a general governance approach, management control systems have to be implemented. Regular performance measurement should be conducted, including measurement of partnership quality. Professional partnering relationships have to develop through attraction, communication and bargaining, expectations development, norm development, and power and justice.

CONCLUSION

The interaction approach to outsourcing governance focuses both on short-term episodes with exchanges and general long-term relationships with cooperation in dyadic buyer-supplier ventures. In addition to understand and apply a general governance approach, management control systems have to be implemented. Regular performance measurement should be conducted, including measurement of partnership quality (as presented in Chapter 8). Professional partnering relationships have to develop through mutual attraction, communication and bargaining, as well as expectations development, norm development, and power and justice. All stakeholders have to be considered and included in the governance structures. Both hard and soft sides of outsourcing have to be included in the governance structures to be successful.

REFERENCES

Ang, S., & Cummings, L. L. (1997). Strategic Response to Institutional Influence on Information Systems Outsourcing. *Organization Science*, *8*(3), 235–256. doi:10.1287/orsc.8.3.235

Barthélemy, J. (2003). The Hard and Soft Sides of IT Outsourcing Management. *European Management Journal*, *21*(5), 539–548. doi:10.1016/S0263-2373(03)00103-8

Blois, K. (2002). Business to business exchanges: a rich descriptive apparatus derived from MacNail's and Menger's analysis. *Journal of Management Studies*, *30*(4), 523–551. doi:10.1111/1467-6486.t01-1-00302

Cannon, J. P., Achrol, R. S., & Gundlach, G. T. (2000). Contracts, Norms, and Plural Form Governance. *Journal of the Academy of Marketing Science*, *28*(2), 180–194. doi:10.1177/0092070300282001

Cannon, J. P., & Homburg, C. (2001). Buyer-Supplier Relationships and Customer Firm Costs. *Journal of Marketing*, *65*, 29–43. doi:10.1509/jmkg.65.1.29.18136

Cernat, L. (2004). The emerging European corporate governance model: Anglo-Saxon, Continental, or still the century of diversity. *Journal of European Public Policy*, *11*(1), 147–166. doi:10.1080/1350176042000164343

Evans, P., & Wurster, T. S. (1999). Getting real About Virtual Commerce. *Harvard Business Review*, *77*(6), 84–94.

Håkansson, H. (1982). *International Marketing and Purchasing of Industrial Goods: An Interaction Approach*. Chichester, UK: John Wiley & Sons.

Kern, T., & Willcocks, L. P. (2002). Exploring relationship in information technology outsourcing: the interaction approach. *European Journal of Information Systems*, *11*(1), 3–19. doi:10.1057/palgrave/ejis/3000415

Klepper, R. (1998). The Management of Partnering Development in IS Outsourcing. In L. P. Willcocks & M. C. Lacity (Eds.), *Strategic Sourcing of Information Systems. Perspectives and Practices* (pp. 305-325). Chichester, UK: John Wiley & Sons.

Lacity, M. C., & Willcocks, L. P. (2000). Relationships in IT Outsourcing: A Stakeholder Perspective. In R. W. Zmud (Ed.), *Framing the Domains of IT Management: Projecting the Future Through the Past*. Cincinnati, OH: Pinnaflex Educational Resources.

Langfield-Smith, K., & Smith, D. (2003). Management control systems and trust in outsourcing relationships. *Management Accounting Research*, *14*(3), 281–307. doi:10.1016/S1044-5005(03)00046-5

Sveiby, K. E. (2001). A knowledge-based theory of the firm to guide in strategy formulation. *Journal of Intellectual Capital*, *2*(4), 344–358. doi:10.1108/14691930110409651

Useem, M., & Harder, J. (2000). Leading Laterally in Company Outsourcing. *Sloan Management Review*, *41*(2), 25–36.

Weill, P., & Ross, J. W. (2004). *IT Governance*. Boston: Harvard Business School Press.

Williamson, O. E. (1979). Transaction-Cost Economics: The Governance of Contractual Relations. *The Journal of Law & Economics*, *22*(2), 233–261. doi:10.1086/466942

Williamson, O. E. (1991). Comparative Economic Organization: The Analysis of Discrete Structural Alternatives. *Administrative Science Quarterly*, *36*(2), 269–296. doi:10.2307/2393356

Williamson, O. E. (2000). The New Institutional Economics: Taking Stock, Looking Ahead. *Journal of Economic Literature*, *38*(3), 595–613.

Chapter 10
Case Study Research

In order to understand the inherent complexities and the underlying constructs of managing IT outsourcing relationships and the performance of these relationships, empirical research was conducted. The empirical research in terms of an exploratory case study had the following guiding research questions: 1) How do client and vendor organizations manage their IT outsourcing relationship? 2) How do different stakeholders influence, or get influenced by, the IT outsourcing relationship? In this research context, the unit of analysis was both the relationship (question 1) and the individual stakeholders (question 2). As our goal was to explore managerial and individual issues, rather than analytical generalization, no research propositions or hypotheses were developed in advance of the empirical study.

First in this chapter, we present the methodology applied in the case study process. Next, we present three internationally based IT outsourcing relationships that were studied (Solli-Sæther, 2006). In the following section, data collected are put into cross-case issues of managing IT outsourcing relationships. Finally, we use the theoretical framework developed in Chapter 2 for evaluating different aspects of the cases studied.

DOI: 10.4018/978-1-60566-796-6.ch010

THE CASE STUDY PROCESS

The selection of cases was based on an instrumental approach, which means that the case study was carried out to provide insight into issue or refinement of theory. "The case is of secondary interest; it plays a supportive role, facilitating our understanding of something else. The choice of case is made because it is expected to advance our understanding of that other interest" (Stake, 1994, p. 237). All three cases were selected for their paradigmatic characteristics in terms of their outsourcing undertaking. In other words, the cases were selected because, the ABB – IBM is a global one; the SAS – CSC contract belongs to one of the largest buy-outs in Europe; the Rolls-Royce – EDS contract is a mature one. All cases are unique, with global client companies from different industries, and all vendor companies are global service providers. In all three international based cases more than a thousand employees were transferred from client to vendor organizations. They provide a broad base of relationship practice, suggesting that a case in each company would be of interest and value to this research study.

Data collection was done through interviews, with questions addressing relationship management issues: enter and exit strategies, activities and phases, contract and contract management, governance structures and relationship management, personnel issues, and knowledge management, with a strong emphasis on what characteristics influenced IT outsourcing relationship. A certain group of questions were addressing individual stakeholder attitude, behavior, and performance. Thus, interviews were focused directly on case study topics. For each client-vendor outsourcing relationship, 2 – 3 interviewees were selected from each of the two parties.

The interviews were scheduled for 1 hour, but some lasted for 90 minutes. All interviewees were assured anonymity to promote openness. Interviews were personal meetings or held as telephone conferences. The exploratory case studies were conducted through July – September 2004. All interviews were tape-recorded and transcribed immediately afterwards. Transcripts from the 16 interviews comprised 65,342 words and 108 pages of text. The analysis of each case was focused essentially on transcripts of the interviews, but to some extent on other materials made available to the researcher (e.g., presentations, internal reports, press releases, annual reports, the Internet). An abbreviation of each case was written and sent to a contact person of each participating company for approval. The individual cases serve only as the evidentiary base for the study and were used in a cross-case analysis. The purpose was not to portray any single one of the relationships. Rather, it was to synthesize the lessons learned from all of them, dispersed throughout separate cross-case issues.

According to Yin (2003), the case study is preferred in examining contemporary events and when the focus is on a contemporary phenomenon within some real-life context. The case study's unique strength is its ability to deal with a full variety of evidence, like documents, artifacts, interviews, and observations. For case studies, five components of research design are especially important: a study's questions, its propositions (if any), its unit(s) of analysis, the logic linking the data to the propositions, and the criteria for interpreting the findings (Yin, 2003, p. 21). In designing the case study, all these components have been dealt with.

THREE INTERNATIONAL BASED IT OUTSOURCING RELATIONSHIPS

The following three subsections have the purpose of presenting the outsourcing ventures and revealing company specific data from the discussions of the outsourcing relationships. The overview essentially

Table 1. Three international based case studies

Client company	Industry	Origin	Outsourced	Start of deal	Length of deal	Value	No of people transferred	Vendor company
Rolls-Royce	Power for civil aerospace, defence aerospace, marine and energy markets	UK	Infrastructure, application support and development	2000 (1996)	144 months	$2,1M	1220	EDS
ABB	Power and automation technologies	Switzerland	Data centre, infrastructure, desktop	2003	120 moths	$1,1M	1200	IBM
Scandinavian Airlines	Air travel and airline related businesses	Nordic	Infrastructure management, application development and support	2003	60 moths	$1,47M	1150	CSC

outlines a brief description of the institution, the role and influence of IT, and the degree/extent of the outsourcing. Table 1 shows some characteristics of the IT outsourcing relationships studied.

A Mature Relationship

Rolls-Royce is a global power systems company providing power for land, sea and air, with leading positions in civil aerospace, defence, marine and energy markets. Rolls-Royce is also one of the most famous names in engineering throughout the world. The history of Rolls-Royce starts back in 1884, when Henry Royce and Charles Royce start to build, manufacture and sell quality cars. Success with the cars led to the formation of the Rolls-Royce Company in March 1906 and to the launch of the six-cylinder Silver Ghost, which, within a year, was hailed as "the best car in the world". At the start of the First World War, Charles Royce designed his first aero engine, used in the air war by the allies. Demand for the Merlin engine, which powered the Spitfire during the Second World War transformed Rolls-Royce from a relatively small company into a major contender in aero propulsion. Rolls-Royce entered the civil aviation market in 1953, and the company has become a major player within this market. In the 1980s and 1990s Rolls-Royce has been undergoing a number of mergers and acquisitions to create the only company in Britain capable of delivering power for use in air, at sea and on land (Rolls-Royce, 2004b). Today, there are some 54,000 Rolls-Royce gas turbines in service and these generate a demand for high-value service throughout their operational life. Rolls-Royce is a technology leader, employing 35,200 employees and operating in 48 countries. Group turnover in 2003 ended at £ 5,645 million (Rolls-Royce, 2004a).

Until 1996 Rolls-Royce had its own information technology operation. The company was growing rapidly in the 1990s, and both IT costs and the number of IT employees were increasing dramatically. In the IT business, there was a change between large mainframes and green screens to GUI and clustered server environments. The company got to a point where they had to manage both environments. The, then, CIO did a study of the capability of the IT function. He had serious doubts about the in-house team's ability to handle the change, both on a capability and scale prospective. In addition, Rolls-Royce was strapped financially. They considered outsourcing as one way, at least in a short term, to help the company deliver its results. Rolls-Royce also needed a change agent. The company began to look outside for a partner to deal with those aspects.

The first outsourcing deal was done in 1996, and was renewed in 2000 for 12 more years. Rolls-Royce outsourced the basic operation of the complete infrastructure – the management of networks, data centers, servers, and so on. And they outsourced the application support for most of their major applications, and the application development function. What was kept was development of internal software at the control level, such as control systems for jet engines. All major assets were transferred, like computers, software, and people. More than 1200 people were transferred from Rolls-Royce to Electronic Data Systems Corporation (EDS). As almost 90% of the IT budget goes with the outsourcer, we may regard this as a total outsourcing. Total outsourcing transfers IT assets, leases, staff and management responsibility for delivery of IT services from internal IT function to a third-party vendor, which represents at least 80 percent of the IT budget (Lacity, Willcocks, & Feeny, 1996). The intention was to put a long-term agreement in place, and to build a close relationship.

In the early years, after the initial outsourcing, Rolls-Royce kept very little competence in-house. But they realized that was unhelpful, because it created naivety on their side and created a degree of frustration on the outsourcer's side. This was later corrected and now they have senior people with experience in managing outsourcers. The central staff, doing information technology, covers the architecture, the oversight of projects, and the management of service levels. Today, Rolls-Royce has around 30,000 computer users, and a lot of the staff are using ERP systems.

In 1999, when Rolls-Royce acquired Vickers (now Rolls-Royce Commercial Marine) the company got a strong in-house IT group with more than 70 professionals. This group provided operational IT services for more than 3200 people at 50 locations worldwide. A memorandum of understanding was signed in 2000, between Rolls-Royce and EDS, to evaluate outsourcing of this group. The process was stopped, concluding that outsourcing was not profitable for Rolls-Royce. The in-house IT group of Rolls-Royce Commercial Marine was a self-efficient group with very significant geographic boundaries, located in Norway, and serving small business units primarily in Norway, Sweden, and Finland. They had just over 10% of the overall IT budget. They were kept in-house for two reasons. First of all, they were not in the natural environment for an outsourcer. And second, maintaining a complete vertical capability in IT was healthy in a CIO perspective. It was possible to build on that group to bring services back in-house, and they provided Rolls-Royce with direct cost comparison versus the outsourcer.

The Largest Buy-Out in Europe 2003

The SAS Group serves northern Europe with air travel and airline related businesses. SAS' parent companies were founded in Denmark (1918), Sweden (1924), and Norway (1927). Scandinavian Airlines System (SAS) was founded August 1, 1946, to co-ordinate flights from Scandinavia to the USA. They have more than half a century of aviation experience. SAS airline companies are flying to more than 80 major destinations in Scandinavia and in Europe. In addition, there are also flights to the United States and to Asia (Scandinavian Airlines System, 2004a). Through partnership in Star Alliance, the SAS Group can offer a worldwide network covering a total of 673 airports in 127 countries. Today, the SAS Group is Europe's 4th largest airline group, carrying more than 31 million passengers in 2003. The SAS Group 2003 revenue was Skr 58,000 million employing more than 33,000 people in five business areas – Scandinavian Airlines, Subsidiary & Affiliated Airlines, Airline Support Businesses, Airline Related Businesses, and Hotels (Scandinavian Airlines System, 2004b).

SAS started a huge cost reduction program called "turn around 2005", due to the state of the airline market after September 11, 2001. The group looked at all kinds of costs, including IT costs. The goal was to reduce IT costs significantly within a few years, partly by reducing costs directly and partly by exchanging old legacy systems with new standardized ones. Scandinavian IT Group (SIG) was sold out of Airline Related Business during the forth quarter of 2003, and the SAS Group entered into an IT outsourcing agreement with Computer Science Corporation (CSC). Under the terms of the contract, CSC provides IT consulting, systems integration, application development and maintenance, and IT infrastructure services for mission-critical SAS business needs, including booking and ticket reservation systems, ticket-free travel technologies, self-service check-in, flight maintenance and cargo control systems. All SAS destination airports were included in the services of the outsourcing deal, as they were previously serviced by SIG.

A Global Deal

The history of ABB goes back to the late nineteenth century, and is a long and illustrious record of innovation and technological leadership in many industries. Elektriska Aktiebolaget was established in Stockholm in 1883 as manufacturers of electrical lighting and generators. Some years later in 1990 a merger founded Allmänna Svenska Elektriska Aktiebolaget (Asea). In the beginning of 1900, Asea played a major role in the electrification of Swedish industry, railways and homes. They expanded their business internationally and in the 1980s Asea was one of the top ten companies in the world in power technologies. In 1986, the year prior to its merger with Brown, Boveri & Cie, Asea had revenues of Skr 46 billion, and 71,000 employees (ABB Group, 2004a).

Brown, Boveri & Cie (BBC) was established in Baden, Switzerland, in 1891. Shortly afterwards, BBC was the first company to transmit high-voltage AC power. The company has since continued to invent a number of major new technologies – like electrical machines in motors and generators, combustion gas turbines for generating electricity, locomotive technology, transformers and control systems. In 1986, the year prior to its merger with Asea, BBC had revenues of Skr 58 billion, and 97,000 employees worldwide (ABB Group, 2004a).

In 1988 Asea and BBC merged to form ABB (Asea Brown Boveri Ltd.), one of the largest electrical engineering companies in the world. A large-scale program of expansion resulted in several acquisitions in the following years. In 2002 ABB streamlined its divisional structure to focus on two core areas of business: power technologies and automation technologies. ABB sold its Financial Services division, its Oil, Gas & Petrochemicals division, and its Building Systems business area. A divestment program of non-core business continued in 2003. Today, ABB is a leader in power and automation technologies that enable utility and industry customers to improve performance while lowering environmental impact. The ABB Group of companies operates in around 100 countries and employs around 105,000 people. The parent company is located in Switzerland. ABB Group revenues for 2003 ended at $18.8 billion (ABB Group, 2004b).

By July 28, 2003, ABB and IBM had signed a ten-year agreement to outsource close to 90 percent of ABB's information systems infrastructure operations – including the transfer to IBM of more than 1,200 employees. The agreement was valued at US$ 1.1 billion and built on a well-established relationship between the two companies. The contract was part of ABB's strategy to focus on its core industrial businesses and would help ABB significantly reduce costs over the period. Combined with pilot contracts signed in the fourth quarter of 2001 for approximately US$ 600 million the full value of the relationship approached US$ 1.7 billion over ten years. IBM Global Services took responsibility for the operation and support of information technology infrastructure in 14 countries in Europe and North America – representing some 90 percent of ABB's information technology infrastructure. The deal included taking over the management of servers, operating systems, and corporate networks, personal computers, and help desks. Control systems within power and automation technologies were regarded as a part of ABB's core business, and were kept in-house. The company had several laboratories developing such industrial IT solutions. Industrial IT solutions enabled ABB customers to manage their installations better and to link up in real time with their own suppliers and customers. Standard applications, such as ERP systems, were not a part of the outsourcing deal.

CROSS-CASE ISSUES

In the below subsections, empirical data collected are put into cross-case issues of managing IT outsourcing relationships. These issues are enter strategies, phases and activities, contract development and management, transfer of IT employees, governance structures, outsourcing costs, retained skills, and exit strategies. This is done in order to get a rich representation of the cases studied, and to explain the complexity and variety of the arrangements.

Enter Strategies

Rolls-Royce did a capability study previous to the outsourcing. It may be regarded as a strategy process. Although none of the interviewees used the term "enter strategy" for what was happening at that point in time: the decision to outsource was regarded as a strategic decision. None of the interviewees were involved in the capability study, as this was done many years ago, and before the interviewees entered the companies. The strategic issues told to be underlying the outsourcing decision were costs, capabilities, and the need for a change agent. Rolls-Royce wanted a 10% reduction in IT costs. The criteria that were presented for vendor selection were pretty clear: around maximum service levels, being able to handle large, skilled contracts of that size, and also pretty clear around costs. EDS had generally been competitive on costs, and they demonstrated that they could provide capability for large scale contracts. Rolls-Royce doubted they had necessary in-house capabilities to do the required step change from managing large mainframe systems to GUI based client-server systems. A change, which was believed to require both human capabilities and financial capabilities to succeed. Rolls-Royce was looking for a company they might discuss as the change agent, a company somewhat different to themselves. They were not looking for a traditional outsourcer, but a very service oriented company. A major transformation seemed to be a part of the plan, a transformation of Rolls-Royce from a manufacturing oriented company to a service oriented company. The culture that EDS was bringing was part of what Rolls-Royce was looking for; a service oriented, global, and people oriented company.

SAS outsourced for three main reasons. First, they wanted to benefit from economies of scale offered by an external service provider and to realize corresponding cost reduction. Compared with other airliners, the cost and efficiency of their internal IT group were far too high. Second, they wanted to lift their existing technologies to new platforms and replace their old legacy systems with standard application in order to establish a more cost-effective platform. And third, they wanted to offer the employees in their internal IT group better development opportunities for their professional careers. Information technology was the core competence of CSC, but it was not at the core of the airliner. SIG management group and their Chairman of the Board took the initiative to start the process.

We were in financial pressure, our bankers pushed the outsourcing forward. (Client IT Manager)

Global IT management at ABB started to develop a strategy document before the outsourcing, which later was signed by senior management. It was never an outsourcing strategy, but a strategy for how to achieve a number of aims. It was at the time when ABB had strong financial difficulties. Because of this, cost reduction was a significant aim to achieve, and was a factor provoking outsourcing. One of the things the CIO did, was to use a lot of time assuring that the countries in ABB were aligned to the outsourcing project. The starting point was a strategy document, but it ended up as a pure cost case, affected by external environment. During the last few years ABB had been through several organizational changes. Focusing on two core business areas, power and automation technologies, they sold away other business. But, remaining internal functions were huge and inflexible. Simultaneously, the requirements from business unit areas were full transparency regarding IT. ABB's financial difficulties at that time and their restructuring around two core business areas pushed the IT outsourcing.

Phases and Activities

Six relationship phases of IT outsourcing are defined as scooping, evaluation, negotiation, transition, middle, and mature phase (Lacity & Willcocks, 2000). These phases are discussed in this section as they were recognized at the three international based IT outsourcing relationships studied.

Prior to the outsourcing, Rolls-Royce did a capability study of the company's IT function, identifying core competence and activities. The capability study raised doubts about the in-house IT function's ability to handle the challenges of the company. This was the scooping phase, establishing a goal or vision for the outsourcing. Evaluation and negotiation phases were limited in a time perspective. Rolls-Royce went through a very standard procurement process of defining all the pieces that needed to be outsourced, defining what was required, and then inviting bids to the standard request for proposal. All the big external outsourcing vendors were involved in the bidding. The first contract with EDS, the one for the aero business, was negotiated in 1996. The second contract for the industrial business was signed in 1997. The goal of these phases was first to select the best vendor and then to sign the contract. In the transition phase the major goal of the two parties was to establish agreed upon operational performance. After the contract was signed, there was a "honeymoon period," during which the outsourcer gave Rolls-Royce "anything." The outsourcer put a new desktop on, because it was more efficient and because they had got the know-how to standardize. The users got lucky; they got something quick and fashionable, and faster than what the IT department could deliver. All major IT assets and more than a thousand people got transferred to the outsourcer. As service levels were established, the parties moved into the improvement phase, where the overall goal was to achieve value-added services above operational performance. The IT department thought they had got a partner they could manage and control. Problems arose when Rolls-Royce started to add new services and remove old services from the original contract. Rolls-Royce had to pay extra for everything, and the parties had to refer to the contract, and they started quarrelling. Rolls-Royce merged the aero business and the industrial business, and in 2000 they had to realign the contracts to reflect changes in technology, services, and business. The original contracts were made a "foot" thick. Then in 2000, they tried to make it a trusted one, and they actually went to buy services. It was widely reported in the press that it was a 1.3 billion pound deal over 12 years. When the relationship was extended, the mature phase provided an opportunity for the two parties to learn from past experiences as well as to explore creative options when constructing the new deal.

In the scooping phase, SAS used business, economic and technical criteria to identify potentials for outsourcing. As a part of the company's huge cost reduction program, the group looked at all kinds of costs, including IT costs. SIG was at that point of time already a stand-alone company, wholly owned by its largest customer, SAS. The management of SIG looked at different scenarios for survival; one of them was to sell the company to an external service provider. This way SIG could continue to serve its largest customer, and with possibilities of gaining large-scale opportunities, and access IT capabilities. SIG management meant an outsourcer would be a better place for SIG employees. Thus they made a suggestion for their board of directors to sell the company. Selective outsourcing was also considered, but they concluded it would require too much management attention. The objective of the evaluation phase was to select the best and final offer. The SAS board of directors decided in August 2003, to start the process of selling SIG and to establish a frame agreement for buy-back of services. First step was to develop an information memorandum describing SAS' IT governance structure, including a description of SIG as a company in terms of economic conditions, assets, and management. An investment banker was also chosen, a short time after the decision, who handled the formalities of the bidding process. Several vendors signed the confidentiality statement and they received the information memorandum. A few vendors delivered a non-binding bid. All the Nordic vendors quit, first of all because of the size of the deal. The steering committee decided which four vendors should be invited to give binding-bids. One of the invited vendors quit and one of them was later removed from the list. SAS started negotiation with two vendors. Important evaluation criteria were economy, financial strength and perseverance of partner, sensitivity to SAS' proposed conditions, and handling of SIG personnel. By December 18, 2004, the outsourcing agreement between SAS and CSC was signed. Due to the fact that SIG was a stand-alone company, they were delivering services to SAS on already established agreements, and thus the evaluation and negotiation phases could be done in a relatively short period of time. The outsourcing deal was partly a take-over, and partly a buy-back of services. Technically the transition of shares took place at February 1, 2004. And by this transaction, SAS were transferring IT assets, leases, staff, and management responsibility for delivery of services from an internal IT function to a third-party vendor. About 1100 employees got CSC as a new employer. Intellectual property rights for business applications were kept in SAS. As SAS had already been treating SIG as an external supplier, the scope, costs, levels and responsibilities of the baseline services were already established, but of course some changes were made during negotiation. Later, there was some disagreement around contractual interpretations, but no serious problems. And thus, the objective of the transition phase, to establish operational performance, was going relatively straightforward. Transforming SIG into CSC's global operating model was, however, a huge program involving a lot of people from the vendor organization. Although operational performance was not affected, the internal focus of the transformation period took focus away from value-added services.

In the scooping phase, ABB identified IT activities for potential outsourcing. Although ABB global senior IT management set forth to create a strategic vision of IT in the company, the IT sourcing decisions ended up as a business decision. As the overall organizational goal was to cut costs, there was also a pressure for significant cost reduction within IT. And a few months later, close to 90% of ABB's information technology infrastructure operations were outsourced to IBM, including more than 1200 employees in 14 different countries. In the evaluation phase a few potential suppliers were invited to bid for the infrastructure operations. There were not many service providers that could deliver services to a large number of locations in many different countries. ABB were aiming for competition, but one service provider after the other dropped out. In ABB's opinion one service provider was not capable of delivering the required services at that time, and they were also not focused sufficiently hard on cost reduction. They were disqualified. Another one declined to bid, because they didn't believe their chances of success were high enough to justify the investment in bid time and quest. A third one was interested in making the investment and attempt to win the business, but they needed to know ABB as an organization. Due to the very difficult financial situation in ABB, it was difficult for senior executives to spend time with the service provider. Consequently they lost the third one. ABB already had a long lasting relationship with IBM. A pilot outsourcing to IBM in Sweden and India twelve months before was at that time going reasonably well. And thus, IBM was selected as the best and final offer. Negotiation was done in two major areas. The first element was the core contract, which was the core service specification. This was negotiated and developed centrally by a global team. The other element was that the ABB countries negotiated their own versions of the contract, underlying the core documents. During the local negotiations, changes to the standard documents were kept at a minimum. This was done to obtain economies of scale. One basic country contract was negotiated globally, with very small country variations. Global sign-off of the agreement was done July 28, 2003. Country agreements were signed locally. Transfer of responsibilities took place in September 2003. It was a ten-year contract helping ABB significantly reduce costs. In the transition phase, the main focus was to establish agreed upon operational performance, including consolidation, rationalization, and standardization of infrastructure. Another important issue was to establish a post-contract management infrastructure and processes. A relationship alignment project between the ABB team and IBM team was set up to take care of this.

Contract Development and Management

In the original outsourcing agreement between Rolls-Royce and EDS, assets were transferred, and services bought back through two different contracts, one for the aero and one for the industrial business. In 2000 these two contracts were merged into one contract. During the time that Rolls-Royce had been in the arrangement, services had been taken away and new services were added. The result was that the outsourcing contract had been more complicated. In the beginning, the two contracts were arrangements around capability and scale. What they were doing in 2000 was to organize the new contract around services that could be provided. The new structure was an overall master services contract, and then services were grained and managed in so called towers – e.g., data centers, networks, application support. Having had a period where they spent a lot of time arguing around interpretations of contractual clauses, Rolls-Royce and EDS had reached the point where they hardly used the contract in the day-to-day operations. The two parties understood each other's goals. If there were changes required in the contract, then they instructed the lawyers to make them. Rolls-Royce had an IT procurement team, a dozen people who were part of the central procurement unit, but had a functional accountability to the IT community. These people did follow-up on the commercial part of the contract.

Concurrent to asking for binding bid, SAS sent contractual suggestions to potential vendors, and they asked for remarks on suggested contractual conditions. The previously contractual relationship between SAS and SIG served as a base for the new outsourcing contracts. Reviewing both binding bids and contractual comments was a learning process for both client and vendor, as they learned more about each other and the services to be delivered. All information around systems solutions – e.g., source codes, costs, and service levels – was accessible for bidders in certain "data rooms." SAS were well prepared in the contractual negotiations as they used both internal and external expertise, e.g., lawyers, purchasers, and financial experts. The contract was structured in four parts. First there was an overall Master Service Agreement, which lay out the length of the relationship, minimum level of services for the five year agreement, and options for extending the agreement. Then there was a Share Purchase Agreement, which regulated the sale of shares, price of shares, balance sheets, bonds, pensions, etc. Subsequently there was a Transition Agreement describing activities tied to the transfer of assets, e.g., transferring of IT employees, facilities, hardware, and software licenses. This agreement lasted for six months, and then all major transition activities were finished. Finally, there was a Frame Agreement, which laid out terms and conditions for buy-back of services. This agreement was a traditional service agreement deal with service description, service levels, prices, conditions, templates, etc. The deal was a five-year contract, starting February 1, 2004, with options for extension. CSC must make an effort to get SAS to provoke the option. On the other hand SAS had the freedom to evaluate the quality of services delivered and to pick a new supplier without being locked for a too long period of time. There had been some contractual interpretation issues, especially concerning price and service clauses. But these issues had been handled successfully of by the relationship steering committee, in which both parties were represented. Each business unit in SAS was responsible for its own use of IT services and its own costs, and thus they had a business relationship with CSC. Contract managers at CIO's staff did contractual follow-up at corporate level.

Both parties had accepted the agreement, but they also tried to get the maximum out of situations where contractual clauses opened up for interpretations. (Vendor Account Manager)

At ABB, core contract documents were negotiated globally, because the service provider could only leverage economies of scale if there were some similarities in the environment. The global teams also negotiated one basic country contract, which was used in the local negotiations, e.g., between ABB Norway and IBM Norway. Statement of work was negotiated globally. Country adjustments contained local supplements and further details where needed. Responsibility for country agreements was distributed, but supported with expertise from the global team. Each contract had several exhibits and schedules. Exhibits included, e.g., form of country agreement, country agreement, and country adjustment. There were several schedules – e.g., acquired assets, employees, facilities, software, transition, service recipients, charges, governance, security, business continuity, exit management, subcontractors, and service measurements. The two parties were trying to verify as much as possible, and "nothing" should be left to coincidence. It was a very complex contractual set up, with one global agreement and 14 separate country agreements operating under it, and there were some very complex linkages. It was really a global agreement, meaning that the country agreements did not operate independently. If IBM, for example defaulted in one country, consequently ABB had the right to terminate in that country, and then they had the right to terminate in all countries participating in the agreement.

Transfer of IT Employees

A thousand people in the aero deal, and an around 200 people in the industrial business deal, were transferred from Rolls-Royce to EDS during 1996 – 1997. The jobs were transferred to the outsourcer, and the terms and the conditions were transferred for a period. This was done in the context of a project, where the services and the management of the services were moved across in about six months. The standard process in accordance with British law was followed. Less than half of those original individuals transferred were still involved in service deliveries to Rolls-Royce. EDS had a normal turnover rate, and they moved people around in projects. There were people no longer interacting with Rolls-Royce, and there were people who had skills that were useful serving Rolls-Royce. Transfer of people in an outsourcing agreement was an issue that EDS as a company had to be very good at. This was stated as the number one risk of an outsourcer. The ability to take over the people, keep some of them on the account, and give the others opportunities to move elsewhere, was emphasized as fundamental for the outsourcer. Another issue stated as critical, was the ability for a client to understand the skills to be retained: "You won't necessarily find the management skills to manage outsourcers within a client organization, because (by definition) they have not done that before within their internal IT." Certainly an IT director, who had previously run an IT department, might not always be the right person to run an outsourcing arrangement. Rolls-Royce realized it was difficult to run an outsourcer, and it was very different in terms of skills.

The top management of the SAS Group handled the sales process of the shares, while the management group of SIG had to handle their employees. As this was a friendly take over, there were no immediate changes for the employees. All conditions of employment were carried on. About 1100 people were transferred from the SAS Group as CSC took over SIG businesses. The employees of SIG were informed about the process, the necessity of the take over, and they got an understanding there was no other way to keep SIG together. During the process, employees did not know the name of the bidders, but of course there were some rumors. Top management of SIG and the labor union were involved, but lower level employees and mid-level managers were not. The employees were loyal to their management and to the process, and they understood the reason why. Regardless of that, there was some frustration and the situation stressed them. The sales process did not last for more than six months, but the transformation continued when SIG was taken over by CSC. Job insecurity was obviously an issue, because some places there were double sets of managers and functions.

We joined a collective job application, without knowing to whom we applied and without any opportunity to influence. (Transferred IT Employee)

As a consequence of the outsourcing, more than 1200 employees were transferred from ABB to IBM. Around 510 of these were transferred under the Sweden and India pilots, and the rest were transferred in September 2003. Because of the global deal, each country had to follow its local laws for transfer of people. ABB countries had to handle the transfer separately, involving human resource managers, labor unions, employees, and information, according to local laws. In Norway for example, 35 people had to change employer. It was a process where nobody quit or got fired as a consequence of the outsourcing. IBM had experience taking over people and they had a procedure for how to handle the following transformation. Old organizational structures among transferred people were broken down, and the employees were replaced into IBM according to their competencies. This meant new managers, new colleagues, and to some extent new clients to support. According to a project executive of ABB, the quality of the technical people who were transferred to IBM was generally high; "A number of them had, even in a short period, done extremely well at IBM."

Governance Structures

Rolls-Royce had a small corporate staff doing information technology and that covered the architecture, the oversight of projects, and the management of service levels. And they were relatively senior people. Rolls-Royce owned the project management overall, and they also owned the IT architecture. They had an IT procurement team that was part of the procurement unit, but had a functional accountability to the IT community. There was a tight top management relationship between the two parties. The CIO of Rolls-Royce met EDS' board members once a year for a couple of days, where they discussed the progress of the contract and the overall relationship in a formal sense. Rolls-Royce also had a "hot line," where the CIO could pick up the phone and get straight through to the CEO of EDS, if something was disastrous. There were regular monthly meetings between the CIO of Rolls-Royce and those that oversaw the accounts of EDS. One of them was account manager and the other was responsible for all the projects and all the services. In addition to that, there were a number of meetings. There were commercial review boards, the review on expenditure, and there were service review boards that managed the quality of the services against the service level and the individual performance of the projects. Where the services were provided directly to Rolls-Royce lines of business, the IT head in the businesses would work out what was needed for the business and would communicate that back to the central IT unit, which in turn brought this back to EDS. Thus, the lines of business had a stake holding in defining the standards. However, managing the services was done centrally. When EDS were attempting to manage all the services and interact with all the business divisions, it actually got quite complicated and expensive in terms of manpower. So, the management of the services on a day-to-day basis took place from Rolls-Royce centrally with experienced service management teams.

Rolls-Royce had more than 70 IT employees in an in-house team in the Commercial Marine business, and this team was a self-efficient group mainly serving their own division. But the in-house team was also involved in some of the central projects, and thus they cooperated with EDS to some extent. Rolls-Royce had a benchmarking process built into the contract where they could take the services to a third party to benchmark against other companies. However, they had found that to be unsatisfactory, because it was very difficult to compare like with like, apples with apples. The in-house IT department kept in the Commercial Marine division gave a value assurance, in the sense that they knew the costs having their own people to do the services, which gave Rolls-Royce an opportunity to measure that against the outsourcer.

In the SAS – CSC case, a steering committee was established for an overall governance of the relationship. The committee had three members from SAS and two members from CSC. From the client side, participants were the CIO, the vice president of the airline business, and the manager of IT purchasing. From the vendor side, participants were the account executive and the operations manager. There were also established some functional groups reporting to the steering committee, and they were working with standardization, security, etc. Each business unit in SAS had a relationship with CSC as the responsibility for IT services and costs were delegated to the consumers of IT services.

At ABB they realized that outsourcing relationships might be extremely dynamic, which was one of the reasons why they tried to develop a contract and a governance approach to these contracts that itself was dynamic. As a client manager at ABB stated: "Within ten years ABB will be a different company than it is today, and so will technology." A real challenge was to develop a contract and a relationship to satisfy a violent cost reduction environment, but also at the same time to serve a business expansion environment. Despite this, the governance model put in place was rather simple. Basically it was local meetings with global escalating. Each country was responsible for their operations (service levels) and their financials. Take Norway as an example; there were two meetings each week between ABB and IBM. First, there was the operational meeting, where technical personnel met. And second, there was the commercial meeting, where project executives met. The intention of the deal was that everything was to be solved locally. Each month every country reported its costs to headquarters. And once a month there was the project executive meeting, either by phone or physically, where all the country executives participated.

Outsourcing Costs

Due to their financial conditions, Rolls-Royce was looking for a 10% reduction of IT costs. But the strategic issues underlying the outsourcing decision were also internal IT capabilities, and the need for a change agent. Due to fact that the decision was made a long time ago, and none of the interviewees were involved in the decision-making process, it was difficult to state what criteria were the most important. A large company such as Rolls-Royce can (to some extent) generate economies of scale and scope internally by reproducing methods of vendors. And thus, defining outsourcing simply in terms of procurements activities seems not to capture the true strategic discussion of the Rolls-Royce IT outsourcing. What Rolls-Royce had done, on the premises of managing information technology services from the board perspectives, was to look at their total IT costs as a percentage of sales. They were moving with EDS towards being at least as competitive as the best of competitors in terms of low costs as a percentage of sales. The two parties were attempting to drive operational costs as low as they could, to open up for new investments spent at the highest possible level.

In the SAS – CSC case it was obvious that IT costs was an important issue. Benchmarking of SIG showed that costs were far too high. Enquiring the market of IT services, bidders showed that SAS could benefit from economies of scale by outsourcing IT to an external service provider. In neo-classical economic theories, outsourcing may be regarded as the substitution of external purchase for internal activities and an initiation of procurement from outside suppliers (Gilley & Rasheed, 2000). By selling SIG and buying services back, the outsourcing reduced SAS' involvement in successive stages of production, and thus the outsourcing might be viewed as vertical disintegration. SAS had estimated a turnover of around Skr 10 billion in the five-year period of the outsourcing deal. They had gained a 20% cost reduction, partly taken up-front as a share price, and partly negotiated through lower service prices. SAS had estimated its total IT budget to be decreasing year by year for the time period 2004 – 2008. For each year in the deal, SAS had committed a level of IT purchase from CSC. The committed level could be a composite of different services, defined in the Frame Agreement by service descriptions, levels, and prices, or it could be new projects and services as well. By the end of each year all services bought from all the different lines of business in SAS were counted. If the total level of services did not exceed the committed level, an additional fee was calculated. There were, however, several mechanisms regulating what was inside the deal and what was outside the deal, and how to transfer services between years.

This long-term deal allows us to significantly take down costs, while benefiting from vendors global expertise. (Client CFO)

There is no doubt ABB had a very strong focus on reducing IT costs. They invited the largest outsourcers in the world to bid for their information technology infrastructure. The scope was defined and the goal was to obtain economies of scale. Neo-classical economic theory suggests that all IT functions, which an external vendor can operate at lower costs than the company, should be outsourced. Selecting IBM as vendor, ABB would obtain better cost-performance of their IT infrastructure. Whatever service IBM provided under the contract, they were committed to provide competitiveness compared to the market. The ABB – IBM contract contained a basic volume for each of the ten years. For each year there was an estimate of the number of users, and with defined decreasing unit prices. By the agreed upon decrease in unit prices, ABB had already pocketed the cost savings.

Retained Skills

When the initial outsourcing took place, Rolls-Royce kept very few skills in-house. They realized that was unhelpful, because it created naivety on Rolls-Royce's side and created a degree of frustration on the outsourcer side. Rolls-Royce had to rebuild a team with very experienced IT outsourcing managers. Teams were built around managing the services and the projects, and managing the procurement activities. Rolls-Royce found that the best way of arriving at a strong relationship with the outsourcer was to have people who deeply understood the business; meaning, to be an intelligent buyer you need to understand your own business. Rolls-Royce realized that they needed to keep knowledge about the business processes and how they were built up, which included the applications and their architecture. They had to rebuild that knowledge in-house – overall architecture skills, solution architecture skills, contract management skills, strategic management skills, and skills to manage top-down governance.

Failure to set up retained IT management is probably one of the key success crushers. We have a lot of problems with it, and the outsourcer does not feel it is on their span of influence, because you cannot yet tell the client how you should be managed. It requires a lot of trust to do that. (Vendor Account Manager)

The top management decision of SAS was to sell SIG, and not to touch other IT communities in the SAS Group. In this way the transfer of SIG could be handled clean and fast. Corporate IT, the CIO's staff, was a small group of people. They had gradually built management capacity, contract management skills, and service level management skills. They had the responsibility for the Frame Agreements with SIG for several years, being more professional and market oriented year by year. SAS kept around 300 IT employees in the airline businesses, ground handling, and technical services. As an example, the common function Airline IT was a competence center focusing on airline business applications. They had the necessary resources to manage and follow-up services, analyze new requirements, and to purchase from CSC. The Airline IT organization had more than 100 employees. This kind of common function was not expected to be very numerous in the future. As the vendor organization was expected to be more professional, SAS would continue to professionalize itself as a buyer of business application services.

The ABB countries were locally responsible for their country agreements, and they had the responsibility for operations management, contract management, and for their business applications, which were not outsourced. ABB kept in-house senior sourcing managers following up the commercial and economic sides of the deal, and they also kept operational managers following up service levels. Globally there was a small group of people handling the global deal.

Exit Strategies

Rolls-Royce had an exit strategy, because of the length and size of the contract. These plans already existed, the resources were already identified, and the major activities were all in place. In the context of commitment to the board, the CIO was the risk owner. He reported up to an overall risk committee. Directors in the company had the responsibility to identify all major risks in the business, and to have plans in place to both contain them when they occur and to avoid them happening. Exit strategies were important both from a risk perspective and from a performance failure perspective.

In the SAS – CSC deal there were agreed upon termination clauses which, to a certain level, described rules and procedures for termination. In the Transition Agreement there were identified activities, which should refine the operational description of the parties' obligations if termination occurs. SAS were discussing possible exit scenarios, any they had started to work with an exit strategy.

The global deal of ABB – IBM had a schedule called Exit Management, where termination clauses were defined as the two parties' rights and obligations in case of exit. The bottom line of the schedule was the costs of quitting. For each year there were defined costs, sinking as the years go by. If several countries used the termination clause, this would release a global renegotiation. Beyond the economic clauses of termination, there had not yet been developed exit plans.

EVALUATING THE IT OUTSOURCING RELATIONSHIPS

In this section we will use the analytical framework presented in Chapter 2 for evaluating the case study of IT outsourcing relationships. These different theoretical lenses are used to enhance the understanding of the relationships on topics such as: high economic benefits, low transaction costs, effective contracts, good principal-agent cooperation, efficient division of labor, development of skills and capabilities, access to vendor resources, alliance performance, social and economic exchange, and balancing stakeholder interest. Of course the researchers are omnipresent in the description, but the theoretical lenses give room for different positions or opinions.

In this form of writing case studies the focus is on interaction between multiple voices (Van der Blonk, 2003). The empirical case material is not approached as a neutral collection of facts, but as an ongoing outcome of the interaction between the diverse actors and events. The chapter is, in this sense, the result of a complex construction of influences and interpretations, and where the researchers' own voices are not the least important one.

Production Costs Reduction

According to neo-classical economic theory, firms outsource IT to attain cost advantages from assumed economies of scale and scope possessed by vendors (Ang & Straub, 1998). Neo-classical economic theory regards every business organization as a production function (Williamson, 2000), and where their motivation is driven by profit maximization. This means that companies offer products and services to the market where they have a cost or production advantage. They rely on the marketplace where they have disadvantages. According to neo-classical economic theory, companies will justify their sourcing strategy based on evaluating possibilities for production cost savings. Thus, the question whether to outsource, is a question whether the marketplace can produce products and services at a lower price than internal production. In the context of IT outsourcing, a company will keep its IT function internally if this has production cost advantages, and it will outsource when the marketplace can offer production cost savings.

In all three cases, an important driver of outsourcing was cost reduction. Rolls-Royce was looking for a 10% reduction of costs. In the SAS – CSC case it was obvious that IT costs was an important issue. Bidders showed that SAS could obtain a 20% cost reduction, benefiting from economies of scale by outsourcing IT to an external service provider. There was no doubt ABB had a very strong focus on reducing IT costs. They invited the largest outsourcers in the world to bid for their information technology infrastructure. The scope was defined and the goal was to obtain economies of scale. As stated by ABB's CFO: "This long-term deal allows us to significantly take down costs, while benefiting from IBM's global expertise." *(Source: press release of July 2003).* Client companies reported reduction of costs, better cost-performance, economies of scale and scope, compared to internal IT function. Selecting global outsourcing vendors, the client companies could obtain better cost-performance of their IT functions.

Principles of neo-classical economic theory were recognized in the decision making process of outsourcing. Client companies outsourced their IT function to gain IT cost savings. The IT function, including IT assets such as employees, was nothing but a production function, which an external service provider could handle more effectively than the client company. As such, the only concern of the client company was costs of services, and they were handling responsibility of transferred employees to the vendor company. For the purpose of this study we notice that neo-classical economic theory does not pay very much attention to the human side of IT outsourcing.

Transaction Cost Reduction

IT outsourcing causes additional costs to occur that are labeled transaction costs. Transaction costs occur in the exchange between client and vendor. According to transaction cost theory, transaction costs are positively associated with (1) the necessity of investments in durable, specific assets, (2) infrequency of transacting, (3) task complexity and uncertainty, (4) difficulty in measuring task performance; and (5) independencies with other transactions. Organizations choose to source via their own hierarchy or via the market based on relative costs, which has two components: production costs and transactions costs. In every IT outsourcing transactions costs are present in terms of effort, time and money incurred in searching, creating, negotiation, monitoring, and enforcing service contracts between client and vendor. Therefore, transactions costs can erode comparative advantages in production costs of vendors.

Rolls-Royce had no doubt discovered the costs of service and contract management. By outsourcing, Rolls-Royce had transferred to EDS, physical IT assets and almost all resources with IT competencies. What they later realize was that they had a problem understanding what the vendor was doing, what technology and what costs were reasonable. Business needs were of course developing, and these needs had consequences for technology and costs. Rolls-Royce's contract managers were not able to understand and control the development within a complex information technology and business environment. And thus, they had to build strong teams around services and projects, procurement activities, and knowledge about business processes and applications. ABB seemed to be aware of the complexity of their global deal, and they had got management teams with both operational and sourcing expertise locally and globally. Although transaction costs were significant in all three cases, production cost differences seemed to be more influential in the sourcing decision than transaction cost differences.

Case studies recognized human capital as a transaction-specific asset. Vendor investments in human and physical assets may have shifted the balance of power between the transaction participants. Employees transferred from client to vendor during IT outsourcing may contribute to reduction of uncertainties of the outsourcing arrangement. As these employees already know clients infrastructure and systems and how they support client business processes, these employees are able to deliver the required services although they have a new employer. But they may also be exposed to vendor opportunism and bounded rationality. As they learn to know demands and obligations from both client and vendor, it is not unlikely they may feel occupational stress.

Contract Completeness

When entering an IT outsourcing arrangement, vendor and client sign a contract. An outsourcing contract provides a legally bound, institutional framework in which each party's rights, duties, and responsibilities are codified and the goals, policies, and strategies underlying the arrangement are specified. Every outsourcing contract has the purpose of facilitating exchange and preventing opportunism. A complete outsourcing contract reduces uncertainty and risks, but a contract alone is insufficient to guide outsourcing evolution and performance. Luo (2002) argues that contract and cooperation are not substitutes, but complements in relation to performance. Since outsourcing involves repeated inter-organizational exchanges that become socially embedded over time, cooperation is an important safeguard mechanism mitigating external and internal hazards and overcoming adaptive limits of contracts.

The original Rolls-Royce – EDS contract was made a "foot thick," but still they started quarreling. The ABB – IBM outsourcing relationship was based on a complex contractual set up, with both global and local agreements, and complex linkages between them. Although they had tried to cover "everything," contractual completeness was Utopia. For example in Norway there had been more than 80 contractual changes or supplements within the first year of the deal. Because of environmental dynamism, contract and contract governance also had to be dynamic. ABB and IBM had recognized the need to manage the relationship professionally, and a relationship alignment project was the enabler for supporting the contractual and commercial relationship between the two parties. SAS and CSC had a professional attitude developing outsourcing contract. A skilled team from SAS met a special European business development team from CSC. The contract was more complex and comprehensive than any previous deal between SAS and SIG. Despite this, the steering committee with representatives from both parties of the relationship had several times been forced to handle disagreements regarding interpretation of contractual terms.

Transfer of physical and human assets from client to vendor was a part of the outsourcing relationships studied. Typically, the outsourcing contracts were outcome based, specifying service levels of infrastructure and information systems. The contracts were set up to take care of the transactions between the parties (sales and lease back). Human assets were typically IT employees transferred from client to vendor, and which continued to deliver services back to their prior employer. They were an important part of the sale of assets agreement, but they were only an indirect part of the lease back agreement. They became "invisible" as behavioral aspects were left out of the contract. As such, an incomplete contract may bring about ambiguity and raise the likelihood of conflict, which in turn will decrease the outsourcing performance.

Vendor Behavioral Control

In an outsourcing relationship, the cooperating parties engage in an agency relationship defined as a contract under which one organization (the principal) engages another organization (the agent) to perform some service on its behalf which involves delegating some decision-making authority to the agent. Agency theory describes the relationship between the two parties. According to Eisenhardt (1985), agency theory is concerned with resolving two problems that can occur in agency relationships. The first is the agency problem that arises when the desires or goals of the principal and agent conflict, and it is difficult or expensive for the principal to verify what the agent is actually doing. The second is the problem of risk sharing that arises when the principal and agent have different risk preferences (Gonzales, Gasco, & Liopis, 2005). These problems are well known in IT outsourcing. An example might be that the client organization wants to reduce its costs, while the vendor organization wants to maximize profits.

The initial outsourcing contract between Rolls-Royce and EDS had a lack of transparency, which was a potential for mistrust. When something was going wrong the contract played an important role. The contract was reviewed in 2000, and the parties were putting a new long-term arrangement in place and built a pretty close relationship. A high degree of transparency of difficulties like finance, should remove mistrust. In both cases ABB – IBM and SAS – CSC, the parties agreed upon the service levels and their prices. As outsourcing contracts were outcome based, client companies were not intended to do behavioral control of vendors or their IT employees

Before outsourcing, from a principal-agent perspective, client organization was principal and IT employees served as agents in the same organization. After the outsourcing, relationships changed. IT employees were no longer agents of the client organization, but they became agents of a new principal, the vendor organization. The vendor organization contracted its services to client organization and operated as an agent of the client organization. IT employees transferred became contractors to the client organization, and they were only indirectly agents of their former employer. As such, transferred employees of IT outsourcing must adopt new attitudes towards their previous principal (client organization), their new principal (vendor organization), and towards the outsourcing arrangement (where they serve as contractor).

Ho et al. (2003) examined client managerial attitudes and expectations toward employees in IT spin-off arrangements. Specifically, they focused on the phenomenon of persistent client managerial expectations by exploring the conditions under which client managerial expectations persist and the effect on client managerial evaluation of transplant performance. They posit that client managers will expect former subordinates to perform their duties and contribute much as they did in the past, even though these duties and responsibilities may not be included in the new outsourcing contractual arrangement.

Demarcation of Labor

Firm boundaries – defined as the scope of revenue-sharing arrangements across individuals – reflect trade-offs associated with referral problems, which are problems of matching economic opportunities to individuals' efficiency (Garicano & Hubbard, 2003). A large theoretical literature focuses on the question, "What determines firms' boundaries?" In our case of IT outsourcing, firms' boundaries are determined by the extent to which there are large markets for specialization. If there are large markets for IT services available from vendors, then a client company will tend to outsource more of its internal IT function.

In the case of SAS, one of the arguments for outsourcing was that the internal IT Group had better development opportunities for their professional careers at an outsourcer. During the transformation program, employees were replaced according to their competencies. In the case of ABB, IT employees were transferred into IBM according to their competencies. Outsourcing information technology infrastructure and the people operating it, ABB and IBM obtained a clear and unambiguous division of labor. The idea was that individuals transferred to IBM would increase their efficiency through specialization, and this would benefit ABB through cost reduction. EDS stated that the ability to take over people, keeping some of them at the account, and giving others the opportunity to move elsewhere (specialize), is the number one risk of an outsourcer.

One of the oldest ideas in economics is that returns to specialization increase with market size. If there are large markets for IT services available from vendors, then a client company will tend to outsource more of its internal IT function. In our case of IT outsourcing, firms' boundaries were determined by the extent to which there were large markets for specialization. As IT workers get transferred to vendors they have an opportunity to become even more specialized, working for an IT service provider.

Core Competence Management

After outsourcing, the client organization will typically focus on and strengthen its core competencies. Core competencies can be defined as the skills that are the determinant resources for a firm's competitive advantage. Quinn (1999) argues that core competencies are not products or "those things we do relatively well." They are the set of skills and systems that a company does at best-in-the-world levels and through which a company creates uniquely high value for customers. According to the theory of core competencies, developing best-in-the-world capabilities is crucial in designing a core competency strategy. Long-term advantage will depend on identifying the next unique combination no one else is exploiting in the marketplace; however, sustainable competitive advantage is strongest if tied to firm-specific capabilities.

In case studies, production cost reduction was not the only reasons for outsourcing. New business strategies and restructuring of client companies were also important drivers. ABB was restructuring around two core business areas, and SAS admitted that information technology was not at the core of the airliner. Core competencies theory suggests activities which are none-core should be considered for outsourcing with best-in-the-world suppliers. ABB's and SAS' outsourcing vendors, IBM and CSC respectively, are large IT service companies with information technology and systems as their core competence. Client managers interviewed in case studies expected their vendor organizations to influence Transferred employees' work outcome. They expected these employees to become more professional service providers.

According to Levina and Ross (2003), client and vendor should develop complementary core competencies. A vendor's efficiency is based on the economic benefits derived from the ability to develop a complementary set of core competencies. This ability, in turn, is based on the centralization of decision rights, and shared with clients through formal and informal relationship management structures. An outsourcing vendor must develop different competencies, as suggested by Levina and Ross: IT personnel development, methodology development and dissemination, and customer relationship management. As such, the role of IT employees may change as they get transferred from client to vendor.

Vendor Resource Exploitation

With resource-based theory, organizations are viewed as a collection of resources that are heterogeneously distributed within and across industries. The value generation potential from vendor resources can be significant for the client. If the vendor has strategic resources, applications of these resources for the client can provide the client organization with sustained competitive advantage. Strategic resources are characterized by being valuable, rare, non-imitable, non-transferable, non-substitutable, combinable, and exploitable (Barney, 2002) .

The ability to handle technological change was reported as a major issue for outsourcing, as both Rolls-Royce and SAS had a challenge, handling cost reduction and new technologies at the same time. According to resource-based theory, outsourcing is a strategic decision that can be used to fill gaps in the firm's IS resources and capabilities. In the case of Rolls-Royce and SAS, there was a difference between desired capabilities and actual capabilities. Both companies needed external resources to implement the required technological changes.

But the transferred IT employees also represented an important resource in the outsourcing arrangements. A unique combination of transferred IT employees, infrastructure and systems, were required to secure the delivery of services from vendor back to client company. In the short-term, the vendor company needed these employees to do infrastructure operation and management, and systems development and support. For the client company, they served as a safeguard for the delivery of services. And thus, transferred IT employees work outcome affects the success of the relationship.

Interesting to notice, the transforming of Rolls-Royce from a manufacturing oriented company to a service oriented company, seemed to be a part of the plan. According to Linder (2004), vendor resources can be brought to the organization to facilitate rapid organizational change, which might be important for long-term survival of the client. In this specific case of Rolls-Royce, the vendor's ability to do change agentry was an important criterion for vendor selection. EDS were engaged for IS/IT outsourcing and for transformational outsourcing.

Alliance Exploitation

Partnership, often referred to as an alliance, has frequently been noted as a major feature of IT outsourcing. Alliances are broadly defined as collaborative efforts between two or more firms in which the firms cooperate in an effort to achieve mutually compatible goals that they could not achieve easily alone (Koh, Ang, & Straub, 2004).

The outsourcing arrangement studied was based on tightly defined contracts, and where the main goals were not necessarily shared. For example, ABB had a contract that locked in their cost savings. IBM, on their side, had to balance profit with customer satisfaction, and internal business control. The IT outsourcing relationship seemed to be an arm's length cooperative relationship, rather than one of strategic partnership. ABB needs IBM to provide the IT infrastructure service; IBM needs ABB to pay the fee. While it is clear that these goals are not shared, each party has a vested interest in the other's success. This type of cooperative relationships manifests itself when goals are complementary, and when each party needs something from the other party to succeed (Lacity & Willcocks, 2000).

According to Lambe et al. (2002), competence in finding, developing, and managing alliances is recognized as important to alliance success. This will also apply for an IT outsourcing relationship. Relationship managers are higher order resources, who must develop their understanding of how to facilitate the combining of the distinct lower order complementary resources contributed by the outsourcing parties. Transferred employees of IT outsourcing had competencies which client organization no longer posited. IT assets were transferred from client to vendor organization, and transferred employees had unique skills and know-how to operate, maintain, and support information technology and systems service delivery back to the client organization. As a result of the outsourcing arrangement, the client organization no longer had these competencies in-house. Thus, it is reasonable to state that the transferred IT employees contribute to distinctive client – vendor complementary resources. Transferred employees' competencies may be considered as vital for service delivery in the outsourcing arrangement, especially in the first phase after contract signing. For the client organization, transferred employees may contribute to reduction of uncertainty and improve the communication between vendor and client organization. For the vendor organization, transferred employees may secure the ability to fulfill contract agreements.

Relationship Exploitation

According to relational exchange theory, a partnership is dependent on relational norms. Norms are expectations about behavior that are at least partially shared by a group of decision makers. Norms are important in relational exchange because they provide the governance rules of the game. Relational norms are based on the expectation of mutuality of interest, essentially prescribing stewardship behavior, and are designed to enhance the wellbeing of the relationship as a whole (Lambe, Spekman, & Hunt, 2000). Kern and Blois (2002) have studied norm development in a major IT outsourcing relationship. Their findings suggest: 1) where unusual organizational structure is proposed, management must recognize the possibility that norms dominant within the constituent organizations will not necessarily be compatible, 2) where norms are not compatible the action must be taken through changing management schemes in order to develop appropriate norms, and 3) the development and initialization of new norms takes time. Norm development becomes more salient as the relationship matures.

The relationship alignment project of ABB and IBM is one example of development of new norms. The project was seen as a key success factor to create and maintain a good working relationship between the two parties. The objective of the project was (among others) to create a framework to manage the natural tension between both parties, to find an agreement on a vision of how the parties needed to work together, to build a strong working relationship between the teams in the various countries, to build and commit to an appropriate strategic relationship structure and enabling mechanisms, to support a group-wide collaborative approach, to review and refine roles & responsibilities, and to align across all countries.

Businesses recognize the impossibility of a contract meeting every eventuality so that there is a need for adaptability within a contract and the completion of a contract is frequently dependent upon workers being able to take up a lot of the uncertainty. Both the normal economic models of a market transaction and the legal model of a contract tend to obscure the degree to which large numbers of contracts are agreements to deliver an indefinite good or service for an indefinite price. Without such willingness to be adaptable many business relationships would grind rapidly and regularly to a halt. Norms are in a sense the lubricants that keep relationships from being stymied by their contractual terms (Kern & Blois, 2002). In case studies, outsourcing contracts were outcome based, measuring agreed upon levels of specified services for an agreed upon price. Transferred employees of IT outsourcing were the contractors to deliver the services. They were the employees ultimately faced with uncertainty of indefinite services. Developing and securing relational norms will guide transferred employees with regard to how to behave if and when exchange issues occur. Prescribed behavior shared by the parties will reduce transferred employees' uncertainty of their new role. And thus, relational norm will supplement the outcome-based contractual agreements and benefit the relationship as a whole.

Social Exchange Exploitation

Social exchange theory assumes self-interested actors who transact with other self-interested actors to accomplish individual goals that they cannot achieve alone. Self-interest and interdependence are central properties of social exchange. Two or more actors, each of whom has something of value to the other, decide whether to exchange and in what amounts. Thus, a critical success factor becomes the enabling of social and economic outcomes that outperform alternatives. This applies both at individual level and inter-organizational level.

Outsourcing may have a negative impact on employees' sense of job security and loyalty. Barthélemy (2003) defined overlooking personnel issues as a deadly sin of outsourcing. Meaning, there is more to outsourcing than transferring people and renegotiating their pay and benefits. Transferred employees of IT outsourcing not only change employer, but as a result their social network and outcome may also change.

Stakeholder Management

The following stakeholder theory recommendations for successful IT outsourcing relationships are meant to create efficient and effective communication with and between stakeholders to secure continued support from all stakeholders, to balance their interests and to make the IT outsourcing arrangement such that all stakeholders achieve their goals. During the case studies several stakeholder groups were identified – client senior management, client business management, client retained IT management, client IT users, transferred IT employees, vendor senior management, vendor account management, and vendor IT employees – each group with its own expectations and goals.

- *Client senior management* was driven by the overall financial goals of their companies, and typically their main interest was to gain economic benefits from the outsourcing. As contracts were signed, senior managers lost their interest in the outsourcing relationship.
- *Client business management* was constantly seeking more efficient IT services. They expected better service quality at lower prices, and a professional client-vendor relationship. Business managers also expected the vendor to be innovative, coming up with new solutions. After all, vendor was a world-class outsourcing company.
- *Client retained IT management* initially expected the same service levels and the same accessibility to their service provider as prior to outsourcing. Their experience was however a more formal and commercial relationship. Running an IT outsourcer was very different from running an internal IT department, different in terms of skills and emphasis. Senior project executives, sourcing managers, and operations managers were first of all responsible for systems and infrastructure service delivery, and to secure commercial and contractual agreements.
- *Client IT users* typically expected better IT services. But very soon they realized that a professional service provider required a more formalistic interaction. Taking away a lot of legacy and non-standard IT from the users, the outsourcer had to be careful not to make a bad name for itself.

- *IT employees transferred from client to vendor (transplants)* represented a huge group in all three cases. First they were doing business as usual, but after some time they got redeployed into competencies and they got new colleagues. The transition of employees from the internal IT department to the global business of the outsourcer was an important issue, as some employees liked it and others did not. Some looked forward to work as an IT professional within an organization where IT was core competence. The *transplant* group, is defined as those IT employees who get transferred from the client company to the vendor company (Ho et al., 2003). These employees formally leave their organization and are transplanted into the vendor company, which employs them and offers their services back to the original employer for a service fee. Even though these transplants still provide services to the original organization, it no longer directly employs them.
- *Vendor senior management* was driven by growth and profit expectations. Thus, the initial analysis up-front (due-diligence) was fundamental. Their investments in such deals were huge, and their number one priority was on safeguarding their investments.
- *Vendor account management* had to balance profit, customer satisfaction, and business control procedures.
- *Vendor IT employees* were those people doing the job (sometimes called factory or delivery unit). Their mission was to deliver agreed upon service levels, neither more, nor less. To some extent they were involved up-front to see how easy the transferred IT department could be built into their own factory.
- *Third party suppliers* had more or less no influence in the process. Some of them regarded the outsourcing as a threat because it reduced their turnover; others saw it as an opportunity as they got more sales. Regardless of that, they had to spend time transferring leases and licences from one company to the other.

Some other stakeholder groups were also identified, such as vendor transition groups, labor unions, and even client customers. In one organization, a vendor transition group was established having a standardize process for transition, and they were HR oriented types of people. Labor unions were representatives for the IT employees, but they also represented a power base in themselves, which they would like to maintain. Client customers were also mentioned as a stakeholder group. Although they could not influence the process, some of the consequences might hit them.

These stakeholder groups are different from those identified by Lacity and Willcocks (2000) at one important point: interviewees recognize and emphasized the important group of transplants. In all three cases the transplant group counted more than 1000 people. Transplants were not recognized in the study of Lacity and Willcocks (2000). Another interesting observation was that the interviewees seemed to be aware of other stakeholders' expectations and goals. Transplants were a necessary precondition for the success of the deal. And thus, their contribution must be seen in the light of costs and risks. This requires efficient and effective communication with and between stakeholders. Neglecting the moral principles that underlie stakeholder theory, vendor companies will have less satisfied transplants, and transplants will show performance that is consistently below industry average. Vendor (and client) organizations have responsibilities to transplants for moral reasons. Upholding moral principles is a necessary precondition for transplants' efficient working.

CONCLUSIONS FROM CASE STUDY RESEARCH

This chapter presented and discussed three paradigmatic case studies that broadly span the most common outsourcing arrangements in today's industry. They were conducted to investigate outsourcing relationship, its development, configuration, costs, and performance, and investigated how individuals affect or get affected by the relationship. The rich qualitative data illustrated the complexities inherent to relationship management, revealing in particular the difficulties various stakeholders encountered.

The three internationally based outsourcing cases studied in this research followed two guiding research questions, an interview protocol was designed and handed out before the interviews, and the analysis of each case focused essentially on transcripts of interviews. Regarding scientific generalization, the aim of the case studies was twofold: 1) to identify characteristics influencing and creating successful IT outsourcing relationships, and 2) to identify individual level attitude, behavior, and performance. The purpose of the case study was to obtain a richer description and understanding not only of how to manage successful IT outsourcing relationships.

Two major themes emerged from the qualitative study. First, stakeholders interviewed emphasized the following issues as important in managing successful IT outsourcing relationships: clear enter strategies; relationship building activities are important after contract signing; specialist resources needed for contract development and management; the ability to handle transfer of IT employees is critical; establishment of new governance structures; the economy of outsourcing is not only an issue of production cost reduction; client skills have to be rebuilt to handle the outsourcer, establishment of exit strategies serve as a safeguarding mechanism making the client able to handle difficult situations.

And second, stakeholders emphasized the unique position of the transplants – the IT employees transferred from client to vendor. Occupational stress was recognized among transplants. That is, transplants perceived different expectations and demands from stakeholders they dealt with. The identified outsourcing arrangement stressors included such factors as client managerial persistent expectations, relational norms, and complementary core competencies. Transplants interviewed reported different attitudes, behavior and task performance, and also different perception of occupational stress.

REFERENCES

Ang, S., & Straub, D. W. (1998). Production and Transaction Economics and IS Outsourcing: A study of the U.S. Banking Industry. *MIS Quarterly, 22*(4), 535–552. doi:10.2307/249554

Barney, J. B. (2002). *Gaining and Sustaining Competitive Advantage*. Upper Saddle River, NJ: Prentice Hall.

Barthélemy, J. (2003). The Seven Deadly Sins of Outsourcing. *The Academy of Management Executive, 17*(2), 87–100.

Eisenhardt, K. M. (1985). Control: organizational and economic approaches. *Management Science, 31*(2), 134–149. doi:10.1287/mnsc.31.2.134

Garicano, L., & Hubbard, T. N. (2003). Firms' Boundaries and the Division of Labor: Empirical Strategies. *Journal of the European Economic Association, 1*(2/3), 495–502. doi:10.1162/154247603322391134

Gilley, M. K., & Rasheed, A. (2000). Making More By Doing Less: An Analysis of Outsourcing and its Effects on Firm Performance. *Journal of Management, 26*(4), 763–790. doi:10.1016/S0149-2063(00)00055-6

Gonzales, R., Gasco, J., & Liopis, J. (2005). Information systems outsourcing risks: a study of large firms. *Industrial Management & Data Systems, 105*(1), 45–61. doi:10.1108/02635570510575180

Group, A. B. B. (2004a). *120 years of technological leadership*. Retrieved September 28, 2004, from www.abb.com

Group, A. B. B. (2004b). *Group Annual Report 2003*. Retrieved September 28, 2004, from www.abb.com

Ho, V. T., Ang, S., & Straub, D. (2003). When Subordinates Become IT Contractors: Persistent Managerial Expectations in IT Outsourcing. *Information Systems Research, 14*(1), 66–86. doi:10.1287/isre.14.1.66.14764

Kern, T., & Blois, K. (2002). Norm development in outsourcing relationship. *Journal of Information Technology, 17*(1), 32–42. doi:10.1080/02683960210137174

Kern, T., & Willcocks, L. P. (2002). Exploring relationship in information technology outsourcing: the interaction approach. *European Journal of Information Systems, 11*(1), 3–19. doi:10.1057/palgrave/ejis/3000415

Koh, C., Ang, S., & Straub, D. W. (2004). IT Outsourcing Success: A Psychological Contract Perspective. *Information Systems Research, 15*(4), 356–373. doi:10.1287/isre.1040.0035

Lacity, M. C., & Willcocks, L. P. (2000). Relationships in IT Outsourcing: A Stakeholder Perspective. In R. W. Zmud (Ed.), *Framing the Domains of IT Management: Projecting the Future Through the Past*. Cincinnati, OH: Pinnaflex Educational Resources.

Lacity, M. C., Willcocks, L. P., & Feeny, D. F. (1996). The Value of Selective IT Sourcing. *Sloan Management Review, 37*(3), 13–25.

Lambe, C. J., Spekman, R. E., & Hunt, S. D. (2000). Interimistic Relational Exchange: Conceptualization and Propositional Development. *Journal of the Academy of Marketing Science, 28*(2), 212–225. doi:10.1177/0092070300282003

Lambe, C. J., Spekman, R. E., & Hunt, S. D. (2002). Alliance Competence, Resources, and Alliance Success: Conceptualization, Measurement, and Initial Test. *Journal of the Academy of Marketing Science, 30*(2), 141–158. doi:10.1177/03079459994399

Levina, N., & Ross, J. W. (2003). From the Vendor's Perspective: Exploring the Value Proposition in Information Technology Outsourcing. *MIS Quarterly, 27*(3), 331–364.

Linder, J. (2004). Transformational Outsourcing. *MIT Sloan Management Review, 45*(2), 52–58.

Luo, Y. (2002). Contract, cooperation, and performance in international joint ventures. *Strategic Management Journal, 23*(10), 903–919. doi:10.1002/smj.261

Quinn, J. B. (1999). Strategic Outsourcing: Leveraging Knowledge Capabilities. *Sloan Management Review, 40*(4), 9–21.

Rolls-Royce. (2004a). *Annual Report 2003*. Retrieved October 25, 2004, from www.rolls-royce.com

Rolls-Royce. (2004b). *History of Rolls-Royce*. Retrieved July 1, 2004, from www.rolls-royce.com

Scandinavian Airlines System. (2004a). *About SAS*. Retrieved August 16, 2004, from www.scandinavian.net

Scandinavian Airlines System. (2004b). *The SAS Group Annual Report 2003*. Retrieved August 16, 2004, from www.scandinavian.net

Solli-Sæther, H. (2006). *Transplants' role stress and work performance in IT outsourcing relationships*. Unpublished PhD thesis, BI Norwegian School of Management, Oslo.

Stake, R. E. (1994). Case studies. In N. K. Denzin & Y. S. Lincoln (Eds.), *Handbook of Qualitative Research* (pp. 236-247). Thousand Oaks, CA: Sage Publications.

Van der Blonk, H. (2003). Writing case studies in information systems research. *Journal of Information Technology, 18*(1), 45–52. doi:10.1080/0268396031000077440

Williamson, O. E. (2000). The New Institutional Economics: Taking Stock, Looking Ahead. *Journal of Economic Literature, 38*(3), 595–613.

Yin, R. K. (2003). *Case Study Research: Design and Methods* (3rd ed.). Thousand Oaks, CA: Sage Publications, Inc.

Chapter 11
Conclusion

Achieving superior performance in IT outsourcing relationships is both a demanding and a rewarding activity. To perform well managers need to understand outsourcing opportunities, critical success factors, company value configuration and maturity for outsourcing, the need for knowledge transfer, and management and control of outsourcing arrangement.

Outsourcing opportunities can be derived from resource-based theory, transaction cost theory, activity theory, agency theory, or other theories of the firm. Based on such opportunities, companies develop business-oriented enter strategies. A strategy defines vision, mission and objectives of the firm. It includes changes in electronic business and other important business areas that impact future use of information technology. The strategy analyzes business direction, information management strategy, and ambition level for IT outsourcing.

The theoretical and empirical based *critical success factors* serve as recommendations for what to outsource and how to succeed in managing IT outsourcing relationships.

Outsourcing business functions, managers must first understand – the underlying business logic of their firm, the company's *value configuration*, and how resources such as information systems affect the performance of various component activities.

The *maturity model* can be applied for strategic planning to understand both state and direction of development in client-vendor relationships. To guide developmental energies at lower levels of orienta-

DOI: 10.4018/978-1-60566-796-6.ch011

tion, which provide additional understanding of the transitional events, individuals and organizations have to accumulate experience in order to move and grow from one stage of development to the next, i.e., from cost stage, through resource stage and into partner stage.

Knowledge management is important to strengthen know-what, know-how and know-why at both the vendor and the client. Knowledge transfer mechanisms have to be installed to handle troubleshooting, technology upgrades and emerging business needs.

Cost controls include both production and transaction economics. Hidden costs are of particular interest, as well as contract development and management costs. To appreciate the cost benefit ratio of outsourcing, both planned and unplanned benefits have to be included in the equation.

Managing IT outsourcing performance is concerned with exploiting outsourcing opportunities and avoiding outsourcing threats. We should remind our self of some of the outsourcing threats suggested by Barthélemy (2003) to avoid them. Outsourcing activities that should not be outsourced can be avoided by thorough understanding of business goals, company boundaries and resources. Selecting the wrong vendor can be avoided by exploring both contractual and relational reactions of potential vendors. Writing a poor contract can be avoided by organizing a qualified contract team that includes a good lawyer. Overlooking personnel issues can be avoided by retaining key employees and securing transfer of employees to the vendor. Losing control of the outsourced activity can be avoided by complementing vendor management skills with technical skills. Overlooking hidden costs of outsourcing can be avoided by identifying search and contracting costs, vendor management costs and other potentially hidden costs. Failing to plan an exit strategy can be avoided by explicitly anticipating the end of an outsourcing contract before it is signed.

An important part of managing successful IT outsourcing relationships is to secure strategic, economic, and technological benefits. This cannot be achieved and controlled without some kind of *performance measurement*, e.g., in terms of service quality, client satisfaction, partnership quality, and overall success of the outsourcing relationship.

Transparent *governance structures* may be based on the interaction approach. Management control systems have to be implemented, including regular performance measurements. Partnering relationships have to be defined, and acceptable partnership quality has to be achieved. All stakeholders have to be considered and included in the governance structures. Both hard and soft sides of outsourcing have to be included in the governance structures.

Effective handling of personnel issues includes humane and predictable human resources management in times of IT staff reduction and transfer, employment protection, pension considerations and handling of persistent managerial expectations. For example, transferred IT personnel from client to vendor may not be employed to work with the previous employer. Rather, a contingent approach can imply that transferred personnel are trained in new areas to serve other vendor clients.

REFERENCES

Barthélemy, J. (2003). The Seven Deadly Sins of Outsourcing. *The Academy of Management Executive*, *17*(2), 87–100.

Selected Readings

Chapter 12
Dynamics of Outsourcing Relationships

Given the potential headaches of managing IT, it is tempting to hand the job over to someone else. Indeed, outsourcing once appeared to be a simple solution to management frustrations, and senior management teams at many companies negotiated contracts with large service providers to run their entire IT functions (Gottschalk & Solli-Sæther, 2006). At a minimum, these providers were often able to provide IT capabilities for a lower cost and with fewer hassles than the companies had been able to themselves. But many of these outsourcing arrangements resulted in dissatisfaction, particularly as a company's business needs changed.

Service providers, with their standard offerings and detailed contracts, provided IT capabilities that were not flexible enough to meet changing requirements, and they often seemed slow to respond to problems. Furthermore, a relationship with a supplier often required substantial investments of money and time, which entrenched that supplier in the company's strategic planning and business processes. The company then became particularly vulnerable if the supplier failed to meet its contractual obligations (Ross & Weill, 2002).

In our dynamic perspective of knowledge resources, outsourcing relationships are not just about transactions between a vendor and a supplier. The resource-based theory argues that the firm's ability to mobilize and utilize both internal and externally available resources determines its ability to succeed in the market place. If the firm is short of important resources such as IT resources, an outsourcing arrangement might help overcome the problem as the vendor makes IT resources available to the firm for a price.

The quality of an outsourcing relationship will vary over time. For example, when the client's behavior in the relationship changes, then a reaction from the vendor should be expected. The vendor's reaction will have to be responded to by the client. In this manner, the relationship might dynamically improve or deteriorate over time. We apply system dynamics to understand such developments over time.

Often, the vendor will have a different value configuration than the client. The vendor being a solutions provider makes it a value shop, while the client might be a value chain, value shop, or value network. Understanding how different value configurations interact will improve the relationship. For example, if the client is a value chain, then information systems operated by the vendor have the main purpose of making production more efficient and effective at the client site. If the client is also a value shop, the information systems operated by the vendor have the main purpose of adding value to the problem solution work done by the client for its customers.

AGENCY THEORY

Agency theory has broadened the risk-sharing literature to include the agency problem that occurs when cooperating parties have different goals and division of labor. The cooperating parties are engaged in an agency relationship defined as a contract under which one or more persons (the principal/s) engage another person (agent) to perform some service on their behalf which involves delegating some decision-making authority to the agent (Jensen & Meckling, 1976). Agency theory describes the relationship between the two parties using the metaphor of a contract. In an IT outsourcing relationship this is a client-vendor relationship and an outsourcing contract.

According to Eisenhardt (1985), agency theory is concerned with resolving two problems that can occur in agency relationships. The first is the agency problem that arises when the desires or goals of the principal and agent conflict and it is difficult or expensive for the principal to verify what the agent is actually doing. The second is the problem of risk sharing that arises when the principal and agent have different risk preferences. These problems are well known in IT outsourcing. An example might be that the client organization wants to reduce its IT costs, while the vendor organization wants to maximize profits. The agency problem arises when the two parties do not share productivity gains. The risk-sharing problem might be the result of different attitudes toward the use of new technologies. Because the unit of analysis is the contract governing the relationship between the two parties, the focus of the theory is on determining the most efficient contract governing the principal-agent relationship given assumptions about people (e.g., self-interest, bounded rationality, risk aversion), organizations (e.g., goal conflict of members), and information (e.g., information is a commodity which can be purchased). Thus the question becomes: Is a behavior-oriented contract more efficient than an outcome-oriented contract? Outsourcing contracts are to a great extent tied up to service-level agreements, where the outcome of the service is the focal point.

The agency theory is applicable when describing client-vendor relationships in IT outsourcing arrangements. Typically, the client organization (principal) transfers property rights to the vendor organization (agent). In the context of IT, assets transferred might be infrastructure, systems and documentation, and employees. For a certain amount of money, the vendor organization provides services to the client organization. This implies a change in legal relationships, and IT services are carried out using a more formal transaction process. The status of personal relationships also changes, from that of a manager and a subordinate, to that of a client-manager and a vendor. According to agency theory, control mechanisms also change, from that of behavioral control, to that of outcome-based control. If both parties to the relationship are trying to maximize their utility, there is good reason to believe that the vendor organization will not always act in the best interests of the client. Monitoring and bonding activities in reducing agency costs include auditing, formal control systems, budget restrictions, and the establishment of incentive compensation systems which serve to more closely identify the manager's interests with those of the outside equity holder.

The original impetus for the development of agency theory was large corporations' separation of control from ownership. Thus, its focus was never on organizational boundaries, as with transaction cost theory. Agency theory's primary interest is not the decision to source via the hierarchy or via the market. Although all contractual arrangements contain important elements of agency, agency theory is essentially concerned with the delegation of work by the principal to the agent via a contract, whether or not they are both within the same organization. However, agency and transaction cost theories share several concepts, such as opportunism, uncertainty, and bounded rationality, and there is a rough correspondence between transaction cost economics' hierarchies and markets and agency theory's behavior-based contracts and outcome-based contracts.

According to Hancox and Hackney (2000), the choice of contract type depends on the agency costs, which include the principal's effort in assessing the agent's performance and the agent's efforts in assuring the principal of his commitment. Agency theory holds that human beings act through self-interest and therefore, as contracting parties, they may have divergent goals. An important aspect of the theory is that both principal and agent wish to avoid risk when dealing with each other. The principal may prefer to place risk with the agent via an outcome-based contract, whereas the agent may prefer to avoid risk by having a behavior-based contract.

Outcome-based contracts are claimed to reduce agent opportunism because the rewards of both agent and principal depend on the same actions. Behavior-based contracts need the principal to have sufficient information to identify two possible dangers: First, whether there is adverse selection (the agent does not possess the skills he claims), and second, whether there is a moral hazard—the agent is shirking. Overall risk may be reduced by sourcing via the hierarchy, but agency costs also exist in hierarchies. Problems between agents and principals are greater in complex organizations with many managerial layers. Given that many public sector bodies are large and complicated both in the range of their activities and the structures adopted to manage and account for those activities, it may be that agency costs are inclined to be higher in the public sector. Nonmarket organizations may be especially susceptible to influence costs, where employees pursue their own agenda. This might imply that within a public sector organization, if the employees of one department were motivated by self-interest, then workers in other departments would be inconvenienced and resent the action, unless, perhaps, they themselves were pursuing a similar or compatible agenda.

The technological and business complexity of IT means that there may be major problems for the principal in choosing a suitable agent and in monitoring the agent's work. Only the agent knows how hard he is working, and that can be especially important in multilateral contracting where one agent acts for several principals. This is often the case in IT outsourcing because of the market dominance of one large firm. Given the difficulties of behavior-based contracts suggested by agency theory, it is reasonable to assume that the overwhelming majority of clients would insist on outcome-based contracts when acquiring IT products and services. Such a strategy can only succeed if the client can confidently specify current and future requirements. But accurate predictions by the client may not always be in the vendor's interests, since vendor account managers often are rewarded according to contract profitability, which is principally achieved through charging the client extra for anything, which is not in the contract.

Hancox and Hackney (2000) interviewed IT managers to find support for the agency theory in IT outsourcing. In their interviews, it was difficult to find examples of some of the ideas from agency theory, although a minority of the organizations had been disappointed with aspects of vendor performance and behavior.

PARTNERSHIP AND ALLIANCE THEORY

Partnership appears to be a less rigorously defined analytical framework than the theories of core competencies, transaction cost economics, and theories that are typically applied to explain outsourcing (Gottschalk & Solli-Sæther, 2006). Indeed, the very word "partnership" has a more everyday ring to it and is associated with the readily understood characteristics, which may be found in a relationship between two or more parties in a particular context. Partnership's treatment in the information systems literature seems largely nontheoretical, perhaps reflecting a wide diversity of practical arrangements and the absence of a single commonly recognized theory. Although the sharing of risk and reward is sometimes mentioned in the information systems literature, often the emphasis is on intangibles such as trust, comfort, understanding, flexibility, cooperation, shared values, goals, and problem solving, good interpersonal relations, and regular communication. The influential Kodak-IBM outsourcing deal had much to do with a sense of honor and a chemistry between the parties, and changed the common perception of IT outsourcing from an arm's length relationship to one of strategic partnership (Hancox & Hackney, 2000).

Partnership, often referred to as an alliance, has frequently been noted as a major feature of IT outsourcing. Partnership can reduce the risk of inadequate contractual provision, which may be comforting for clients about to outsource a complex and high-cost activity such as IT. However, in the relationship between vendor and client, the latter may be overly dependent on the former, and goals are not necessarily shared. A client may be more comfortable if he knows the vendor already. In partner selection, cultural compatibility is vital and shared values and objectives inform all stages of the partnership development process. This may make a successful relationship especially difficult if the putative partners are from fundamentally different domains and bring fundamentally different perspectives, as might well be argued is the case in a private sector/public sector arrangement. The difficulty may be compounded where, as in the UK government's compulsory competitive tendering policy, the outsourcing can be involuntary.

Hancox and Hackney (2000) found that few organizations claim to be in a strategic partnership with their IT suppliers. The contract is more likely to favor the vendor because he has greater experience in negotiation. Clients with loose contracts were more likely to regard outsourcing as a failure; yet most respondents in a study used the vendor's standard contract as a basis for outsourcing agreement and most did not use external technical or legal advice. It was found that 80% of clients wished that they had more tightly defined contracts. Partly the client's view of IT influences its relationship with the vendor, such that firms regarding IT as a core competence capability are more likely to look upon outsourcing as an alliance. Clients who view IT as a core are also more likely to be satisfied with the outsourcing arrangements because they negotiate from a more knowledgeable position.

Hancox and Hackney (2000) interviewed IT managers to find support for the partnership theory in IT outsourcing. Despite assurances found in vendors' marketing literature, most clients were skeptical about partnership. If partnership did exist, it was usually as a collection of some of the intangibles mentioned earlier, rather than as a formalized arrangement. Partnership was more likely to be claimed in the area of systems development, where vendors needed to have a greater understanding of the organization, than in outsourcing of operations and IT infrastructure support. There seemed to be no correlation between those organizations regarding IT as strategic and those regarding relationships with vendors as partnerships.

Das and Teng (2002) studied how alliance conditions change over the different stages of alliance development to understand the development processes of strategic alliances such as an IT outsourcing relationship. They defined the following stages in the alliance development process:

- **Formation stage:** Partner firms approach each other and negotiate the alliance. Partner firms then carry out the agreement and set up the alliance by committing various types of resources. The alliance is initiated and put into operation. Alliances will be formed only under certain conditions. These conditions include a relatively high level of collective strengths, a low level of inter partner conflicts, and a high level of interdependencies.
- **Operation stage:** Not only is the formation stage directly influenced by alliance conditions, the transition from the formation stage to the operation stage is also dictated by the same alliance conditions variables. During the operation stage, partner firms collaborate and implement all agreements of the alliance. The alliance will likely grow rapidly in size during this stage, somewhat akin to the growth stage of organizational life cycles. Other than the growth route, an alliance may also be reformed and/or terminated at this stage.
- **Outcome stage:** During this stage, alliance performance becomes tangible, and can thus be evaluated with some certainty. There are four possible outcomes for an alliance at this stage: stabilization, reformation, decline, and termination. A combination of outcomes is also possible, such as a termination after reformation. Alliance reformation and alliance termination do not necessarily signal alliance failure. Reformation and termination may be the best option under certain circumstances, such as the achievement of preset alliance objectives. Alliance condition variables continue to play a decisive role in the outcome stage. The particular alliance outcome will depend on the condition of the alliance.

Das and Teng (2003) discussed partner analysis and alliance performance. An important stream of research in the alliance literature is about partner selection. It emphasizes the desirability of a match between the partners, mainly in terms of their resource profiles. The approach is consistent with the resource-based theory of the firm, which suggests that competitors are defined by their resources profiles. They found a lack of agreement concerning alliance performance. This lack of agreement reflects an underlying conceptual puzzle: What does effective alliance performance mean? There are two distinct loci of alliance performance in the literature: the alliance itself and the partners forming the alliance. On the one hand, when alliances are viewed as separate entities, alliance performance is the success of these separate entities, in terms of, say, profitability or growth rate. On the other hand, because partner firms use alliances to achieve certain strategic objectives, alliance performance ought to be measured in terms of the aggregated results for the partner firms.

Alliances are broadly defined as collaborative efforts between two or more firms in which the firms pool their resources in an effort to achieve mutually compatible goals that they could not easily achieve alone. Resources here are defined as any tangible or intangible entity available for use by a firm to compete in its marketplace. When interfirm business relationships are collaborative, rather than adversarial, in nature, a variety of types of these relationships may be classified as alliances, for example outsourcing. According to Lambe, Spekman, and Hunt (2002), the popularity of alliances is growing. Alliances account for anywhere from 6 to 25%of the market value of the typical company. Yet alliance success remains elusive. Studies find that as many as 70%of alliances are not successful. Thus, an important question for researchers and practicing managers is, what makes alliances succeed? They argue that alliance competence contributes to alliance success, both directly and through acquisition and creation of resources. Using survey data gathered from 145 alliances, empirical tests provide support for the posited explanation of alliance success.

Alliance competence has three facets, which Lambe et al. (2002) labeled alliance experience, alliance manager development capability, and partner identification propensity. Furthermore, consistent with competence-based theory and resource-advantage theory conceptualizations of a competence (a higher-order resource that is a distinct combination of lower-order resources), the researchers proposed that these three facets are the three lower-order resources that collectively comprise the higher-order resource of an alliance competence. That is, more of each of these three lower-order resources will contribute to increasing a firm's competence in finding, developing, and managing alliances:

- **Alliance experience** is a resource that can be leveraged across an organization because it contributes to knowledge about how to manage and use alliances.
- **Alliance manager development capability** enables firms to plan and navigate the mechanisms of an alliance so that roles and responsibilities are clearly articulated and agreed upon. In addition, these managers have the ability to review continually the fit of the alliance to the changing environment to make modifications as necessary.
- **Partner identification propensity** enables firms to systematically and proactively scan for and identify partners that have the complementary resources that are needed to develop a relationship portfolio or mix that complements existing competencies and enables them to occupy positions of competitive advantage.

Lambe et al. (2002) posited that two specific types of resources affect alliance success: idiosyncratic and complementary resources. In terms of resource-advantage theory, complementary resources may be thought of as lower-order resources that are brought to the alliance and idiosyncratic resources as the higher-order resources that are developed by the alliance through the process of combining the complementary resources of the partner firms. Idiosyncratic resources are resources that are developed during the life of the alliance, are unique to the alliance, and facilitate the combining of the distinct lower-order resources contributed by the partner firms. Idiosyncratic resources may be tangible, such as computers and cables, or intangible, such as developing a methodology or a process together. Similarly, some researchers refer to idiosyncratic investments or assets.

RELATIONAL EXCHANGE THEORY

Contracts are often extremely imperfect tools for controlling opportunism. While relational contracts may mitigate some opportunistic behavior, significant residual opportunism may remain. It is possible that transactors using relational contracts may incur significant ex-post bargaining costs as they periodically negotiate contract adjustments (Artz & Brush, 2000). Relational exchange theory is based on relational norms. According to this theory, the key to determining how efficiently contract governance is carried out lies in the relational norms between the transactors. For example, the degree to which transactors engage in joint planning or their extent of interfirm information sharing are process elements that determine the costs associated with periodically renegotiating contracts. Those transactors who have established behavioral norms that can simplify and smooth the renegotiation process can reasonably expect to incur lower ex post bargaining costs than those who have not.

Artz and Brush (2000) examined supplier relationships that were governed by relational contracts, and they found support for the relational exchange theory. By altering the behavioral orientation of the alliance, relational norms lowered exchange costs. In their measurement of relational norm, Artz and Brush (2000) included collaboration, continuity expectations, and communication strategies. Collaboration refers to the willingness of the client and vendor to work together to create a positive exchange relationship and improve alliance performance. Collaborative actions can act to enhance the client-vendor relationship as a whole and curtail opportunistic behaviors. For example, joint planning and forecasting can allow both the customer and the supplier to participate in determining the roles and responsibilities of each and foster mutually beneficial expectations. Continuity expectations refer to the extent to which the customer and the supplier expect the relationship to continue for the foreseeable future. Expectations of a long-term supply relationship can encourage cooperation by providing the opportunity for one alliance partner to retaliate if the other behaved opportunistically. Specifically, opportunistic behavior by one party in one period can be matched by opportunistic behavior by the other partner in the next. Similarly, cooperation can be met with cooperation. "Communication strategies" refers to the type of communications the customer and vendor use in their bargaining sessions to try to influence the negotiations. Such strategies can be grouped into either coercive or noncoercive communications. Partners using coercive communications attempt to achieve their desired goals by applying direct pressure with adverse consequences of noncompliance stressed. Examples of coercive communications include using threats or legalistic pleas, in which one party argues that compliance is required by the formal contract terms. When one firm attempts to coerce another in order to gain a more favorable negotiation outcome, that firm is likely to be viewed by its alliance partner as exploitative rather than accommodative, and retaliatory behavior often results. In contrast, noncoercive strategies attempt to persuade rather than demand. Noncoercive communications center on beliefs about business issues and involve little direct pressure. Examples include simple requests or recommendations, in which one party stresses the benefits the other party will receive by complying.

Kern and Blois (2002) considered the role of norms within networks by describing how BP Exploration outsourced its information technology function,a major business activity. This outsourcing venture led to the formation of a consortium of vendors. However, this attempt was found to have failed. They suggested that central to the failure of the consortium, as an outsourcing arrangement was the issue of norms. Norms create expectations of behavior and imply a certain action and are shared by the actors. It is believed that society shares a number of common norms that make it necessary for contracts to contain certain features but not necessary to include statements about others. Yet norms vary a great deal between and within societies, as is illustrated by international contracts in which a foreigner's requirements as to what should go into a contract will often surprise us but what we would not consider necessary to include may surprise them.

Businesses recognize the impossibility of a contract meeting every eventuality, so there is a need for adaptability within a contract and the completion of a contract is frequently dependent upon workers being able to take up a lot of the uncertainty. Both the normal economic models of a market transaction and the legal model of a contract tend to obscure the degree to which large numbers of contracts are agreements to deliver an indefinite good or service for an indefinite price. Without such willingness to be adaptable many business relationships would grind rapidly and regularly to a halt. Norms are in a sense the lubricants that keep relationships from being stymied by their contractual terms.

In the case of BP Exploration, three problems arose. First, the consortium's members, though competitors, were expected to work closely with each other as the senior partner on some sites and as the junior partner on others. Yet neither BP Exploration nor any member of the consortium recognized in advance that the norms that they usually applied in their relationships with their clients would not be applicable to this situation. Consequently, their staff was working with norms that were at best not appropriate to the new situation and at worst made for difficulties. For example, a company's norms do not normally encourage the acceptance of flexibility, information exchange, and solidarity in contacts with competitors, all of which are needed if sound relationships are to be developed between organizations. Second, BP Exploration's line managers conducted their relationships with the consortium members as if they were buying a commodity service. Yet a major reason for outsourcing was BP Exploration's desire to obtain a state-of-the-art IT service. Its behavior toward the consortium was therefore based on norms that were inappropriate relative to its stated objectives. The third problem was that one of the vendors was not familiar with European modes of operations and had a horrendous job trying to adapt to a non-U.S. culture.

Norms are formed in different ways. Some norms' roots can be related to cultural backgrounds, but the roots of others are more difficult to identify. However, how norms develop when new industries or, as in the case of BP, new forms of organization evolve is far from apparent. In relationships such as the one described in this case, which develop in a new environment, the relative power of the parties involved is presumably a major factor. Thus, where one organization is very dominant in a new market it seems probable that their values and approaches to business will be very influential. Within business relationships the nature of exchanges that occur between the personnel involved can vary a great deal. Sometimes the relationships at a senior level are more relaxed than those at a junior level. Yet the opposite can be true with junior staff making the relationship work on a day-to-day level in spite of adversarial behavior among the directors. Many classifications of norms have been proposed, but no one is regarded as dominant. It has been proposed that relational norms are a higher-order construct consisting of three dimensions (Kern & Blois, 2002):

- **Flexibility**, which defines a bilateral expectation of the willingness to make adaptations as circumstances change.
- **Information exchange**, which defines a bilateral expectation that parties will proactively provide information useful to the partner.
- **Solidarity**, which defines a bilateral expectation that a high value is placed on the relationship. It prescribes behaviors directed specifically toward relationship maintenance.

Many factors led to BP Exploration being a less than successful experiment in outsourcing. However, a major contribution was a failure to recognize the need for establishing norms of behavior that were appropriate to the consortium form of organization (Kern & Blois, 2002).

Norms are expectations about behavior that are at least partially shared by a group of decision makers. Norms are important in relational exchange because they provide the governance rules of the game. These rules depend on the game, which from an exchange perspective has been described as either discrete or relational. Discrete exchange norms contain expectations about an individualistic or competitive interaction between exchange partners. The individual parties are expected to remain autonomous and pursue strategies aimed at the attainment of their individual goals. In contrast, relational exchange norms are based on the expectation of mutuality of interest, essentially prescribing stewardship behavior, and are designed to enhance the well-being of the relationship as a whole. In the evolutionary model of relational exchange, relational norm development takes place during an extended period of time through many interactions between the partners. For example, tacit relational norms emerge as partners interact during the exploration stage of relational development (Lambe, Spekman, & Hunt, 2000).

Relational exchange is an interactive process where commitments are made, outcomes are observed, and further investments are made, if outcomes meet or exceed expectations. Based on previous interactions as well as expectations about the future, a mutual orientation develops resulting in a common language and mutual knowledge. The exchange is embedded in a normative structure that determines the functioning of the system. Patterns of behavior are taken for granted. The actors share common expectations about expected and accepted behavior, and collective interests are incorporated into the preferences and belief structures of the actors (Rokkan & Haugland, 2002). Discrete and relational exchange can be regarded as polar cases. Pure discrete exchange is consistent with the underlying assumptions of neoclassical economic theory. Relational exchange, on the other hand, accounts for the social and historical context in which exchange takes place. The fundamental norms of discrete exchange are discreteness and presentation, which means that any transaction is separated from all else between the participants at the same time and before and after, and that all future obligations and actions are brought into the present. Relational exchange, on the other hand, is based on norms such as role integrity, conflict resolution, and preservation of the relationship.

Rokkan and Haugland (2002) studied the effect of power on relational exchange. Power is related to whether the relationship is symmetrical or unbalanced. A key characteristic of long-term relationships is mutual power relations. Actor A's power in the relationship with actor B is the inverse of B's dependence upon A. Dependence or interdependence thus affects and constrains the behavior of the actors, but it may also create opportunities. This factor is important in relation to relational exchange, as it is closely linked to the question of equity or fair dealing. They hypothesized that dependence asymmetry would have a negative effect on relational exchange, but they did not find empirical support in their survey for this hypothesis.

PARTNERSHIP QUALITY DETERMINANTS

Increasing attention is paid to building successful partnerships in information technology outsourcing. Lee and Kim (1999) have studied the effect of partnership quality on IS outsourcing success. They define partnership as an interorganizational relationship to achieve the participants' shared goals. Partnership is not a new concept in the management area. Marketing and interorganizational systems research has explored relationships between customer and vendor, buyer and seller, manufacturer and distributor, or auditor and client, and so on. A number of different views emerged concerning interorganizational relationships.

Research has classified the relationship between organizations into two types: transactional style and partnership style. A transactional style relationship develops through the formal contract in which rules of the game are well-specified and the failure to deliver on commitments by either party should be resolved through litigation or penalty clauses in the contract. In contrast, the requirements of a partnership style relationship include risk and benefit sharing, the need to view the relationship as a series of exchanges without a definite endpoint, and the need to establish a range of mechanisms to monitor and execute its operations.

In traditional IS management, the role of a service provider was limited in terms of the size of the contract and the type of service. Maintenance of hardware or program subcontracting has traditionally been the typical IS service provider. However, the type of relationship in outsourcing is changing from such buyer-seller relationships to the more strategic partnership relationship. Therefore, a necessary condition to move away from self-interest is a belief that the exchange relationship is a win-win situation for organizations to gain competitive advantages.

Relevant theories to analyze the interorganizational relationship include the resource-dependency theory, transaction-cost theory, and agent-cost theory from the economic viewpoint, and social exchange theory and power-political theory from the social viewpoint. Economic theories aim at explaining the characteristics of governance or contract. They treat each sourcing decision as an independent event regardless of prior relationships that affect the ongoing sourcing decision. This treatment may be inappropriate where organizations repeatedly enter transactions with each other. Explaining the relationship between organizations from a purely economic point of view is unjustifiable because interorganizational relationships form from the social learning experiences based on specific sequential interactions (Lee & Kim, 1999).

Social theorists assume that processes evolve over time as participants mutually and sequentially demonstrate their trustworthiness, whereas in the economic perspective, the organization's exchange activities are enforceable. Social theorists understand a relationship as a dynamic process through specific sequential interactions in which two participants carry out activities toward one another. However, a good relationship does not always bring about the participants' desired results. According to social theories, two mechanisms, trust and power, can explain the relationship between organizations. Trust, a feature of relationship quality, has been conceptualized as the firm's belief that the other company will perform actions that will result in a positive outcome for the firm, and will not take unexpected actions that would result in negative outcomes for the firm. Power is determined by the relative dependence between two actors in an exchange relationship, and the concept of power is only meaningful when compared with another organization. While social exchange theory uses the concept of trust to explain interactions between participants, power-political theory relies on the power derived from offering valuable resources that few other sources can provide (Lee & Kim, 1999).

Partnership is an effective way to improve economies of scale and scope provided by the traditional modes of organization. However, partnership does not guarantee a desired outcome. Therefore, careful attention needs to be paid to the partnership problems that may lead to an unstable and conflicting relationship. Partnership quality is an important concept in this respect. Quality is treated as having two dimensions: fitness of use (does the product or service does what it is supposed to do? Does it possess the features that meet the customer's needs?), and reliability (to what extent is the product free from deficiencies?) If we apply the first dimension to partnership, partnership quality may be expressed as how well the outcome of a partnership matches the participants' expectations (Lee & Kim, 1999).

From this outset, partnership quality can be viewed as an antecedent of the outsourcing success. High partnership quality may be a necessary condition for outsourcing success, but not a sufficient condition. For instance, if the main objective of the outsourcing was cost reduction but the outsourcing vendor failed to meet the objective, such an outsourcing project would be a failure regardless of the partnership quality between the service receiver and provider. Thus, Lee and Kim (1999) distinguish the concept of partnership quality from that of outsourcing success, and empirically tested whether outsourcing is successful when high-quality partnership exists. They identified the following five factors that make up partnership quality: trust (degree of confidence and willingness between partners), business understanding (degree of understanding of behaviors, goals, and policies between partners), benefit/risk share (degree of articulation and agreement on benefit and risk between partners), conflict (degree of incompatibility of activities, resource share, and goals between partners), and commitment (degree of the pledge of relationship continuity between partners).

Partnership quality is affected by organizational, human, and environmental factors. However, most literature does not explicitly distinguish the components of partnership quality from the factors that affect it. Lee and Kim (1999) introduced the factors from previous literature as potential determinants of partnership quality and presented the hypotheses related to each factor. They expected to find a positive relationship between each of the hypothesized determinants of partnership quality and trust, business understanding, benefit/risk share, and commitment among the components of partnership quality, and a negative relationship between each of the hypothesized determinants of partnership quality and conflict.

Figure 1 illustrates their findings. Participation was found to be significantly related to partnership quality. From a social perspective, participation is prescribed as a remedy when there is conflict, frustration, and vacillation in the group. Active participation of the partnership members plays a major part in enhancing the sustainability of their partnerships over time. When one partner's actions influence the ability of the other to compete effectively, the need for participation in specifying roles, responsibilities, and expectations increases. Accordingly, the higher the degree of participation, the higher the quality of partnership. Communication quality was found to be significantly related to partnership quality. According to the social exchange literature, effective communication between partners is essential in order to achieve the intended objectives. Intensive communication should lead to better-informed

Figure 1. Partnership quality affected by determinants and effecting outsourcing success

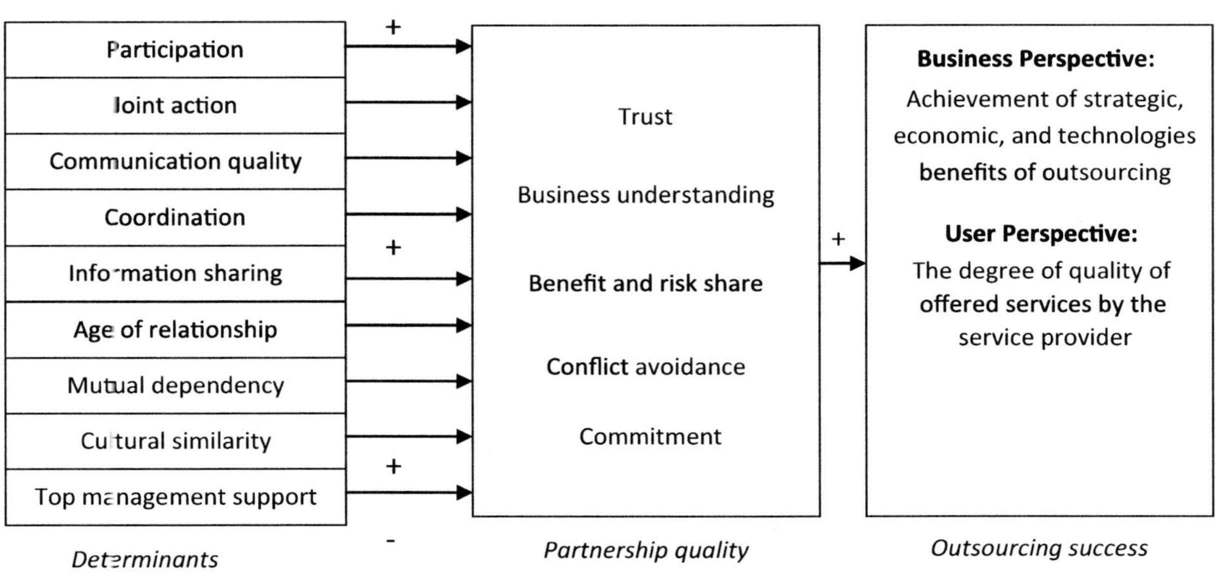

parties, which in turn should make each party more confident in the relationship and more willing to keep it alive. Communication quality is treated as an antecedent of trust in the research literature. Accordingly, higher communication quality is believed to enhance the quality of partnership. Information sharing is the third significant determinant in Figure 1. Information sharing is the extent to which critical or proprietary information is communicated to one's partner. Partnerships can create a competitive advantage through the strategic sharing of organizations' key information. Closer relationships result from more frequent and relevant information exchanges among high-performance partners. Participants are expected to sustain more effective relationships over time by sharing information and by being knowledgeable about each other's organization.

Age of relationship had a significant negative effect on the partnership quality. Among the components of partnership quality, conflict and commitment were significantly associated with age of relationship. However, contrary to many expectations, age of relationship had a positive effect on conflict and a negative effect on commitment. Interestingly, mutual dependency was also negatively associated with partnership quality. This means that the degree of partnership quality was lower when mutual dependency was higher. Although mutual dependency had a significant effect on business understanding, benefit and risk share, and conflict, these results were contrary to the researchers' expectation. The relationship between top management support and partnership quality was significant. Top management support also was significantly associated with trust and business understanding, while it was not related to benefit and risk share, conflict, or commitment.

In Figure 8.6, there is a causal relationship between partnership quality and outsourcing success. Successful partnership enables participants to achieve organizational objectives and to build a competitive advantage that each organization could not easily attain by itself. To gain these advantages of partnership, participants should try to enhance their partnership quality to reflect the extent of intimacy between partners. Therefore, a higher quality of partnership is likely to lead to a successful outsourcing relationship.

Outsourcing success can be viewed as the level of fitness between the customer's requirements and the outsourcing outcomes. Lee and Kim (1999) measured outsourcing success in terms of both business and user perspectives in the following way: They expected to find a positive relationship between outsourcing success and components of partnership quality such as trust, business understanding, benefit/risk share, and commitment, and a negative relationship between outsourcing success and conflict. In a business perspective, outsourcing is motivated by the promise of strategic, economic, and technological benefits. The success of outsourcing, then, should be assessed in terms of attainment of these benefits. Strategic benefits refer to the ability of a firm to focus on its core business by outsourcing routine information technology activities. Economic benefits refer to the ability of a firm to use expertise and economies of scale in human and technological resources of the service provider and to manage its cost structure through unambiguous contractual arrangements. Technological benefits refer to the ability of a firm to gain access to leading edge IT and to avoid the risk of technological obsolescence that results from dynamic changes in IT. From a user perspective, outsourcing success may also be the level of quality of offered services. A decision to outsource on the basis of saving costs without analysis of the quality of service frequently leads to higher costs and lower user satisfaction. Therefore, it is imperative to conduct a proper analysis of the service quality before building a relationship with a service provider for a successful outsourcing project.

In their statistical analysis, Lee and Kim (1999) found that the quality of outsourcing partnership had a strong positive relationship with both business satisfaction and user satisfaction, as well as with overall outsourcing success. Trust showed a strong positive relationship with business satisfaction, while it had no effect on user satisfaction. This indicates that trust is a critical predictor of outsourcing success in terms of the business perspective, as opposed to the user perspective. Unlike the result with trust, business understanding was not a good predictor of business satisfaction, while it significantly influenced user satisfaction. This means that the outsourcing outcome matched the users' requirements as understanding of its partner's business increased. Benefit and risk share showed a strong positive relationship with both business satisfaction and user satisfaction, as well as with overall outsourcing success. Although conflict was a predictor of business satisfaction, it had no effect on the overall outsourcing success and user satisfaction. Lee and Kim's (1999) finding for the conflict variable indicated that outsourcing success was not affected by the degree of conflict between the service receiver and provider. Their study also indicated that commitment was significantly associated with outsourcing success in terms of both the business and the user perspective. In summary, all partnership quality variables except conflict were significantly related to outsourcing success.

PARTNERSHIP QUALITY DYNAMICS

As has become quite well known by reading this book so far, the findings in Figure 1 have obvious limitations. Rather than focusing on determinants that have a one-on-one relationship with partnership quality, there are interactions, as illustrated in Figure 2. Figure 2 illustrates some of the cause and effect relationships and feedback loops when partnership quality is studied as a function of time.

Figure 2. Causal loop diagram for outsourcing partnership quality dynamics

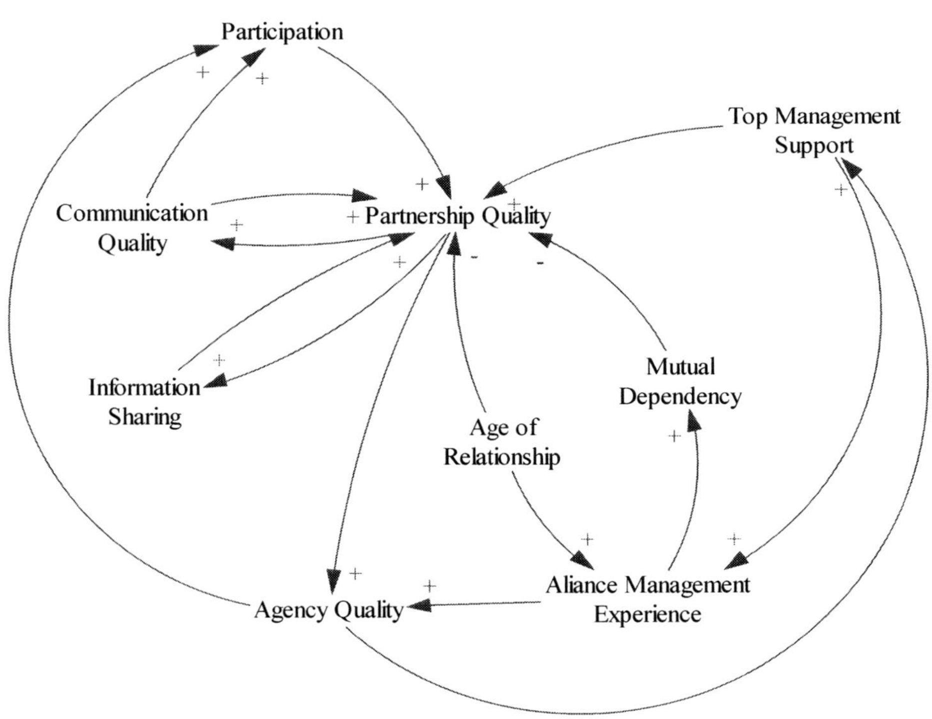

Figure 3. Reference mode for outsourcing partnership quality

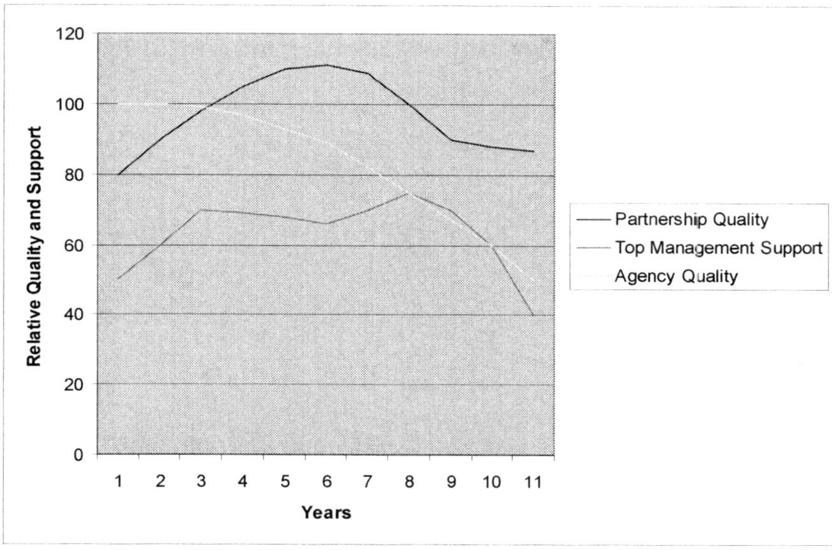

The causal loop diagram in Figure 2 might produce different simulation results depending on parameters for quantitative relationships. One possible outcome is illustrated in Figure 3. We see partnership quality initially rising in the first years of the outsourcing relationship. In year 6, the relationship reaches its top quality, before it starts to deteriorate. Top management support for the outsourcing arrangement remains for 2s more years, but this variable as well starts to deteriorate in year 8. Because of such developments, the vendor starts to practice opportunistic behavior, causing a fast deterioration in agency quality.

REFERENCES

Artz, K. W., & Brush, T. H. (2000). Asset specificity, uncertainty and relational norms: An examination of coordination costs in collaborative strategic alliances. *Journal of Economic Behavior & Organization, 41,* 337-362.

Das, T. K., & Teng, B.-S. (2002). The dynamics of alliance conditions in the alliance development process. *Journal of Management Studies,* 39(5), 725-746.

Das, T. K., & Teng, B.-S. (2003). Partner analysis and alliance performance. *Scandinavian Journal of Management, 19,* 279-308.

Eisenhardt, K. M. (1985). Control: Organizational and economic approaches. *Management Science, 31*(2), 134-149.

Gottschalk, P., & Solli-Sæther, H. (2006). *Managing successful IT outsourcing relationships.* Hershey, PA: Idea Group Publishing.

Hancox, M., & Hackney, R. (2000). IT outsourcing: Frameworks for conceptualizing practice and perception. *Information Systems Journal, 10*(3), 217-237.

Jensen, M. C., & Meckling, W. H. (1976). Theory of the firm: Managerial behavior, agency costs and ownership structures. *Journal of Financial Economics, 3*(4), 305-360.

Kern, T., & Blois, K. (2002). Norm development in outsourcing relationship. *Journal of Information Technology, 17,* 32-42.

Lambe, C. J., Spekman, R. E., & Hunt, S. D. (2000). Interimistic relational exchange: Conceptualization and propositional development. *Journal of the Academy of Marketing Science, 28*(2), 212-225.

Lambe, C. J., Spekman, R. E., & Hunt, S. D. (2002). Alliance competence, resources, and alliance success: Conceptualization, measurement, and initial test. *Journal of the Academy of Marketing Science, 30*(2), 141-158.

Lee, J.-N., & Kim, Y.-G. (1999). Effect of partnership quality on IS outsourcing success: Conceptual framework and empirical validation. *Journal of Management Information Systems, 15*(4), 29-61.

Rokkan, A. I., & Haugland, S. A. (2002). Developing relational exchange: Effectiveness and power. *European Journal of Marketing, 36*(1), 211-230.

Ross, J. W., & Weill, P. (2002, November). Six IT decisions your IT people shouldn't make. *Harvard Business Review*, 84-91.

This work was previously published in Business Dynamics in Information Technology, by P. Gottschalk, pp. 153-173, copyright 2007 by IGI Publishing (an imprint of IGI Global).

Chapter 13
The Role of the CIO

THE ROLE OF THE CIO

The CIO can be defined as the highest-ranking IT executive who typically exhibits managerial roles requiring effective communication with top management, a broad corporate perspective in managing information resources, influence on organizational strategy, and responsibility for the planning of IT. This definition is in line with research; which applied the following criteria when selecting CIOs for empirical observation: i) highest-ranking information technology executive; ii) reports no more than two levels from the CEO, that is, either reports to the CEO or reports to one of the CEOs direct reports, iii) areas of responsibility include information systems, computer operations, telecommunications and networks, office automation, end-user computing, help desks, computer software and applications; and iv) responsibility for strategic IS/IT planning. The CIO plays a vital role in every interoperability project in digital government. There may be a CIO in each involved public agency as well as a CIO for the whole of government. For example in Hong Kong, there is an office of the government chief officer, which developed the interoperability framework for all agencies and other public organizations to follow (2007).

In this chapter we start by defining the position of the CIO. CIOs are playing a key role sourcing IT resources and enabling IT governance. These topics are covered in the next sections. Then, we continue discussing CIO leadership roles. As organizations expand their use of the Internet, the CIO emerges as an important executive for developing digital government, competitive strategy and Internet strategy. We are also looking into the CIO selecting e-business model.

The CIO Position

The CIO position emerged in the 1970s as a result of increased importance placed on IT. In the early 1980s, the CIO was often portrayed as the corporate savior who was to align the worlds of business and technology. CIOs were described as the new breed of information managers who were businessmen first, managers second, and technologists third. It was even postulated that in the 1990s, as information became an organization's critical resource, the CIO would become the logical choice for the chief executive officer (CEO) position.

Job advertisements for information systems positions from 1970 to 1990 were reviewed by Todd, McKeen and Gallupe (1995). They investigated specific positions related to programmers, systems analysts and information systems managers. It is the latter position that is of interest here. At the time of the research, it was considered that successful information systems managers should have a blend of technical knowledge and sound business related skills. Further, in general, they should possess effective interpersonal skills. Over the twenty-year period, Todd et al. (1995) determined that there had not been much change in the required skills indicated in job advertisements.

Benjamin, Dickinson and Rockart (1985) suggested that the emergence of the CIO role represented the recognition of the importance of the role to be played within the organization. Kaarst-Brown (2005), however, suggested it is unfortunate that twenty years later, in 2005, the CIO is still held in lower regard than those senior managers of other more traditional business units. Kaarst-Brown (2005) suggested the reasons for this gap might be attributed to some of the items on the following list:

- Personality conflicts
- Lack of corporate technology vision
- Poorly aligned IT goals
- Lack of business knowledge
- Lack of IT awareness among the business executives
- Incorrect formal structure and reporting relationships

However, Kolbasuk (2005) reported that the perception of CIOs within organizations may be evolving. She suggests they may finally be getting the respect they deserve as they become members of the board of directors of large companies. This movement to the board level in the organization indicates the perception of the CIO role is evolving from a manager primarily focused on regulations, back office operations, and administrative duties to applying information technology at a strategic level to facilitate competitive advantage through an understanding of how business processes function and may be adapted to a changing corporate environment.

As a manager of people, the CIO faces the usual human resource roles of recruiting, staff training, and retention, and the financial roles of budget determination, forecasting and authorization. As the provider of technological services to user departments, there remains a significant amount of work in publicity, promotion, and internal relations with user management. As a manager of an often-virtual information organization, the CIO has to coordinate sources of information services spread throughout and beyond the boundaries of the organization. The CIO is thus concerned with a wider group of issues than are most managers.

While information systems executives share several similarities with the general manager, notable differences are apparent. The CIO is not only concerned with a wider group of issues than most managers, but also, as the chief information systems strategist, has a set of responsibilities that must constantly evolve with the corporate information needs and with information technology itself. It has been suggested that the IT director's ability to add value is the biggest single factor in determining whether the organization views information technology as an asset or a liability. According to Earl and Feeny (1994, p. 11), chief information officers have a difficult job:

Chief information officers have the difficult job of running a function that uses a lot of resources but that offers little measurable evidence of its value. To make the information systems department an asset to their companies – and to keep their jobs – CIOs should think of their work as adding value in certain key areas.

Creation of the CIO role was driven in part by two organizational needs. First, accountability is increased when a single executive is responsible for the organization's processing needs. Second, creation of the CIO position facilitates the closing of the gap between organizational and IT strategies which has long been cited as a primary business concern.

Alignment of business and IT objectives is not only a matter of achieving competitive advantage, but is essential for the organization's very survival. Though the importance of IT in creating competitive advantage has been widely noted, achieving these gains has proven elusive. Sustained competitive advantage requires not only the development of a single system, but the ability to consistently deploy IT faster, cheaper, and more strategically than one's competitors. IT departments play a critical role in realizing the potential of IT. The performance of IT functions, in turn, often centers on the quality of leadership, i.e., the CIO.

Figure 1. Sourcing options for IT resources and services

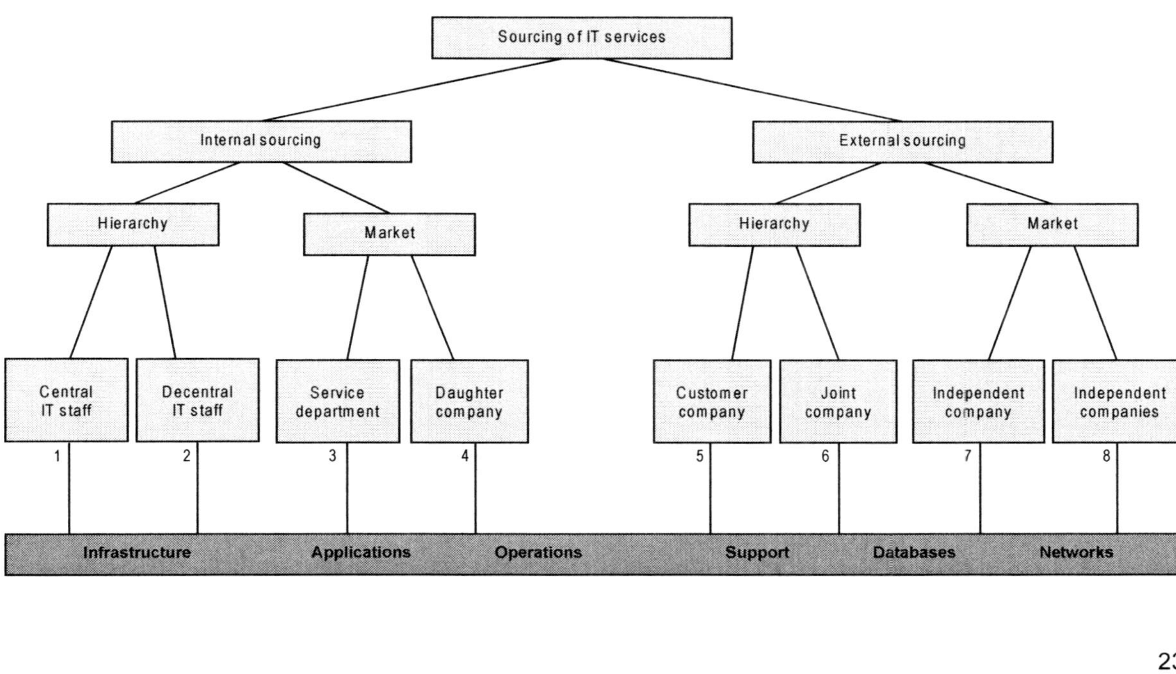

The CIO Sourcing IT Resources

IT sourcing is concerned with defining, planning and managing how an enterprise deploys internal and external resources and services to ensure the continuous fulfillment of its business objectives. A variety of sources have emerged. This variety is illustrated in Figure 1. Here we find internal sourcing and external sourcing. Both can be managed either through organizational hierarchy or through market mechanism.

In general, organizations have three basic alternatives for acquiring technological know-how. They can (1) develop the technology independently, (2) acquire another company that already has the technology, or (3) enter into a technology-sourcing arrangement. If a firm lacks the capabilities needed to develop a technology independently and other organizations already have the technology, management can consider external sourcing. There is a continuum of external sourcing methods based on the level of mutual commitment between the firm that has the technology (the source firm) and the firm that desires the know-how (the sourcing firm). These methods range from arms-length licensing contracts, through more tightly coupled co development partnerships and joint ventures, to the outright acquisition of the source firm (Steensma & Corley, 2001).

Steensma and Corley (2001) focused on the two polar extremes in their study of technology sourcing: market contracting through licensing versus the use of firm hierarchy through acquisition. The polar cases are basic particles from which more elaborate arrangements are constructed. Hierarchy implies that the sourcing firm can hierarchically control the technology, personnel, and other assets of the IT function and apply it to its current needs at its discretion.

Internal market as illustrated with numbers 3 and 4 in the figure has a different sourcing logic. The concept of internal market is not new. The concept was first perceived to have radical implications eliminating superior-subordinate relationships, organizing all activity in terms of self-responsible profit centers, determining compensation objectively, eliminating internal monopolies, allowing freedom of access to information, and establishing a corporate constitution (King & Malhotra, 2000).

These appear to be less radical in today's environment of matrix organizations, self-managed teams, and re-engineered business processes. However, the notion of internal markets is not as simples as first suggested. The internal market is a mechanism for unleashing market forces inside the firm. Firms selecting this alternative might be able to retain control of the function while achieving the objectives of cost savings and service-responsiveness that are often ascribed to an external vendor (King & Malhotra, 2000).

According to King and Malhotra (2000), the internal market within an organization is characterized by a setup in which internal units are enabled to act autonomously by exerting self-control in conducting transactions with other internal units and with external entities within a framework of an overarching corporate vision, values and precepts. This notion of internal markets may be best understood in terms of its potential broad applicability in an organizational context.

Implementation of the internal market concept requires the creation of a market economy inside a firm. In this, organizational units buy and sell goods and services among themselves and to others outside the firm at prices established in the open market. In contrast, the transfer prices that are used for internal transactions often represent a simulation of a marketing-clearing mechanism (King & Malhotra, 2000).

The CIO Enabling IT Governance

Monnoyer and Willmott (2005) are skeptical of IT governance. They argue that something is gone very wrong with the structures, processes, and policies that govern how a business makes IT decisions and who within the organization makes them. They find that IT governance arrangements have become a substitute for real leadership. Companies are relying on tightly scripted meetings, analyses, and decision frameworks to unite CIOs and business executives around a common vision for IT. But committee meetings and processes are poor stand-ins for executives who can forge a clear agreement among their peers about IT investment choices and drive the senior-level conversations needed to make tough trade-offs. Monnoyer and Willmott (2005) find that in companies with strong IT leaders, governance constitutes a much more flexible set of managerial activities, involves fewer people and fewer meetings, and is typically tailored to fit the IT leader's style, much as executive committee activities often reflect a CEO's leadership approach.

To play a key role in developing IT governance arrangements is important for the CIO to increase his or her chances for becoming the next CEO. While corporate governance allocates decision rights in the overall company affecting the CEO position, IT governance allocates decisions rights in all IT-related dimensions affecting the CIO position.

In many organizations, information technology has become crucial in the support, the sustainability and the growth of the business. This pervasive use of technology has created a critical dependency on IT that calls for a specific focus on IT governance. IT governance consists of the leadership and organizational structures and processes that ensure that the organization's IT sustains and extends the organization's strategy and objectives (Grembergen, Haes, & Guldentops, 2004).

IT governance matters because it influences the benefits received from IT investments. Through a combination of practices (such as redesigning business processes and well-designed governance mechanisms) and appropriately matched IT investments, top-performing enterprises generate superior returns on their IT investments (Weil, 2004).

CIO Leadership Roles

One approach to understanding the CIO position is to study managerial roles. In this chapter, ten roles by Mintzberg and six roles by Grover (derived from Mintzberg) are presented to shed light on the various leadership roles for CIOs.

Mintzberg (1994) notes a number of different and sometimes conflicting views of the manager's role. He finds that it is a curiosity of the management literature that its best-known writers all seem to emphasize one particular part of the manager's job to the exclusion of the others. Together, perhaps, they cover all the parts, but even that does not describe the whole job of managing. Based on an observational study of chief executives, Mintzberg (1994) concluded that a manager's work could be described in terms of ten job roles. As managers take on these roles, they perform management functions. These ten roles consist of three interpersonal roles (figurehead, leader and liaison), three informational roles (monitor, disseminator, and spokesman), and four decisional roles (entrepreneur, disturbance handler, resource allocator, and negotiator):

- **Figurehead** performs some duties of a ceremonial nature. Examples are greeting visitors, responding to journalists' questions, and visiting customers and allies.

- **Personnel leader** is responsible for motivation of subordinates and for staffing and training. Examples are most activities involving subordinates, such as settling disagreements between subordinates.
- **Liaison** establishes a web of external relationships. Examples are attending conferences and giving presentations.
- **Monitor** seeks and receives information to understand and learn from the environment. Examples are reading journals and listen to external experts.
- **Disseminator** transmits information to other organizational members. Examples include forwarding reports and memos, making phone calls to present information, and holding informational meetings.
- **Spokesman** involves the communication of information and ideas. Examples are speaking to the board of directors and top management, and talking to users.
- **Entrepreneur** acts as initiator and designer of much of the controlled change in the organization. Examples are user ideas converted to systems proposals and management objectives transformed to infrastructure actions.
- **Disturbance handler** is responsible for solving conflicts in the organization.
- **Resource allocator** is responsible for allocation of human, financial, material, and other resources. Examples are working on budgets, developing project proposals, and monitoring information technology projects.
- **Negotiator** is responsible for representing the organization in negotiations. Examples are negotiations with unions concerning wages and with vendors concerning procurements.

According to Mintzberg (1994), these ten roles are common in all managerial jobs regardless of the functional or hierarchical level. However, differences do exist in the importance and effort dedicated to each managerial role based on job content, different skill levels, and expertise. Mintzberg (1994) states that managers are in fact specialists, required to perform a particular set of specialized managerial roles that are dependent upon the functional area and hierarchical level in which they work.

Grover, Jeong, Kettinger and Lee (1993) used the Mintzberg framework to study CIO roles. They selected six of ten roles, which they found relevant for CIOs: personnel leader, liaison, monitor, spokesman, entrepreneur and resource allocator. The four other roles (figurehead, disseminator, disturbance handler, and negotiator) were not operationalized because Grover et al. (1993) found that the activities constituting these roles were correlated with the activities of the other six roles and because they found that the activities that comprised those four roles were consistently important only for certain functions and levels of management. The six selected roles were related to information technology management by rephrasing them:

- As the *personnel leader*, the IS manager is responsible for supervising, hiring, training, and motivating a cadre of specialized personnel. Literature has emphasized the impact of this role on IS personnel. This role is mainly internal to the IS organization.
- The *spokesman* role incorporates activities that require the IS manager to extend organizational contacts outside the department to other areas of the organization. Frequently, he or she must cross traditional departmental boundaries and become involved in affairs of production, distribution, marketing, and finance. This role is mainly external in relation to the intra-organizational environment.

- As the *monitor*, the IS manager must scan the external environment to keep up with technical changes and competition. In acting as the firm's technical innovator, the IS manager uses many sources including vendor contacts, professional relationships, and a network of personal contacts. This role is mainly external in relation to the inter-organizational environment.
- As the *liaison*, the IS manager must communicate with the external environment including exchanging information with IS suppliers, customers, buyers, market analysts, and the media. This role is mainly external in relation to the inter-organizational environment.
- As the *entrepreneur*, the IS manager identifies business needs and develops solutions that change business situations. A major responsibility of the IS manager is to ensure that rapidly evolving technical opportunities are understood, planned, implemented, and strategically exploited in the organization.
- As the *resource allocator*, the IS manager must decide how to allocate human, financial, and information resources. The litany of past discussion on charge-back systems (users have to pay for IT services) and the importance of "fairness" in IS resource allocation decisions speak to the importance of this role. This role is mainly internal to the IS organization.

In Figure 2, the selected six CIO roles are illustrated. The roles of personnel leader and resource allocator are both internal to IT functions. The entrepreneur absorbs ideas from the intra-organizational environment, while the spokesman influences the intra-organizational environment. The liaison informs the external environment, while the monitor absorbs ideas from the external environment.

A survey was conducted in Norway to investigate CIO roles (Gottschalk, 2007). CIOs were asked questions about the importance of the different roles. Survey results indicate some variation in the importance of roles. Responding CIOs found the role of entrepreneur most important and the role of liaison least important. This is indicated with numbers in Figure 2, where the scale went from 1 (not important) to 6 (very important).

Figure 2. CIO roles on different arenas

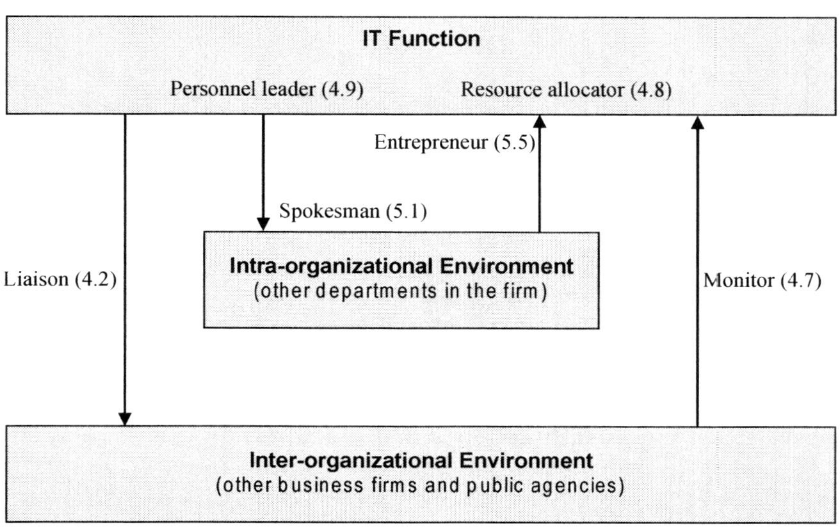

The CIO Developing Digital Government

As organizations expand their use of the Internet from electronic commerce to electronic business, the CIO emerges as the most important executive for performance improvements when selecting business models.

Electronic commerce (EC) is an important concept that describes the process of buying, selling, or exchanging products, services, and information, via computer networks, including the Internet (Turban, King, Lee, Warkentin, & Chung, 2002). From a communications perspective, EC is the delivery of goods, services, information, or payments over computer networks or by any other electronic means. From a business process perspective, EC is the application of technology toward the automation of business transactions and workflow. From a service perspective, EC is a tool that addresses the desire of firms, consumers, and management to cut service costs while improving the quality of goods and increasing the speed of service delivery. From an online perspective, EC provides the capability of buying and selling products and information on the Internet and other online services. From a collaboration perspective, EC is the framework for inter- and intra-organizational collaboration. From a community perspective, EC provides a gathering place for community members, to learn, transact, and collaborate.

Electronic commerce over large ubiquitous networks will soon be conducted in routine fashion. While some may question the timeframe involved, few will question its imminence. In this transient phase of rapid technological change, it is difficult to see the real implications of these changes for both business and society. Recent writings have elaborated on the power of information technologies to reduce the costs of coordination and transactions and consequently to influence governance structures between buyers and sellers. Much of the popular press is also fairly aggressive in providing anecdotes of innovative companies that have leveraged Web-based technologies by expanding, improving, or modifying product and service offerings. A subliminal theme in all this hyperbole is the notion that these technologies are good and will provide the consumer with many more options, services and advantages. Grover and Ramanlal (1999) challenged this theme by presenting alternative scenarios in which these technologies did not necessarily work in the best interest of the customer. For example, product customization, enabled by IT networks, can allow sellers to exploit buyers rather than benefit buyers.

The emergence of e-commerce is creating fundamental change to the way that business is conducted. These changes are altering the way in which every enterprise acquires wealth and creates shareholder value. The myriad of powerful computing and communications technology enabling e-commerce allow organizations to streamline their business processes, enhance customer service and offer digital products and services. This shift underlying marketing fundamentals is now the driving force that is luring many organizations to embrace e-commerce. However, as they are learning, organizations must proceed with caution, as the road to e-commerce is littered with failed initiatives (Chang, Jackson, & Grover, 2003).

While engaging in e-commerce undoubtedly has substantial benefits, this marketplace is also quite competitive. E-commerce reduces customer search and switching costs, has the ability to distribute information on new products, access new sales channels and reduce entry-level capital requirements, thereby lowering barriers to entry. Companies, which exhibit a market orientation, by being vigilant regarding the needs of customers and the actions of competitors, tend to achieve better performance. Overemphasizing one dimension at the cost of the other tend to lead to sub-optimization in an environment that rewards the ability to sense and respond to a variety of information cues (Chang et al., 2003).

Figure 3. E-Commerce is part of E-business

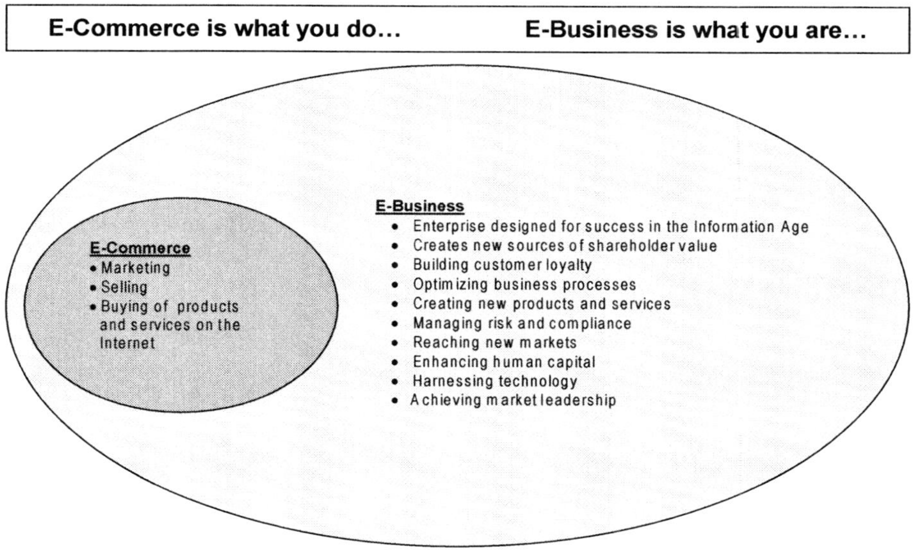

The term commerce is defined by some as describing transactions conducted between business partners. When this definition of commerce is used, some people find the term electronic commerce to be fairly narrow. Thus, many use the term e-business. E-business refers to a broader definition of EC, not just the buying and selling of goods and services, but also servicing customers, collaborating with business partners, and conducting electronic transactions within an organization (Turban et al., 2002).

E-commerce is part of e-business, as illustrated in Figure 3. The difference can be demonstrated using a business example. The business example is concerned with handling of customer complaints. As long as customers do not complain, then e-commerce may be sufficient for electronic transactions with customers. The front end of the business is electronic, and this front end is the only contact customers have with the business. However, if a customer complains, then other parts of the business may have to get involved. For example, if the customer has received a computer which is found deficient. Then the customer gets in touch with the vendor. The vendor has to decide whether the complaint is justified. If it is, then the vendor has to decide whether to (a) fix the product, (b) replace the product, or (c) refund the money paid for the product.

This kind of decision-making will typically involve other departments in addition to marketing and sales departments. These other departments may be the technical department, the production department and the finance department. While the marketing and sales departments have electronic communication with the customer using information systems, other departments may not be connected to the same information systems. In this situation, the internal handling of a customer complaint in the business is not transparent to and accessible for the customer. The customer may experience time passing by, without any information from the vendor. A complaining customer was angry already at the time of the complaint. The anger and frustration are rising as the customer receives no response. The customer is unable to obtain information from the vendor by electronic means, since the vendor is doing e-commerce, not e-business.

Figure 4. Customer complaint handling business process in company with e-commerce but no e-business

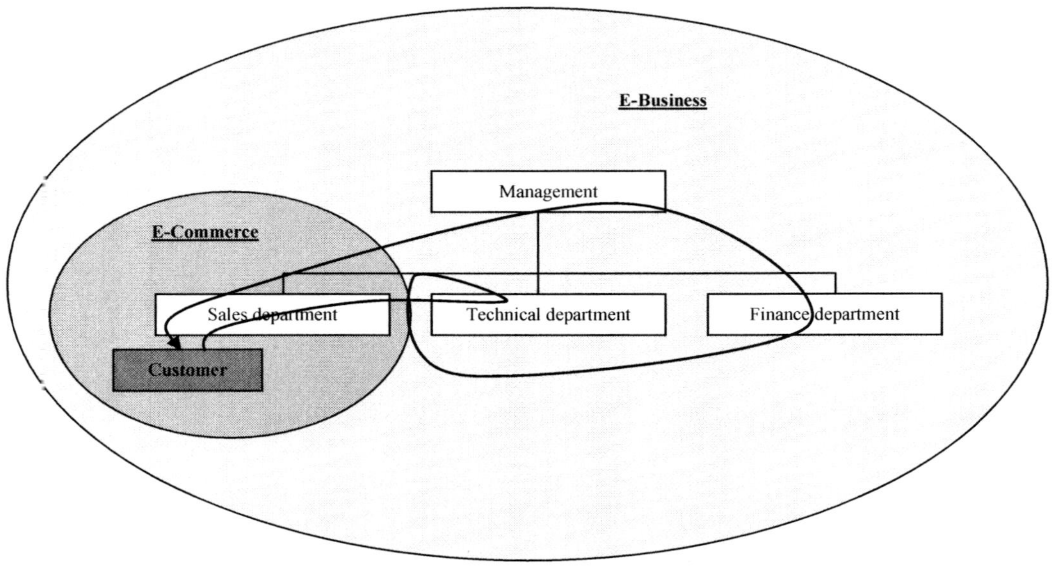

If the vendor would be an e-business, then the business process of customer complaints handling would be an integrated information system to which the customer has access. Then it is possible for the customer to follow the complaint handling process, and it is possible for other departments than marketing and sales, to stay in direct contact with the complaining customer to resolve the issues. This business process is illustrated in Figure 4.

Weill and Vitale (2002) uses the following working definition of e-business: Marketing, buying, selling, delivering, servicing, and paying for products, services, and information across (nonproprietary) networks linking an enterprise and its prospects, customers, agents, suppliers, competitors, allies, and complementors. The essence of this definition is the conduct of business and business processes over computer networks based on nonproprietary standards. The Internet is the exemplar of a nonproprietary network used today for e-business. Given its low cost and universal access, the Internet will be the major infrastructure for the foreseeable future. However, new access technologies already on the horizon (e.g., use of wireless application protocol from mobile telephones) will supplement the Internet.

E-business embodies the most challenging, pervasive, disruptive, and disconcerting form of change: it leaves no aspect of managing organizations untouched, it challenges long-accepted business models, and organization leaders have little to draw on from their past experience to manage its effects (Fahey, Srivastava, Sharon, & Smith, 2001). When starting on an e-government voyage little do executives know about where to go and how to do it. In particular, e-government capacity to transform business processes is no longer in dispute. The new technologies at the heart of e-business open up a number of possibilities not just to reconsider in terms of re-engineering existing processes, but also to design, develop, implement and deploy fundamentally new ways of conceiving and executing business processes. Senior executives in every organization are thus confronted with a central challenge: How should they move to learn, capture, analyze, and project the transformational impact of e-government on their organization's most critical or core processes?

Fahey et al. (2001) argue that in spite of its pervasiveness, visibility, and impact, e-business in industries and government often remains a poorly understood phenomenon. E-government constitutes the ability of an agency or public service provider to electronically connect, in multiple ways, many organizations, both internal and external, for many different purposes. It allows an organization to execute electronic transactions with any individual entity along the value creation – authorities, citizens, municipalities, hospitals, police, and courts. Increasingly, e-business allows an organization to establish real-time connections simultaneously among numerous entities for some specific purpose, such as optimizing the flow of cases, document production and decision-making in the value shop configuration.

The CIO Developing Competitive Strategy

A study conducted by Chang et al. (2003) proposed that e-commerce initiatives are important strategic initiatives and that firms with a stronger e-commerce market orientation will be more successful. Content analysis of CEO's letter to shareholders of 145 Fortune 500 firms was conducted to evaluate the importance of e-commerce and strategic orientation. The results provide support to the studies proposition and indicate that e-commerce must be pursued carefully as a strategic initiative rather than as an appendage to an existing organization.

Strategy is an ongoing process of evaluating purpose as well as questioning, verifying and redefining the manner of interaction with the competitive environment. Complexity of the strategy process can be simplified by searching for patterns of behavior in organizations. These patterns of emergent behavior can be used to describe the underlying processes of organizational adaptation. Basic strategic orientation of organizations can be described in terms of a typology of defenders, prospectors, analyzers and reactors. Each orientation differs with respect to risk disposition, innovativeness and operational efficiencies. Strategic orientation such as low cost or differentiation is means of altering the firm's position vis-à-vis competitors and suppliers. Strategy involves mustering resources and creating capabilities that are difficult to imitate by competitors, resulting in superior rents. Strategic orientation is both an issue of how firms position themselves with respect to competitors and an issue of how firm-specific resources are exploited.

Much strategic management literature has been devoted to identifying attributes or dimensions of a company's strategic orientation. Internet-based businesses include portals, travel sites, e-tailers, and providers of financial and informational services. These businesses attempt to leverage the Internet infrastructure and digital economics in order to gain strategic positioning within the marketplace. For Internet-based businesses, four major dimensions of strategic orientation are particularly pertinent: risk disposition, innovativeness, operational efficiency and marketing intensity (Grover & Saeed, 2004).

The CIO Developing an Internet Strategy

Many of the pioneers of Internet business, both dot-coms and established companies, have competed in ways that violate nearly every precept of good strategy. There was for a long time an absence of strategy. According to Porter (Porter, 2001), the time has come to take a clearer view of the Internet. It is necessary to move away from rhetoric–such as Internet industries, e-business strategies, and a new economy–and see the Internet for what it is. It is an enabling technology, a powerful set of tools that can be used, wisely or unwisely, in almost any industry and as part of almost any strategy.

Strategy is neither the quest for the universally best way of competing nor an effort to be all things to every customer. It defines a way of competing that delivers unique value in a particular set of uses or for a particular set of customers. To establish and maintain a distinctive strategic positioning, a company needs to follow six fundamental principles (Porter, 2001):

- It must start with the *right goal*: superior long-term return on investment. Only by grounding strategy in sustained profitability will real economic value be generated. Economic value is created when customers are willing to pay a price for a product or service that exceeds the cost of producing it.
- A company's strategy must enable it to deliver a *value proposition*, or set of benefits, different from those that competitors offer.
- Strategy needs to be reflected in a *distinctive value configuration*. To establish a sustainable competitive advantage, a company must perform different activities than rivals or perform similar activities in different ways.
- Robust strategies involve *trade-offs*. A company must abandon or forgo some product features, services, or activities in order to be unique at others.
- Strategy defines how all the elements of what a company does *fit* together. A strategy involves making choices throughout the value configuration that are independent; all a company's activities must be mutually reinforcing.
- Strategy involves *continuity* of direction. A company must define a distinctive value proposition that it will stand for, even if that means forgoing certain opportunities.

The absence of strategy in many pioneering Internet businesses, have mislead them to focus on revenues rather than profits, indirect values rather than real value, every conceivable product rather than trade-offs, activities of rivals rather than tailor the value configuration, and rash of partnerships rather than build control. To capitalize on the Internet's strategic potential, executives and entrepreneurs alike will need to develop a strategy that exploits this potential. In some industries, the use of the Internet represents only a modest shift from well-established practices. Virtual activities do not eliminate the need for physical activities, but often amplify their importance. The complementarity between Internet activities and traditional activities arises for a number of reasons. First, introducing Internet applications in one activity often places greater demands on physical activities elsewhere in the value configuration. Second, using the Internet in one activity can have systemic consequences, requiring new or enhanced physical activities that are often unanticipated. Third, most Internet applications have some shortcomings in comparison with conventional methods, such as customers being unable to physically examine products (Porter, 2001).

The CIO Selecting E-Business Model

A business model can be defined as the method by which an organization builds and uses its resources to offer its customers better value than its competitors and to take money doing so. It details how a firm makes money now and how it plans to do so in the long run. The model is what enables a firm to have a sustainable competitive advantage, to perform better than its rivals in the long term. A business model can be conceptualized as a system that is made up of components, linkages between the components, and dynamics (Afuah & Tucci, 2003).

Weill and Vitale (2001) define an e-business model as a description of the roles and relationships among a firm's consumers, customers, allies, and suppliers that identifies the major flows of product, information, and money, and the major benefits to participants. There are many different ways to describe and classify e-business models. Weill and Vitale (2001) propose that there are a finite number of atomic e-business models, each of which captures a different way to conduct e-business. Firms can combine atomic e-business models as building blocks to create tailored e-business models and initiatives, using their competencies as their guide. Weill and Vitale (2001) identified a small number of 8 atomic e-business models, each of which describes the essence of conducting business electronically:

1. **Direct to Customer.** The distinguishing characteristic of this model is that buyer and seller communicate directly, rather than through an intermediary. The seller may be a retailer, a wholesaler or a manufacturer. The customer may be an individual or a business. Examples of the direct-to-customer model are Dell Computer Corporation (www.dell.com) and Gap, Inc. (www.gap.com).

Infrastructure. The direct-to-customer model requires extensive electronic connection with the customer, including online payment systems. Many direct-to-customer implementations include an extranet to allow customized Web pages for major B2B customers. Operating a direct-to-customer e-business requires significant investment in the equivalent of the store: the Web site. Direct-to-customer businesses spend millions of dollars developing easy-to-navigate and easy-to-use Web sites with the goal of improving the B2B or B2C shopping experience online. Lands End (www.landsend.com) has devised a feature by which women can build and store a three-dimensional model of themselves to "try on" clothes electronically. In their field research, Weill and Vitale (2001) found that firms with e-business initiatives containing the direct-to-customer e-business model needed and were investing more heavily in three areas of infrastructure services: application infrastructure, communications, and IT management. Direct-to-customer firms particularly needed payment transaction processing to process online customer payments, enterprise-wide resource planning (ERP) to process customer transactions, workflow infrastructure to optimize business process performance, communication network services linking all points in the enterprise to each other and the outside world (often using TCP/IP protocol), the installation and maintenance of workstations and local area networks supporting the large number of people required to operate a direct-to-customer model, and service-level agreements between the business and the IT group or outsourcer to ensure, monitor, and improve the systems necessary for the model.

Sources of Revenue. The main source of revenue in the direct-to-customer model is usually direct sales to customers. Supplemental revenues come from advertising, the sale of customer information, and product placement fees.

Critical Success Factors. Critical success factors are the things a firm must do well to flourish. The following list shows the critical success factors for the direct-to-customer model: create and maintain customer awareness, in order to build a critical mass of users to cover the fixed cost of building an electronic presence; reduce customer acquisition costs; strive to own the customer relationship and understand individual customer needs; increase repeat purchases and average transaction size; provide fast and efficient transaction processing, fulfillment, and payment; ensure adequate security for the organization and its customers; and provide interfaces that combine ease of use with richness of experience, integrating multiple channels.

2. **Full-Service Provider.** A firm using the full-service provider model provides total coverage of customer needs in a particular domain, consolidated via a single point of contact. The domain could

be any major area of customer needs requiring multiple products and services, for example, financial services, health care, or industrial chemicals. The full-service provider adds value by providing a full range of products, sourced both internally and externally, and consolidated them using the channel chosen by the customer. Examples of the full-service provider are the Prudential Advisor (www.prusec.com) and GE Supply Company (www.gesupply.com).

Infrastructure. Virtually all businesses aspire to getting hundred percent of their customers' business, or at least to getting as much of that business as they can profitably handle. Yet the number of full-service providers remains small. Part of the reason for this is required infrastructure. The missing piece of infrastructure in many businesses is often a database containing information about the customer and the products that the customer owns. Without owning these data, a provider does not own the customer relationship, and therefore some of the customer's transactions are likely to take place directly with other providers. All of the important interactions with customers occurring across any channel or business unit must be recorded in the firm wide customer database. Weill and Vitale (2001) identified in their field research databases and data warehouses as some of the most important infrastructure services associated with the full-service provider model. Other important infrastructure services included the following: the ability to evaluate proposals for new information systems initiatives to coordinate IT investments across a multi-business-unit firm with the goal of a single point of contact for the customer; centralized management of IT infrastructure capacity to integrate across multiple business units within the firm and third-party providers, the full-service provider model is not readily workable if each business unit optimizes its own IT needs; installation and maintenance of workstations and local area networks to operate the online business linking all the business units and third-party providers; electronic support for groups to coordinate the cross-functional teams required to implement this model; and the identification and testing of new technologies to find cost-effective ways to deliver this complex business model to the customer across multiple channels.

Sources of Revenue. A full-service provider gains revenues from selling its own products and those of others, and possibly also from annual membership fees, management fees, transaction fees, commissions on third-party products, advertising or listing fees from third-party providers, and fees for selling aggregated data about customers.

Critical Success Factors. One important critical success factor is the brand, credibility and trust necessary for a customer to look to the firm for its complete needs in an area. Another is owning the customer relationship in one domain and integrating and consolidating the offering of many third parties into a single channel or multiple channels. A third factor is owning more of the customer data in the relevant domain than any other player. A final factor is enforcement of policies to protect the interests of internal and external suppliers, as well as customers.

3. **Whole of Enterprise.** The single point of contact for the e-business customer is the essence of the whole-of-enterprise atomic business model. Although many of this model's breakthrough innovations have occurred in public-sector organizations, the model is applicable in both the for-profit and the public sectors. An example of this model is the Australian state of Victoria with its Business Channel (www.business.channel.vic.gov.au) and Health Channel (www.betterhealth.vic.gov.au).

Infrastructure. For the whole-of-enterprise model, infrastructure needs to link the different systems in the various business units and provide a firm wide perspective for management. The field research by Weill and Vitale (2001) revealed that the following infrastructure services are the most important for implementing this model: centralized management of infrastructure capacity to facilitate integration and capture economies of scale; identification and testing of new technologies to find new ways to integrate the often different systems in many business units into a single point of customer contact; management of key data independent of applications and the creation of a centralized repository for firm wide information; electronic means of summarizing data from different applications and platforms to manage the complexity arising from a single point of contact for multiple business units; development of an ERP service to process the transactions instigated by customers interacting with several different business units, often requiring consolidating or linking several ERPs in the firm; payment transaction processing, either on a firm wide basis or by linking several systems across the business units; large-scale data-processing facilities to process transactions from multiple business units, often centralized to achieve economies of scale; and integrated mobile computing applications, which provide another channel to the customer.

Sources of Revenue. In the for-profit sector, revenues are generated by provision of goods and services to the customer by the business units. There may also be the opportunity to charge an annual service or membership fee for this level of service. In the government sector, the motivation is usually twofold: improved service and reduced cost. Service to the community is improved through continuous, round-the-clock operation and faster service times. Government costs can potentially be reduced by sharing more infrastructures and eliminating the need to perform the same transaction in multiple agencies.

Critical Success Factors. The following list details the critical success factors for the whole-of-enterprise model: changing customer behavior to make use of the new model, as opposed to the customer continuing to interact directly with individual units; reducing costs in the individual business units as the direct demands on them fall, and managing the transfer pricing issues that will inevitably arise; altering the perspective of the business units to take an enterprise-wide view, which includes broad product awareness, training, and cross-selling; in the integrated implementation, reengineering the business processes to link into life events at the front end and existing legacy processes and systems at the back end; and finding compelling and practical life events that customers can use as triggers to access the enterprise.

4. **Intermediaries** such as portals, agents, auctions, aggregators, and other intermediaries. E-business is often promoted as an ideal way for sellers and buyers to interact directly, shortening old-economy value chains by disintermediating some of their members. Yet some of the most popular sites on the Internet, both for consumers and for business users, are in fact intermediaries – sites that stand between the buyer and the seller. The services of intermediaries include search (to locate providers of products and services), specification (to identify important product attributes), price (to establish the price, including optional extras such as warranties), sale (to complete the sales transaction, including payment and settlement), fulfillment (to fulfill the purchase by delivering the product or service), surveillance (to conduct surveillance of the activities of buyers and sellers in order to report aggregate activity and prices and to inform and regulate the market), and enforcement (to enforce proper conduct by buyers and sellers). Examples of intermediaries are electronic malls, shopping agents, specialty auctions, electronic markets, electronic auctions and portals.

Infrastructure. Intermediaries generate value by concentrating information and bringing together buyers and sellers, operating entirely in space and thus relying on IT as the primary infrastructure. Weill and Vitale (2001) found in their field interviews that the most important infrastructure services for firms pursuing the intermediary atomic business model are the following: knowledge management, including knowledge databases and contact databases that enable the codification and sharing of knowledge in this highly information-intensive business; enforcing Internet and email policies to ensure proper and consistent use of electronic channels to buyers, sellers, and intermediaries; workstation networks to support the products and services of this all-electronic business model; centralized management of e-business applications, ensuring consistency and integration across product offerings; information systems planning to identify the most effective uses of IT in the business; and information systems project management to ensure that business value is achieved from IT investments.

Sources of Revenue. An intermediary may earn revenues from buyers, sellers, or both. Sellers may pay a listing fee, a transaction fee, a sales commission, or some combination. Similarly, buyers may pay a subscription fee, a success fee, or a sales commission.

Critical Success Factors. The chief requirement for survival as an intermediary is sufficient volume of usage to cover the fixed costs of establishing the business and the required infrastructure. Attracting and retaining a critical mass of customers is therefore the primary critical success factor. Another important critical success factor is building up infrastructure just quickly enough to meet demand as it increases.

5. Shared Infrastructure. The firm provides infrastructure shared by its owners. Other suppliers, who are users of the shared infrastructure, but not owners, can also be included. Customers who access the shared infrastructure directly are given a choice of suppliers and value propositions. The owner and the non-owner suppliers are generally represented objectively. In some situations, goods or services flow directly from the shared infrastructure to the customer. In other situations, a message is sent by the shared infrastructure to the supplier, who then completes the transaction by providing the goods or services to the customer. An example illustrating the features of the shared-infrastructure business model is the system from 2000 by America's largest automakers, some of their dealers, and IBM, Motorola, and Intel. The initiative was named Covisint (collaboration vision integrity). General Motors, Ford and DaimlerChrysler see stronger potential benefits from cooperating on supply-chain logistics than from competing.

Infrastructure. The shared-infrastructure business model requires competitors to cooperate by sharing IT infrastructure and information. This level of cooperation requires agreement on high-level IT architectures as well as operational standards for applications, data communications, and technology. Effective implementation of the shared-infrastructure model also requires enforcement of these standards, and most shared-infrastructure models have a joint committee to set and enforce standards. Another role of these committees is to implement the policies of the shared infrastructure about what information, if any, is shared and what information is confidential to partner firms. Weill and Vitale (2001) found in their field research that the most important infrastructure services required by firms implementing the shared-infrastructure atomic business model all concerned architectures and standards: specification and enforcement of high-level architectures for data, technology, applications, communications, and work that are agreed to by alliance partners; and specification and enforcement of detailed standards for the high-level architectures.

Sources of Revenue. Revenues can be generated both from membership fees and from transaction fees. The alliance may be run on a nonprofit basis or on a profit-making basis. Not-for-profit shared infrastructures are typically open to all eligible organizations and distribute any excess revenues back to their members. The for-profit models are typically owned by a subset of the firms in a given segment, which split up any profits among themselves.

Critical Success Factors. Critical success factors for the shared-infrastructure model include the following: no dominant partner that gains more than any other partner; an unbiased channel and objective presentation of product and service information; critical mass of both alliance partners and customers; management of conflict among the ongoing e-business initiatives of the alliance partners; compilation and delivery of accurate and timely statements of the services and benefits provided to each member of the alliance; and interoperability of systems.

6. Virtual Community. Virtual communities deserve our attention, and not only because they are the clearest, and perhaps the last, surviving embodiment of the original intent of the Internet. By using IT to leverage the fundamental human desire for communication with peers, virtual communities can create significant value for their owners as well as for their members. Once established, a virtual community is less susceptible to competition by imitation than any of the other atomic business models. In this business model, the firm of interest – the sponsor of the virtual community – sits in the center, positioned between members of the community and suppliers. Fundamental to the success of this model is that members are able, and in fact are encouraged, to communicate with one another directly. Communication between members may be vial email, bulletin boards, online chat, Web-based conferencing, or other computer-based media, and it is the distinguishing feature of this model. Examples of this model are Parent Soup (www.parentsoup.com), a virtual community for parents, and Motley Fool (www.motleyfool.com), a virtual community of investors.

Infrastructure. Virtual communities depend on IT to exist. In particular, the creation and continual enhancement of an Internet site is essential if a virtual community is to survive. Many virtual-community sites include not just static content and links, but also tools of interest to potential members. Weill and Vitale (2001) found in their field research that the infrastructure services most important for the virtual-community business model are the following: training in the use of IT for members of the community; application service provision (ASP) to provide specialized systems virtual communities need such as bulletin boards, email, and ISP access; IT research and development, including infrastructure services for identifying and testing new technologies and for evaluating proposals for new information systems initiatives; information systems planning to identify and prioritize potential investments in IT in this completely online business; and installation and maintenance of workstations and local area networks to support the electronic world of the virtual community.

Sources of Revenue. A sponsoring firm can gain revenue from membership fees, direct sales of goods and services, advertising, clickthroughs and sales commissions. A firm sponsoring a virtual community as an adjunct to its other activities may receive no direct revenue at all from the virtual community. Rather, the firm receives less tangible benefits, such as customer loyalty and increased knowledge about its customer base.

Critical Success Factors. The critical success factors for a virtual community include finding and retaining a critical mass of members; building and maintaining loyalty with an appropriate mix of content and features; maintaining privacy and security for member information; balancing commercial potential and members' interests; leveraging member profile information with advertisers and merchants; and engendering a feeling of trust in the community by its members.

7. Value Net Integrator. Traditionally, most firms operate simultaneously in two worlds: the physical and the virtual. In the physical world, goods and services are created in a series of value-adding activities connecting the supply side (suppliers, procurement, and logistics) with the demand side (customers, marketing, and shipping). In the virtual world, information about the members of the physical value chain are gathered, synthesized, and distributed along the virtual value chain. E-business provides the opportunity to separate the physical and virtual value chains. Value net integrators take advantage of that split and attempt to control the virtual value chain in their industries by gathering, synthesizing, and distributing information. Value net integrators add value by improving the effectiveness of the value chain by coordinating information. A pure value net integrator operates exclusively in the virtual value chain, owning a few physical assets. To achieve the gathering, synthesizing, and distributing of information, the value net integrator receives and sends information to all other players in the model. The value net integrator coordinates product flows form suppliers to allies and customers. The product flows from the suppliers to customers may be direct or via allies. In some cases the value net integrator may sell information or other products to the customer. The value net integrator always strives to own the customer relationship with the other participants in the model, thus knowing more about their operations than any other player. Examples of value net integrators are Seven-Eleven Japan and Cisco Systems (www.cisco.com).

Infrastructure. The value net integrator succeeds in its role by gathering, synthesizing, and distributing information. Thus, for a value net integrator, data and electronic connectivity with allies and other players are very important assets. Field research carried out by Weill and Vitale (2001) suggests that the most important infrastructure services required for a value net integrator include middleware, linking systems on different platforms across the many players in the value net; a centralized data warehouse that collects and summarizes key information for analysis from decentralized databases held by several players across the value net; specification and enforcement of high-level architectures and detailed standards for data, technology, applications, and communications to link together different technology platforms owned by different firms; call centers to provide advice and guidance for partners and allies in getting the most value from the information provided by the value net generator; and high-capacity communications network service to support the high volumes of information flowing across the value net.

Sources of Revenue. In this model, revenues are generally earned by fees or margins on the physical goods that pass through the industry value net. By using information about consumers, the value net integrator is able to increase prices by meeting consumer demand. By using information about suppliers, the value net integrator reduces costs by cutting inventories and lead times.

Critical Success Factors. The critical success factors for the value net integrator atomic business model are as follows: reducing ownership of physical assets while retaining ownership of data; owning or having access to the complete industry virtual value chain; establishing a trusted brand recognized at all places in the value chain; operating in markets where information can add significant value, such as those that are complex, fragmented, regulated, multilayered, inefficient, and large with many sources of information; presenting the information to customers, allies, partners, and suppliers in clear and innovative ways that provide value; and helping other value chain participants capitalize on the information provided by the value net integrator.

8. Content Provider. Like many terms associated with e-business, content provider has different meanings to different people. We define content provider as a firm that creates and provides content (information, products, or services) in digital form to customers via third parties. The physical-world analogy of a content provider is a journalist, recording artist, or stock analyst. Digital products such as software, electronic travel guides, and digital music and video are examples of content. A virtual-world example of a content provider is weather forecasters such as Storm Weather Center (www.storm.no).

Infrastructure. Content providers must excel at tailoring and manipulating their core content to meet the specific needs of customers. Content providers must categorize and store their content in well-indexed modules so it can be combined and customized to meet customer needs via a wide variety of channels. Customers and transactions tend to be relatively few, at least compared with the number of end consumers and their transactions. Often complex and unique IT infrastructures are needed to support the particular needs of the specialized professionals employed by the content provider. Field research by Weill and Vitale (2001) identified the most important infrastructure services: multimedia storage farms or storage area network infrastructures to deal with large amounts of information; a strong focus on architecture, including setting and enforcing standards particularly for work; detailed data architectures to structure, specify, link manipulate, and manage the core intellectual property; workstation network infrastructures to enable the fundamentally online business of a content provider; and a common systems development environment to provide compatible and integrated systems, ensuring the systems can provide content across multiple channels to their customers.

Sources of Revenue. The primary source of revenue for a content provider is fees from its third parties or allies. These fees may be based on a fixed price per month or year, or on the number of times the third party's own customers access the content. In some situations, the fees paid are lower for content branded by the provider, and higher for unbranded content, which then appears to the customer to have been generated by the third party itself.

Critical Success Factors. To succeed, a content provider must provide reliable, timely content in the right format and at the right price. The critical success factors for this model include the following: branding (the value of content is due in part to reputation), recognized as best in class (the business of

Figure 5. E-business models integration with customers versus partners

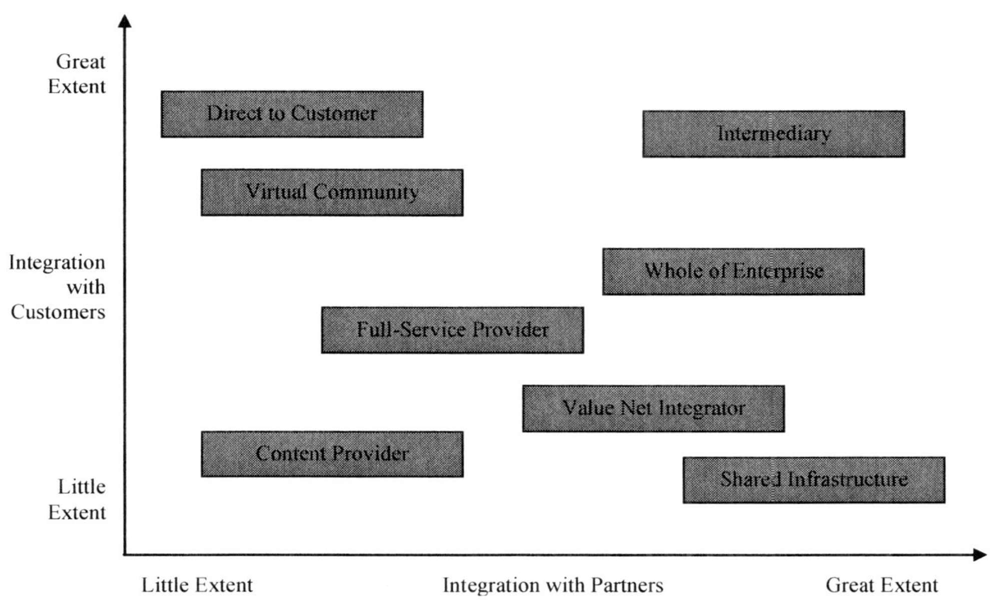

content provision will be global and competitive), and network (establishing and maintaining a network of third parties through which content is distributed.

One way of comparing these e-business models is to analyze to what extent each model creates integration with customers and to what extent each model creates integration with partners. As illustrated in Figure 5, the business model of Direct to Customer creates mainly integration with customers, while Shared Infrastructure creates mainly integration with partners.

CONCLUSION

As the highest-ranking IT executive the CIO has an important role in the organization requiring effective communication with top management. The CIO has to deal with sourcing options for IT resources and services. In an IT governance perspective the CIO must establish structures, processes, and politics that govern how and who within the organization that makes IT decisions. The CIO may take on different roles related to information technology management – as a personnel leader, spokesman, monitor, liaison, entrepreneur, and resource allocator. As organizations expand their use of the Internet, CIOs play a central role in selecting and developing business models.

In a survey of state government CIOs on collaborative government and e-government, Reddick (2008) found that collaboration stimulated and supported by CIOs is an important approach to enhance the successful adoption of electronic government and e-government projects. One of the findings indicates a high level of agreement that collaboration is having an impact on communication, trust and standards within state governments.

REFERENCES

Afuah, A., & Tucci, C. L. (2003). *Internet business models and strategies* (2nd ed.). New York: McGraw-Hill.

Benjamin, R. I., Dickinson, C., & Rockart, J. F. (1985). Changing tole of the corporate information systems officer. *MIS Quarterly, 9*(3), 177-197.

Chang, K., Jackson, J., & Grover, V. (2003). E-commerce and corporate strategy: An executive perspective. *Information & Management, 40*(7), 663-675.

Earl, M. J., & Feeny, D. F. (1994). Is your CIO adding value? *Sloan Management Review, 35*(3), 11-20.

Fahey, L., Srivastava, R., Sharon, J. S., & Smith, D. E. (2001). Linking e-business and operating processes: The role of knowledge management. *IBM Systems Journal, 40*(4), 889-907.

Gottschalk, P. (2007). *CIO and corporate strategic management: Changing role of CIO to CEO*. Hershey, PA:IGI Global Publishing.

Grembergen, W. V., Haes, S. D., & Guldentops, E. (2004). Structures, processes and relational mechanisms for IT governance. In W. V. Grembergen (Ed.), *Strategies for information technology governance* (pp. 1-36). Hershey, PA:IGI Global Publishing.

Grover, V., Jeong, S. R., Kettinger, W. J., & Lee, C. C. (1993). The chief information officer: A study of managerial roles. *Journal of Management Information Systems, 10*(2), 107-130.

Grover, V., & Ramanlal, P. (1999). Six myths of information and markets: Information technology networks, electronic commerce, and the battle for consumer surplus. *MIS Quarterly, 23*(4), 456-495.

Grover, V., & Saeed, K. A. (2004). Strategic orientation and performance of Internet-based businesses. *Information Systems Journal, 14*(1), 23-42.

King, W. R., & Malhotra, Y. (2000). Developing a framework for analyzing IS sourcing. *Information & Management, 37*(6), 323-334.

Kolbasuk, M. (2005). CIOs get respect. *Insurance and Technology, 30*(9), 18.

Kaarst-Brown, M. (2005). Understanding an organization's view of the CIO: The role of assumptions about IT. *MIS Quarterly Executive, 4*(2), 287-301.

Mintzberg, H. (1994). Rounding out the manager's job. *Sloan Management Review, 36*(1), 11-26.

Monnoyer, E., & Willmott, P. (2005). What IT leaders do [Electronic Version]. *McKinsey Quarterly*, 5 pages. Retrieved August, 2008 from www.mckinseyquarterly.com

Office of the Government Chief Information Officer. (2007). *The HKSARG Interoperability Framework*. Government of the Hong Kong Special Administrative Region.

Porter, M. E. (2001). Strategy and the Internet. *Harvard Business Review, 79*(3), 62-78.

Reddick, C. G. (2008). Collaborative management and e-government: A survey of state government CIOs. *Electronic Government, an International Journal, 5*(2), 146-161.

Steensma, H. K., & Corley, K. G. (2001). Organizational context as moderator of theories on firm boundaries for technology sourcing. *Academy of Management Journal, 44*(2), 271-291.

Todd, P. A., McKeen, J. D., & Gallupe, R. B. (1995). The evolution of IS job skills: A content analysis of IS job advertisements from 1970 to 1990. *MIS Quarterly, 19*(1), 1-27.

Turban, E., King, D., Lee, J., Warkentin, M., & Chung, H. M. (2002). *Electronic commerce: A managerial perspective*. Sidney, Australia: Pearson Education, Prentice Hall.

Weil, P. (2004). *Don't just lead, govern: How top-performing firms govern IT* (No. CISR WP No. 341): Center for Information Systems Research, Sloan School of Management, Massachusetts Institute of Technology.

Weill, P., & Vitale, M. R. (2001). *Place to space. Migrating to eBusiness models*. Boston: Harvard Business School Press.

Weill, P., & Vitale, M. R. (2002). What IT infrastructure capabilities are needed to implement e-business models? *MIS Quarterly Executive, 1*(1), 17-34.

This work was previously published in E-Government Interoperability and Information Resource Integration: Frameworks for Aligned Development, by P. Gottschalk and H. Solli-Sæther, pp. 190-216, copyright 2009 by IGI Publishing (an imprint of IGI Global).

About the Authors

Hans Solli-Sæther has a MSc degree from the University of Oslo and a PhD degree from the Norwegian School of Management. He has been the CIO of Norway Post and has several years of practical experience with outsourcing. Dr. Solli-Sæther has published several research articles and books on this topic. His current research interests are outsourcing and organizational interoperability. See http://www.bi.no/homepage/fgl99031/ for a detailed description of education, publications and management experience.

Petter Gottschalk is Professor of Information Systems and Knowledge Management in the Department of Leadership and Organizational Management at the Norwegian School of Management. He is the author of several books on these subjects, and he has published in major journals. Professor Gottschalk earned his MBA at the Technical University Berlin, Germany, his MSc at Dartmouth College and Sloan School, MIT and his DBA at Henley Management College, Brunel University, UK. His executive experience includes CIO at ABB and CEO at ABB Datacables. See http://www.bi.no/homepage/fgl98023/ for a detailed description of education, publications and management experience.

Index